Sandra Danneil
Trick, Treat, Transgress
THE SIMPSONS' TREEHOUSE OF HORROR as a Popular-Culture History
of the Digital Age

Marburger Schriften zur Medienforschung 89
ISSN 1867–5131

The author

Sandra Danneil has a master's degree in Cinema and Television Studies from Ruhr-University Bochum, Germany, and a Bachelor's degree in education. In 2020, she successfully defended her dissertation project entitled "Trick, Treat, Transgress: The Simpsons' Treehouse of Horror as a Popular-Culture History of the Digital Age" and was awarded with summa cum laude. Sandra Danneil works as a Postdoc in the British and American Studies Department at TU Dortmund University where she teaches courses in Cultural and Media Studies. She worked in the film- and television industry for several years, is currently producing her own horror-film podcast and spends much of her time working in the field of horror media studies, and doing research in genre studies with a focus on female serial killers and the new final girl, contemporary horror fiction, cinematic (un)pleasure, complex seriality, and sound cinema.

Sandra Danneil

Trick, Treat, Transgress

The Simpsons' Treehouse of Horror as a Popular-Culture History of the Digital Age

Bibliografische Information der Deutschen Nationalbibliothek
Die Deutsche Nationalbibliothek verzeichnet diese Publikation in der Deutschen Nationalbibliografie; detaillierte bibliografische Daten sind im Internet über http://dnb.d-nb.de abrufbar.

Abbildungsnachweis
20th Century Fox (1–3, 6, 8, 10–14, 17–19, 23–27, 30–33, 35–40); Bongo Comics (16); Brainpickings.org: "Gustave Doré's Beautiful 1883 Illustrations for Edgar-Allen Poe's 'The Raven'" (34); Disney Corp. (4, 5, 7); EC Comics (15); Bill Plympton (22); riptapparel.com (FUTURAMA inspired T-shirt print) (41); Viacom/Paramount (20, 21); Duke Wellington Photographs, Margaret Herrick Library, Academy of Motion Picture Arts and Sciences, Beverly Hills, CA; qtd. in Phillips 2018: 3 (9); YouTube (28–29).

Schüren Verlag GmbH
Universitätsstr. 55 | D-35037 Marburg
www.schueren-verlag.de
© Schüren 2021
Alle Rechte vorbehalten
Gestaltung: Erik Schüßler
Umschlaggestaltung: Wolfgang Diemer, Frechen
Coverfotodesign von Christine Schube
Druck: Booksfactory, Stettin
Printed in Poland
ISBN 978-3-7410-0389-9 (Print)
ISBN 978-3-7410-0145-1 (eBook)

Table of Contents

Danksagung	7
1 Introduction	9
2 Theory | THE SIMPSONS and Postmodernity	29
Umberto Eco: THE SIMPSONS as the 'Low' Ground of 'High' Art	41
Angela McRobbie: Popular-Culture Representations in THE SIMPSONS	52
Linda Hutcheon: Postmodern Parody in THE SIMPSONS	64
Michel Foucault: Reading TREEHOUSE OF HORROR as Popular-Culture History Archive	86
THE SIMPSONS, A Funhouse Mirror: A Conclusion	101
3 Analysis | TREEHOUSE OF HORROR: Lessons to Remember	105
Opening Credits | THE SIMPSONS' TREEHOUSE OF HORROR Teaches Lessons to Remember	105
History Lesson No. 1 | Animation Auteurs and Auteur Television: Analyzing the Couch Gag as Participatory Culture	137
History Lesson No. 2 | The Literary Legacy of American Gothic Fiction: Complex Television & TREEHOUSE OF HORROR	170
History Lesson No. 3 | Exotic Islands, Haunted Houses, and Home Invasions: TREEHOUSE OF HORROR's History of Film Horror	197

Table of Contents

History Lesson No. 4 | 'A Treehouse Full of Twilight Zones' – The Legacy of Anthology Storytelling, Science-Fiction TV, and TREEHOUSE OF HORROR's Love Letter to Rod Serling's THE TWILIGHT ZONE   232

4 Conclusion | A Popular-Culture History of the Digital Age   261

5 References   273

6 Appendix   287
TREEHOUSE OF HORROR Episode Guide   287
TREEHOUSE OF HORROR Reference Guide   291
THE SIMPSONS & TREEHOUSE OF HORROR: Guest-Animated Couch Gags   300

List of Figures   301

Index   303

Danksagung

DIE SIMPSONS sind weltberühmt und berüchtigt dafür, die Zukunft vorhersehen zu können. Innerhalb diverser Episoden der vergangenen 33 Jahre schockierte die Serie Fans beispielsweise damit, schon zwei Jahre zuvor das unerwartete Serienfinale von GAME OF THRONES gezeigt zu haben. Die Simpsons wussten auch schon in den Neunzigern, dass es einmal Smartwatches, dreiäugige Fische oder den Coronavirus geben würde. Das Visionäre der SIMPSONS zu untersuchen, d. h. zu überlegen, wie es einer TV-Serie schon vor langer Zeit gelingen konnte, uns zu weitsichtigen Fans heranzuziehen, ist auch in vielerlei Hinsicht Inhalt dieses Buches. Gleichermaßen visionär waren viele meiner Weggefährt:innen, die stets daran glaubten, dass die Simpsons nicht nur die Zukunft des Higgs-Bosons oder die von Donald Trump gezeichnet haben, sondern auch ein wesentlicher Bestandteil meiner Zukunft sein würden.

Mein besonderster Dank gilt daher meiner Doktormutter, Randi Gunzenhäuser, die mir in all den Jahren mental und kognitiv immer einen Schritt voraus war, zu erkennen, was ich eigentlich sagen will; und meinem Doktorvater, Walter Grünzweig, der mir maximale Freiheiten und Möglichkeiten gab, meine Gedanken schließlich auf gedrucktem Papier sehen zu können. Eine tiefe Verbundenheit und maßloser Dank gilt meinen geschätzten Freunde-Kolleg*innen Iris-Aya Laemmerhirt, die endlose Stunden mit der Korrektur meiner Kapitel verbrachte; Mark Schmitt und Sarah Reininghaus, deren professionelle Klarheit und wunderbare Art, mich zu kritisieren, mein Antrieb waren; und natürlich Martina Pfeiler, die immer herzliche, Mut machende Worte für mich übrig hatte. Dazu möchte ich mich bedanken bei meinen schlauen wie schönen Kolleginnen aus der Dortmunder Amerikanistik. In den zahlreichen Oberseminaren und Promotionskolloquien habe ich stets konstruktives Feedback, manchmal fragende Gesichter, aber

Danksagung

bestimmt Hunderte von Lach-Smileys und Daumen-Hoch-Emojis bekommen von Hanna Rodewald, Tanja Ferreira, Julia Sattler, Kim Gass, Laura Kost, Sibylle Klemm, Jana Stormanns, Christine Vennemann und sicher noch einigen mehr. Meine Lebensgefährtin und große Liebe, Tabea Frank, hat wahrscheinlich den größten Beitrag zur Fertigstellung dieses Buches geleistet. Meine endlosen Klagelieder über den Zustand meines Körpers hat sie stets ertragen; für die Schmerzen in meinem Rücken und die Krämpfe in meinem Kopf hatte sie immer einen Trainingsplan, Dehnübungen und zahllose physiotherapeutische Anwendungen. Aber am dankbarsten bin ich ihr für ihre Geduld und ihren Siegeswillen, um mit mir da durch zu gehen und schließlich am Ziel anzukommen. Dem visionären, Künstler-Verständnis und der Beharrlichkeit meiner Freundin Christine Schube, ihres Zeichens Diplom-Fotografin und Spezialistin für Foto-Inszenierungen, ist zu verdanken, dass dieses Buch das wahrscheinlich wunderbarste Cover-Design hat, das ein kulturwissenschaftliches Buch je gesehen hat. Ohne meine Mutter wäre ich höchstwahrscheinlich nicht da, wo ich jetzt bin, denn ohne eine langfristige finanzielle Unterstützung ist der Traum einer akademischen Karriere erfahrungsgemäß ein Alptraum. Meinem Sohn Rocko möchte ich dafür danken, dass er mir mit seiner unverstellten, kindlichen Sicht auf die Welt der SIMPSONS immer eine Inspiration war. Vielen Dank an alle, dass ich nun nicht „D'Oh!" sagen muss, sondern aus voller Brust „Cowubunga" rufen darf!

1 Introduction

This introduction will present my topic, THE SIMPSONS, which many scholars and fans call the most exciting U.S.-American TV production of the 1990s if not of all times; among them is the famous TV scholar Jason Mittell in one of his best-known essays, "Cartoon Realism: Genre Mixing and the Cultural Life of THE SIMPSONS" from 2001 which he begins with the following words: "Few television programs exemplify 1990s media like THE SIMPSONS – popular culture sensation, marketing phenomenon, generic mixture, (alleged) embodiment of postmodernism, and representative of the post-Fordist network era." (15) But whereas the regular SIMPSONS series is also one of the most discussed TV shows ever, its TREEHOUSE OF HORROR (ToH) annual Halloween cycle so far hasn't caught the critics' attention. In this initial chapter I hypothesize that THE SIMPSONS' Halloween special is well worth academic attention because it has established its very own narrative strategies, aesthetic principles, as well as its generic set up; it approaches U.S.-American popular culture and its history in unique ways. The concentration on TREEHOUSE OF HORROR necessitates the use of different reading strategies and theoretical approaches than the analysis of the main SIMPSONS series. I will show that when read closely, the Halloween Special will reveal the distinctive way it works and how it works differently than THE SIMPSONS. I consider TREEHOUSE OF HORROR a most innovative series: For me, it works as no less than a popular-culture history of the digital age. But let's start at the very beginning.

1 Introduction

The Beginnings: Fox & THE SIMPSONS

The beginnings of THE SIMPSONS as a media phenomenon are part of a well-known story. When in 1986 Rupert Murdoch founded the Fox Broadcasting Company (formerly known as FBC) as the subsidiary of the media conglomerate News Corporation, Fox became an innovative media company (see Abelman/Atkin 2011: 81 ff.). Fox was announced as a complement to the U.S. network market of the so-called Big Three of NBC, ABC, and CBS, with Fox as the fourth big cable network. In order to successfully establish Fox on the market, Murdoch hired James L. Brooks, who at that time was an acclaimed Hollywood screenwriter, director, and producer, for example of the awarded TV series THE MARY TYLER MOORE SHOW (CBS 1970–1977).

Chris Turner, author of the acclaimed SIMPSONS historiography *Planet Simpson* (2004), explains: "According to legend, according to the press, according to the word of its creator, THE SIMPSONS was born in a single fevered moment" (16). Brooks, who had just founded the Gracie Films production company, became Fox's executive producer of the variety format THE TRACEY ULLMAN SHOW (Fox, 1987–1990) for which he hired 33-year-old underground cartoonist Matt Groening to create a series of animated shorts. Legend has it that during one of their first meetings Brooks wanted to produce Groening's comic strip *Life in Hell* (since 1977) that starred the one-eared nihilist bunny Binky as Fox, but Groening gave him 'the Simpsons' instead (cf. Turner 2004: 17). Brooks asked Groening for the names of the new, crudely sketched characters the cartoonist had just drafted in the waiting room in front of Brooks' office. For lack of a better idea, Groening spontaneously gave the first names of his own family members. The father was named after Groening's dad Homer, the mother after his mother Margret, and his sisters stood in for the eight-year-old second-grader Lisa and the one-year-old toddler Maggie. The oldest son of the Simpsons he named Bart, an anagram of 'brat,' the character Groening envisioned as America's nastiest ten-year-old and the most menacing child of the Simpson family. Brooks was thrilled.

What began as rough sketches of a dysfunctional 'white-trash' family in the ULLMAN SHOW in 1987, soon was turned into a television program and became one of the first prime-time formats on the infant Fox Network in 1989 (cf. Turner 2004: 18). After 48 shorts had aired on the ULLMAN SHOW, "something unexceptional was happening," remembers the music journalist Turner (18). Although the ULLMAN shorts were only coarse drafts, the Simpsons introduced audiences to their "somewhat unorthodox but ultimately rudimentary theme" (18) giving a rough idea of where the American family would be going on late 20th-century television. Among the saccharine family sitcoms of THE COSBY SHOW (NBC 1984–1992) and FAMILY TIES (NBC 1982–1989) that dominated the American TV screens in the 1980s, THE SIMPSONS established family life as "loutish and vulgar, a slow-burn nightmare" that offered viewers "a quick Tpeek into a nasty world where stories didn't inevitably have morals and Father emphatically did not Know Best. THE SIMPSONS as we know it was about to emerge from the womb." (Turner 18–19)

THE SIMPSONS: A Non-Affirmative Part of Popular Culture

For people of my generation, i. e. those who were born around 1980, THE SIMPSONS has always been there. When I tell people about what has kept me busy in the last years, I can be sure that, unexceptionally, people of all ages know who the Simpsons are and what THE SIMPSONS is. But THE SIMPSONS is not only familiar to viewers across generations. What *The Guardian* once termed the "trailblazer in TV's blue-collar renaissance" (2000) has been appealing to popular-culture- and media-studies scholars of the past twenty-five years too. In other words, it will be a crucial question of this project to ask how come THE SIMPSONS is more than an unorthodox part of popular culture and how its Halloween show TREEHOUSE OF HORROR contributed to this success? In which respect does TREEHOUSE stand for a new tradition within popular culture, a tradition that started to question U.S.-American media myths in the late 1980s?

On American TV in the 1980s, myths were braced and intensified by the wisecracking Bill Cosby and his white-washed approach to African American middle-class family life in THE COSBY SHOW among others. In the sitcom FAMILY TIES, the family's conservative offspring Alex played by Michael J. Fox educated his liberal, ex-hippie parents Steven and Elyse Keaton with affirmative messages for the Reagan era. As a contrastive alternative, THE SIMPSONS gave its audience burping contests and showed that it was cool to act coarsely and be ordinary and upfront (cf. Turner 18; Bhattacharya 2000). Matt Groening once told a reporter: "We were definitely at the right place at the right time; at the end of a decade of real complacence, a lot of upper-middle-class family comedy. So we gave them a dose of something really crude and unglamorous." (Qtd. in Bhattacharya 2000) However, THE SIMPSONS are not only crude and unglamorous. And so during my academic journey I not only did research on thirty years of THE SIMPSONS and its untamable corpus of anecdotes in 673 episodes within 31 seasons. I also became involved in roughly thirty years of American popular-culture research which began to appreciate THE SIMPSONS as late as in the mid-1990s.

The Beginning of Thinking Seriously About Television

Long before THE SIMPSONS was developed, already in the 1970s, the American cultural-studies- and media scholar Horace M. Newcomb paved the way for 'serious' television programs to enter the academy as he began to "think seriously about television" (1986: 217). In his numerous publications, Newcomb explores television, firstly, by means of a sociological approach as in his book *TV: The Most Popular Art* from 1974, secondly, by means of a critical journalistic analysis as in *Television: The Critical View* from 1976, and thirdly, by studying the growing significance of television authorship and media convergence as in *The Producer's Medium* which he published in 1983.

Newcomb's academic interests were confirmed and further expanded by feminist television scholar Charlotte Brunsdon among others. In the "Introduction to the Second Edition" of her reader on feminist TV criticism from 2008 [1997], Brunsdon notes that TV studies in the humanities roughly developed as an interdisciplinary field from the three branches of the social sciences, critical journalism, and film studies (cf. 2008: 1). This early academic interest in American television criticism and history paved the way for what followed. In the early 1990s, television scholarship was preoccupied with the analysis of audiences in the context of Pierre Bourdieu's guiding structuralist concept of 'social habitus' (see his *Outline of a Theory of Practice*, 1977) and poststructural theories of 'everyday life' (see Michel de Certeau, *The Practice of Everyday Life*, 1984; John Fiske, *Television Culture*, 1987; Roger Silverstone, *Television and Everyday Life*, 1994).

In the "Introduction" to her volume *Television after TV* co-edited with Jan Olsson in 2004, professor of screen cultures Lynn Spigel sees early-television scholars often being at odds with each other. Whereas the Frankfurt School was preoccupied with intellectually deconstructing TV and its criticism with the help of concepts such as "mass society," popular-culture theorist John Hartley associated the "textual tradition" of TV texts with literary and film theory. Journalistic criticism based its television critique on performance studies and theater criticism, and cultural-studies research showed a major interest in the relationship of television to other media and their audiences (cf. Spigel 2004: 8). Spigel emphasizes that "although these traditions developed differently in different national contexts, they all formed a discourse field – a set of interrelated ways of speaking about TV – that continue to affect the way we frame television as an academic object of study" (8).

TV Studies; or, How to Establish an Independent Discipline

The interrelated ways to speak about TV culminated in a debate that focused on what has become known as "quality TV" in the late 1980s and early 1990s. In 1996, Robert J. Thompson wrote about 'quality TV' as 'not-conventional TV' and described contemporary TV as making up television's *Second Golden Age* in his book of the same name. Thompson remembers that, since the late 1980s, the quality profile of more and more continuity formats "has come to refer more to a generic style than to an aesthetic judgment" (13). Although Picket Fences (CBS

1992–1996) or TWIN PEAKS (ABC 1990–1991) were unconventional, slow-burn narratives with bittersweet humor labeled as 'quality drama,' they were broadly considered far ahead of their time. However, the term quality TV emerged because these series showed a special way to enlighten, enrich, challenge, involve, and confront fans, as well as to appeal to their intellect and touch their emotions (cf. Thompson 13). Based on this, the American film theorist Kristin Thompson extended her research interest from 'art film' to what she termed 'quality television' in her book *Storytelling in Film and Television* in 2003. Here, Thompson describes BUFFY THE VAMPIRE SLAYER (The WB 1997–2003), THE SOPRANOS (HBO 1999–2007), but also THE SIMPSONS to have altered the TV landscape and its traditional narrative forms. Slowly but steadily, television was established as an art form both on the screen and in the academy, where scholars in the field of TV studies pushed television's potential.

One push happened in 2001, when one of America's most acclaimed TV scholars, Jason Mittell, associate professor of American studies as well as film and media culture at Middlebury College, published an early essay on the complexity and innovation of TV programs such as THE SIMPSONS. Mittell's insights into the cultural life of THE SIMPSONS were not only indispensable for his book. His writings also influenced the discussion about quality TV, which he later replaced by the term 'complex TV' in his 2015 study *Complex TV: The Poetics of Contemporary Television Storytelling*. Mittell avoided to judge THE SIMPSONS by its cinematic or literary qualities only; rather he praised its medial qualities, such as its 'cartoon realism' and genre status.

In other words, THE SIMPSONS has contributed to the fact that TV studies became acknowledged as an academic discipline independent from film- or other forms of popular-media studies. Early scholars of TV studies such as Robert J. Thompson, Kristin Thompson, or Jason Mittell pointed to the cultural value of television with their critical approaches in the mid-1990s to early 2000s. Based on their texts, this book is dedicated to the cultural value of THE SIMPSONS. Chris Turner argued that THE SIMPSONS was a "cartoon masterpiece" that "documented an era" and "defined a generation:" now this book wants to investigate what the show has further contributed to the study and reception of American popular culture. How did not only THE SIMPSONS, but, more importantly, its Halloween off-shoot TREEHOUSE OF HORROR teach us to become members of a more thoughtful, actively participating audience, how did it extend our critical view to American pop-culture history? By addressing all those who have been watching THE SIMPSONS since their childhood, this text alludes to the fact that nothing about watching THE SIMPSONS is simple. I want to show that it is necessary to distinguish THE SIMPSONS from its pop-historical archive TREEHOUSE OF HORROR from which we can learn that watching television can inspire the dialogue between viewers in the digital age and the visual culture of the past.

The Simpsons is 'Us:' The Early Days of Participatory Culture

Another issue "to emerge from the womb" of American popular television in the 1990s is television's development from a consumers' to a users' medium. Horace M. Newcomb observed that 1980s' television, "however trivial it might have seemed to some" (1986: 217), trained not only a new generation of researchers, but also a new generation of television viewers, for example by subverting traditional forms of TV storytelling from live-action sitcoms to children's Saturday-morning cartoons. In addition to that, THE SIMPSONS appreciated both the intelligence of its increasing fan audience and the status of popular culture in the world. The show started to reach out to its audience in a new way.

When scholars and critics began "to think seriously about television," as Newcomb suggested in 1986 (217), they may have felt as 'fans' of their favorite TV programs but, according to Henry Jenkins, they were "marginal to the operations of our culture, ridiculed in the media, shrouded with social stigma, pushed underground by legal threats, and often depicted as brainless and inarticulate" (*Fans, Blogger, and Gamers*, 2006a: 1). To fight this traditional contempt for TV and its fans, Henry Jenkins, one of the foremost American communication and media theorists, drew his inspiration from British cultural-studies approaches of the Birmingham School as well as from youth- and subcultures in order to radically change the image of fan cultures in the U.S.

In his first book project about new directions in participatory culture, *Textual Poachers* from 1992, Henry Jenkins aimed to "construct an alternative image of fan cultures, one that saw media consumers as active, critically engaged, and creative" (2006a: 1). In 2006, Jenkins extended the concept in his sequel book *Convergence Culture*. *Convergence Culture* largely builds on the insight that fans are increasingly central to how culture operates as new technologies 'enable' the average consumers to "archive, annotate, appropriate, and recirculate media content" (2006a: 1). At the conjunction between textual poaching and media convergence, Jenkins defines "the terms of our participation in contemporary popular culture," stressing the "interplay between media industries and their consumers" (2006a: 2). His approach to the participatory quality of late 20th-century popular culture leads to a new, participatory reading of the Simpson family at the end of the opening sequence of their show. The family's taking a seat on their brown couch and switching on the TV can now be read as a moment of self-reflexivity: In postmodern terms, the Simpsons are 'us'; they know we are watching them watching television.

In pop-cultural terms, Jenkins argues that "participatory culture is anything but fringe or underground today" (2006a: 2). THE SIMPSONS know this. From the start, the show has established a respectful, intimate connection to its fans. In contrast to the practice of lecturing viewers in THE COSBY SHOW or FAMILY TIES,

THE SIMPSONS actively engaged and addressed its fans and turned them into a group of 'us.' As far as I am concerned, the show's inclusive approach leaves no other option than to feel enabled as an "active, critically engaged, and creative" addressee of the show's vast field of media content. It seems that before popular-culture studies were able to "formulate and reformulate" (Jenkins 2006a: 2) how television and consumers interact, THE SIMPSONS had already proved that it is possible to take one's fans and their response seriously. It will be part of this project to investigate how THE SIMPSONS accomplished to establish an intimate and appreciative connection to a new generation of fans.

Why This Book Needs to be Written

At this point readers may question if it is necessary to write yet another book on a television cartoon show which today some may call an old hat and which much has been written about in the past. THE SIMPSONS "made its way to the very heart of mainstream" a long time ago so that the show, compared to more recent animated shows, has become "relatively conventional these days," as cartoon artist Matt Groening self-critically said about his own invention in 2018 (qtd. in *Newsweek* 2018). However, it should not be ignored that in thirty years of THE SIMPSONS, research largely investigated how the show turned into a mainstream TV institution. The existing academic research on THE SIMPSONS improves our understanding of how the show reflects on Western everyday life by exploring discourses on gender roles or class issues as well as contemporary themes such as politics, religion, digital media, and many more.

But, I argue, it has largely been unnoticed that very early on THE SIMPSONS has started to contribute to a new understanding of popular culture, "however trivial it might have seemed to some" as Horace Newcomb diagnosed for TV in the 1980s (cf. 1986: 217). In other words, this project will discuss in which ways THE SIMPSONS along with other popular shows of the 1980s and 1990s affected the way we frame television as an academic object of study. At the same time, my quest will investigate in how far the comedy series – just like more 'serious' shows such as HILL STREET BLUES (NBC 1981–1987) or TWIN PEAKS – contributed to how we study all forms of pop culture, from popular literature across radio and cinema to digital media in the 21st century.

Since THE SIMPSONS premiered as a stand-alone program on Christmas 1989 with "The Simpsons Roasting On an Open Fire," the show has been raising questions about family and politics, about social equality and racial difference, about issues of gender, class and labor. THE SIMPSONS exemplified how animation as a mode of production much older than digital media was nevertheless able "to combine the aesthetic and the social in a way the old mass media, such as theatre,

1 Introduction

movies, TV shows and novels never could", as Espen J. Aarseth, professor of humanistic informatics at the University of Bergen, said about digital media in 2001, actually indicating not so much the newness of the digital media, but rather the new academic approach to the popular after the scholars' first encounters with 'new,' or rather, newly seen popular media.

By the end of the millennium, THE SIMPSONS had become one of the early texts by help of which a new generation of scholars learned to read popular culture and sharpen their eye for its intricacies. Popular-culture scholars Henry Jenkins, Tara McPherson, and Jane Shattuc call their introductory chapter to *Hop on Pop: The Politics and Pleasures of Popular Culture* from 2002 "The Culture that Sticks to Your Skin: A Manifesto for a New Cultural Studies." In this introduction they formulate much the same argument as the game-studies scholar Espen Aarseth shortly before them, but this time with respect to the fundamentally new ways in which a new generation of scholars now defined their relationship to a new generation of pop:

> [...] we are interested in the everyday, the intimate, the immediate; we reject the monumentalism of canon formation and the distant authority of traditional academic writing. We engage with popular culture as a culture that "sticks to the skin," that becomes so much a part of us that it becomes increasingly difficult to examine it from a distance. *(2002: 3)*

As "defining characteristics" (2002: 6) of popular culture as they understand it, the authors foreground the aspects "immediacy," "multivalence," "accessibility," "particularity," "contextualism," and "situationalism" (*ibid.*: 6ff.) – all characteristics THE SIMPSONS have made use of in exemplary ways from its very beginning.

Since 2006, Henry Jenkins has been publishing a blog called "Confessions of an ACA Fan," and the title in which he refers to himself as an "ACA Fan," an academic fan, already circumscribes what the relationship between today's popular culture and its academic scholars is. On October 5, 2012, Jenkins describes one of the many powerful characteristics of THE SIMPSONS at the occasion of meeting Moritz Fink, who later authored *THE SIMPSONS: A Cultural History* published in 2019:

> [Fink looks at] THE SIMPSONS in relation to the larger history of cultural jamming politics, a project which seeks to rethink culture jamming not simply as a disruption or interruption of mass media feeds but also as having the potential to "jam with" popular culture, creating something new out of the raw materials provided us by mass media producers. Anyone who has thought about THE SIMPSONS and especially its relationship with Rupert Murdoch's Fox Network recognize [*sic!*] that there's something curious going on here: THE SIMPSONS both embodies a highly successful commercial franchise,

one which extends across conglomerate media, and at the same time, it often models subversive and resistant relationships to corporate culture, going back to its roots in alternative comics. Early on, Matt Groening embraced the grassroots entrepreneurialism represented by the "Black Bart" T-shirts which transformed the Simpsons [sic!] into a vehicle for Afro-centric critique of white culture.

This quote from Jenkins' blog shows why many ACA fans concentrate on THE SIMPSONS: The series' producers have always been experts at culture jamming, a guerrilla tactics formerly restricted to anti-consumerist texts, as Mark Dery's pamphlet title *Culture Jamming: Hacking, Slashing, and Sniping in the Empire of Signs* from 1993 demonstrates. But with late-20th-century media and, I would say, with THE SIMPSONS, that changed.

Accordingly, in his book *Fans, Bloggers, and Gamers: Exploring Participatory Culture,* published in 2006, Henry Jenkins looks back on the 1990s as a cultural moment of great importance for "mass media," or, as we would say today, popular media and popular-culture studies at the same time (cf. 2006b). In the 1990s, consumerist media texts changed: they addressed their formerly passive viewers as participating fans, and, on these grounds, academics started to take them seriously. Thus I claim that, seen from a 21st-century perspective, THE SIMPSONS, from the 1990s onwards, have significantly helped pushing forward not only pop culture, but also U.S.-American popular-culture studies and helped television studies make considerable progress.

Therefore, the question whether it is necessary to write yet another book on THE SIMPSONS has to be answered with a yes. By looking at THE SIMPSONS' varied incarnations within the special cycle TREEHOUSE OF HORROR, this book will show that THE SIMPSONS practiced media jamming long before the cultural practices of the digital age were hailed by Espen Aarseth in sentences such as: digital media are able "to combine the aesthetic and the social in a way the old mass media, such as theatre, movies, TV shows and novels never could." With respect to culture-jamming practices of TV among other media, Aarseth is actually proven wrong by the popular-culture scholars of his time, although he is, of course, right when it comes to his media-related analyses of the digital age.

As will be demonstrated at several points in this book, in the late 1980s, THE SIMPSONS were new pop material and thus gave observant readers the opportunity to develop new theories of media convergence and participatory culture (Henry Jenkins), remediation and hypermediality (Jay David Bolter and Richard Grusin), or mediascapes (Arjun Appadurai), and of Jean Baudrillard's simulations from 1981 as reformulated in the context of videogames by Espen J. Aarseth in 2001. By way of these new pop-cultural terms I will first be looking at how THE SIMPSONS travels from one medium to another. In a second step, however, I will shift focus to the ways TREEHOUSE OF HORROR uses the Simpsons as characters to self-reflexively think about the visual culture from which the series emerged, about other mediascapes as well as about the conditions of their production and perception.

THE SIMPSONS, Postmodernism, and Popular-Culture Studies: Between Fans and the ACAdemy

Existing scholarship on THE SIMPSONS can be subdivided into two larger categories. The first category includes, among others, officially 'licensed' merchandise such as THE SIMPSONS Bongo Comic book series and SIMPSONS-creator Matt Groening's own publications of the SIMPSONS Forever books (1997, 1999). These are "color-coded" (1997: 13) episode guide books that chronicle detailed readings of SIMPSONS' "characters, episodes, and secret jokes you might have missed" (cover text, 1997).

In addition, the first category also comprises the broad creative output by fans including 'unlicensed' (also online) articles and books. Significant sources are fashion journalist John Ortved's *SIMPSONS Confidential: The uncensored, totally unauthorized history of the world's greatest TV show by the people that made it* (2009), music journalist Chris Turner's bulky volume *Planet Simpson* (2012 [2004]), and stand-up comedienne Allie Goertz's and Julia Prescott's *(Totally Unofficial) 100 Things THE SIMPSONS Fans Should Know & Do Before They Die* (2018). Chris Turner, for example, justifies his almost 500-pages SIMPSONS manifesto by the fact that, in contemporary culture, THE SIMPSONS is probably cited more often than the Bible or Shakespeare (cf. 55). The recent retrospective *'THE SIMPSONS': A Cultural History* by the librarian and scholar Moritz Fink from 2019 offers an affectionate look back on thirty years of "lasting influence of the show" (Bosky 2019). All of these texts offer erudite tongue-in-cheek explorations of and much background stories on THE SIMPSONS and those who stand behind the show.

The second group of SIMPSONS research comprises texts which not only better the academic understanding of THE SIMPSONS as a cultural and media phenomenon. These texts also improve the understanding of contemporary American popular culture by means of THE SIMPSONS. Noteworthy sources are the two books by the self-proclaimed 'Simpsonologists' and popular-culture experts Carma Waltonen and Denise Du Vernay. In 2010, they co-authored their collection *THE SIMPSONS in the Classroom: Embiggening the Learning Experience with the Wisdom of Springfield* (2010). Waltonen and Du Vernay demonstrate how THE SIMPSONS has become a great asset to the learning experience across a variety of different disciplines, from American cultural studies across linguistics to literary- and media studies. Their second book from 2019 is dedicated to *THE SIMPSONS' Beloved Springfield: Essays on the TV Series and Town that Are a Part of Us All.*

1 Introduction

In cooperation with a range of different contributors, Waltonen and Du Vernay base their essay collection on the belief that it is not the show that has changed so much since its heyday, but 'us.' Not only would the show have changed popular culture, but, more importantly, its viewers' ability *to look at* popular culture. From this point of departure, the essays in the volume shed a quite intimate light on THE SIMPSONS' everyday culture that is part of us all, on Springfield's "rhetorics of death," on "commercials and consumerism," or on "banal environmentalism." The essays offer an advanced, elaborate, sometimes polemic perspective of 'fan academics' who work in a variety of different fields and who justifiably can define themselves as Simpsonian natives. A review in the *Library Journal* writes that the book is a "fun read" both for SIMPSONS' fans "who will appreciate academics geeking out," but also for scholars who "will benefit from this embiggening of Simpson-ology" (Bosky 2019).

With regard to THE SIMPSONS' educational value, it should be noted that already some years earlier Jonathan Gray, a communication and media-studies scholar at the Jesuit Fordham University in New York, referred to the social role of THE SIMPSONS' comedy for teaching purposes. In 2006, Gray published the reception study *Watching With 'THE SIMPSONS': Television, Parody, and Intertextuality* that was preceded by his article "Television Teaching: Parody, THE SIMPSONS, and Media Literacy Education" he had published in 2005. In both texts Gray examines to what extent THE SIMPSONS' use of intertextual parody can function as a "media literacy educator" (2005: 223), for example of rhetorical techniques that are genuine to television. However, Gray does not open THE SIMPSONS' scope towards other areas of media. Instead, he limits the show to a "parodic sitcom" that offers "a playful critique of television from within the television frame" (2005: 223).

Further research between fandom and academic interest in THE SIMPSONS was done within a range of niche disciplines; 'niche' at least in relation to a popular animated-television show. THE SIMPSONS was read through the lens of behavioral psychology, for example, in *The Psychology of THE SIMPSONS' D'oh!* (Brown/Logan 2009). But the show also raised the attention of contemporary philosophers who looked at *THE SIMPSONS and Philosophy* (Irwin/Conard/Skoble 2010), or of mathematicians as proved by the German publication *Homers letzter Satz: DIE SIMPSONS und die Mathematik* (Singh 2013). Both categories of literature on THE SIMPSONS helped to open what Spigel terms a "discourse field," (8) reducing the formerly insurmountable distance between fan response and academic analysis. However, within both fan-centered- and ACA-fan categories no research was conducted on TREEHOUSE OF HORROR, THE SIMPSONS' annual Halloween special cycle.

In the following two subchapters, I will discuss three SIMPSONS-focused secondary sources in greater detail that had an essential influence on American popular culture as dominated by postmodern theories: firstly, by former Fulbright professor of American literature Matthew A. Henry, secondly, by John Alberti, popular-culture and television scholar at Northern Kentucky University, as well as, thirdly, by television scholar Jason Mittell from Middlebury College. Those scholars were among the first to spawn a new way of thinking about popular culture and television and a reading of THE SIMPSONS in line with postmodern thought. I will use their approaches to non-affirmative, postmodern storytelling in order to proceed to TREEHOUSE OF HORROR and its relation to American popular-culture history in the digital age.

THE SIMPSONS, Popular Culture, and Postmodern Theory: Matthew A. Henry and John Alberti

As one of the first SIMPSONS scholars, Matthew A. Henry established a connection between postmodern cultural theories and the study of pop-culture representations in his 1994 essay "The Triumph of Popular Culture: Situation Comedy, Postmodernism, and THE SIMPSONS". In comparison, the already mentioned 'Simpsonologists' Carma Waltonen and Denise Du Vernay belong to the group of more recent scholars who look back at THE SIMPSONS' history from a current point of view. Matthew Henry, however, was one of the first academics who used THE SIMPSONS in the mid-1990s to speculate about the difference THE SIMPSONS would make in the future of U. S.-American culture.

The essay is based on a quote by *The New Yorker* journalist Tad Friend about popular culture and the "conceptual crisis" of art in 1993 (Henry 1994: 85). Friend suggests that in the late 20th century, "good art that reaches millions and makes them feel connected may have more to offer us than great art that reaches three thousand and makes them feel more or less alone" (qtd. in Henry 1994: 85). That said, Friend claims that in 1993 the standards for what is perceived as 'good art' are determined by popular culture, i. e. by millions of television viewers and internet users, and that "the future belongs to Bart Simpson" (qtd. in Henry 85). In 2012, Henry published his essay as part of his monograph *The Simpsons, Satire, and American Culture* which he dedicates to the question what makes THE SIMPSONS so significant. Already in his 1994 essay, he celebrates THE SIMPSONS for disputing "the need for critical distance" which "makes people feel connected in society" (cf. Henry 1994: 85). Henry confirms that the show's animation, its humor, satire, and 'realistic' approach to everyday culture encourages its fans to feel as members of a group when they refer to their fandom.

Building on Henry's notions about THE SIMPSONS' influence on American postmodern pop culture, I suggest to now take a closer look at TREEHOUSE OF HORROR and to investigate whether the show offers a take on popular culture that exceeds the scope of THE SIMPSONS. Whereas the secondary literature on THE SIMPSONS inquires how the series broadens people's view on American culture, I will ask if

Treehouse of Horror further improves our understanding of U.S.-America's popular narratives, its art, and media history. If The Simpsons has taught its fans how to watch postmodern television, I argue that Treehouse of Horror has taught us fans how to make sense of American popular media culture in general.

Postmodernism & Popular Satire

In 2004, John Alberti from Northern Kentucky University invited contributors to realize a book project in celebration of The Simpsons series. The essays in the collection *Leaving Springfield: The Simpsons and the Possibility of Oppositional Culture* read the show as political, and its writers, show runners, and animators as activists. In his introduction, Alberti explains that, from the beginning, the show's key attraction has been "the sense of 'getting away with something'" (Alberti xii). The editor insists that The Simpsons has managed to become a highly popular prime-time program while, at the same time, promoting "the subversive and the transgressive" (*ibid*.: xii). He describes The Simpsons as subversive because it consciously undermines the of the upper-middle-class television shows that dominated the TV screens in the 1980s. Groening's animated series transgressed the moral standards of traditional television comedy. Alberti suggests that The Simpsons defined new standards for biting satirical comedy on prime-time network television. He regards The Simpsons as pioneers of political satire long before 'satire TV' conquered the airwaves in the post-network era with the hugely successful The Daily Show that premiered in 1996 on Comedy Central. The essays hold the opinion that The Simpsons taught Stephen Colbert, Jon Stewart, and Rick Mercer how to do TV satire. According to them, everybody who wants to have a lasting impact on their audience should live up to Matt Groening's central and oft-cited motto: be entertaining and subversive (cf. Bhattacharya 2000).

From The Simpsons to Treehouse of Horror: Popular Genre Mixing & Adult Animation

Television scholar Jason Mittell published texts "in formal academic publications and informally on blogs" (2015: 4) on the changing landscape of television storytelling around the turn of the millennium, a landscape to which The Simpsons had decisively contributed. Most of Mittell's writings represent his attempt "to engage with television's formal dimensions in concert with a broader approach to television as a cultural phenomenon" (2015: 4). The Simpsons has been a central object in his scrutiny of today's television. In his article "Cartoon Realism" from 2001, Mittell analyzes The Simpsons' 'cartoon realism,' the way The Simpsons set the standard for a new type of adult-animation programs. Then Mittell related animation to 'genre mixing,' i. e. to the way the show made ample use of different genres to establish THE SIMPSONS as something totally new, as a genre that was directed at adults.

In his article "Making Fun of Genres" from 2004, Mittell further extends the strategy of genre mixing. He examines whether THE SIMPSONS' politics of (postmodern) parody has an influence on American culture in general. Mittell later includes THE SIMPSONS in his various considerations about seriality and television genres, and refers to it in his much-acclaimed article "Narrative Complexity in Contemporary American Television" from 2006. The TV scholar also uses THE SIMPSONS to define the transition to a new TV culture in *Television and American Culture* (2010). In *Complex TV: The Poetics of Contemporary Television* from 2015 he elaborates on why the notion of 'quality TV' needs a re-evaluation and should be measured by the poetics of narrative complexity rather than by its politics.

Mittell reads THE SIMPSONS' "postmodern textual aesthetic" as having revolutionized the sitcom's formulaic limits (2004: 180). His enthusiasm towards the animated series encouraged me in my quest of finding a proper category for TREEHOUSE OF HORROR. Mittell's most recent study on *Complex TV* also inspired me to investigate whether TREEHOUSE OF HORROR is even more innovative than THE SIMPSONS, if it adds up to the complex forms of television storytelling by mixing different popular-culture languages that far exceed the frame of 20th-century television. Does TREEHOUSE OF HORROR use different, new ways to appeal to fans than its main series? What effects does the Halloween Special create with its unusual narrative approach, its constant remediation of different media, and its genre mixing when compared to other complex-TV formats and to THE SIMPSONS? Do the TREEHOUSE OF HORROR episodes mix genres in the same way as THE SIMPSONS which mix sitcom with children's cartoon? Or does TREEHOUSE OF HORROR offer us even more innovate techniques and aesthetics that anticipated digital media layering and other complex forms of blending genres which predominated in later animation shows of the digital age?

Mittell argues that complexity in TV series depends on narrative special effects, i. e. on aesthetics which a television narrative employs to "flex its storytelling muscles" in order to "confound and amaze a viewer" (2015: 43). Yet, neither Jason Mittell nor any other scholar so far has realized that TREEHOUSE OF HORROR does not need any explosive pyro techniques to leave its viewers awestruck. I have always been most impressed by the way TREEHOUSE OF HORROR references media and genres from across history. It does this differently than THE SIMPSONS, or the action-oriented television series ALIAS (ABC 2001–2006), the cinephile thriller anthology FARGO (Netflix 2014–2017), or LOST (ABC 2004–2010) with its fast oscillation between different temporal levels. But so far no one has written about the specific techniques TREEHOUSE OF HORROR makes use of to, for example, foreground all kinds of different readings that Edgar Allen Poe's classic 19th-century Gothic poem "The Raven" can evoke.

Treehouse of Horror's "The Raven" (1990) raises attention to the changing interpretations of literary texts across time. Lisa begins to solemnly read out the poem to her brother from a school book, while Bart sarcastically comments on the canon text from a 20th-century perspective in return. Another reading is given in James Earl Jones' voice-over interpretation (he lent his voice to Darth Vader in the Star Wars prequel trilogy, 1977–1983) of Poe's text while the animation takes up the perspectives and aesthetics of the poem's late-19th-century illustrator, Gustave Doré. His engravings obviously influenced the mise-en-scène of Treehouse of Horror's animated segment, an early moment of Treehouse of Horror's spectacular storytelling.

Treehouse's "The Raven" introduced innovative techniques that appealed not only to cine aficionados, but also to avid readers of 19th-century literature, to cartoon- and comedy fans, historians, sound designers, and many more. Beginning with the first Halloween episode from 1990, I will investigate the techniques and aesthetics Treehouse of Horror has been working with to shame conventional television. I ask how Treehouse of Horror managed to sharpen many viewers' senses for popular culture. How is it different from any animation series following the lead of The Simpsons, from South Park (Comedy Central, since 1997) to Family Guy (Fox, since 1999). Treehouse of Horror is much more than an audacious half-hour obscene-comedy program for adults. Does it suffice, then, to define the Halloween series as a one-off seasonal special or an anthology series for adults? As the first scholar to concentrate on Treehouse of Horror as a cycle with its own history, aesthetic standards, genre parameters, and 'narrative special effects' I aim at finding a category for this anthology series.

The Simpsons' Halloween Special Cycle

It is a well-established tradition on American television that the Big Four networks, Fox, ABC, NBC, and CBS, but also streaming- and other broadcasting services offer special programs for special occasions. Special occasions are, of course, public holidays, days when a large amount of American households is assumed to have considerable time to spend in front of the television. Thus, the networks seek to sell season-relevant products especially through special programming that is supposed to get consumers in the right mood for Christmas, Thanksgiving, or Halloween. I have, of course, always had special appreciation for the Halloween episodes of my favorite sitcoms. Even today, Roseanne's "Boo" (ABC 1989) or Home Improvement's "Haunting of Taylor House" (ABC 1992) give me fond memories of their one-off seasonal take on Halloween with their exciting costumes, the scary make-up, and the excessive Halloween decoration inside and outside the families' home. Therefore, it doesn't come as a surprise that these episodes commonly are the most watched and thus best-rated episodes of a sitcom season.

Of course THE SIMPSONS also has 'special' episodes that center on traditional American holidays like Thanksgiving and Christmas, but none of these are as noteworthy as the annual Halloween attraction of TREEHOUSE OF HORROR. One crucial distinguishing factor that sets TREEHOUSE OF HORROR apart from the 'normal' sitcom special is that THE SIMPSONS' Halloween series is the only holiday special with an uninterrupted continuity of thirty episodes between 1990 and 2020. In comparison, ABC produced eight Halloween episodes altogether in ten seasons of ROSEANNE between 1988 and 1997; and HOME IMPROVEMENT comprises seven Halloween specials in eight seasons between 1991 and 1999.

A second determining characteristic of TREEHOUSE OF HORROR's non-canonical continuity is the segments' focus on a plot-based structure. This narrative pattern sets it apart from those of the Connors and the Taylors; their traditional character-centered plots about loyalty and bonding are simply set among Halloween decoration. Metaphorically speaking, TREEHOUSE OF HORROR episodes uproot their characters, tear them from their regular roles and positions in order to replace the protective safety of the 'family' and the 'home' by the wonky and draughty 'treehouse' in which the horror stories are assumedly told. The series' mini-horror stories revolve around the most familiar narratives from different media and varying forms of genre-horror. For thirty years, TREEHOUSE OF HORROR has been paying animated homage to genre texts from Gothic, fantasy, horror, and science fiction. In these episodes, the Simpson characters can die (see "Wanted Dead, Then Alive," 2015), and play varying roles (e. g. Marge and her sisters act as witches in "Easy-Bake Coven," 1997), mutate to monsters (see "Married to the Blob," 2006), or turn all kinds of familiar film horror scenarios into a family matter as in "The Shinning" and "Bad Dream House" (both 1990).

TREEHOUSE OF HORROR: Time Travel through American Pop-Culture History

The overall ninety segments of the thirty TREEHOUSE OF HORROR episodes plus couch gag (i. e. opening sequence plus three segments per episode) take you out of your TV comfort zone in order to abduct you to a completely different time and place. When I noticed that THE SIMPSONS' Halloween episodes send their fans on time travels through American popular-culture history, I knew that the moment had come to devote my book entirely to TREEHOUSE OF HORROR. In a collaborative effort, the show's various writers, show runners, and executive producers make careful use of popular texts and media from the past and thus create a "rich, primary-colour dystopia," as Sanjiv Bhattacharya writes in *The Guardian* in 2000. And it became my aim to explore these rich dystopias. My questions are: Why does TREEHOUSE take up such diverse texts as E. A. Poe's Gothic poem *The Raven* from 1845, Stuart Rosenberg's horror movie AMITYVILLE HORROR from 1979, or Rod Serling's TWILIGHT ZONE episode "To Serve Man" from 1962? Which texts were privileged and how were they dealt with? What were the show's creators trying to tell present-day fans about the past?

One of my colleagues at university once told me that when she was younger she didn't like the TREEHOUSE OF HORROR show, although she was a fan of the regular THE SIMPSONS series; she was terrified because she simply didn't understand the Halloween special. Her example illustrates that TREEHOUSE OF HORROR obviously follows a different strategy than the seasonal episodes of my beloved sitcoms ROSEANNE or HOME IMPROVEMENT. TREEHOUSE OF HORROR in fact doesn't have much to do with regular television programming or other one-off seasonal sitcom specials. Thus a large part of my investigation will be dedicated to finding out which traditions of television storytelling TREEHOUSE OF HORROR can be attributed to. If THE SIMPSONS is dealing with current events in American culture such as television shows, politics, or everyday phenomena like Black Friday shopping, what is the prime concern of TREEHOUSE OF HORROR? What are its functions?

Popular-Culture History of the Digital Age: Theory, History, Analysis

Now, at the end of my introduction, I will introduce the structure of the following text. The book is divided into three larger parts; in accordance with the introduction, the second part consists of a theoretical and the third part of an analytical section. Whereas part two, "THE SIMPSONS & Postmodern Theory," introduces the foundation of my thinking about THE SIMPSONS, the analytical part three is subsequently preoccupied with negotiating theory and history in four close readings exploring the genres of TREEHOUSE OF HORROR. The four different analyses are introduced in 3.1 . This subchapter equips the reader with the necessary background to understand TREEHOUSE's conceptual framework of lessons to remember, that help to make sense of the ways historical bits and textual pieces were used to create something entirely new.

The existing research on THE SIMPSONS led me to believe that the show arouses the fan in the academic scholar, but frequently also evokes the academic scholar in the fan. Based on this observation, the following chapter two discusses four highly influential postmodern theories closely read through the lenses of THE SIMPSONS and TREEHOUSE OF HORROR: Umberto Eco's notions of popular art (2.1), Angela

McRobbie's contributions to representations within popular culture (2.2), Linda Hutcheon's emphasis on the significance of postmodern parody (2.3), and lastly, Michel Foucault's view on the concept of the archive which I will contextualize as a popular-culture archive (2.4). These approaches will help me to examine how the perspectives on the digital age that the Halloween series offers to its fans are different from those of THE SIMPSONS.

As mentioned above, part three is introduced by how the show "teaches lessons to remember" and then continues with detailed analyses of the four individual sections which make up a typical TREEHOUSE OF HORROR episode. The first Halloween episode from 1990, for example, begins with the opening sequence also known as the 'couch gag.' What follows are three mini-stories, one of which (to stick to a chronological order of artistic development in the first episode) deals with a literary example from 19th-century Gothic fiction, another continues with a cinematic example, in this case a horror-movie mash-up of films from the 1980s, and the last one ends with an adaptation of the television anthology THE TWILIGHT ZONE from the 1960s. These genre markers provide the basic structure for my close reading of more than one hundred years of pop-culture media content. The frame of reference given in 3.1 splits TREEHOUSE OF HORROR into its typical components from which the show was assembled during different 'golden ages of horror' that once were defined for the radio and for cinema, had their respective heydays in comics culture and Gothic literature, and even on television. In chapter 3.2, I will discuss the couch gag as a prototypical example of participatory culture by means of what I define as the 'cartoon auteur.' Subchapter 3.3 invites a look at the literary legacy of TREEHOUSE OF HORROR; the show teaches the audience not only about European and American Gothic fiction, but also about performative media literacy and the popular-culture practice of transmedia adaptation. Part 3.4 puts TREEHOUSE OF HORROR's filmic archive under the microscope and discusses the relationship between television and cinema as an example of media convergence. My final analysis in 3.5 explores the lasting influence of the broadcasting tradition of the radio play and more specifically TREEHOUSE OF HORROR's repurposing of Rod Serling's TV anthology THE TWILIGHT ZONE from the 1960s.

Exploring my appendix is worthwhile for those who find pleasure in comprehensive contexts of TREEHOUSE OF HORROR. I give hitherto new overviews of the show's complex setup in "TREEHOUSE OF HORROR Episode Guide" (5.1) and "TREEHOUSE OF HORROR Reference Guide" (5.2) as well as a "List of Guest-Animated Couch Gags" (5.3) from THE SIMPSONS and TREEHOUSE OF HORROR. The appendices provide interesting information, for example, on the titles and original airdates, shed light on the themes, motifs, and sources of each segment, and give information on the who-is-who of guest animators who have submitted contributions to both shows.

To Be Continued?

This book will fill a gap that still exists in Simpsons criticism and cultural-studies analysis. After having watched The Simpsons on television for thirty years, I consider myself one of the "Simpsonian natives," as Michael Gruteser and his co-editors call us in *Subversion zur Prime-Time* (2013: 11). I am an ACA fan whose mission is to document what lessons about popular-culture history and -theory we have learned from Treehouse of Horror in particular. My strategic focus on Treehouse of Horror will open a chapter of The Simpsons that was long overdue to be written.

1 Screenshot from THE SIMPSONS' original opening sequence since 2004 with a close-up of the brass plate underneath the Springfield's alleged town founder Jebediah Springfield.

2 Theory | THE SIMPSONS and Postmodernity

"A noble spirit embiggens the smallest man!" This is the inscription on the brass plate below the statue of Springfield's founding father, Jebediah Springfield (see Fig. 1). Cultural studies- and media scholars who work with THE SIMPSONS often read the uplifting quote along the lines of other Simpsons neologisms (e.g. Homer's "D'oh!" or "Mmm… donuts") as a lesson in linguistics. I will take a look at this quote from a postmodern popular-culture perspective to investigate what else can be learned from it beyond a lesson in grammar, phonology, and semantics.

From this point of departure a number of questions come to mind: Does the quote help us to understand the show's approach to the U.S.-American culture in which it is set, from which it emerged, and which it is about? Does the quote mirror the show's agenda as enlightening even its 'smallest' fan?[2] Does it want to enlighten or embiggen its fans? Whose 'noble spirit' is meant? Does the adjective 'noble' refer to somebody's honorable and altruistic character? Does 'embiggen' imply that a noble spirit will improve the spiritual wealth of every small man? What does 'small' mean in this context? 'Small' in mind or in power, low in need or in taste, physically small or spiritually limited as in the Bible's beatitude of "the poor in spirit"? As of yet, unanswered questions abound.

I suggest to read the inscription in THE SIMPSONS' opening sequence differently. For me, it rather exemplifies THE SIMPSONS' basic principle of irritating

---

1   Unless otherwise specified, the images are screenshots from episodes of the Fox series THE SIMPSONS.
2   German media critic Diedrich Diedrichsen reads THE SIMPSONS' subversion as part of "postmodern enlightenment" as it is quoted in Gruteser *et al.* 2002: 18.

the viewing habits of TV consumers. By this quote, the series shows that, in the 1980s, it presents something entirely new. When the show started as a primetime series, it confronted TV audiences with a viewing experience other sitcoms of the time had not prepared them for. In applying an inclusive, dialogical approach to America's (popular) cultural history, THE SIMPSONS' mission to embiggen the minds of its audience manifests a far more complex form of serial storytelling than originally assumed in early research on THE SIMPSONS, for example, in linguistics.[3]

Postmodernism: A Perfect Cromulent Wor(l)d?

Before THE SIMPSONS were launched, the neologism 'embiggen' had not existed in common parlance, and made it into the Merriam Webster and the OED Dictionaries first in 2018. The word's etymology is explained in the 1996 episode, "Lisa the Iconoclast," in which Springfield's school children watch a film about the founding father of their hometown, Jebediah Springfield, which the teachers, Ms. Krabappel and Ms. Hoover, comment on with the following dialogue:

> MS. KRABAPPEL: 'Embiggen'? – Mm. Never heard that word before I moved to Springfield.
> MS. HOOVER: I don't know why?! It's a perfect cromulent word.

An article on the Merriam Webster explains that the writers of the episode were asked to create these nonce words – words that only sound as if they could be in actual use. According to the DVD audio commentary to "Lisa the Iconoclast," David X. Cohen, writer of the episode, coined 'cromulent' which he translates as 'acceptable' and 'fine'.[4] The subtlety of this joke was that its viewers didn't know it was a joke. Both 'cromulent' and 'embiggen' are sly expressions that, according to the author of the article in Merriam Webster's "Words We're Watching," have "crept into the language" (undated). This inconspicuous example of how things invented in THE SIMPSONS crept into U.S.-American parlance encourages me to look for and analyze what cultural influence Matt Groening's yellow five have not only had on generations of audiences, but also on 21st-century cultural-studies re-

---

3   Heidi Harley, professor of linguistics at the University of Arizona, holds a blog in which she posts "annual Simpson's linguistic joke collections" since 2005. See her Blogpost "Beyond beyond beyond beyond 'Beyond embiggens and cromulent'", posted on August 23, 2016 (URL: https://bit.ly/3jsosbQ). The two often cited authors of *The Simpsons in the Classroom* from 2010, Carma Waltonen and Denise du Vernay, dedicate a chapter to THE SIMPSONS and linguistics in "A Noble Spirit Embiggens the Smallest Man, or THE SIMPSONS and Linguistics", 159–178.
4   Cohen, David X. THE SIMPSONS season 7 DVD commentary for the episode "Lisa the Iconoclast" (DVD). 20th Century Fox, 2005.

search. I would even go so far as to claim that THE SIMPSONS' creators employ such nonce words to direct the viewers' attention to the show's exceptional status in the history of American network television.

In "Mr. Lisa Goes to Washington",[5] Homer is depicted with his plumber's crack peeping out of his pants when ironically commenting that "cartoons are just stupid drawings that give you a cheap laugh." Metaphorically, however, the notion of emboldening, i.e. equipping someone quite common with additional courage and grandeur illustrates that THE SIMPSONS' cartoon art is exceptional and pursues higher goals than to provide "cheap laughs" only. The indefinable quality of the statue's inscription hints at THE SIMPSONS' inventiveness and its quite coarse straightforwardness when it comes to humor. But at the same time this example speaks of a cultural sensibility testifying to its creators' knowledge of theory.

From the very beginning of SIMPSONS academic research, scholars showed a tendency to discuss the show under premises from postmodern cultural theory as can be demonstrated by titles such as Matthew Henry's 1994 article "The Triumph of Popular Culture: Situation Comedy, Postmodernism, and THE SIMPSONS," Jason Mittell's "Cartoon Realism" from 2001, and John Alberti's *Leaving Springfield* from 2006. However, the longer I thought about the 'noble spirit that embiggens even the smallest man,' the clearer it became that this cartoon show can also be read as a disturbance, an irritation of postmodernist assumptions. In the following section, I will focus on THE SIMPSONS' irritation strategies in greater detail.

When Postmodernism went Popular Culture

In how far is THE SIMPSONS a prototypically postmodern example? Already in 1999, the German cultural-studies scholar Diedrich Diederichsen described THE SIMPSONS as "das kompletteste postmoderne Kunstwerk" and its aim as "postmoderne Aufklärung" (Diederichsen 2013: 15). He was convinced that the show was in fact the only 'enlightening' piece of art that 'understood' what postmodernism was (cf. *ibid*.: 15).

Postmodernism is often seen as a period practicing extensive citation. THE SIMPSONS are a popular example to illustrate this. Australian art historian Daniel Palmer explains that the very structure of THE SIMPSONS quotes not only the classic live-action family sitcom; in order to ridicule all forms of institutional authority – patriarchal, political, religious – the show endlessly quotes from other media texts and thus establishes intertextual relations between itself and other texts. Palmer is convinced that the show "generates a relentlessly ironic or postmodern worldview" by the help of its "hyperconscious intertextuality" (Palmer 2014).

---

5   Cf. THE SIMPSONS, dir. Wes Archer, s03e02, Fox 1991.

Yet, THE SIMPSONS (so-called 'canon')[6] and its annual Halloween special TREEHOUSE OF HORROR (so-called 'non-canon') make different use of hyperconscious intertextuality than other TV shows because both series offer different "push-button options" of recognizing how different texts are linked to one another in their animation as Jim Collins proves in "Postmodernism and Television" (1993: 167). THE SIMPSONS, for example, is famous for mocking almost every American president, dead or alive, such as Richard Nixon in "Whacking Day,"[7] or George Bush, Sr., in "Two Bad Neighbors,"[8] not to mention the many instances that play on the Donald Trump administration as in the YouTube short film "Trumptastic Voyage" (2015). American presidents are popular targets of the show because they exemplify the contradictory ideological foundation of American institutions, each functions as "Hohlspiegel gesellschaftlicher Realitäten" ("concave mirror of societal realities," my transl.), as the German media scholar Andreas Rauscher calls such figures (2013: 154).

TREEHOUSE OF HORROR doesn't make use of individual characters as mirrors of societal realities; rather the show works with familiar plots from written texts, television formats, and films, foregrounding fictional characters such as monsters in order to hold up the mirror to American society and look at it through the lens of popular culture. According to film theorist Jim Collins, the decision in favor of these narrative, say 'push-button options' requires that a text presupposes that its audience has reading competence and understands what constitutes both entertainment and cultural literacy in the age of information (cf. Collins 1993: 167).

What will be shown at various moments in this book is how THE SIMPSONS validated the study of popular culture by challenging the priority of high art through the versatility of popular mass entertainment. It will further be analyzed what precisely are the different 'push-button options' in THE SIMPSONS and TREEHOUSE OF HORROR respectively, and how each show uses its own hyperconscious intertextuality not to mark intellectual decay or the end of great ideas in mass entertainment, but to be read as a site of re-membering popular-culture history differently in and through animation. How, then, could THE SIMPSONS exemplify a new

6   When discussing TV series as fictitious continuity narratives the 'canon' label defines a consistency of all characters, locations, and relationships that create the fictional universe of, for example, THE SIMPSONS. TREEHOUSE OF HORROR is defined as 'non-canon' because as seasonal Halloween special that is produced once a year, the series, or cycle, might contain moments that extend beyond the borders of the regular canon, including new characters and locations, killing-off stock characters, or experimenting with other forms of continuity storytelling to depart from sitcom formulaic conventions, e.g. as the show does with the anthology narration. For the matter of this project, however, I aim to demonstrate that TREEHOUSE OF HORROR needs to be analyzed as an independent continuity with an individual fictional universe.

7   Cf. THE SIMPSONS, dir. Jeff Lynch, s04e20, Fox 1993.

8   Cf. THE SIMPSONS, dir. Wes Archer, s07e13, Fox 1996.

zeitgeist by operating with parody as well as satire in a time when postmodernism and its citation practices had already become the dominant discourse in Western culture of the 1980s?

Before THE SIMPSONS became a cultural phenomenon, cultural-studies scholars were preoccupied with the question whether postmodern cultural representations such as paintings, literature, film, or television, should still be legitimized by way of modernist values and ideals or not. The art critic and historian Hal Foster, for example, remarks in the preface to his book *Anti-Aesthetic* from 1983 that postmodernism aims to deconstruct or rewrite modernism in order to "open its closed systems" (xi). From the perspective of 2021, the differences between modernism and postmodernism are not of great interest. For me it is more compelling to investigate how popular media has enlightened postmodern culture and theories. TREEHOUSE OF HORROR aims at deconstructing *and* rewriting historical media texts in order to embiggen or complement contemporary culture with an open repository of popular-culture production. The TREEHOUSE SERIES does not simply quote from other media texts, but discursively commemorates them. As a consequence, the TREEHOUSE OF HORROR texts re-negotiate, re-mediate, and re-member their historical material for the present, it re-purposes older texts, and re-creates an archive of American popular-culture history.

The constructivist philosopher Siegfried J. Schmidt offers an interesting approach to the discursive practice of re-membering in his essay "Gedächtnis – Erzählen – Identität" from 1993. He claims that memory solely exists in relation to the here and now of remembering, producing a sense which is necessitated by the present and conditioned by the past (cf. 1993: 76). Following Schmidt's reasoning, TREEHOUSE OF HORROR, for example, uses animation for the "now of remembering" by which the show constructs its own particular interpretation within a history of ordering practices (cf. *ibid*.: 76). Using Schmidt as a point of departure, the German media scholar Randi Gunzenhäuser writes:

> Remembering can be read as the continual re-membering, the re-cognition, and re-building of structure, and the re-establishing of a coherent order in the light of present interests. [...] Remembering constructs a 'present' past aiming at a future, a chronology in which past, present, and future relate to one another, depending on, and constructing, certain points of view. These points of view are intertextual; they construct and present particular moments and places within and as discourse. *(1998: 76–77)*

In the 1990s, when the first special episode of TREEHOUSE was produced, the idea to re-mediate historical texts and re-constitute intertextual points of view on particular moments within and of American popular-culture history was new in television. One of the best-known and most-referenced examples is the animation of "The Raven" from the first TREEHOUSE OF HORROR episode (1990). Following Gunzenhäuser's idea of re-membering as a continual process, the segment shows an interest in re-membering, re-constructing, or re-reading E. A. Poe's narrative poem *The Raven* to construct an intertextual chronology from a variety of different points of view. The segment thus re-constitutes a past for Poe's text, which the TREEHOUSE writers saw as being 'necessitated by the present and conditioned by the past.'[9] In contrast to THE SIMPSONS, TREEHOUSE OF HORROR has created its own discursive moment and place to re-member texts and media of the past; an animated destination on television that offers to re-experience American (popular) culture in a new way.

The cultural climate in which THE SIMPSONS was born marked the beginning of a new era of critical thinking about and through popular-culture representations. At the beginning of what Douglas Kellner labels the "postmodern turn," the 1970s and 1980s became the "time of the posts," which called for an overcoming of early 20th-century modernist ideas. Kellner, a third-generation Frankfurt School theorist, considered the times as marked by the "call for new theories and politics to deal with the striking novelties of the present" (Kellner 1997: 3–4). 'Overcoming' here meant to accelerate the 'becoming' of a new generation who, instead of being able to actively master the narratives, was itself more and more passively mastered *by* the narratives.

The generation's urge for a new social order brought along a belief in significant historical changes, a hope for post-war, post-colonialization, post-capitalism, and other revolutionizing 'post' times. In the preface to *The Empire Writes Back: Theory and Practice in Post-Colonial Literatures* (2002 [1989]), American Shakespeare scholar Terence Hawkes remembers that, although in his book *New Accents* from 1977,[10] he himself spoke darkly of a time of rapid and radical social change and regretted that modes and categories inherited from the past no longer seemed

9   This indicates that TREEHOUSE OF HORROR metaphorically speaking, paved the way for what would in the internet age become known as the "post-television era," in which networks offer their online-streaming services to viewers so they can binge-watch their favorite series in a bundle. After Disney's purchase of Rupert Murdoch's Fox corp. in 2017, the new streaming service Disney+ launched its program with airing THE SIMPSONS. According to the online newsfeeds of *The Los Angeles Times* (2019) or *The Hollywood Reporter* (2019), Disney+ upset fans of THE SIMPSONS because the show not only had to be adapted from a 4:3 ratio to Disney+'s 16:9 format, which partly cuts out essential details from the images. *Disney+* is also taunted for having cleaned the SIMPSONS catalogue. Some episodes do obviously not fit the family-friendly policy of Disney so that, for example, the Michael Jackson episode "Stark Raving Dad" (1991) was taken off the canon. For more information see Ryan Faughnder's "Don't have a cow, 'Simpsons' fans. Disney+ will offer 'original' aspect ratios in early 2020." *Los Angeles Times.com*, 15 Nov. 2019. 04 Jan. 2020. Parker, Ryan. "'Simpsons' Episode Featuring Michael Jackson Kept Off Disney+." *The Hollywood Reporter.com*, 13 Nov. 2019. 04 Jan. 2020.

10 For more information see Terence Hawkes' *Structuralism and Semiotics (New Accents)*. U of California Press, 1977; and "Preface" in *The Empire Writes Back: Theory and Practice in Post-*

to fit the reality experienced by a new generation, it would have been important to encourage, not resist the process of change (cf. 2002: ix). Hawkes' observation matches a quote from Chris Turner's *Planet Simpsons* in which the music journalist explains the impact of THE SIMPSONS on the 1980s cultural landscape:

> THE SIMPSONS was like climate change: it built incrementally, week by week, episode by episode, weaving itself into the cultural landscape slowly but surely until it became a permanent feature, a constant reminder that just beneath the luxurious surface of the prosperous time lurked much uglier truths.
> *(Turner 2004: 5)*

Chris Turner's comparison of THE SIMPSONS with climate change is helpful here: Some people may still try to refuse any belief in THE SIMPSONS, but nevertheless the series slowly but surely changed the cultural landscape until it has become a permanent feature whose importance today even non-believers have to accept (cf. Turner 2004: 5).

Douglas Kellner defines the decade of the 1980s as primarily surfing on the "vogue of deconstruction," which he describes as having "challenged the very premises of modern thought" (1997: 6) on academic and intellectual grounds. At the end of the decade, THE SIMPSONS proved that animation on primetime television was capable of questioning the myths of American culture and challenge the very premises of its ideological superstructure. "The show has had a pervasive influence on the broader culture, particularly in setting the default tone of its discourse," argues Chris Tuner (2004: 5). THE SIMPSONS presented a unique form of criticism with regard to American politics, social issues, corporate culture, identity, religion, gender, education, and many more points, which was unique among animated television shows of the 1980s.

Throughout the decade, identity and bodies as well as art had been deconstructed which influenced the response to popular-culture production both in positive and negative terms. The British cultural theorist Angela McRobbie reads the popular-culture explosion of the 1980s as an "implosion," because in the 1980s "images have pushed their way into the fabric of our social lives" (1994: 17). And by the end of the 1980s through the implosion of mass-media influence, from MTV as the voice of a new generation to the cyberpunk movement, from Thomas Pynchon's fiction between "pulp and Joyce"[11] to THE SIMPSONS' cartoon-

---

Colonial Literatures. 2nd ed. by Bill Ashcroft, Gareth Griffiths, and Helen Tiffin. London / New York: Routledge, 2002 [1989].

11 On the occasion of Thomas Pynchon's 80th anniversary in 2017, Andreas Platthaus praises Pynchon in the German *FAZ* for having invented something entirely new in the 1960s. Pynchon's novels *V* (1963), *The Crying of Lot 49* (1966), and *Gravity's Rainbow* (1973) set new standards for American fiction writing: According to Platthaus, Pynchon takes the structural

and comedy innovations, postmodernism had become an integral part of Western everyday life and the study of culture.

When people speak about popular culture, they in all probability refer to U.S.-American popular culture. In 2019, I taught a seminar on "1980s Cinema" and was startled to observe to which extent the idea of a 1980s America had influenced my students, although most of them were born around the 2000s. Although none of my students had a personal memory of this decade, the majority had an impressive media- and cultural literacy of the 1980s, primarily of films, styles, and music. This observation brought me to believe that Western popular culture is significantly shaped by the high-concept Hollywood cinema of the 1980s. The high-concept movie category includes, for example, the universe of the STAR WARS space opera that premiered in 1977, Steven Spielberg's cult characters of Indiana Jones from 1981,[12] E. T. from 1982,[13] and Gizmo from 1984,[14] as well as John Hughes' redefinition of the 1980s teen-drama,[15] a genre that addressed a new, commercially increasingly significant adolescent demographic.

Western popular culture was also influenced by the rise of cable television and American syndication of popular TV shows such as the American-Canadian cartoon series HE-MAN AND THE MASTERS OF THE UNIVERSE (Cartoon Network 1983–1985), the U.S. sitcoms CHEERS (NBC 1982–1993) and ALF (NBC 1986–1990), the TV drama DALLAS (CBS 1978–1991) and thriving game shows such as WHEEL OF FORTUNE (since NBC 1975). These television shows started in the U.S., spread throughout the globe and during my childhood became the most popular television programs of the decade in Germany. Specific product placement sold

---

    middle ground between "pulp and Joyce," in makes use of stock characters known from pulp fiction of the 1940s and embedded them in a rich referential universe between everyday banality and stylistic virtuosity. This structural principle would have been introduced in James Joyce's *Ulysses*. Cf. Andreas Platthaus article "Der Anti-Paranoiker" unter *FAZ.com*, rev. in 08 May 2017. 02 Jan. 2020.

12 The character Indiana Jones was introduced in Stephen Spielberg's RAIDERS OF THE LOST ARK (1981).

13 E. T. is the extraterrestrial protagonist of Stephen Spielberg's E.T.–THE EXTRATERRESTRIAL (1982).

14 Gizmo is the furry figure of Stephen Spielberg's horror comedy GREMLINS (1984), for which Spielberg ushered a new rating category of PG-13 to appeal to distributors and a broader audience demographic. For more information see James Kendrick's essay "Children in Danger: Screen Violence, Steven Spielberg, and the PG-13 Rating." *Hollywood Bloodshed: Violence in 1980s American Cinema*. Carbondale: Southern Illinois UP, 2009, 170–203.

15 John Hughes' teen-drama film cycle, also known as high school movies or coming-of-age drama films, consists of six films between 1984 and 1987, in which he defined 'youth in film' from an 1980s' perspective in terms of "suburbia, high school, and adolescent identity formation" (Driscoll 46). Hughes' teen-movie cycle includes, for example, THE BREAKFAST CLUB (1985), PRETTY IN PINK (1986) and FERRIS BUELLER'S DAY OFF (1986). For more information see Catherine Driscoll's *Teen Film: A Critical Introduction* from 2011.

the American way of life to me, a young German consumer; for me the American Dream consisted in drinking Coke, wearing Levi Strauss jeans, and eating McDonald's burgers. "First Time, First Love" became the song of Coca Cola's 1988 advertising campaign and one of Robin Beck's greatest hits, a song that still echoes my feelings of that time. The U.S. entertainment industry of Hollywood and broadcast media propelled a booming consumer culture. Movies and television shows of the time were successful in promoting American brands such as Steven Spielberg's 1985 all-time favorite movie BACK TO THE FUTURE and its placement of Nike Airs, Pepsi Max soft drinks, and the skateboarding of hero Marty McFly (Michael J. Fox) who pushed the social factor of "coolness."[16]

The effects of American popular culture on people's everyday lives in the Western world also affected academic research in the discipline of cultural studies. During the 1980s, popular culture developed into consumer culture, and identity, social values, and everyday practices were increasingly based on forms of consumption. When facing the "daunting task" of mapping the conceptual landscape of popular culture, British popular-studies theorist John Storey remarks in *Cultural Theory and Popular Culture* that "popular is in effect an *empty* conceptual category, one that can be filled in a variety of often conflicting ways, depending on the context of use" (2015: 1, *ital. in orig.*).

Studying popular culture, according to Storey, first means to think about 'culture' as, for example, a set of signifying practices like structuralists and post-structuralists generally argue (cf. 2015: 3). In this context the French Marxist philosopher Louis Althusser and his concept of "material practice" became highly influential. Althusser stresses that rituals and customs – such as the holiday traditions of trick'r'treating on Halloween or decorating a pine tree for Christmas – have the effect of binding us to the social order. The philosopher also argues that ideology is encountered in the practices *of* everyday life and not only in specific ideas *about* everyday life. Accordingly, 'ideology' is another concept crucial for the study of popular culture (qtd. in Storey 2015: 3).

When dealing with American culture, capitalist ideology is considered to be formative. John Storey argues that capitalist ideology builds on the power of the economy and can be characterized by

> […] a certain masking, distortion, or concealment. Ideology is used here to indicate how some texts and practices present distorted images of reality. They produce what is sometimes called 'false consciousness.' Such distortions, it is argued, work in the interests of the powerful against the interests of the powerless.
> *(Storey 2015: 3)*

---

16   For more information on the cultural logic of 'coolness' read the Canadian journalist Naomi Klein who provides insightful approaches in her mind-blowing book *No Logo!* from 1999.

This approach towards ideology follows the basic assumptions of classical Marxism, i. e. that "the way a society organizes the means of its economic production will have a determining effect on the type of culture that society produces" (Storey 2015: 3). The 20-year-old students in my "1980s Cinema" class proved that although they have no point of personal reference to the decade of 1980s, they operate on the basis of a collective memory characterized by a capitalist ideology, a culture that is based on 1980s American popular representations. MTV, Pepsi Max, and Marty McFly obviously have had a determining effect on the type of culture that Western societies have produced; a culture which I see located between an ideological sell-out of the American Dream and a narrative squeeze-out of the rags-to-riches story. Based on what the epic playwright Bertolt Brecht said about stage plays, namely that a play always includes an image of the world, no matter whether good or bad, John Storey enlarged the scope of Brecht's understanding of drama and Marx's understanding of ideological practices to all texts. Storey points to Brecht's statement that "art is never without consequences" which Storey rephrases as "all texts are ultimately political" (2015: 4).

In conclusion, I want to come to British cultural-studies theorist Stuart Hall who already in 1964 had published a book with Paddy Whannel on *The Popular Arts*. Hall gave one of the most comprehensive definitions of popular culture in 2009. He claims that popular culture is a site "where collective social understandings are created; a terrain on which the politics of signification are played out in attempts to win people to particular ways of seeing the world" (2009: 122–123). What terrain would be more suitable than television in order to direct a global audience's attention to the way that, for example, the white, middle-class sitcom presents a particular image of American life and wins people to its consumer-oriented ways of seeing the world through the windows of a suburban family home?

As one answer to Margaret Thatcher's neo-liberal conservatism, Stuart Hall suggests in "Gramsci and U. S.:" "I do believe that we must 'think' our problems in a Gramscian way" (see *The Hard Road to Renewal*, 1988: 161). Here Hall refers to Antonio Gramsci's concept of hegemony (1971, 2009),[17] and describes it as a way of control by those in power that functions at the same time as a power from above and from below. With respect to my examples, the white middle-class sitcom family can serve as a representative example of how the hegemony works through popular culture. From a Gramscian point of view, the traditional sitcom is one example for the hegemonic way in which "through a process of 'intellectual and moral leadership'" a dominant group in society (in this case: WASP) takes

---

17   For further discussion of Gramsci's definition of 'hegemony' in the context of cultural studies, see also, for example, Chris Barker's comprehensive reader *Cultural Studies: Theory and Practice* from 2007 or Jeff Lewis' *Cultural Studies: The Basics* from 2008.

over "intellectual and moral leadership" and "seeks to win the consent of subordinate groups in society" (Gramsci qtd. in Storey 2009: 10). By means of the concept 'hegemony,' Storey explains that Gramsci sought to elaborate the nature and politics of popular culture, which he saw as a "terrain of exchange and negotiation" between a pop culture that is dominated and incorporated by hegemonic forces and a pop culture of struggle and resistance.

The emergence of the cable-TV channel MTV (acronym for Music Television) in 1981 became significant for 1980s popular culture because it established the music video as an art form between protest and sell-out in the television landscape of the late 20th century. The niche channel MTV presented pop, hip-hop and rock music along with music videos and thus pushed a new art form with a distinct visual language. The mixed-performance style and fast-paced editing of MTV's premiering music video clip, The Buggles' "Video Killed the Radio Star" from 1979, already made clear that the approach was experimental. In his book *Legitimating Television: Media Convergence and Cultural Status* from 2012, music journalist Michael Z. Newman explores how television could develop from a "plug-in drug" to a "sophisticated high-tech gadget" in the 21st century (2014: 1). In his next book, *Video Revolutions: On the History of a Medium* from 2014, the television scholar considers, for example, the historical significance of MTV's first aired music video to be its comment on the ambivalent remediation that takes place when the televisual medium replaces the radio (cf. *ibid*.: 20). MTV had obviously understood how to appeal to a new generation of consuming viewers and from now on played a major role in establishing a global visual pop culture.

Similarly to MTV, Matt Groening felt a need to experiment with new concepts of television production. In *Planet Simpsons*, Turner quotes The Simpsons' inventor as wondering in a 1989 interview about

> [...] how few cartoonists in print or animation go after the bigger issues, the kinds of things that keep you lying awake in the middle of the night. Questions about death and love and sex and work and relationships. And that's what I try to do, inject the stuff that people really care about into [The Simpsons].
> *(2004: 6)*

The underground cartoonist Groening belongs to a generation of artists who resisted the formulaic stagnation of cartoons and their incorporation into hegemonic visual media. From the beginning, Groening's motto was to create a show that entertains and subverts, and thus he consciously used The Simpsons as a terrain on which to experiment with the forces of hegemonic incorporation and resistance. Accordingly, the question that will return over and over again in this book is whether The Simpsons plays the part of popular hegemonic incorporation that views the audience as devoted to passive consumption; or rather that of subversion in the mass-culture medium of television that enables viewers to actively participate and become critical and media literate fans.

Looking back to my initial thoughts on what is meant by Springfield's motto "a noble spirit embiggens the smallest men," I suggest the following reading: Whereas the town's foundation myth is based on the "noble spirit" of Jebediah Springfield who led the settlers to the New World, THE SIMPSONS' 'foundation myth' is based on Matt Groening's similarly noble spirit. Groening set out to 'embiggen' the perception on American popular culture and led a new generation of television viewers into an animated world which mobilized them to look through animation onto American everyday life with THE SIMPSONS and onto American visual pop-culture practice with TREEHOUSE OF HORROR. Chris Turner argues that, in its early period, THE SIMPSONS had to learn "how to hone its satirical edge into a mighty samurai sword" (2004: 8). Yet, by the end of the 1990s, a period which Turner calls the "Golden Age" of THE SIMPSONS (1992–1997), the series already had the function of a cultural warrior machine. The show had made clear that it was not the product of a single fevered mind. Rather, THE SIMPSONS had become a unique collaborative enterprise of dozens of producers, writers, and animators who created "a stretch of sustained brilliance" (Turner 2004: 7).

The German media scholars Michael Gruteser, Thomas Klein, and Andreas Rauscher attest in the third edition of *Subversion zur Prime-Time*: "DIE SIMPSONS ist selbst bereits ein kulturwissenschaftlicher Reader." (Gruteser/Klein/Rauscher 2014: editorial, unpaged) The authors' observation points to the possibility of treating the show as a cultural-studies archive, a repository of academic concepts on culture, ideology, and hegemonic practices. Turner remarks that fans soon began to realize that their favorite television show had become "a treasure trove of obscure references and incidental details – the very sort of things, in fact, that were becoming prime commodities on the Internet, which had just begun to emerge as a mass medium in the mid-1990s" (2004: 13).

THE SIMPSONS helped to make Western cultural-studies scholars aware of the 'popular' factor and contributed to a shift of paradigms in cultural studies (cf. McRobbie 1994: 2). Since THE SIMPSONS' inception as a half-hour program on the infant Fox network in 1989, the show has been creating a terrain on which entertainment and subversion, resistance and incorporation, conformity and controversy could be played out. I advise to watch THE SIMPSONS if you want to learn something about postmodern pop culture. Diederich Diederichsen, (who defines himself as "durchschnittlichen postmodernen zwangsassoziativen Alltagskulturwissenschaftler," a character that can be described as the prototype of Jenkins' concept of the "ACA fan") writes about THE SIMPSONS in his acclaimed article "Die Simpsons der Gesellschaft:" "Sie erinnern mich an mein altes, geerbtes Sachkundebuch 'Wege in die Welt', [durch] das man immer wusste, man kann noch viel mehr wissen." (2014: 19). For the 'average everyday cultural studies scholar' Diederichsen, "die gelben Fünf aus Springfield sind wohl am nächsten dran amerikanische Kultur und Gesellschaft als Ganzes darzustellen" (2013: 20).

As I pointed out in this section, THE SIMPSONS' first appeared in the period of late 1980s cultural-studies research during which, as Douglas Kellner notes, the few defenders of the critical popular-culture project wrote against those theorists who were denigrating popular culture as anti-intellectual. In the next subchapter, I will demonstrate how, since THE SIMPSONS' inception, not only postmodern popular-culture theory has changed in the past thirty years, but also argue that THE SIMPSONS and TREEHOUSE OF HORROR have historically evolved along substantial criticism *of* and critical thinking *about* popular culture. In order to distinguish TREEHOUSE OF HORROR from THE SIMPSONS, I started my observations with the historical evolution of THE SIMPSONS to then, step by step, develop an individual model for exploring the Halloween Special TREEHOUSE OF HORROR.

In order to contextualize some of the theories of the time, I picked from among the politically engaged scholars of the time the Italian semiotician Umberto Eco, the British feminist cultural-studies scholar Angela McRobbie, the Canadian literary-studies specialist Linda Hutcheon, and the French philosopher Michel Foucault. In the following section, they will serve as inspiring sources to further develop my own critical thinking about THE SIMPSONS and help me to spawn new thinking about TREEHOUSE OF HORROR. The four theorists have two important things in common: Firstly, their discussions of distinct postmodern cultural practices benefit from their outside perspective onto American popular culture. And secondly, their contributions exhibit how hard thinkers were trying to make sense of the paradigmatic shifts in the increasingly complex study of culture and everyday life since the 1980s.

Asking with Umberto Eco:
Is THE SIMPSONS as the 'Low' Ground of 'High' Art?

Umberto Eco still is one of popular-cultural studies' exemplary figures, because he had a highly positive and enthusiastic understanding of postmodern popular culture.[18] Throughout his long career of non-fictional as well as fictional writing, Eco was specifically productive in the 1980s and 1990s, when he advocated that all kinds of postmodern art can subvert conventional formulae and raise corrosive critique. He was convinced that without a reliable consent about what art is and how it is defined, everything can move up and down the cultural escalator at

---

18 As one of the first theorists, Eco integrated semiotics into a Post-Marxist approach which had much influence on the leftist criticism in most of his writing. See, for example, Umberto Eco's *Semiotics and the Philosophy of Language* from 1984.

a time when recoding has become a daily cultural practice to form, reform, and transform meanings of objects.

In his ironic reading of postmodern art as 'Kitsch,' which he talks about in his essay collection *Apocalypse Postponed* (1994), Eco sees the same aesthetic and social effects in popular everyday-culture artifacts of Charlie Brown or James Bond as in those produced by the cultural elites during their times. In short, Eco understood Kitsch as provoking modernist theories of originality, as "innovative antiforms," and, thus, as a material expression of cultural capital (Bouchard 2009: 14).[19] In *New Essays on Umberto Eco* (2009), cultural- and comparative-literary scholar Norma Bouchard, for example, emphasizes Eco's "unexpected words of praise" for popular products like Michael Curtiz's CASABLANCA (1942) or the *Superman* comics (DC, since 1938), which other critics completely disregarded. In her essay "Eco and Popular Culture," Bouchard provides an insightful discussion of how Eco uses Kitsch to tear down the academic walls between high art and popular- or mass culture because he understood that this binary tension was one of cultural theory's as well as semiotic studies' heaviest burdens.

Eco translated postmodernism's radical cultural project into what he calls "semiological guerrilla warfare" when he, for example, named Donatello's David statue in the same breath as plastic garden furniture.[20] In "Towards a Semiological Guerrilla Warfare" (1997 [1976]), Eco applied his guerrilla ideas to other scholars' thinking: to Marshall McLuhan's ideas about mass media's "call for narcotic passiveness," to Susan Sontag's notion of "camp,"[21] and to Jean Baudrillard's contempt for contemporary culture as "the desert of the real itself" (2009: 389).[22] Eco engaged in what those intellectuals wrote about their individual cultural experiences, no matter whether they embraced or feared postmodernity's excessive production of signs.

The semiotician contests McLuhan by writing that "the medium is *not* the message; the message becomes what the receiver makes of it" (1997: 235). Message and meaning had become the chief commodities of the late 20th century (cf. Eco 1997: 137), but the new messages brought with them new readers. For this reason, *The Guardian* hails Eco's "intellectual [...] slumming," the fact that he calls high

---

19   See Eco's discussion of Kitsch between art and the trivial in his essay "Apocalyptic and Integrated Intellectuals: Mass Communication and Theories of Mass Culture." Robert Lumley, ed. *Umberto Eco: Apocalypse Postponed* from 1994.
20   For more information, see Umberto Eco's essay "Towards a Semiological Guerrilla Warfare" in *Travels in Hyperreality* from 1997.
21   See Eco's chapter "The Ugliness of Others, Kitsch and Camp" in his book *On Ugliness* from 2007, in which he refers to Susan Sontag's famous essay "Notes on Camp" in *Against Interpretation and Other Essays*, first published in 1966.
22   See Jean Baudrillard's article "The Precession of Simulacra" in John Storey's fourth edition of the edited essay collection *Cultural Theory and Popular Culture: A Reader* from 2009.

art fake,[23] and praises his efforts of "applying literary judgement to ephemera" (Thompson 2016). Eco pushed the limits of culture theory and moved beyond traditional concepts of art, media, and mass culture, to exemplify that popular culture consists of the symbolic expressions of our collective lives (cf. Bouchard 2009: 3, 9). In *Faith in Fakes* (1998 [1986]), he argues that the public gains more pleasure from the perfection of "total fake" than from what might be verified as real, such as, for example, a "dinosaur," a "Polynesian restaurant" or "Disneyland," any of which "corresponds much more to our daydream demands" (Eco 1998: 34–36, 43–44). To him, Hollywood film classics such as CASABLANCA (1942), novels such as Joseph Heller's war satire *Catch-22* (1961), or Charles M. Schultz's *Peanuts* cartoon (1950) equally function as "textual syllabuses" produced by the endless recycling of cultural works (cf. Bouchard 10).

In her essay "Eco and Popular Culture," Bouchard further interprets Eco's 'textual syllabus' as consisting of indefinite fractured historical units forming a collage or rather bricolage that provides the audience with constant *déjà vu* moments and with a consolatory structure for their pleasure in fake. In spite of highlighting redundancy in these *déjà vu* moments, Eco paved the way for a concept that, in contemporary reception studies, has been coined "performative literacy" by education scholar Sheridan Blau (2003). Transferring this concept to THE SIMPSONS, Valerie Chow, author of the essay "Homer Erectus: Homer Simpson As Everyman... and Every Woman" from 2004, defines the show's "pop irony" as a move towards encouraging the audience to know it better (cf. 113). In his publication "Performative Literacy: The Habits of Mind of Highly Literate Readers," Blau defines performative literacy as a "habit of mind" that elevates readers' advanced knowledge and their quasi-active engagement in the text (2003: 18). This 'habit of mind' can open up the text towards the reader to such an extent that Eco argues: "[…] when all the archetypes burst out shamelessly, we plumb Homeric profundity. Two clichés make us laugh but a hundred clichés move us because we sense dimly that the clichés are talking among themselves, celebrating a reunion (1986: 209).[24] When Eco speaks of "Homeric profundity," he means that Kitsch can be 'epic,' that "banality allows us to catch a glimpse of the sublime," and may have a lasting impact of heroic proportions (Eco 1986: 209). The author's prime example is CASABLANCA, which is known to cite from countless other films, copying dialogues from many other cinematic moments, and thus offering to viewers the chance to choose from numerous push-button options – to indulge in CASABLANCA means to indulge in Hollywood itself.

It is interesting to observe how the term 'cliché' keeps changing its meaning in contemporary contexts. For example, in video game culture, clichés refer to over-

---

23   See Umberto Eco's essays about the concept of 'fake' *Faith in Fakes: Travels in Hyperreality.* Trans. William Weaver. London: Vintage, 1986.
24   See Eco's essay "Reading Things" in *Travels in Hyperreality* from 1986.

used elements in video games that have become recurrent stereotypes or conventionalized motifs such as certain heroic characters, memes such as zombies, and thematic missions such as 'rescue the princess' or 'save the world.' In comics culture, clichés mean overused expressions that have lost their former effect and irritate readers now. For example when the eyeballs pop out of a cartoon character's head. At the same time, such techniques can still be used for comic effect exactly because they are clichés. Then such an element can talk back to readers, made a pact and reassure them in their belief that everything is a "total fake." It challenges their media literacy and plays with the eternal possibilities of intertextual re-reading. I catch the opportunity to make such clichés and their 'Homeric profundity' visible in the reading of the crossover episode "The Simpsons Guy" from the TV series FAMILY GUY (2014).

Cartoon Clichés and Homeric Profundity in "The Simpsons Guy"

Fox's two animated series THE SIMPSONS and FAMILY GUY are broadly regarded as two sides of the same animated medal. Although Matt Groening's THE SIMPSONS (since 1989) went on air ten years ahead of Seth McFarlane's FAMILY GUY (since 1999), the conflict between the two shows basically consists in the question whether the latter is a clone of the first, although the jokes in FAMILY GUY are often packed with racist cynicism and sexist humor. Both shows have often "thrown barbs at each other," as Gavin Jasper writes in a review on the media website *Den of Geek* (2014). In earlier episodes, THE SIMPSONS frequently joked about FAMILY GUY being a rip-off of their show, while, in return, FAMILY GUY mocked how THE SIMPSONS became a sell-out at the expense of its original charm (cf. Jasper 2014). Hence, "The Simpsons Guy"[25] crossover episode is basically about getting the record straight. First I thought that the crossover episode had been an idea of the SIMPSONS writers; yet the opposite is the case. Although we see FAMILY GUY's Griffin family enter THE SIMPSONS' Springfield, the episode's writer, Patrick Meighan, hijacked the Simpsons and placed them within FAMILY GUY's 13th season's premiering episode, with an extended or rather duplicated running time of 44 minutes.

For those who do not know FAMILY GUY, here is a short introduction to the family: The Griffins have the same number of family members as the Simpsons (see Fig. 2). Peter Griffin is the obese father and head of the family who works in the local beer factory, the Pawtucket Brewery. He is married to wife Lois, has three children, Chris, Meg, and toddler Stewie, and a dog named Brian, who is the intellectual of the family. Together they live in a small town named Quahog, a state of Rhode Island, and are known among their fans for their substantial exaggeration

---

25   Cf. FAMILY GUY. "The Simpsons Guy," dir. Peter Shin, s13e01, Fox 2014.

2 The Griffins meet The Simpsons in Family Guy's crossover episode "The Simpsons Guy" (s13e01, Fox 2014)

of everyday situations which are commonly drawn out into absurdity. In comparison to The Simpsons, Family Guy's humor is slightly more obnoxious, obscene, vulgar, and coarse which creates a difference in off-color jokes and bad-taste comedy that has fed much of the rivalry between the two series. Mutual forms of referencing can be traced in various episodes. The Simpsons' episode "The Italian Bob"[26] shows a picture of Peter in a book about American criminals, and when Homer clones himself in the episode "Send in the Clones"[27] one clone looks like Peter. In return, the Family Guy episode "PTV"[28] shows how Stewie, with his toy bike, runs over Homer in his garage so that he escapes from the attack like he does in The Simpsons' opening sequence. Soon after, Peter enters the garage, pejoratively asking Stewie "who the hell is this?".

However, for my comparative analysis I chose one of the best-known and richest examples of references. In "The Simpsons' Guy," the Simpson family accommodates the Griffins for as long as it takes the Springfield police to find their stolen car. Both families stand in the living room when the dialogue presents one of multiple moments in which one comedy series reflects on the other's clichés, for example, concerning characteristic catchphrases of Bart Simpson.

> MARGE: Honey, your hands are filthy. Go wash up for lunch!
> BART: Eat my shorts!
> STEWIE: (*amused*) 'Eat – my – shorts'! I love that. Is that a popular expression, like "what the deuce"?
> BRIAN: Probably more popular. Probably… Probably way more popular.[29]

---

26 Cf. The Simpsons, dir. Mark Kirkland, s17e08, Fox 2005.
27 Cf. Treehouse of Horror XIII, dir. David Silverman, s14e01, Fox 2002.
28 Cf. Family Guy, dir. Dan Povenmire, s04e14, Fox 2005.
29 Unless otherwise noted, the transcripts of "The Simpsons Guy" episode are taken from the community content of The Simpsons Wiki powered by Fandom (undated). URL: https://bit.ly/3tHFCGW.

Brian, of course, comments on the popularity of Bart's character, on his omnipresence during the era of 1990s 'Bartmania.' The period of Bartmania roughly comprises the first ten years of THE SIMPSONS. During this time, Bart played the leading role in the plots of most SIMPSONS episodes. As a comic device, several of his recurring catchphrases such as "Eat my shorts!," "Don't have a cow, man!" or the recycled surfer word from the 1960s, "Cowabunga,"[30] became iconic memes for the 1990s MTV generation. Many of Bart's teenage slang statements were printed on shirts as a commentary against parental monitoring. Speaking with his usual, disarming British accent, Stewie's eccentric reaction apparently compromises Bart and his wacky, simple-minded sayings, although Stewie's character is much younger than Bart.

Stewie is the Griffin's wicked toddler who remains misunderstood or rather literally unheard by the other family members so that he is just able to have conversations with the family's intellectual dog Brian. After Bart has taken Stewie to his room, Stewie recognizes that he shares some characteristics with Bart's 'meanness' when he gets introduced to Bart's collection of weapons which consists of only one slingshot:

> STEWIE: A slingshot! It's so simple and pure. He doesn't need lasers or time machines, just gumballs and marbles and balls of string. He's like something out of Mark Twain!
> BRIAN: Whose real name was Samuel Clemens.
> STEWIE: How… How does that further this conversation?

By equating Bart and his 'simple' armament with Mark Twain's *The Adventures of Tom Sawyer* from 1876, Stewie brings up another instance in which FAMILY GUY competes with THE SIMPSONS. He questions the other show's alleged timeliness by hinting at its lost former charm or, like in this case, by joking about Bart's character being based on a classic 19th-century figure. Although Bart's social background resembles Twain's middle-class character of Tom Sawyer, he used to be read as the counter example to American children's bourgeois alignment. According to turn-of-the-century standards, Bart Simpson, however, rather equals Tom Sawyer because both are boyish pseudo-rascals, who, compared to the one-year-old Stewie, have always been more assimilated to their familial surrounding than Huckleberry Finn. Huck Finn is Tom Sawyer's friend, but Twain wrote him as a character

---

30 To be more precise, the neologism was originally coined by "The Howdy Doody Show" (1960) and appeared five years later in a PEANUTS comic, depicting a surfing Snoopy who says "Cowabunga" while riding a wave. In comic history, the word later gained increased popularity through the 1990s extremely popular film franchise TEENAGE MUTANT NINJA TURTLES, to which the term is commonly credited. In THE SIMPSONS, Bart used 'Cowabunga' in the same context as the previous sources to approve of something as more than 'cool.'

3 In "The Simpson's Guy" THE SIMPSONS leave Springfield and enter the basement of adult animation: Stewie shackles and gags Nelson Muntz in a cellar full of torture tools.

who grows up under socially precarious conditions. For this reason, Huck Finn has nothing in common with Stewie, but rather resembles THE SIMPSONS' character of Bart's on-/off-friend Nelson Muntz. Stewie obviously mocks Bart's subversive *façade,* indicating that the gumballs and marbles reveal that Bart maintains a 'fake' identity. Stewie points at the irony that Bart is actually constructed in a similar way as Tom Sawyer since both perform as 'heroic' characters in their respective medium and celebrate their pseudo-heroism at any given moment. According to my reading, Stewie only pretends his admiration for Bart, exposing his character as just a dazzling surface behind which the controversy is not more than an exchange of bullets with slingshots. This confrontation further reveals that Stewie's character is drawn to defy comparison to other child characters from popular culture. The toddler's utter madness rather reminds me of THE SIMPSONS' character Sideshow Bob in his profound contempt for Bart Simpson.

Bart takes Stewie to the local skatepark, where the toddler witnesses how the white outsider with the tattered vest, the Huck Finn of the 20th century, Nelson Muntz, punches Bart and leaves him lying on the ground while dropping his famous 'Ha-Ha!'. Nelson Muntz's antisocial aggression towards his schoolmates is well known to stem from his 'white-trash' social background and his need to compensate for his absent father and prostitute mother. If Nelson is similarly non-conformist as his assumed 19th-century role model Huckleberry Finn, Stewie's antisocial behavior is rather premature and motivated by the psyche of a megalomaniac genius. Nelson is consequently shown being ambushed by Stewie, who, in the next moment, has shackled and gagged Nelson in a dark room. The scene evokes the feeling that the episode now definitely wants to 'leave Springfield' aesthetically as well as thematically, since the location is drawn with a cinephile horror-genre atmosphere. (See Fig. 3)

Viewers indeed enter a psycho-horror story when Nelson realizes that he is surrounded by a whip, a chainsaw, jumper cables attached to a car battery, dental tools, and a clown painting. The audience's eerie feeling is further confirmed by Stewie's freakish monologue. Here the outdated cliché of one of Bart's 1990s catchphrases becomes a literal threat. The way Stewie takes revenge on Nelson by literally making him 'eat his shorts' stresses FAMILY GUY's aim not to be seen as fake. The sequence emphasizes FAMILY GUY's claim to use violence and sexual connotations as building blocks of the show's dark humor.

> STEWIE: Wakey, wakey. Good morning. You and I have quite a day ahead of us... – Oh, that's a clown I painted, so you know I'm truly insane. You know, Nelson. I don't doubt that you've had a twisted childhood. Most evil people have. Hitler, Manson, Jaden Smith. But you're different from them, aren't you? Because they're rail-thin, and you're fat. You're a little piggy, aren't you, Nelson? In fact, I bet you're hungry now. (*Stewie takes the ball gag out of Nelson's mouth.*)
> NELSON: I could eat.
> STEWIE: Good. Because you're going to eat... my... shorts! (*He shoves his shorts into Nelson's mouth.*)

Extending the comedy with a literal 'ball gag' and Charles Manson's "piggies," the cartoon becomes an animated version of the 'torture porn' genre (starting with Eli Roth's HOSTEL in 2005), which is a relatively young subgenre of the horror film with characteristically explicit depictions of sadism. FAMILY GUY's pushing of genre borders almost evokes pity for Springfield's archetypal bully Nelson Muntz.

The sequence demonstrates to what extent FAMILY GUY conceives of itself as more up-to-date than THE SIMPSONS, raising the pulse of younger audiences. Most of the times, the FAMILY GUY writers expose the primetime cartoon rivals to ridicule. Springfield thus becomes FAMILY GUY's battleground on which both formats fight for predominance to show, for example, which series is culturally more significant, which one is smarter (Brian knows Mark Twain's birth name) with more state-of-the-art humor and more visibility, which one deserves to receive greater public appraisal, academic attention, or a PG-13 rating label. Once more, the FAMILY GUY creators reveal that THE SIMPSONS characters are only recycled American archetypes from 19th-century literature and FAMILY GUY is the true innovator of the adult-animation campaign.

Stewie's eccentric flamboyance and his upper-class British accent confirm that his character is inspired by Bart's nemesis, Sideshow Bob, THE SIMPSONS' self-proclaimed genius and Yale University graduate. Bob received his name at his job as a TV sidekick of Krusty the Clown and his television show of the same name. Time and again, Krusty's former assistant attempts to brutally murder Bart Simpson to take revenge on the ten-year-old who thwarted Bob's plan to bust his employer and become the admired star-clown instead. Since the episode "Krusty Gets Busted,"[31] Bart is Sideshow Bob's declared arch-enemy.

---

31 Cf. THE SIMPSONS, dir. Brad Bird, s01e12, Fox 1990.

In contrast to Stewie, however, THE SIMPSONS' evil-spirited genius Sideshow Bob speaks with a 'real' British accent (Bob is voiced by the British actor Kelsey Grammar) to underline his un-American upper-class sensibility. As revealed in the episode "Send in Stewie, Please,"[32] Stewie confesses to a child psychologist that his mundane accent is faked. In the conversation, Stewie admits that he only pretends to be British to mask his true identity and that the accent is part of "a carefully constructed persona" which Stewie claims he has cultivated "to feel special." The voicing of characters with a British accent in an American-language context traditionally makes audiences anticipate that its speaker is educated and has more intellectual appeal. (And, of course, according to Eco, the public enjoys the fake.) Within an American popular culture context, Eco saw 20th-century readers equipped with enough performative literacy to "select their own interpretative codes" to identify the fake and function of such masquerade (Eco qtd. in Bouchard 2009: 9). Stewie's "carefully constructed persona" is a fitting example to how the taxonomy of a pre-established reception and the promotion of redundant messages can be challenged.

"The Simpsons Guy" crossover episode can be read as a present for fans of both programs. It is often hard to distinguish between the two shows' different animation styles. The conflict between the two heads of the families from FAMILY GUY and THE SIMPSONS eventually turns into a metaphorical battle between Peter Griffin and Homer Simpson. In appreciation of Homer's help to retrieve Peter's stolen car, Griffin gives Simpson his emergency six-pack of Pawtucket Patriot Ale from the brewery in Quahog where he is employed. While sitting at the bar in Moe's Tavern, Homer drinks the bottle in one go, which is followed by the subsequent lines:

PETER: Yeah, it's pretty good, right?
HOMER: No. It's not good. This beer tastes exactly like Duff. It's just a lousy rip-off!
PETER: Hey, whoa, whoa, whoa! It's not a rip-off of Duff. It may have been inspired by Duff, but I like to think it goes in a different direction.
HOMER: No, this is just the same as Duff, but, like, worse!
PETER: Hey, come on, now, this is my favorite beer you're talking about! Hell, I work for the company. It's my livelihood.
MOE: (*Moe snatches the bottle.*) Oh, yeah? Well, your livelihood is based on fraud. Look at this! (*The barkeeper rips off the label, revealing that it's Duff.*) Huh?
HOMER:(*gasps*) It is Duff! Your beer is in big trouble! You can't just slap a new label on omething and call it your own!

---

32 Cf. FAMILY GUY, dir. Joe Vaux, s16e12, Fox 2018.

PETER: Well, maybe Duff should be in trouble for… You know, not being that great.
HOMER: Duff is an icon!
PETER: Yeah, but some folks prefer Pawtucket Pat. I mean, don't get me wrong, I used to love Duff when I was younger, but I haven't even had it in, like, 13 years.

It should be clear that the two characters' debate is about more than beer because of two reasons. Firstly, I like the idea that if the tenor of the two cartoon shows is delivered by the vehicle of 'beer,' the message is that both shows have become more enjoyable over time. The cultural myth that beer is something that gets better with age can be read as a means to prevent children and adolescents from drinking alcohol until they turn 21 in most American states since the 1980s.[33] So, replace any 'Duff' with THE SIMPSONS and any 'Pawtucket Pat' with FAMILY GUY and you got the argument right: Homer's and Peter's obsession with beer mocks America's moral standards not only to prevent younger viewers from drinking beer, but also from learning too early in their lives what is behind the myth, what is the tenor of the 'beer' metaphor.

Secondly, this example shows that the viewer needs an increased literacy compared to those of older series to decode the beer analogy. The viewer is required to develop an understanding for what media scholar Jim Collins defines as ironic hyperconsciousness of the overarching conflict between THE SIMPSONS and FAMILY GUY (cf. 1992: 335). In his essay "Postmodernism and Television" from 1992, Jim Collins defines hyperconsciousness as a "hyperawareness on the part of the text itself, of its cultural status, function, and history" (335), which further extends to the realm of audience reception. Read with Collins in mind, the conversation between Peter and Homer exemplifies that THE SIMPSONS falls into the "meta-pop text" category that focuses on involving fans.

The meta-pop text improves our ability to read the beer-based conflict because first through the beer, as Collins suggests, "we encounter, not avant-gardists who give 'genuine' significance to the merely mass cultural, but a hyperconscious rearticulation of media culture by media culture" (335). This way viewers of "The Simpsons Guy" can oscillate between the inherently hyperconscious comedy and the meta-discussion which Homer has with Peter to fight out the beer question.

---

33 The Wikipedia article "U.S. history of alcohol minimum purchase age by state" informs that the age limit has changed over time. Whereas several states had pre-prohibition acts that go back to the 19th century, Congress passed the National Minimum Drinking Act, which includes that U.S. states had to raise the age for the purchase of alcohol to 21 until 1986 or lose 10 % of their federal highway funds. The mythologizing of beer can in this instance be read as mockery towards the American moral system. See https://bit.ly/2NprG43.

Eco's claim that 20th-century readers can select their own interpretative codes is further elaborated in Collins' text. He writes:

> The self-reflexivity of these popular texts of the later eighties and early nineties does not revolve around the problems of self-expression experienced by the anguished creative artist so ubiquitous in modernism but instead focuses on antecedent and competing programs, on the ways television programs circulate and are given meaning by viewers, and on the nature of television popularity.
> *(1992: 335)*

The competing strategy employed in "The Simpsons Guy" precisely revolves around the popularity status of two animation programs, partly by means of how their fan audiences are assumed to read them. The episode reflects the fans' quarrels over deciding which show is the better one in terms of recurrent clichés, audience appeal, topicality, and unconventionality. Eco's diagnosis of such a competing reading experience was that the reader "continuously recovers, point by point, what he already knows, what he wants to know again" (qtd. in Bouchard 10). Eco would probably read THE SIMPSONS as a clever work of popular art which often uses overused clichés, exaggerations, and fake, in order to encourage fans to perform their literacy. In this sense, to indulge in THE SIMPSONS means to indulge in digital age popular-culture practices. At the same time, these techniques ironize common beliefs about American consumer culture, both in terms of brands of beer and brands of animated TV shows. Pawtucket Ale and Duff Beer are Kitsch because "The Simpsons Guy" episode self-consciously uses beer as a provocation of both shows' claim to originality. The ongoing rivalry between Groening and McFarlane so becomes a hyperconscious re-articulation of media culture by media culture.

I used the dispute between FAMILY GUY and THE SIMPSONS to exemplify Eco's approaches to popular culture, which helped me to circumscribe the high-/low-conflict on the level of popular-culture analysis. By using the crossover episode "The Simpsons Guy" as an exemplary text, I discussed Eco's notions of 'fake' and 'Kitsch' in order show how popular texts can move up and down the cultural scale to challenge the viewers' capacity to find their own interpretive codes. My next theoretical subchapter will explore how THE SIMPSONS' signifying practices might have influenced people's imaginations by means of different character concepts. Angela McRobbie's approaches will help me to closely read popular-culture representations of the 1990s and how they are related to the cultural life of the Simpson family.

Angela McRobbie: Popular-Culture Representations in THE SIMPSONS

The British cultural theorist Angela McRobbie combines the study of youth culture, feminist theory, and popular-media culture. Since she is Professor of Communications at the University of London, Goldsmith, and her research is strongly influenced by Stuart Hall and the Birmingham School of Cultural Studies, Marxism, and feminist theory. She describes her critical gaze in books and articles as engaging "with everyday life as an eclectic and invigorating interplay of different cultures and identities" (1994: x). In 1980, McRobbie published the article "Settling Accounts with Subculture: A Feminist Critique," in which she argues against Dick Hebdige's *Subculture: The Meaning of Style* from 1979 from a feminist discourse on female subcultures in post-war Britain. During the 1990s, she claimed popular culture as a space for social change and political transformation (cf. 1994: x), and began to write against the rather pessimistic readings of postmodernity which culminated in her 1994 publication *Postmodernism and Popular Culture*. The book includes eleven essays in which McRobbie not only makes use of "a feminist postmodernism [which] forces us to confront questions which otherwise remain unasked" (1994: 1); she also raises questions about shifting academic practices and paradigms in cultural studies and sociology which, in her opinion, should be "doing that kind of intellectual work which inevitably provokes controversy and protest" (*ibid.*: 2). According to McRobbie, "living along the faultlines of the postmodern condition means engaging with questions and dilemmas which were there on the surface and no longer hidden from history" (*ibid.*: 2).

McRobbie encouraged the process of change, while French theorist Jean Baudrillard and American post-Marxist literary critic Fredric Jameson resisted such developments in cultural studies. In order to make her position clear, McRobbie refers to Baudrillard's "catastrophe scenarios" (*ibid.*: 2) from his 1983 text *In the Shadow of Silent Majorities* and foregrounds Jameson's desire to return to the strong values of modernity; she argues against the notion that "the superficial [...] necessarily represents a decline into meaninglessness or valuelessness in culture" (*ibid.*: 4). The feminist rather seeks new meaning and value in the "glossy surface of pop," using "all this criss-crossing and fast cutting" of the popular-culture kaleidoscope in the 1990s "to develop a critical vocabulary which can take this rapid movement into account" (*ibid.*: 4). According to McRobbie, postmodernism had moved on from the field of the arts and visual high culture to the music of Blondie and the Talking Heads, to the cinema of David Lynch, as well as to the adverts of Levi Strauss – in which pop music from the 1960s was revived for 1980s' jeans commercials, and of Apple Macintosh Computers – in which Orwell's 1949 dystopian novel *Nineteen Eighty-Four* served as a motif in Apple's 1984 Super-Bowl Ad. The shift from snob to pop led to "thinking seriously about the trivial" (*ibid.*: 3).

The massive explosion of the media industries in the 1980s and the increasing production of ever new and sparkling surfaces produced a wave of moving images all over the Western world. Matt Groening[34] once used a similar metaphor in an interview. With respect to popular culture's concern with surfaces, he said: "I can't stop a tidal wave, but I can surf on it." (Qtd. in McClellan 67) Groening indicates that he doesn't think of himself as the producer of surfaces, nor does he see himself in control of their meanings. As a surfer on the wave of surfaces Groening suggested that THE SIMPSONS should go with the flow. THE SIMPSONS became a prototypical example of postmodernism because Groening aimed at giving surfaces new social and political meaning by using fast-moving animation as his critical vocabulary (cf. McRobbie 1994: 4).

At several instances of the SIMPSONS' floating timeline, flashback episodes were common to irritate critics and fans with several period settings. The episode "The Way We Was" from 1991 recapitulates Homer and Marge's first acquaintance as a wild ride through the pop culture of the 1970s replete with the men's long sideburns and tacky tuxedos at the prom, with '70s music of the Steve Miller Band and posters of Pink Floyd, or with Homer and Barney as the pot-smoking Cheech and Chong of their high school. "That '90s Show" from 2008 shifts to one of Homer and Marge's darker points of their relationship when the newlyweds move into the residential complex from MELROSE PLACE (Fox 1992–1999). While Marge enthuses her radical feminist revisionist history professor Steffan August and makes a degree in Cultural and Art History at the prestigious Springfield University, Homer takes a job at his father's popular laser tag warehouse, then gets addicted to Frappuccinos – a trademarked brand of the Starbucks Coffee Corporation since 1994 – , and ultimately invents the new sound of "Guitar Rock Utilizing Nihilist Grunge Energy" – better known as '90s "grunge." The surfaces in both episodes consolidate the language of popular culture of each respective decade to say something about the conditions of higher education, marriage, an increasing low-wage sector, corporate media, and the trends of youth culture; and, if that weren't enough, to say further something about cult TV shows, remember iconic sounds, and evoke nostalgic feelings. If THE SIMPSONS had for a long time been read as the 'yellow peril' of serious academic research, Angela McRobbie's *Postmodernism and Popular Culture* took Matt Groening and his fellow artists seriously as organizers of surfaces. She writes:

> Rather than starting with a definition of postmodernism as referring either to a condition of contemporary life, or to a textual, aesthetic practice, I want to begin by suggesting that the recent debates on postmodernism both possess a positive attraction and a usefulness to the analyst of popular culture. This is

---

34 See interview with Matt Groening in Jim McClellan. "Who the Hell is [sic] Bart Simpson?" *The Face.com*, No. 30 (1991): 66–67. 17 Apr. 2019. 9 May 2019. URL: https://bit.ly/3a6VSJU.

because they offer a wider, and more dynamic, understanding of contemporary representation than other accounts to date. *(1994: 13)*

McRobbie continues: that "[pop] has never signified within one discrete discourse, but instead combines images with performance" to speak in "multi-media tongues" (1994: 13). If "the recent debates on postmodernism possess both a positive attraction and a usefulness to the analyst of popular culture" (*ibid.*: 13), then THE SIMPSONS do, too. And Groening uses THE SIMPSONS' multi-media tongue as an analytical tool to further explore the surfaces of popular culture. In my opinion, the Simpson characters have indeed contributed to the postmodern debates of the 1990s by promoting "a wider and more dynamic perception of contemporary representation" (*ibid.*: 13). McRobbie's vision of the trivial with and through postmodern theory serves as a suitable tool to read THE SIMPSONS, too. Moving towards the postmodern strategy of analyzing how surfaces are described by the image of a "criss-crossing and fast-cutting" "pop culture kaleidoscope" (*ibid.*: 4), McRobbie opens her investigation of 1990s popular culture which she describes as "a multiplicity of fragmented, and frequently interrupted, 'looks'" (*ibid.*: 13). I will take up her idea and examine which different, fragmented looks exist in THE SIMPSONS that create the "visual density of everyday life" (*ibid.*: 13).

Comparable to Eco, McRobbie saw the surfaces of everyday culture as permeated by a new form of complexity, a complexity which I argue can also be found in the construction and use of the leading characters of the Simpsons family. Angela McRobbie argues with the help of Susan Sontag's famous essay "Notes on Camp" from 1967 to query Fredric Jameson's critique of surfaces. Sontag theorizes the producers of camp culture (i.e. gay men) by paying close attention to their social practices, e.g. to how their use of "tinsel and glitter can produce meaning" (*ibid.*: 4). In Sontag's opinion, obvious questions to ask are, firstly, whether camp surfaces can be a deliberate political strategy, and secondly, which social subjects are indeed privileged to "represent the voice of their generation in culture?" (*ibid.*: 4, 13). In the following paragraphs, I will use the yellow characters from Springfield to explore how they have inscribed themselves into popular culture. Can their 'surface' as animated television characters and products of consumer culture serve as a popular form of critical action? Or should their surfaces not better be seen as insertions? The Simpsons characters are critical elements whose performance mirrors our fragmented look on culture, invites specific ways of critical reading, and exposes a fresh attempt to make sense of the world. The question remains they represent different generational voices that hint at the complexity of the superficial?

The creation of the underground cartoonist Matt Groening soon turned into a marketable brand, a commodity of corporate capitalism with high economic value. In the last thirty years, THE SIMPSONS has become a popular-culture enterprise that created a multi-million dollar merchandise empire, one that has often been criticized for being a "mass-marketed money machine" (Rabin 2011). THE SIMPSONS, then, are both, an economically successful brand and a set of characters which can do (self-)critical cultural work depending on the ways fans and critics read them.

Back in the early 1990s, THE SIMPSONS' popularity stirred up questions about their position in a series of debates (cf. Henry 2012: 2) which were called "culture wars" by American sociologist James D. Hunter in *The Struggle to Define America* (1991). According to Hunter, the 'culture wars' of the Reagan-Bush era were waged between proponents of political orthodoxy and promoters of social change regarding race and ethnicity, class, gender, and sexuality. During the 'culture wars' the involvement of pop-culture producers and artifacts became increasingly obvious. Accordingly, critics and scholars began to systematically examine the ways in which a show like THE SIMPSONS participated in the discussion of what Matthew A. Henry calls "hot-button social, political, and moral issues" (e.g. immigration reform, education policy, same-sex marriage, abortion, etc.) which had dominated U.S.-American culture since the 1960s (cf. Henry 2012: 135).

Along with comparative-literary theorist Andreas Huyssen, McRobbie convincingly argues in 1994 that "pop in the broadest sense was the context in which a notion of the postmodern first took shape," and according to Huyssen, whom McRobbie quotes in *Postmodernism and Popular Culture*, "high theory was simply not equipped to deal with multilayered pop" (Huyssen 1984 qtd. in McRobbie 13). I will take a closer look at the 'glossy pop' surface of the two-dimensional Simpson characters and how they stirred up popular culture theory in the 1980s. The following close reading of Lisa, Bart, and Homer Simpson will show how THE SIMPSONS participated in the culture wars and continued to give greater depth to the multilayered pop-political project in the 1990s.

Lisa the Wholesome: Feminist Representations in 1990s America

> Well, I'm going to be a famous jazz musician. I've got it all figured out. I'll be unappreciated in my own country, but my guts blues styling will electrify the French. I'll avoid the horrors of drug abuse, but I do plan to have several torrid love affairs, and I may or may not die young. I haven't decided.
> *(Lisa Simpson in "Separate Vocation").*[35]

> Mom, romance is dead. It was acquired by Hallmark and Disney in a hostile takeover, homogenized, and sold off piece by piece.
> *(Lisa Simpson in "Another Simpsons Clip Show").*[36]

---

35 Cf. THE SIMPSONS, dir. Jeffrey Lynch, s03e18, Fox 1992.
36 Cf. THE SIMPSONS, dir. David Silverman, s06e03, Fox 1994.

The quotes by Lisa Simpson evidence that her character shows self-reflection which makes her commonly question her persona, for example, when imagining herself as an unappreciated jazz talent in America but at the same time envisioning being an object marketed by the entertainment industry. In the following character analysis, I will explore which 'looks' Lisa Simpson offers at American everyday culture. During the years of "The Simpsons Shorts" as part of THE TRACEY ULLMAN SHOW (1987–1989), Lisa appeared as the female equivalent of Bart, but was soon equipped with more unique attributes and greater emotional depth.

The eight-year-old middle child of the Simpsons is the politically engaged, intellectual moral center and voice of reason of the family, who, in the course of the series, converts to Buddhism,[37] becomes a vegetarian,[38] and successfully plays the saxophone. Lisa is a child prodigy who loves Jazz music,[39] fights for women's rights,[40] and far exceeds the standards of other second graders of her age, which makes her a social outsider and nerdy overachiever with only few friends. Future-predicting episodes such as "Bart to the Future"[41] portray Lisa's ambitious import when she, at the age of 38, becomes America's youngest and first female president, or when she is accepted by Harvard University in "Mr. Lisa's Opus."[42] Due to her strong moral and ethical compass, Lisa personifies a kind of woman whom leftist bourgeois intellectuals imagined as curing an over-saturated American culture from its maladies.

Yet, Lisa tends to be too ambitious for her own good as her efforts in Springfield's version of the world's oldest high-IQ society MENSA evidence. The episode "They Saved Lisa's Brain"[43] shows how she and the other MENSA members (including Stephen Hawking as himself) instigate a revolution against the growing stupidity of Springfieldians, but ultimately lose the battle against the town's angry mob. Lisa's frequent failures counterbalance the too mature appearance of her eight-year-old character as Lisa in this episode finally appears more reliable and believable. Although Lisa usually behaves like a grown-up, she can only dream of being a successful adult who is trapped in a child's body (cf. Turner 2004: 203). But back to questions Angela McRobbie keeps returning to: Firstly, can Lisa's 'surface' be read as a deliberate political strategy? And secondly, does she represent the voice of postmodern feminism? Does her character participate in the culture wars between intellectual elitism and trivial consumption and subvert traditional images of 'wholesome' female representations?

---

37 "She of Little Faith" THE SIMPSONS, s06e13, dir. Stephen Dean Moore. Fox 2001.
38 "Lisa the Vegetarian." THE SIMPSONS, s05e07, dir. Mark Kirkland. Fox 1995.
39 "Moaning Lisa." THE SIMPSONS, s01e06, dir. Wes Archer. Fox 1990.
40 "Lisa vs. Malibu Stacy." THE SIMPSONS, s14e05, dir. Jeff Lynch. Fox 1994.
41 Cf. THE SIMPSONS, dir. Michael Marcantel, s11e17, Fox 2000.
42 Cf. THE SIMPSONS, dir. Steven Dean Moore, s29e08, Fox 2017.
43 Cf. THE SIMPSONS, dir. Pete Michels, s10e22, Fox 1999.

In the episode "Lisa vs. Malibu Stacy"[44] Lisa Simpson presents a feminist perspective on American consumer culture. Lisa is upset by the, in her view, misogynistic traits of the Malibu Stacy toy doll which was inspired by the Mattel's 'Teen Talk Barbie' doll edition from 1992. Malibu Stacy contains a voice box programmed with sexist phrases such as "Don't ask me, I'm just a girl!" and "Thinking too much gives you wrinkles!". Lisa decides that she needs to change the misleading and outworn concept of femininity girls are taught to pursue and approaches the inventor of Malibu Stacy, the business woman Stacy Lovell voiced by Hollywood actress Kathleen Turner. Lisa convinces Lovell to create a new doll that, as Lisa believes, suits her time better. Together they create 'Lisa Lionheart,' who Lisa imagines "to have the wisdom of Gertrude Stein, the wit of Cathy Guisewhite, the tenacity of Nina Totenberg, the common sense of Elizabeth Cady Stanton, and to top it off, the down-to-earth good looks of Eleanor Roosevelt." Therefore, after Lisa has programmed Lisa Lionheart's voice box herself, the doll says things like "Trust in yourself and you can achieve anything!" According to Lisa's feminist idealism, Lisa Lionheart combines 'wisdom,' 'wit,' 'tenacity,' 'common sense,' and more realistic 'good looks' which supposedly will teach girls that they "can be more than vacuous ninnies whose only goal is to look pretty," as the Simpson feminist says.

14 years later, another sketch in TREEHOUSE OF HORROR XIX (2008) shows Lisa wearing a witch costume for Halloween. When Bart's best friend Milhouse van Houten makes a compliment about the costume, Lisa replies: "Why is it when a woman is confident and powerful, they call her a witch?" Lisa also stands up against other sexist clichés. In the episode "To Surveil with Love,"[45] her intelligence is not taken seriously because she has blonde hair. Here, Lisa demonstrates that she rather acts as a mature feminist 'woman' and campaigns for tolerance by instructing her biased surroundings not to think that all blondes are dumb, all fat people are jolly, and all old people are bad drivers. Altogether, Lisa Simpson is probably not only one of the most persistent feminist characters in American television history, she is also the first vegetarian character on primetime television, as the animal rights organization PETA reports (Savage 2017). The character of Lisa indeed represents an idealized feminist image, combining traits of bourgeois intellectuals such as the modernist poet Stein, the feminist cartoonist Guisewhite, the legal-affair correspondent Totenberg, the 19th-century social activist, abolitionist, and suffragist Stanton, as well as Civil-Rights activist and former first lady Roosevelt. But her character moreover reflects the *zeitgeist* of a younger generation which participated in the 1990s culture-war debates on issues such as religion, social equality, nutrition, education, and animal rights.

---

44   Cf. THE SIMPSONS, dir. Jeff Lynch, s05e14, Fox 1994.
45   Cf. THE SIMPSONS, dir. Mark Kirkland, s21e21, Fox 2010.

Bart The Trickster: 1990s' Boyhood between Boomer Enthusiasm and the Age of Innocence Lost

In the early days of the show, Bart Simpson, the older brother of Lisa and Maggie and first-born son of Marge and Homer, quickly turned into a cultural icon. It is common knowledge that soon after THE SIMPSONS premiered, Bart became a best-selling commodity of THE SIMPSONS and a star of its mass-marketed merchandising. In 1991, the hype around his character entered the American feuilleton under the catchy term Bartmania. Thanks to Bart's immediate success, Nathan Rabin writes on *The A. V. Club*, "the show evolved from a success to a hit and then into something much bigger – a pop culture phenomenon so huge it transcended television and cultural boundaries – and then something much crasser: a mass-marketed money machine" (2011). While Bart was instantly admired by children, he became a thorn in the side of parental, political, and religious interest groups. In short, Bart offered the ideal projection surface on which both young generations and educators could project mainly bad external influences on the American youth.

Interpreting him according to Baudrillard's understanding of simulacra, of an image's artificial overexposure, Bart's character showed how television blurred the line between meaningful images and negative commodities limited to their commercial value. But Bart is more than that. In "THE SIMPSONS: Atomistic Politics and the Nuclear Family" (1999), American literary- and media critic Paul A. Cantor points to Bart as a character blending archetypal American characteristics and writes: "Bart is an American icon, an updated version of Tom Sawyer and Huckleberry Finn rolled into one" (748). However, it seems important to look behind Bart's self-assertive "Cowabunga!"-*façade*. Caught between Tom Sawyer and Huckleberry Finn, he is not allowed to be either, and I read him as a character who shows how the youth of the time oscillates between the status of both archetypal American characters of boyhood. McRobbie says about youth-culture scholar Dick Hebdige, that he, in her words, described the "landscape of the present" (i. e. the cultural landscape in post-war Britain) as amalgamating various surfaces (i. e. pop, music, style, fashion) and thus creating an indefinite and heterogenous terrain of "fragmented subjectivity" (1994: 14). Accordingly, McRobbie's comments on the rise and rediscovery of "drowned voices" in popular culture reminded me of the portrayal of Bart Simpson. The British scholar traces the

> landscape of the present… with […] its exploration of fragmented subjectivity – all of this articulates more precisely with the wider conditions of present 'reality:' with unemployment, with education, […] and with the coming into being of those whose voices were historically drowned by the (modernist) meta-narratives' mastery, which were in turn both patriarchal and imperialist.
> *(McRobbie 1994: 14)*

In my opinion, Bart can be read as a character on which various surfaces accumulate and who demonstrates "the wider conditions of present 'reality'." Bart acts as the voice of a "drowned" generation. Some of THE SIMPSONS' postmodern techniques of the 1980s and early 1990s are illustrated by him. To a greater extent than Lisa, Bart is representative of a Western generation of 'innocence lost,' caught in the limbo between baby-boomer idealism and Gen Xers'[46] 'No Future' cynicism. As Bart's massive appeal on American television demonstrates, the character plausibly embodied the generation's fragmented subjectivity which 1990s' fans welcomed like a breath of fresh air. Bart's archetypal subjectivity helped to highlight cultural diversity and to express a need to think seriously about the trivial and about the generation that celebrated pop culture. Bart showed how it had become impossible to establish stable moral hierarchies within a new pluralist American society. Configured as Lisa's direct opposite, he is the archetypal postmodern trickster, a cheating anti-hero, a detached millennial, who disobeys the rules of conformity, openly mocks authorities (Principal Skinner, Homer, etc.), and promotes chaos and unrest in his environment. Yet, Bart's trickster qualities often speak of integrity, for example, when his character is used to negotiate current social- and political issues.

Furthermore, in the Reagan-Bush era of the late 1980s, Bart Simpson's anarchic underachiever identity was set up against political orthodoxy which pushed the trend of political correctness and parental advisories. During the first period of 'Making America Great Again,' conservatives ignored the effects which a cartoon show could have on the collective political consciousness of a mainstream audience. Until the late 1980s, "Saturday morning cartoons" had solely been kids' innocuous pleasure. Even THE SIMPSONS' primetime predecessors, THE FLINTSTONES (ABC 1960–1966) and THE JETSONS (ABC 1962–1963; 1985–1987), literally reanimated the industry's mantra by wallowing in familiar domestic ideology. In contrast to that, Paul Cantor suggests that Bart's characteristic rebelliousness and disrespect for authorities goes back to an older tradition on which America was built: that of its disobedient founding fathers (1999: 748).

On the other hand, German television scholar Michael Gruteser sees Bart's underachiever subtext motto, "… and proud of it, man!", as "nationale Bedrohung", a 'national threat' to the success-ridden nation of the 1980s (2014: 57). As I read Bart Simpson, by the mid-1990s his character led America into a new era of a deliberate from-rags-to-loser attitude. Reagan's propagandistic "It's morning in America"-rhetoric was built on the myth of a restored white masculinity, on fictional Hollywood 'hard bodies' which feminist film theorist Susan Jeffords finds in Rocky

---

46 'Gen X' and its members, the 'Gen Xers,' are commonly used abbreviations to refer to the Generation X – a sociological definition of social cohorts which Douglas Coupland particularly popularized in his novel *Generation X* from 1991.

Balboa of 1976, the box champion both on the big screen and on the national stage, and in Rambo, the Vietnam veteran from 1982. She writes in her seminal book *Hard Bodies* from 1994:

> Reagan's policies were geared not so much to the individual human body as it might be the material location of suffering, pain, or deprivation, as they were to the control of the *idea* of the body, as the Reagan ideology vied for and captured power to define how bodies were to be perceived, touched, fed, regulated, and counted. *(24, ital. in orig.)*

According to Jeffords, during the 1980s masculinity was defined by a spectacular surface that reproduced the mainframe of masculine authority (Jeffords 1994: 176).

In opposition to that, McRobbie suggests that in 1990s popular culture was "full of jokes:" "It refused to take itself seriously and for this reason found itself subject to criticism." (3) Bart Simpson is, like Charlie Brown from 1948, an underachiever; but Bart does not resign like Charlie Brown. Instead he shows America his naked butt. Bart's bottom is a frequently referenced body part standing for the character's anarchic, non-affirmative attitude against political regulation. Michael Gruteser reads Bart as an old form of subversion that has already been assimilated by the mainstream: "Das Subversive abseits des Etablierten hat für die Kulturindustrie einen so hohen Marktwert, [dass das Subversive] erst im etablierten Status jene puristische Oberfläche [erhält], über die *sellout* betrieben wird" (2014: 57, *ital. in orig.*). Bart's anarchic attitude was absorbed when the merchandise industry turned his cartoon protest into a popular motif printed on bed cloth and coffee mugs. Nathan Rabin remembers that already in 1991, "audiences couldn't hit a K-Mart without being inundated with shelf upon shelf of SIMPSONS merchandise, each piece [...] more shameless than the last" (2011). Catching up on the shamelessness of THE SIMPSONS, Chris Turner writes about Bart's personality in *Planet SIMPSONS* (2004):

> Like any good punk rocker, Bart had the nihilism thing down from the very beginning. Though not so much pissed off as extremely undisciplined, the Bart Simpson of the ULLMAN short is either fighting with his sister, inciting his father into murderous levels of rage, executing dangerous stunts that end in cartoonish levels of disaster, or simply spitting snarky one-liners at whatever authority figures cross his path. This appetite for destruction continued to be the defining feature of the smart-assed kid who dominated many episodes of the first few seasons of THE SIMPSONS – the version that spawned Bart-mania – though his methods and motivations show considerably more nuance than the white-trash Bart of the ULLMAN era. *(12)*

Succeeding the Ullman era, Bart's later, more nuanced persona shows him as a descendant of the baby boomers. Bart was born into the "lackadaisical nonchalance" of Gen Xers whose legacy the postmodern theorist Douglas Kellner sees manifest in the "discourses associated with postmodern emphasis on the margins, differences, excluded voices and new subjects of revolt" (1997: 9). Bart's irreverence and nihilism were translated into a philosophical position. In his philosophical essay "Thus Spake Bart," co-editor of THE SIMPSONS and Philosophy, Mark T. Conard, for example, sees Friedrich Nietzsche's "bad boy" immorality as reflected in Bart's disobedience (cf. 2001: 86). Season four's episode "Homer's Triple Bypass"[47] can be read as capturing the "spirit of that generation" (Conard 2001: 86). Homer is afraid that Lisa and Bart may be troubled by the news of their father's heart surgery; here is their response:

BART: Nothing you can say can upset us. We're the MTV generation.
LISA: We feel neither highs nor lows.
HOMER: Really? What's it like?
LISA: Ehh.[48]

Following Turner's 'punk' characterization, Bart surfs on the wave of surfaces not as a meaningless action in the present, but as a conscious move to confront the double standards of the past. Growing up under the influence of Generation X, 1990s teenagers are not afraid of losing their fathers; the quote above shows that they already have the attitude of the generation who has lost their innocence. Matt Groening, himself a father of two boys, once commented that "if you don't want your kids to be like Bart, you don't act like Homer Simpson."[49]

Homer the Everyman: Representations of 1990s' Marginalized Masculinity

Although in the early years of THE SIMPSONS Homer's persona was limited to his angry temperament and boorish behavior, his personality was further explored in the later decades. Homer embodies a number of stereotypes of blue-collar Americans: He is the crude, overweight, borderline alcoholic (Turner 2004: 78–79), and although Matt Groening describes him as "completely ruled by his impulses," Homer is a character with "full desires" (ABC World News 2007) and

---

47 Cf. THE SIMPSONS, dir. David Silverman, s04e11, Fox 1992.
48 Christian Whiton from Fox News writes in his comment to THE SIMPSONS' 30th anniversary in 2018 that Lisa's "'ehh' is more recently cast in everyday parlance as 'meh'," which he defines as the "anthem of Gen X". See "'THE SIMPSONS' turns 30 – a big milestone for Gen X and America." Fox News.com, 30 Sept. 2018. 9 Accessed May 2019 under URL: https://fxn.ws/370PJgb.
49 See the whole interview "Questions for: Matt Groening" in The New York Times Magazine, posted on 27 Dec. 1998. Accessed 22 Aug. 2019 under URL: https://nyti.ms/374Mrsyl.

the one who does not only show great emotions for donuts and beer, but also for Marge.

Homer has had a massive cultural influence. In 2007, *USA Today* cited him as one of "the top 25 most influential people of the past 25 years" (Page 2007), and in 2010, *Entertainment Weekly* ranked him number one of "The 100 Greatest Characters of the Last Twenty Years" (Vary 2010). Media-studies scholar Robert Thompson from Syracuse University believes that "three centuries from now, English professors are going to be regarding Homer Simpson as one of the greatest creations in human storytelling" (qtd. in Baker 2003). In terms of representing white America, Homer Simpson is described as the ultimate embodiment of the American everyman. Over the years, the character has been given enough cultural agency and psychological depth to become an all-American icon.

In terms of identity politics, THE SIMPSONS' radical political project has not only been to decode the 'national body' as a political fake and failed ideology. The show has been deconstructing masculinity at least since the episode "King-Size Homer."[50] Here, Homer's role model as breadwinning patriarch of the family is suspended by his goal to gain three hundred pounds in weight to qualify for disability and claim his legal right not to leave the house for work anymore. Homer discovers that hyper-obesity is the only disability which enables him to fulfill his dream and carry out his work as a Security Inspector of Burns' nuclear power plant from home. In her article "Homer Erectus," Valerie Chow considers Homer Simpson an American "everyman and everywoman" (2004: 107) since Homer's disability equals a "self-abstracted masculinity" which exiles him to the traditionally feminine sphere of the home. Due to his hyper-obesity, Homer's physical appearance blurs the boundaries of male and female gender identities not least because the only piece of clothing that still fits him is women's traditional Hawaiian dress, the so-called muumuu (cf. Chow 2004: 127).

Homer's self-indulgence becomes not only physically pertinent, but is also visible in the context of his not acting as a responsible father figure. Homer has always had a problematic relationship with his son. Most of the time Homer simply does not care about Bart. In the episode "Brother from the Same Planet" (1993), Homer forgets to pick up Bart after soccer practice and does everything to turn his son into a sociopath who does not even care when Homer hangs himself at the end of the episode "Love is a Many-Strangled Thing."[51] Homer's abusive strangling of Bart whenever the ten-year-old does something wrong has become a hallmark routine aiming to prove Homer's lack of educational and social competence.

50 Cf. THE SIMPSONS, dir. Jim Reardon, s07e07, Fox 1995. In the German translation of the episode's title which reads "Der Behinderte Homer," the deconstruction of the character's masculinity becomes even more apparent.
51 Cf. THE SIMPSONS, dir. Michael Polcino, s22e17, Fox 2011.

In order to show disrespect for Homer's role as a patriarch, Bart usually calls his father by his first name instead of calling him Dad. Altogether, Homer's abject body pushes social norms, while Bart is a threat to the public sphere because he is unwilling to adhere to the rules at school and elsewhere. Nevertheless, an in many regards disabled father and the family's 'brat,' an anagram for Bart, become animated symbols of 1990s counter culture and their lack of role models; these symbols serve as what Gruteser calls "respektlos anarchistische Zeitkritiker," 'bluntly anarchic critics of the contemporary age' (57).

The 1990s exposed the hyper-masculine action heroes of the 1980s as representatives of white men who fought against their loss of hegemonic power. After the Reagan administration, the hard body of characters like Rambo shrank to an empty fantasy which soon had to make way for the Homers, the everymen, of the nation. The yellow skin color of THE SIMPSONS' characters represents whiteness, but a form of whiteness which is known from the tabloids, the yellow press. The Simpsons' lower-middle-class whiteness is at stake in a famous quote by Homer when he comments on Bart's obsession with the ultra-violent cat-and-mouse cartoon THE ITCHY AND SCRATCHY SHOW: "Oh Marge, cartoons don't have any deep meaning. They're just stupid drawings that give you a cheap laugh" (1991). Homer and Bart stand for two generations of white American masculinity who debunked Rambo as a national hyper-real fake of the 1980s.

The hard bodies were reversed in the errant bodies of a "King-Size Homer" and of the Simpsons' first-born son, a ten-year-old terror child. In her essay "White Masculinity and the TV Sitcom Dad" from 2010, Cerise L. Glenn argues that Homer and Bart represent a white masculinity marginalized in the public and private spheres. In the 1990s, their characters foster

> identification with Americans who have not been able to achieve the nuclear family and the American dream or who do not believe in these values. [...] THE SIMPSONS [...] shows how unattainable the ideal nuclear family can be for working-class families struggling against failing education systems, corrupt political leaders and over-consumption of popular culture.   *(2010: 184)*

Hence, whereas the abusive Homer Simpson of the 1990s was the opposite of the bombastic fathers of earlier television eras, the Bart Simpson of the 1990s spit on the rotten fruit that Reaganomics had left for Generation X.

Wrapping up McRobbie: Thinking about Culture Wars with THE SIMPSONS

Returning to Groening's metaphor from the beginning, THE SIMPSONS not only rides surfaces like waves. In fact, the show adds a different color to these waves. By now, THE SIMPSONS have become popular culture's tidal wave itself, creating a rich variety of "fragmented looks" by way of its characters. As I illustrated with my character analyses of Lisa, Bart, and Homer, popular culture and postmodern criticism are intersecting where the superficial seems to reign and where the trivial abounds.

But speaking of the fault-lines of the postmodern condition, much of my attention is dedicated to the question of how THE SIMPSONS immerses in this field, indulges in this tension, and invites criticism. As Bart Simpson exemplifies, surfing the wave of hyper-real surfaces does not necessarily mean to get caught up by the trivial and superficial. Surfing the wave indeed means to 'master,' that is to understand and take advantage of the surface by oscillating between the different positions of fragmented subjectivities. For those whom Gruteser, Klein, and Rauscher call "Simpsonian natives" (2014: 11), THE SIMPSONS may by now be a conservative constant that has developed along the lines of postmodern cultural theory, further shifting Gen Xers' coming-of-age narratives to new-age stories of resilience.

In the last section, I explored Angela McRobbie's notions about postmodern subjectivities and about the fragmented look provided by a feminist perspective on how cartoon bodies could become projection surfaces of (counter-)national concerns in 1990s' popular culture. In a next step, I will scrutinize Linda Hutcheon's groundbreaking approaches to a postmodern use of parody for its helpfulness in understanding THE SIMPSONS. More precisely, I will now include TREEHOUSE OF HORROR in my inquiry in order to question whether parody is used as a comedic technique of ridicule and laughter, or whether parody has in fact become a meaningful, critical cultural practice and essential to THE SIMPSONS' multifunctional humor.

Linda Hutcheon: Postmodern Parody in THE SIMPSONS

Critics found many ways to hail THE SIMPSONS' viral "media revolution" (Rushkoff 2004: 292) or celebrated it as "the new repository of the West's common metaphors," if not "a parlance of our times" (Evans 2011: 78). Noëll K. Wolfgram Evans' book *Animators of Film and Television* (2011) includes a chapter on Matt Groening, whom the animation critic calls "The Populist Hippie" (2011: 76). Evans suggests that the two contradictory attributes of 'populist' and 'hippie' make Groening a "modern-era version of Walt Disney" (*ibid.*: 82). My first reaction to Evans' comparison was irritation. For me, setting up a connection between Walt Disney and Matt Groening didn't make sense. After all, THE SIMPSONS rarely bypassed a chance to pull Disney to pieces, especially not after Disney had taken over major shares of Rupert Murdoch's 20th Century Fox to which THE SIMPSONS belongs until 2082, as journalist Michael Hogan claims.[52] Thinking more thoroughly

---

52 Journalist Michael Hogan writes in "21 things you never knew about THE SIMPSONS" (2014) in the *Sydney Morning Herald* that Fox owns the rights to THE SIMPSONS until 2082.

4 The first featurette of the Silly Symphonies Series The Skeleton Dance by Ub Iwerks (1929) showed innovative techniques of mixing classical music with mass-entertaining Animation

about the connection established by Evans, Matt Groening and Walt Disney can both be characterized as restless innovators who managed to push animation as an art form and medium to new heights. Evans also suggests that Matt Groening resembles Walt Disney in that he shares his forerunner's understanding that success is built on story (cf. *ibid*.: 82). Let's first look at how Walt Disney's story began before taking into consideration in how far Matt Groening's can be compared.

Appealing to the Masses: Walt Disney, Matt Groening, and the Different Ways of Cartoon Storytelling

According to "The Serious History of Silly Symphonies," a contribution to the fan base *Oh My Disney.com* (2016), Disney's success story began after Mickey Mouse had become a big sensation following the character's premiere in Steamboat Willie in 1928.[53] Only one year later, Disney and his partner Ub Iwerks sparked the idea of a black-and-white short, The Skeleton Dance (1929),[54] that was, in many regards, highly unusual at the time. It is common knowledge that this first "featurette" was an exceptional film for the Disney canon since the cartoon is based on Saint-Saens' *Danse Macabre* symphony from 1874, to which Disney edited the portrayal of skeletons rising from their graves (Pinsky 109) (see Fig. 4).

After The Skeleton Dance, there followed the beginning of a lasting tradition, the serial Silly Symphonies, which presented animated stories that deliberately denied a deeper meaning, as Walt Disney confirmed in an 1937 interview

---

53   Steamboat Willie can be accessed on the YouTube Channel "Walt Disney Animation Studios," posted on 27 Aug. 2009 under URL: https://bit.ly/2QvPQuR.
54   The Skeleton Dance was directed by Walt Disney with background visuals by Ub Iwerks. The cartoon short can be accessed on the YouTube channel "Walt Disney Animation Studios," URL: https://bit.ly/398DgIn.

5 The 'Big Bad Wolf' in disguise of a Jewish peddler became a lasting symbol for Disney's way of adding 'some meanness'

with *Time* magazine.⁵⁵ Disney specialist Mark I. Pinsky remarks that THE SILLY SYMPHONIES favored "some meanness" (2004: 110) in their portrayal, for example, of Africans as cannibals (see CANNIBAL CAPERS, 1930)⁵⁶ or of a character that is known in Western popular culture as the 'Big Bad Wolf.' In the 1930s, Disney's Wolf did not only become a lasting symbol of the Depression period, a symbol of the hardships threatening the home, but is also interpreted today as giving away Walt Disney's much-discussed anti-Semitic attitude.⁵⁷ After all, the Wolf disguises himself as a Jewish peddler in order to break into the third pig's house (see THE THREE LITTLE PIGS, 1933) (cf. Fig. 5).⁵⁸

In THE SIMPSONS' "Itchy & Scratchy Land,"⁵⁹ the episode's writers refer to the racist accusations against Walt Disney. In a biographical black-and-white footage film, the creator of Itchy & Scratchy, Roger Meyers, Sr., who serves as THE SIMPSONS' equivalent of Walt Disney, is portrayed in an obviously staged and scripted situation which emphasizes that Meyers, Sr., "cared of almost all the

---

55 In 1937, Walt Disney told a journalist from *Time* magazine that throughout his career there was no deeper meaning to his cartoons and shorts because the one time a deeper meaning was given to a cartoon telling of the King Midas story, THE GOLDEN TOUCH (1935), it became "a tremendous flop" (qtd. in Pinsky 2004: 110).

56 See CANNIBAL CAPERS on the YouTube channel "Cartoon Classic Cinema," posted on 12 Jul. 2018 under URL: https://bit.ly/3lMJMts.

57 For more information on the anti-Semite controversy, see the biographies by Mark Eliot, *Walt Disney: Hollywood's Dark Prince* (1993), as well as by Richard Schickel, *The Disney Version: The Life, Times, Art and Commerce of Walt Disney* (1968). In *The Gospel According to Disney* (2004), Mark I. Pinsky writes that many biographers, for example Katherine and Richard Greene, came to the conclusion that "the allegations of Walt Disney's anti-Semitism are a myth" (Pinsky 112).

58 See the cartoon short THE THREE LITTLE PIGS on YouTube, posted on 13 Aug. 2012 by "Roel71" under URL: https://bit.ly/2OVSaex.

59 Cf. THE SIMPSONS, dir. Wes Archer, s06e04, Fox 1994.

peoples of the world and in return was beloved by the world" as the voice-over informs. The voice continues: "Except in 1938, when he was criticized for his controversial cartoon 'Nazi Supermen Are Our Superior Race'." The background story of the "gentle genius" Roger Meyers, Sr., strongly resembles the story of Walt Disney. THE SIMPSONS' canon includes various episodes throughout the decades which were meant to mock Walt Disney's assumed anti-Semitism and his conservative political attitude.

With respect to the subsequent SILLY SYMPHONIES series between 1929 and 1935, Walt Disney claimed that instead of including "some social meaning" in the cartoons, they needed something unconventional and original with a wide appeal. At least partly due to their originality, THE SKELETON DANCE, CANNIBAL CAPERS, as well as THE THREE LITTLE PIGS were extremely successful. For the series, the studio produced fifteen- to twenty-five minute long "featurettes" (cf. Pinsky 109) with technological breakthroughs such as continuous movements, dramatic coloring, and experimental content.[60] Furthermore, the studio introduced sound-image compositions to mainstream audiences – a technique which was previously known from experimental-art film contexts. Oscar Fischinger's "Visual Music" studies of the 1920s, for example, show meticulously planned arrangements of abstract animation and classical music which inspired Disney. The producers of SILLY SYMPHONIES used orchestrated classical music that was edited to the cartoon movements in post-production. According to essayist Richard Hildreth, "the most important innovation in SKELETON DANCE is that the musical score and the animated action were planned, designed, and executed in unison" (2006). Disney, just like later Groening, re-purposed techniques from experimental filmmaking for his experimental style and storytelling.

Both Walt Disney and Matt Groening are successful, highly innovative storytellers and had their own way to appeal to the masses. In "Summit Meetings: Mickey Mouse's Culture Wars," film critic and historian John C. Tibbetts remembers that Walt Disney always ignored the distinctions between art and commerce as he supported "a more democratic" possibility to "ring the death knell of an un-American elitist culture" (2011: 206). The Disney biographer Steven Watts notes that "Disney smoothed the jagged transition from the values of the Victorian age to those of a fledgling consumer America" and "helped to dismantle the barriers between highbrow and lowbrow cultural activity" (1997: 163). Disney wanted to help Americans "to accommodate to a new age by appealing to older traditions while forging a new creed of [...] mass consumption" (Watts 1997: 163) – just like Groening later. However, as far as I am concerned, the situation is not as easy as it may appear at first sight. The following analysis will shed light on how THE

---

60 An illustrative example is Ub Iwerk's 1929 Halloween five-minute short HELL'S BELLS on YouTube, posted on 16 Jun. 2016 under URL: https://bit.ly/3cg2VkC.

SIMPSONS makes use of parody to lampoon Walt Disney. Parody according to THE SIMPSONS reveals the difference between Walt Disney's and Matt Groening's approaches to storytelling.

Firstly I argue that Matt Groening does not merely capitalize on adding 'meanness' to his cartoons the way Disney did. Rather Groening finds constructive ways of critically re-evaluating, for example, Disney's dubious political messages in his postmodernist cartoons. For probing into the meanness in Walt Disney's allegedly well-intended cartoons, Groening, according to Noëll Evans, makes use of his "almost psychic connection with the psyche of America" (82). Whereas Disney is known to stand for conservative, white, nationalist values, Groening has less mainstream, left-wing, subversive, and postmodern values. Politically speaking, Disney and Groening are worlds apart, but structurally they both do what it takes to push their ideologies and businesses.

Disney transformed animation into a market force with mass-appeal that could compete with Hollywood's entertainment industry at a time when people had only limited access to visual media. After STEAMBOAT WILLIE, THE SILLY SYMPHONIES series and THREE LITTLE PIGS turned the American public into a Disney audience, ready to learn Disney's moral lessons about American values. Richard Hildreth comments: "During the decade of SILLY SYMPHONIES, Disney and his various collaborators had transformed animated films from novelties to true cinema" (2006). The stratospheric popularity of the early short-film series as well as that of the later full-length features are based on the fact that Walt Disney capitalized on the Americanization of European fairytales and folktales by creating an 'American' way of storytelling. His narratives were unique in being shaped by his understanding of the new character and content of American public culture (cf. Tibbetts 206). When THE SIMPSONS were launched in 1989, national audiences were still on a diet of white, middle-class sitcoms teaching viewers white, middle-class behavior. Groening for his part used animation to re-invent conventional television storytelling and taught THE SIMPSONS' audience how to 'un-learn' formulaic concepts of family and friendship.

A second distinction between Walt Disney and Matt Groening is that their animation seems to emerge from two entirely different national 'psyches.' During the 1930s, Walt Disney established a conservative storytelling tradition that was to contribute to a modern America. Thus, the spirit of the third little pig was supposed to boost the nation's morale. When the Wolf tries to blow off its house in the featurette from 1933, the smart pig sings: "I have no chance to sing and dance, for work and play don't mix." The Disney biographer Richard Schickel reads the pig's song as a political statement and "unofficial anthem" of the Roosevelt administration during the Depression, which emphasized the spirit of "self-reliance, the old virtues of solid, conservative building and of keeping the house [i.e. the nation, ann. SD] in order" (2016: 165). Disney's three little pigs act heroically, their story tells of hard work, steadfastness, and hope. As THE THREE LITTLE PIGS cartoon illustrates, Disney's anthropomorphic wolf and pigs create a myth about reality.

Groening obviously created his yellow American suburbanites with different values and narratives in mind. In times of national crisis, THE SIMPSONS' storytelling is characterized not by affirming, but by questioning traditional morale and outworn orthodoxies. As I have discussed in the chapter above on the 'surface' representations of the U.S. in THE SIMPSONS of the 1990s, Groening uses postmodern storytelling in order to create his characters' fractured perspectives on a crisis-ridden America. THE SIMPSONS' animation style creates a visual parody which is not about reality, but rather rooted in reality; its characters are flawed and contradictory, clearly identifiable as human.

When the Wolf dresses as a Jewish peddler and sells brushes with a thick accent ("I'm the Fuller Brush Man! I'm giving free samples!") it becomes clear to today's viewer that this SILLY SYMPHONIES' episode indeed has a deeper meaning which was often read as bearing anti-Semitic tendencies. On the *Tumblr* blogosphere "Walt Disney Confessions," a still from the cartoon is posted along with a quote from Walt Disney who said about the THREE LITTLE PIGS cartoon: "I personally found the Jewish Peddler scene in THREE LITTLE PIGS pretty funny, and it's a shame that the punchline (pigs aren't Kosher) got lost in a mess of conspiracy theories and accusations of anti-Semitism due to its non-PC and somewhat clumsy delivery" (qtd. on "Walt Disney Confessions," *Tumblr.com* 2011). The Disney biographer Neal Gabler wrote about this issue in his book from 2006:

> As with race, one could certainly point to some casual insensitivity. Shortly after the release of THREE LITTLE PIGS in 1933, Rabbi J.X. Cohen, the director of the American Jewish Congress, wrote Walt angrily that a scene in which the wolf was portrayed as a Jewish peddler was so 'vile, revolting and unnecessary as to constitute a direct affront to the Jews,' especially in light of what was then happening in Germany, and he was asked that the offending scene be removed.
> *(454).*

Blogger Jamie Stewart's posts in "Bibbity Bobbity Bigot: Addressing the Rumors of Walt Disney's Anti-Semitism," part of column "Academic Analyses" that both the stereotypical depiction of ethnicities and the Disney company's efforts to erase their existence were common characteristics of older and not-so-old Disney productions (cf. Stewart 2015). We only have to think of the racism towards indigenous people in PETER PAN (1953), towards African Americans in DUMBO (1941) and SONG OF THE SOUTH (1946), or Middle Eastern people in ALADDIN (1992). However, the punchline that "pigs aren't kosher" does not only impress as anti-Semitic. Even more important for a hegemonic reading of its time is that the Jewish peddler does not live up to the pigs' American work ethic in this, by 1930s' standards, typically melodramatic scene. Accompanied by Practical Pig's dramatic piano music, neither the Wolf nor the peddler are able to penetrate or destroy the 'foundations' on which Practical Pig's solid brick house is built. Even during the time of Depression, external or internal threats cannot harm America which, represented by the earnest and smart Practical Pig and his brothers, rests safe behind steadfast masonry.

On the one hand, THE SIMPSONS was one of the first cartoon series in American animation history that avoided to make use of anthropomorphic characters: the family's pets Snowball III (cat) and Santa's Little Helper (dog) remain speechless, and the only animals which are shown to occasionally use speech are the cartoon-in-the-cartoon cat-and-mouse characters Itchy and Scratchy. On the other hand, I have often asked myself whether the function of 'Simpsonizing' real-life guest cameo characters of American presidents and Hollywood actors is to further expose their supposedly true personality? When, for example, Barbara and George Bush, Sr., move to the Simpsons' neighborhood in the episode "Two Bad Neighbors" (1996), THE SIMPSONS not only secured the Bushes a place in its animated cultural archive. The episode also portrayed George and Barbara Bush as the people next door. When the Simpsons come over to welcome their new neighbors, the ordinariness of the Bushes is defined by supposedly normal things and behavior such as the door's name plate ("The Bushes") or the fact that George Bush holds a hammer in his hand (hands-on mentality) and drinks lemonade with his wife on their veranda.

If the cartoon realism which Disney uses is highly confirmative of conservative values, THE SIMPSONS rather exposes this confirmative function of traditional cartoon realism. By normalizing the former U.S. president and his wife, THE SIMPSONS cartoonists, unlike Disney, use fractal pieces from everyday culture to foreground the relationship between audience and the Bushes; to point to the Bushes' to-be-looked-at-ness as objects of the viewers' critical gaze.[61] Disney uses the Wolf as a metaphor for the evil capitalist and thus invites a normalizing gaze. Although the aesthetics of both animation traditions certainly share many features, their framing works altogether differently: Disney's cartoon films present a straight, unironic reading of conservative values and ideological concepts, which means that the frame of the text is congruent with the subtext; THE SIMPSONS, however, invite a parodic reading, which means that the frame of the text may not be congruent with the subtext.

In the episode "Lisa the Vegetarian,"[62] the Simpson family goes on a trip to "Storytown Village," a small theme park which promises "fun for ages between 1

---

61 In context of the "gaze" as organized within "regimes" in psychoanalytically inspired feminist film theory, see Laura Mulvey's seminal essay "Visual Pleasure and Narrative Cinema" from 1975.
62 Cf. THE SIMPSONS, dir. Mark Kirkland, s07e05, Fox 1995.

6 The Simpsons visit a low-tech animatronics mimicry of Disneyland that has the iconic scene of Disney's The Big Bad Wolf trying to blowdown The Three Little Pigs' house

to 7 ½" and contains animatronic versions of classic fairy-tale characters as imagined by Disney. Animatronics are figures which are electronically, mechanically, or pneumatically controlled and have always been a popular attraction of theme parks and fun-fairs. Animatronics are further commonly used in many Hollywood films of the 1980s and 1990s (e. g. parts of the shark in Jaws, 1975, or the T-Rex in Jurassic Park, 1993). Yet, in contemporary times, animatronics are rather computer- or software-controlled so that "Storytown Village" appears to be just a poor, low-tech imitation of Disneyland. The Simpsons bypass the rather cheap-looking exhibit of "Goldilocks and the Three Bears" and arrive at the fenced-off display of "Three Little Pigs" (see Fig. 6). The following dialogue[63] can be read as a statement on how The Simpsons' creators apply a critical perspective towards Disney's version of Three Little Pigs.

> THE WOLF: Come out, come out, or I'll blooow your house in.
> THE THREE PIGS: Not by the hairs on our chinny-chin-chin.
> BART: What a load of crappy-crap-crap.
> HOMER: Quiet, boy. I have a feeling some bad stuff is about to go down.
> MARGE: This is where the wolf blows down the pigs' house.
> BART: He blows, all right. He blows big time.
> MARGE: That's it, honey! Get into the spirit!

The "bad stuff" that Homer assumes "is about to go down" can be seen as a satirical reference to the Wolf as a symbol for the Depression that was unable to destroy the spirit of the three little pigs, symbolizing the ironic "crappy-crap-crap" of 18 million unemployed Americans according to the "gloomy statistics of 1932" that Schickel vividly remembers in his third edition of *The Disney Version: The Life, Times, Art and Commerce of Walt Disney* (1997: 165).

---

63 The entire transcript of the episode "Lisa the Vegetarian," including annotations, can be found on *Genius.com* under URL: https://bit.ly/3tYJGD0.

In addition, a closer look at the screenshot in Fig. 6 shows the differences concerning the framing of cartoon realism between Disney and Groening. Because of the fact that the exhibited scene is fenced off from the visitors, it will probably only be enchanting for children between 1 and 7 ½. Moreover, the fence makes clear that the scene has no magic at all, but is "crappy crap crap" and thus disenchanting for visitors like Bart. A closer look at the pigs reveals that they have microphones in their snouts, the house is visibly moved by a hydraulic foot, and the construction doesn't hide that the wolf is controlled by a little box connected to a hydraulic hose. The exaggeration of the low-tech solutions in this scene invites the viewers' ironic gaze: The clumsy fakeness of the animatronics exposes the staged quality of Disney's make-believe and ridicules not only the characters of THREE LITTLE PIGS, but also the melodrama that narratively frames them.

Morality according to THE SIMPSONS:
Re-Telling Tales of Human Defectiveness and Mistaken Emancipation

Classical Disney characters such as the seven dwarfs, which materialized in 1937, or Pinocchio, which emerged in 1940, are interpretations of literary protagonists and can be read both as parodies and confirmations of their written version. SNOW WHITE AND THE SEVEN DWARFS was Disney's first full-length animated feature film and is based on the fairytale "Sneewittchen" first published by the Brothers Grimm in 1812. Pinocchio is the protagonist of the Italian children's book *Le Avventure di Pinocchio* by Carlo Collodi from 1883 which Disney's second full-length animated feature film PINOCCHIO is based on. Disney's seven dwarfs are extremely clumsy, his wooden puppet Pinocchio is very naive. I wonder if these traits make the Disney characters more loveable than the originals because of their 'defectiveness'? In the following analysis I will ask whether the dwarfs are 'real men' and Pinocchio a 'real boy' or if both figures are symbolic representations of Disney's concept of morality. Can the seven dwarfs as well as Pinocchio be interpreted as parts of an othering process? Do the malformed community of mine workers and the wooden boy with the long nose fit the norm of late-1930s America?

But first things first. The little people's societal inappropriateness can be seen in the fact that, in opposition to Snow White, the dwarfs as well as Pinocchio are shown to have four instead of five fingers. Thus I asked myself if these characters are actually meant to be read as non-human and if their position as 'others' defines their thoroughly constructed personae. After all, Pinocchio only becomes a human with five instead of four fingers once he has proven worthy of being treated as a boy rather than a toy. Based on this observation, I assumed that Disney's four-fingered characters are portrayed as being stigmatized. Is their status as objects a consequence of their disability and does it make them outsiders? Are they infantilized and belittled to stress that they depend on a wholesome, normal person? Are Snow White, who knows how to clean and cook, and Jiminy Cricket, who can talk but, after all, is a bug, 'normal' and 'real' because they know the difference between right and wrong?

According to Disney biographer Schickel, Disney introduced the recurring device of giving his main characters a "worldly wise mentor, ally and rescuer," "a good-natured lad" (1997: 247) in order to make his movies more easily consumable by family audiences. Pinocchio's mentor Jiminy Cricket helps the main character "to discover the principles of correct behavior" (*ibid*.: 247). The cricket which in Collodi's original *Le Avventure di Pinocchio* should have acted as Pinocchio's conscience, is squashed by the puppet without further ado. In the Disney feature, however, Jiminy Cricket is used to "brighten and lighten" (*ibid*.: 247) the story and to add a moment of comic relief when the narrative develops a too serious tone. The seven dwarfs in SNOW WHITE fulfill a similar function, but do not only act as Snow White's sympathetic sidekicks. The seven dwarfs are stereotyped by diverse disabilities, including dwarfism, deficient learning capabilities (Dopey is the most mentally challenged) and speech difficulties (Doc stutters). As his name already indicates, Grumpey suffers from emotional deficiency. The dwarfs as a group are evidence of defective masculinity, reinforce stereotypical gender- and class behavior and stand in contrast to the physical and mental perfection of fully human characters such as Snow White, the Evil Queen, and the Prince.

In the *Tumblr* blog "Disnability," the ACA fan Jennifer Snow broadly analyzes disability in Disney films. In her "Analysis of the Seven Dwarfs," Snow describes their function in Disney's SNOW WHITE. She argues that the seven dwarfs are depicted as hard workers and suggests that "Disney reinforces gender stereotypes and […] stereotypes associated […] with disabilities. The seven dwarfs are […] unable to live a successful life. […] With Snow White serving a mother-like role, the dwarfs are depicted as finally happy and complete." (Snow, undated)

Whereas Disney's first feature film, SNOW WHITE AND THE SEVEN DWARFS (1937), tells a story of correct feminine and masculine behavior within clearly separated spheres of the home (Snow White) and the workplace (the mine), Disney's second full-length animated feature, PINOCCHIO, is a story about moral education and about withstanding the temptations of evil. In his book *The Gospel According to Disney* (2004), former *L. A. Times* journalist Mark I. Pinsky describes PINOCCHIO as "a simple morality tale – cautionary and schematic –ideal for moral instruction, save for some of its darker moments" (28).

The "darker moments," however, that Pinsky mentions are the subject of "Pinitchio," THE SIMPSONS' parody of Disney's PINOCCHIO. In the episode "Itchy & Scratchy Land" (1994), Lisa and Bart again visit the Simpsonized version of a Disney theme park. Lisa and Bart arrive at a small walk-through cinema, in which a documentary about the Itchy & Scratchy creator, Roger Meyers, Sr., calls "Pinitchio" one of Meyers' first "wildly successful" feature films – of course, a direct parody of Walt Disney's Pinocchio. Next a scene from "Pinitchio" is shown in which the wooden mouse, Pinitchio, promises its creator, Scratchpetto, that it will be "a good boy" and "never hurt" the wood-carver cat again. Yet, "hurting" has a peculiar meaning in Itchy & Scratchy cartoons: Itchy's violence is commonly physical, not emotional. Therefore, Pinitichio's promise instantly turns out to be a lie when its nose grows and pierces Scratchpetto's eye according to the cartoon's usual ultra-violent tone. The scene cuts to Lisa who remains unaffected by the scene and ironically wonders whether "this kind of violence does desensitize." Lisa indicates that "Pinitchio's" lack of melodramatic pathos undermines the character development of the main character, especially in the final, and finally *moral* transformation process from puppet to human boy as shown in Pinocchio's climax. The graphic physical violence shown in the Itchy & Scratchy spoof of Pinocchio creates an ironic contrast to Disney's symbolic morality and his conservative portrayal of children's virtuous behavior.

Disney's pathos becomes evident in the portrayal of Snow White as well, an archetypal Disney character who is defined by purity and innocence. The contrast between the young maiden Snow White and the Seven Dwarfs functions as an othering device just like Pinocchio's deficiency. When the princess reaches the Dwarfs' cottage, Pinsky observes the absurdity behind Snow White's assumption that the filth and disarray of the residents can be attributed to their not having a mother (cf. Pinsky 22). After the Dwarfs' first 'heigh-hoing' back from the mine they enter their now tidy abode, where the innocent victim-heroine Snow White convinces the "little men," as she calls them, to offer her shelter. Pinsky writes: "[A]ccording to story notes in the Disney archive, a sequence in which Snow White teaches the dwarfs how to pray was suggested but never filmed" (24). Even without the prayer scene, it does not take viewers long to discover the moral dimension of Snow White, particularly when the persecuted princess confidently "whistles when she works" in order to forget adversity and "get along somehow." According to Pinsky, her motto must have found deep resonance when first heard during the Depression (cf. Pinsky 2004: 23).

The fact that Snow White falls victim to the wicked queen's poisoned apple heightens the psychological impact on the viewer who feels relieved when at long last the childlike dwarfs are replaced by the able, hyper-masculine Prince who kisses Snow White and wakes her from sleep. Snow White's character stands in stark contrast to the portrayal of the Seven Dwarfs as flawed. Snow White is the "all-American mom," as Katie Croxton suggests, forming the maternal center of what Walt Disney himself considered "a perfect story" that suits "happily ever after desires" (2015: 27), or as Croxton describes it: Snow White foregrounds Walt Disney's "tendencies to highlight a simplified romance between royalty and commoners" (Croxton 2015: 27).

Linda Hutcheon: Postmodern Parody in THE SIMPSONS

7–8 THE SIMPSONS borrowing from Disney's visual inventory: comparison between Disney's SNOW WHITE (1937) and THE SIMPSONS' interpretation of Lisa as the princess In "Four Great Women and a Manicure" (2009)

THE SIMPSONS' version of SNOW WHITE AND THE SEVEN DWARFS, as part of the episode "Four Great Woman and a Manicure,"[64] retells some of the most iconic scenes and ironically even reproduces camera perspectives and distinct visual cues of the Disney feature. Springfield's Blue-Haired Lawyer ironically makes Lisa, the narrator, aware of potential copyright infringements when she retells the fairy-tale and 'borrows' from the visual inventory of the Disney film (cf. Fig. 7 with 8). Among the scenes Lisa adapts from Disney's version are the musical sequence in which Snow White whistles while doing housekeeping for the Dwarfs, the sequence in which the Evil Queen asks, as Lisa comments it, her "magic HDTV-screen on the wall, who's the fairest one of all," and, of course, the moment when Snow White gets poisoned and is laid out in the famous glass coffin in the forest's clearing. But in contrast to Disney's credo "that adversity can *always* be overcome with a song and a smile" (Pinsky 23, *ital. in orig.*), THE SIMPSONS' version deliberately disrupts the melodramatic frame and transforms SNOW WHITE into a femi-

64 Cf. THE SIMPSONS, dir. Raymond S. Persi, s20e20, Fox 2009.

nist "great woman" tale as its title, "Four Great Women and a Manicure," shows. In the episode Lisa Simpson tells her "original" version of what happened to Snow White in Snow White and The Seven Dwarfs.

Whereas Disney films are allegories which are supposed to have some ethical impact and bring about a catharsis in their viewers, Lisa follows a different strategy. In her version, the wicked queen receives cruel punishment when she's lynched by a mob of woodland creatures. The narrator also decides that the "fairytale from hundreds of years ago" has to have a new ending: The princess sleeps and waits for her prince to come, with the slight exception that, according to Lisa, "he never did... because a woman shouldn't have to depend on a man." Lisa's ending is not happy, Disney's is. The Disney film does not end after the Evil Queen accidentally falls from a cliff (as in Grimm's interpretation) to her death because it is an unwritten Disney law that the final scene has to compensate the viewers for their emotional investment. Accordingly, Disney's Snow White ends by showing the princess's perfect happiness when riding into the sunset with her savior Prince. Lisa's version, however, ends with a deer carrying the witch's head on its antlers like a crown; the narrator deliberately foregoes a happy ending and tells a feminist morality tale. Whereas Snow White and the Seven Dwarfs and Pinocchio give "moral instructions" which Pinsky diagnoses as socially appropriate behavior according to Disney, The Simpsons make parodic use of Disney in order to teach viewers to interrogate, or better, un-learn the moral lessons which Disney has been teaching its young audience for ages.

Rethinking The Simpsons' Parody:
The Antithetical Gaze & Cartoon Layering

Disney's animated features are melodramas aiming for emotionally uplifting their viewers. In 2003, animation scholar David Surman argues that this is the function of Disney's animated "pseudorealism" (2003: 14). He criticizes Disney's understanding of animation aesthetics and blames him for having "misrepresented the animated form and its specific capabilities by aligning animation with aspects of photorealism" (Surman 2003: 14). According to Surman, Disney's aesthetics invites a straight, affirmative reading of his narratives' underlying subtext. The animated world imagined in Disney's full-length features creates an "illusion of life" (ibid.: 13) by translating worldly norms into animated images.

Pinocchio and Snow White exemplify the realism which is framed by melodrama, underlining clear distinctions between good and bad as well as between beauty and ugliness. Surman calls this animation strategy "pseudorealism," a cartoon technique which he sees in stark contrast to the animated surrealism of the Popeye (1933–1942) or Betty Boop (1930–1939), cartoons produced by the Fleischer studios around the same time (cf. 13–14). According to Surman, Walt

Disney's desire to express "a plausible, coherent worldview" corresponds to the animation's central "naturalistic idealism" (23). Snow White and The Seven Dwarfs, for example, coerced the animated form from Silly Symphonies' "plasmatic flexibility" into a "neorealist practice" (Wells 1998: 23, qtd. in Surman 25).[65]

Due to what Surman calls "neorealist practice," the portrayal of Snow White's new habitat demands a detailed style of drawing. This style puts emphasis on seemingly trivial, often everyday objects which testify to the "authenticity" of the image and its meaning. Shortly after the Dwarfs have accepted her, Snow White fully assimilates to her new mission as she immerses into the housekeeping, becoming one with herself and with nature. On the one hand, Snow White works in a kitchen which is full of household gadgets that indicate she is a "real" housekeeper. On the other hand, the detailed portrayal of birds, squirrels, and deer enforce the impression of "real" nature. In other words, the "real" is real because it is part of the Disney film's ideological setup: Its clear-cut meaning is that nature is the object of the human subject, while the woman is a domesticated subject who is only armed with kitchen tools.

As early as in the opening of the second Treehouse of Horror episode of 1991 Disney's pseudorealistic morality tales were made fun of. While the camera pans over Springfield cemetery, we see that one of the 'funny tombstones' is inscribed with "Walt Disney" next to one inscribed with "Bambi's Mom," declaring both, quite unemotionally, dead. Unlike Disney's myths of the unified nation and the intact American family, The Simpsons provides a look onto a fragmented, faceted, layered everyday world. The postmodern series refuses to create "a natural fantasy" in which all good creatures act in harmony while the evil ones "stumble through a graceless sideshow of error and petty rancor," as animation scholar Nicholas Sammond argues in *Babes in Tomorrowland: Walt Disney and the Making of the American Child* (2005: 178).

The comparison between Disney's and Groening's Snow White animation style shows that The Simpsons created a new form of 'flexible' realism. The deaths of Disney and Bambi's mother manifest that cartoon storytelling, led by a new generation of storytellers, has entered a new era. I would claim that The Simpsons' realistic animation style framed by a parodic mode is antithetical to Disney's politics of representation. This can be illustrated by way of Lisa Simpson's Snow White version, which is also a site of experimentation directed against traditional conventions and conservative practices.

The narrative frame of The Simpsons episode "Four Great Women and a Manicure" from 2009 shows Marge and Lisa sitting in a beauty salon and receiving a facial treatment, which inspires Lisa to introduce her Snow White version as a tale about the "dangerous obsession with female beauty." Lisa imagines herself

---

65 For more information on the animation style of Disney, see David Surman's book on *CGI Animation: Pseudorealism, Perception and Possible Worlds* (2003) published as ePub on *Academia.edu*.

playing the leading role as the innocent princess Snow White. Lisa, who is known as the intellectual center of THE SIMPSONS, deliberately positions herself in the role of Disney's passive female, which I see as a direct hint at how THE SIMPSONS reimagines the framing of the tale.

I will take a closer look at two distinct moments of Lisa's tale in order to point to a pattern in the antithetical aesthetic of THE SIMPSONS. Firstly, Lisa as Snow White also befriends birds and small animals which help her doing the housekeeping akin to Disney's version (cf. Fig. 8). But instead of exaggerating the stereotypical traits which, in Disney's kitchen scene, exceed the animation and demonstrate the main character's enthusiasm concerning her role as housekeeper, Princess Lisa turns these ideological issues inside out. Supported by a style which animates animals and kitchen tools in equally detailed perfection, the framing invites a parodic reading when Lisa forces a turtle to climb into a pot of boiling water to flavor her soup. The turtle eventually suffers a painful death, which Lisa lightheartedly laughs away.

The second moment of ironic framing happens at the end of THE SIMPSONS' version of SNOW WHITE. THE SIMPSONS episode makes use of the same melodramatic moment as the Disney film and shows Lisa dead in the glass coffin surrounded by the dwarfs. But unlike in SNOW WHITE, the scenario is suddenly interrupted by a deer that redirects our attention away from the pathos in the background and towards the head of the witch on the deer's antler in the foreground.[66] Disney's framing is literally transgressed by a moment that I would define as cartoon realism exposing the ideological patterns of Disney's movies.

But what is THE SIMPSONS' pattern? Whereas Disney uses the turtle in order to show Snow White's unconditional love of animals and, reversely, their love for the innocent Princess, the turtle is used in "Four Great Women and a Manicure" to counterpoint Disney's portrayal of positive emotions between humans and animals. In opposition to this example, the speared head of the brutally murdered Evil Queen blurs the distinction between storytelling modes: comedy exaggerates the use of melodramatic retaliation. Not only does the foregrounding of the Evil Queen's death upstage Snow White's laying out in the glass coffin. The final take of Lisa's narrative further indicates that Disney wantonly changed the Grimm tales' course of events. As I see it, Lisa's additional comment that SNOW WHITE is "a fairy-tale from hundreds of years ago" and that "no one owns that" points to the quality of European folklore, implying that even the fairy-tale ending of the Brothers Grimm is only one in a variety of local versions. In written form, the lore of 'Schneewittchen' (or also 'Sneewittchen'; 'Schneeweißchen') first appeared in the *Kinder- und Hausmärchen* by Brothers' Grimm in 1812 (ATU 709, Nr. 53). Yet the

---

[66] In addition, the Disney movie hides the Evil Queen's death behind the romantic ending of heteronormative love.

story is assumed to originate in 16th-century Germany, when it still was part of the oral tradition of European folktales.⁶⁷

The tradition of folktales suggests a narrational freedom, as Walt Disney acknowledged when he turned *Schneewittchen* into a tale dominated by American morals and ideals of nationhood and gender behavior. Groening's antithetical attitude towards the animation and narrative aesthetics of Walt Disney is part of the artist's general 'rebelliousness' towards what Surman calls "the hegemonic practices of the mid-thirties to the mid-nineties" which made way for his "anti-Disney television animation" (cf. 48). Commenting on the attitude that runs counter to Disney's social contract with his audience, animation scholar Paul Wells writes:

> The deliberate interrogation into the possibilities of the form beyond its application in the Disney-patented full animation style had characterized many approaches in the U.S. and elsewhere, in attempting work which offered a model of "difference" aesthetically, and most importantly, ideologically, from that of the Disney canon. The Disney aesthetic carried with it clear connotations of "state-of-the-art" achievement that […] remains embedded in the popular memory as one of the key illustrations of a conflation of self-evident artistry with a populist, folk, quasi-Republican, middle-American sensibility.
> (Wells 2003: 18)

Lisa's claim that the tale is her "own original creation," mirrors THE SIMPSONS' self-confident ironic reference to Disney. Groening's version is aware of the copyright violation (as proclaimed by the blue-haired lawyer) by the seeming visual proximity to Disney. Lisa's version of SNOW WHITE illustrates to what extent ironic subversion and the blurring of stylistic boundaries allow a critical approach to traditional forms of animation. Groening's techniques set the stage for re-framed aesthetic and ideological differences and deliberately subvert Disney's ideological sensibilities.

So far I focused on THE SIMPSONS' "anti-Disney" attitude at the crossroads between Disney's hegemonic 'larger-than-life' enthusiasm and Groening's 'down-to-earth' subversive parody. Groening's view of Disney is expressed in THE SIMPSONS' art to re-member, to re-collect specific Disney moments and put them together in new ways. The detailed re-drawing of animals and kitchen tools in Lisa's "Snow White" speaks for a layering of cartoon images, a technique which I will discuss in the following paragraphs.

Groening's parodic strategy of expressing his antithetical attitude towards Disney's hegemonic politics consists of revealing Disney's dominant 'image regimes.' This

---

67 For more information on the history of 'Schneewittchen,' see Theodor Ruf's *Die Schöne aus dem Glassarg: Schneewittchens märchenhaftes und wirkliches Leben* from 1995.

strategy had already been used by other postmodern critics of other creative fields, for example, of photography, theater, or performance dance. Inspired by postmodern theorist and conceptual artist Victor Burgin who used photography as a central medium in his book *The End of Art Theory: Criticism and Postmodernity* in 1986, Linda Hutcheon defines the antithetical gaze in Burgin's work as prototypical of postmodernism's "double meaning" and its "politics of representation" (cf. Hutcheon, *Politics* 2002: 3). Many of Burgin's photographs offer viewers the possibility of finding "double meanings." The black-and-white double exposures of his *Fiction Film* collection from 1991, for example, combine at least two antithetical layers, e. g. a static close-up of a face and a dynamic long shot of an arriving train, each dominated by a multiplicity of different tones of color(s) arrived at through duotone printing.[68]

Hutcheon labels Burgin's conceptual photography as prototypical for "the self-reflexive, parodic art of the postmodern" and uses it as an illustration of the fact that "all cultural forms of representation – literary, visual, aural – in high art or mass media are ideologically grounded" (2002: 3). Where Disney, according to Paul Wells, had still favored "overtly moral confrontations within *realistic* scenarios" (1998: 23, *ital. in orig.*), Groening's animation obviously superimposes different layers of meaning to create a critical and oppositional reading. THE SIMPSONS' take on SNOW WHITE can be read as a palimpsest that has a translucent surface because the episode invites viewers to recognize Disney's SNOW WHITE AND THE SEVEN DWARFS in THE SIMPSONS' careful interweaving of visual cues from traditional animation and the modernized version of THE SIMPSONS. But how can this kind of oppositional reading attitude become part of the same image as the 'original' reading?

The postmodern series persistently directs the viewers' attention to Disney's hegemonic and pseudorealistic animation practices. Then the episode counterpoints Disney's take on the fairy-tale with the rather anti-climactic ending presented by Lisa. That final scene of the tale is followed by a cut back to the beauty salon where Lisa tells her mother and the audience that the prince never showed up – but quickly adds that "Snow White was brought back to life by a Lady Doctor." Instead of reaffirming the innocent victim-heroine of Snow White as Disney's passive female who just waits for the prince to rescue her, the feminist Lisa turns herself into the fairy-tale's protagonist. By overwriting Snow White's persona with characteristics that we attribute to Lisa Simpson, the SIMPSONS' narrative ultimately portrays Snow White as a 21st-century heroine and challenges her viewers to come to new conclusions about the character. Lisa becomes the postmodern incarnation of Snow White and thus evokes a critical, feminist perspective onto the fairy-tale in Disney's Americanized guise.

---

68   London's TATE Modern acquired the entire series of Burgin's nine photographs the artist titled *Fiction Film* from 1991 in 1992. The photographs can be accessed on the museum's respective website under URL: https://www.tate.org.uk/art/artworks/burgin-fiction-film-65421.

Lisa's Snow White puts up for discussion whether the new version of Snow White belongs to the group of "Four Great Women" tales. At the same time it stimulates the audience to ask whether the Simpsons version fulfills what Linda Hutcheon claims for postmodern parody, namely that it "cannot but be political" (3). Hutcheon writes:

> While the postmodern has no effective theory of agency that enables a move into political *action*, it does work to turn its inevitable ideological grounding into a site of de-naturalizing critique. To adapt Barthes's general notion of the 'doxa' as public opinion or the 'Voice of Nature' and consensus, postmodernism works to 'de-doxify' our cultural representations and their undeniable political import. *(Politics 2002: 3, ital. in orig.)*

Lisa shows that she's a feminist and an emancipated woman by concluding that "Snow White was fine in a lesbian relationship." Lisa's "Snow White" thus can be regarded as a 'political parody' which interrogates Disney's 'doxa,' i.e. the Disney version's ideological impetus of heterosexual patriarchy. In line with Groening's rebel attitude, The Simpsons refuses to reaffirm the ending of Disney's Americanized Snow White and the Seven Dwarfs from 1937. Rather Groening does what Hutcheon claims for postmodern art: It reads the old story against itself.

Dan Harris' monograph *Film Parody* (2000) helps to explain how Groening's Disney parody articulates its satiric impulse to criticize not only the unity of normative structures. Harris refers to Linda Hutcheon who pointed out that "many parodies today do not ridicule the backgrounded text but use them as standards by which to place the contemporary under scrutiny" (2000: 124). In a nutshell, Groening moreover exposes the insularity of Disney's canon and questions the legitimacy of its normative "constructedness" (*ibid.*: 124). Parody in this regard offers a technique to pry open Disney's "rigid representations" of good and evil and its closed structure of cultural memory. The Simpsons' palimpsest style of superimposing new cartoon layers on older ones, which still shine through as in Burgin's photographs, sets up a new, a postmodern contract with the audience. As The Simpsons' diverse Disney parodies show, Groening's animation artistry questions Disney's 'doxa' by undercutting his straight melodramatic mode and thus criticizing the Disney canon. Parallelly, parody invites viewers to look outside of Disney's morality box and widen their gaze. The Simpsons has helped to established a postmodern form of framing storytelling, a form that appeals to contemporary audiences. Instead of a melodramatic mode, postmodernism prefers a comedic, parodic mode which invites viewers to reconsider their conclusions about the cultural implications and moral legacy which two of Disney's first feature films Pinocchio and Snow White and the Seven Dwarfs left behind.

Parody, Popular History, and TREEHOUSE OF HORROR as Historiographic Metafiction

All of the analyses so far examined to what extent THE SIMPSONS have established a new way of animated storytelling, how to reach out to new generations of audiences, as well as how it helped to popularize postmodern theory. But can Eco's definition of popular culture by means of Kitsch and cliché, McRobbie and her postmodern understanding of surfaces, or Hutcheon's conception of parody as a political instrument also be applied to TREEHOUSE OF HORROR? The longer I thought about a way to distinguish THE SIMPSONS from TREEHOUSE OF HORROR, the clearer it became that the Halloween special confronts its audience with a new reading of the history and tradition of the American horror genre according to the postmodern politics of parody. Linda Hutcheon argues that at the conjunction between genre and parody "representation becomes an exploration of the way in which narratives and images structure how we see ourselves and how we construct our notions of self, in the present and the past" (*Politics* 2002: 7). As I have shown with the comparison between Walt Disney's and Matt Groening's different framing techniques and animation aesthetics, THE SIMPSONS present critical re-animations of what Nicholas Sammond termed Disney's melodramatic, mid-century "assimilationist fables" (2005: 377). But how does TREEHOUSE OF HORROR animate sujets of the Horror genre? And what do its animations of sujets from the domains of popular fiction writing, filmmaking, and television production tell us about American culture? Last, but not least, how can the animation of monsters from the past help us to understand today's viewers?

In her *Poetics of Postmodernism*, Hutcheon sees the need for a new genre that can decenter a purely autotelic form of (post)modernism which has its end in itself: She found this new, genre in "historiographic metafiction" (1988). Hutcheon argues:

> Theorists of metafiction themselves argue that this fiction lo longer attempts to mirror reality or tell any truth about it. This is certainly one of the consequences of what I see, not as postmodernism, but as an extreme of *modernist* autotelic self-reflexion in contemporary metafiction. It is for this reason that I would like to argue […] that the term postmodernism in fiction be reserved to describe the more paradoxical and historically complex form that I have been calling 'historiographic metafiction.' (*Poetics*, 1988: 40; ital. in orig.)

Hutcheon started thinking about specific new writers of "historical" fiction from Atwood across Doctorow and other Jewish writers as well as Vonnegut, Borges, DeLillo, Pynchon, to African American writers such as Morrison. To the Canadian literary scholar these authors wrote against the excesses of U.S.-American culture. The new historical fiction of the 1980s was concerned with the oppression of women and the lower classes, the Holocaust, World War II, 18th-century imperialism, slavery, and many more topics. The postmodern historical writers critically reflected on history by constructing an alternative look at the world from an often oppositional perspective, which Hutcheon called a metafictional stance towards the past in the present.

The same metafictional stance can be found in TREEHOUSE OF HORROR, a television narrative which had different topics and certainly a very different style than Hutcheon's writers of historiographic metafictions. Nevertheless, TREEHOUSE OF HORROR can be distinguished from THE SIMPSONS because it uses the medium of animation no longer to talk critically about American popular culture history only. Rather, the Halloween horror show re-animates historical horror and metacritically investigates its topics and the meanings it creates. The show is concerned with, for example, how the American culture industry deals with literary canons, how WWII or the Cold War gave rise to their own kinds of monsters, but also asks how television evolved as a medium that encourages participation and critical viewing habits. If Hutcheon saw historiographic metafiction as the new literary genre that complemented the autotelic literary landscape of the 1980s, I see TREEHOUSE OF HORROR as a metafiction complementing the autotelic popular media of its time. By means of animation, TREEHOUSE OF HORROR creates alternative realities in order to broaden metafiction's scope to popular art forms.

I hypothesize that by using Hutcheon's concept to examine how the media in the 21st century comment on their past, TREEHOUSE OF HORROR can be seen as a complex narrative machine establishing critical readerly connections to older texts. In this subchapter I will ask how the show tells its stories and what kinds of relations it creates between the past and the present. Also the question will be raised whether the horror episodes shed new light on the respective medium from which the historical texts emerged (i. e. literary fiction, the radio, cinema, television). Lastly, I want to inquire whether cartoon metafiction which uses animation as its visual language functions like a palimpsest.

According to the *Cambridge English Dictionary*, a "palimpsest" refers to "a very old text or document in which writing has been removed and covered or replaced by new writing" (*Cambridge Dictionary.org*, undated). Formally, this definition is also applicable to "a work of art that has many levels of meaning, types of style that build on each other" (*ibid.*). How does TREEHOUSE OF HORROR's animation layer its meanings and styles? How does TREEHOUSE's animation inscribe itself as a new surface on top of older readings of, for instance, historical horror texts? The Halloween show does not stop at using the stylistic conventions from other cartoon genres as THE SIMPSONS does in its Disney example. How, then, does TREEHOUSE visually repurpose written narratives, films from different genres, and television narratives?

The premiering Halloween episode of 1990 establishes the series' operational principle of animating texts from American popular history and squeezing them into three mini-movies per episode. These mini-movies have been referred to as 'segments' that add up to an episodic cartoon collage. The majority of critics and fans regard the first episode as being responsible for the ongoing stratospheric popularity of the Halloween special. Due to its instant success, the show could establish its own off-canon cycle and became an anthology series with three self-contained narratives in each episode.

When putting the segments into chronological order, the first TREEHOUSE OF HORROR episode begins with an homage to Edgar Allen Poe's "The Raven," continues with an adaptation of "To Serve Man," an episode from Rod Serling's THE TWILIGHT ZONE, and closes with an animated collage of American horror films from the 1980s, most prominently of Stuart Rosenberg's AMITYVILLE HORROR from 1979. Parody is a key term when critics write about the way the show treats historical material. On top of that, "The Raven" segment illustrates how its animation is visually both professional and technically clever; aurally, the piece is an atmospheric work of signature voice-acting. The collage re-members the literary American Gothic with all media devices.

The animated homage "The Raven" makes way for a fragmented look, for the various perspectives that include diverse audiences' different receptions of Poe's narrative poem. Bart, for example, has a double function: he both acts as a 'commentator' and as the title character of the poem, the raven. Some may read Bart's disrespectful comments which constantly interrupt Lisa's reading as an attack on the famous atmospheric density of Poe's poem. Others may assume Bart's comments to represent an exercise in storytelling- or radio-play conventions of horror narratives. After all, the listeners of radio, the 'blind medium,' are fed off-voice images of and commentaries on distinct situations in order to move the story (cf. King 78).[69] By distinctly addressing the aural sense, the segment also points to the fact that television often relied on the re-mediation of radio plays which in themselves already were remediated literary- or theater texts.

Bart's second function of acting as the raven itself, his recurring "nevermore" can be read as representative of his generation's denial of the past. Bart contributes to re-membering an old radio tradition and to the raven's conclusion that the past will return 'nevermore.' In this he mirrors Poe's narrator who finds himself drawn between his desire to forget and his urge to remember. Bart himself, a contemporary student, wants to forget what he was taught in school. Yet he is also the character who re-members layers of old text that were in turn replaced, but not completely overwritten by newer layers of text as my detailed analysis of TREEHOUSE

---

69   In his book *Danse Macabre – The World of Horror,* Stephen King dedicates an entire chapter to "Radio and the Set of Reality" (1989: 68–80).

of Horror's literary legacy in general and of "The Raven" in particular in chapter 3.3 will show.

At first glance, the episode's second segment, "Bad Dream House," parodies the iconography of popular 1980s horror franchises from Poltergeist to Amityville Horror. In these films, the haunting of the idealized American middle-class home became a recurring theme that is still employed in contemporary horror films such as The Conjuring from 2013 or Hereditary from 2018. By using a Gothic-style architecture, bleeding walls, and a mysterious Indian burial ground, "Bad Dream House" turns the haunted-house motif into a symbol for the mortgage- and real-estate crisis in America. "Bad Dream House" ends with an anthropomorphized evil house, whose voice is so disgruntled with the Simpsons that it rather implodes upon itself instead of living with this family. I use "Bad Dream House" as a point of departure to analyze how Treehouse of Horror not just parodies 1980s horror cinema, but indeed renegotiates specific motifs from the cycle of haunted-house genre horror. In chapter 3.4 I will inquire what it does to re-member the social and political climate of the decade.

The third segment of the first Treehouse episode shows the Simpsons' encounter with the aliens Kang & Kodos. This segment, "Hungry Are the Damned," can be read as a metafiction which directs the audience's attention to cartoon realism and its potential to switch from a funny mode to a serious one. The episode's writers pay homage to Rod Serling's iconic Twilight Zone episode "To Serve Man" from 1962. Twilight Zone, a television anthology series from the 1960s, was preoccupied with the nation's latent fear of external threats (e. g. alien invasion and abduction). The Treehouse segment's writers employ a metacritical perspective by entering into the critical dispute about collective social anxieties of the Cold War era. The different viewpoints on these fears will receive detailed examination in chapter 3.5.

Once a year, the Halloween special show performs critical readings of historical texts from different media. Linda Hutcheon argues: "[H]istoriographic metafiction does not pretend to reproduce events, but to direct us, instead, to facts, or to new directions in which to think about events" (*Poetics*, 1988: 154). I use Linda Hutcheon's definitions of metafiction to ask how Treehouse of Horror interconnects parody and the re-animation of pop culture, a strategy which stands in the complete opposite to what Disney's animation strategy. After all, the series is a Halloween-based format and on Halloween we remember the dead, a task which Treehouse of Horror metaphorically mirrors by re-membering bygone art and culture.

It is important to note that the three segments in the first Treehouse of Horror episode do not imitate the art of Edgar Allen Poe, copy the 1980s horror-genre trend, or mimic Rod Serling's science-fiction television. My project will bring to light how the three segments and those that followed in the subsequent 29 years of TREEHOUSE OF HORROR gave new directions to thinking about their 'original' texts. Gruteser, Klein, and Rauscher write that THE SIMPSONS operates as a kind of fiction auteur (cf. 15). In their understanding, the show creates its own signature art with its own signature features and unmistakable visual recognition value (see my close-reading of the animation auteur in chapter 3.2). Gruteser, Klein, and Rauscher's description actually fit the aesthetics of TREEHOUSE OF HORROR better than that of the regular SIMPSONS series. The Halloween special departs from Groening's regular animation series by re-membering America's history of popular Gothic. It uses metafictional parody to paint the past of long forgotten or misrepresented horror texts. In postmodern parody, the past only exists "through its textual traces, its often complex and indirect representations in the present," as Hutcheon suggests (*Politics* 2002: 75). TREEHOUSE OF HORROR presents the narrative of history by animating it.

In the upcoming chapters, I will deal with the Halloween special not only as a syntactic repository of pop-culture history. Additionally, the concept of the archive will help to further the understanding of TREEHOUSE OF HORROR's function and complexity. In *The Politics of Postmodernism* Hutcheon suggests:

> If the archive is composed of texts, it is open to all kinds of use and abuse. The archive has always been a site of a lot of activity but rarely of such self-consciously totalizing activity as it is today. Even what is considered acceptable as documentary evidence has changed. And certainly the status of the document has altered: since it is acknowledged that it can offer no direct access to the past, then it must be representation or a replacement through textual refiguring of the brute event.
>
> *(2002: 77)*

Examples from the TREEHOUSE OF HORROR series will show how the series 'uses and abuses' popular fictions to tell about and question pop-cultural authority; the series will be defined as a site of representing or possibly replacing older textual traces by means of animation. My fourth and last excursion into postmodern popular-culture theory leads me to the French philosopher Michel Foucault. His insights will improve the understanding of how Western culture organizes its past within what Foucault defines as the 'archive.'

Michel Foucault: Reading TREEHOUSE OF HORROR as Popular-Culture History Archive

I will take a look at Foucault's ambiguous use of the archive because in postmodern literary and cultural studies, the notion of the archive has been vital in approaching transformations in times of medial and aesthetic change. In 1969, Michel

Foucault approached the archive in *The Archaeology of Knowledge*. Depending on context, the archive as an analytical concept can signify an historically embedded institution that systematically stores knowledge (such as a museum or library), or a socially and historically specific space of aesthetic experience (such as a cinema or theater, but also hospitals and cemeteries), spaces which Foucault refers to as "heterotopias" (cf. his talk "On Other Spaces" from 1967 and his later essay "Of Other Spaces: Utopias and Heterotopias"). In "Of Other Spaces," Foucault describes heterotopias as "realized utopias" (17) (e.g. Disneyland or shopping malls; see also Kern 2008: 106) – spaces that are organized differently than the social world surrounding them. Film theorist Hans Jürgen Wulff writes in *Lexikon der Filmbegriffe*: "Heterotopien sind institutionell oft geschlossene [...] Räume in einer Gesellschaft, die gegen die Unordnung der umgebenden Welt (oder gegen ihre verschiedenen, einander behindernden oder sogar ausschließenden Ordnungen) gestellt sind" (*Filmlexikon.org* 2011). The chapter at hand will discuss why I understand the Treehouse series as an archive that is organized as a heterotopia, a space whose order runs counter to the "Unordnung der umgebenden Welt," the 'disorder of the surrounding world.'

I will investigate how Treehouse of Horror explores horror texts and their organization of power and knowledge, thus becoming an "Order of Disorder" as German media theorist Wolfgang Ernst describes the archival process in the subtitle of his book *Stirrings in the Archive* (2015). My discussion will include Foucault's notion of the archive as a tool for addressing fast-changing aesthetic practices in postmodernism. No matter whether Foucault negotiates archives as discourses in institutions, or as spatially organized practices, the archive is what in his monograph *Michel Foucault: Discourse Theory and the Archive* the German literary scholar Johannes Schlegel calls "a driving force" behind recent transformations and cultural turns (2016).

I will examine how Treehouse of Horror participates in the practice of popular-media archaeology (cf. Heidelberg 2016). In the popular imagination of the digital age, the archive is now a ubiquitous feature in thoughts about, for example, cloud technologies. According to the media theorists Erkki Huhtamo and Jussi Parikka, however, media archaeology has become an emerging field of interdisciplinary theories and methodologies that address history in new, often unconventional ways – both looking for elements of repetition as well as variations in the past.[70] In a nutshell, scholars like Thomas Elsaesser, Siegfried Zielinski, Friedrich

---

70 For more insights into the field, see Erkki Huhtamo and Jussi Parikka's co-edited volume *Media Archaeology: Approaches, Applications, and Implications* from 2011 in which the contributions provide readers with a vast array of directions new media technologies, i.e. the Internet, digital television, interactive multimedia, virtual reality, mobile communication, and video games are taking to create what today is commonly discussed under the umbrella category of 'media culture.' The authors offer different research agendas: "from network analysis to soft-

Kittler, or Wolfgang Ernst have elaborated on media archaeology as a way "to understand new and emerging media cultures through the past" (Huhtamo/Parikka 2011: 3).

In his book *Digital Memory and the Archive* from 2013, Wolfgang Ernst from the Humboldt-University in Berlin asks whether "media archaeology insists on the difference that the media make in cultural construction" (53), to what extent "media archaeology deals with the crisis in the narrative memory of culture," and what is actually done, "in practice, to implement a media-archaeological approach" (both: 70)? In a first attempt to answer his questions, Ernst suggests that the main challenge for media archaeology is to teach traditional scholars how to read and speak about media. Parallel to this, I see the main challenge for TREEHOUSE OF HORROR to teach traditional viewers how to read and speak about its re-mediations. Tracing how the horror series employs methods of storytelling, I argue that TREEHOUSE OF HORROR is part of a transformation of postmodern practices as I have so far introduced them. TREEHOUSE OF HORROR demonstrates how popular culture can be a site that subverts conventional accounts of the past, offers alternative histories, and complicates the notion of origins (cf. Heidelberg 2016).

The archive's theoretical trichotomy of discursive formation, institutionalized space, and aesthetic experience is key to the Foucauldian understanding of power and knowledge and, I would argue, to TREEHOUSE's engagement in history. Foucault scholar Nadine Dannenberg suggests that "to exist means to be archived," so that "the archive, or rather its interpreter, becomes a producer of knowledge" (2016). I understand TREEHOUSE OF HORROR as an archive and the show's writers as its interpreters who deal in alternative views on American media history and its power-knowledge formations. My initial questions are: What is archived? Who controls and collects the material archived in TREEHOUSE OF HORROR? And how can this heterotopian archival space be read?

THE SIMPSONS' Archive: Order of Disorder, or The Re-Organization of History

As already credited earlier, the German media scholar Michael Gruteser once described THE SIMPSONS as "das kompletteste postmoderne Kunstwerk" ('the most complete postmodern piece of art') (2002: 18). With respect to its freedom of animation techniques and of topics, THE SIMPSONS appears as an archive that persistently juggles with massive amounts of knowledge from all kinds of contemporary and past domains. Gruteser's suggestion indicates that THE SIMPSONS' postmodern art is "complete" because it portrays discursive practices and aesthetic experi-

> ware studies; from mappings of the new empire of network economies to analyses of new media as 'ways of seeing' (or hearing, reading, and touching)." (Huhtamo/Parikka 2011: 1). The latter is of special interest for my investigation.

ences about basically everything. This explains why scholars frequently consider THE SIMPSONS as the perfect example for a contemporary approach to America's everyday culture.

In his book *THE SIMPSONS, Satire, and American Culture* from 2012, Matthew A. Henry focuses on the discursive tensions inherent in the show's status as both a commercial and an artistic object, and analyzes how the series uses these tensions in its satirical engagement with highly politicized social and culture issues (cf. 2012: 6). Henry turns THE SIMPSONS into a cartoon "counter-site," a satirical archive which uses political satire to create a kind of critical comic heterotopia in which other sites of culture can be represented, contested, and inverted (6; cf. Foucault 1984: 3). In his article "Commodity Culture and Its Discontents," taking up Freud's *Civilization and Its Discontents* from 1930, Kurt M. Koenigsberger argues that "THE SIMPSONS returns to something like the critical orientation of the pre-modernist British author Arnold Bennett (1867–1931) toward his audience and society" (2012: 31). Similarly to the postmodernist SIMPSONS, Bennett's pre-modernist fictions promoted "the democratisation of art" by which the British writer helped "the crowd… really to see the spectacle of the world" (qtd. in Koenigsberger 2012: 31).[71] In a comparative argument, Kevin Dettmar postulates in his chapter on "Countercultural Literacy: Learning Irony with THE SIMPSONS," that THE SIMPSONS teach their fans media- and countercultural literacy by way of irony.[72]

Henry, Koenigsberger, and Dettmar evoke Foucauldian strategies by analyzing the animated show as an archival discourse formation which goes against hegemonic structures by means of satire, the democratization of art, and irony. One can say with Foucault that THE SIMPSONS are an animated "generator and controller of social meaning" (Foucault 1972: 129; 2006: 28–29). I would argue that THE SIMPSONS, unofficially appointed by its fans, can be considered a new lawmaker concerning what can be said in popular media, how it can be said, and by whom. THE SIMPSONS functions as an archive which shows that oppositional knowledge is possible – against high-cultural and hegemonial texts.[73]

The essays included in John Alberti's collection *Leaving Springfield* from 2012 interrogate whether THE SIMPSONS may indeed be considered an archive that uses

---

71 For more information on the discursive tensions in THE SIMPSONS, see Kurt M. Koenigsberger's "Commodity Culture and Its Discontents: Mr. Bennett, Bart Simpson, and the Rhetoric of Modernism," or Vincent Brook's "Myth or Consequences: Ideological Fault Lines in THE SIMPSONS" in David L.G. Arnold's *Leaving Springfield* (2012), 29–62.
72 Kevin J.H. Dettmar's article "Countercultural Literacy: Learning Irony with THE SIMPSONS" raises the question to what extent viewers enhance their media and cultural literacy by means of irony.
73 For more information on John Alberti's *Leaving Springfield* (2012), see David L.G. Arnold's essay "'Use a Pen, Sideshow Bob': THE SIMPSONS and the Threat of High Culture," 1–28.

oppositional knowledge against hegemonic American media and culture. From their perspective, Homer Simpson can be regarded as representing both the old ideal of patriarchy and its worst enemy – he, the series' most unreliable character, ironically works as a safety inspector of the local nuclear power plant. In a parallel ironic move, Homer is the patriarch who supposedly is in control of the safety and sanity of THE SIMPSONS' all-American nuclear family and thus the center of the family myth; but at the same time his unreliability threatens his family members. This ironic two-sidedness is Homer's main function in THE SIMPSONS. In TREEHOUSE OF HORROR, however, Homer's cartoon persona is far more than that. Here, Homer's appearance is not bound to the physical laws of the real world that THE SIMPSONS usually confirms. Homer contributes monstrous and amputated versions of his body to the archive of horror symbolism which deconstruct straight, hegemonic discourses about, for example, capitalism, heroism, manhood, and fatherhood.[74]

Obviously the archival material of TREEHOUSE OF HORROR belongs to one of America's most versatile genres: horror. TREEHOUSE excavates popular texts that were once associated with the American Gothic and horror genres, including 19th-century literature and 20th-century comic books, but also radio broadcasts and television anthologies as well as a large range of Hollywood movies, and stores them. TREEHOUSE OF HORROR's archive deconstructs what the American literary scholar Ed Folsom defines in his dictionary entry on "Archive" as "the very nature of the 'past'" (2016: 24). According to Folsom's definition, the archive deals with questions such as if and how the past can be accessed via 'memory' and used as 'origin.' Above all, he asks who controls, collects, and organizes "the materials out of which we gather and create the stories of the past" (24). The Halloween special of THE SIMPSONS uses horror and monstrosity as a means to accumulate and organize texts from America's popular culture and proves that an archive can construct and present an alternative version of history and reality.

According to Ed Folsom, the historian Carolyn Steedman offers an interesting interpretation of the Foucauldian archive when she foregrounds the way it exercises power by means of narrativization. Through its narratives, the archive can (re)direct old ways of seeing and knowing (qtd. in Folsom 2016: 24–25). According to Steedman, the archive thus can empower its users to reassemble a story from fragmented pieces and weave a new narrative in animated form "out of the dust" (Steedman qtd. in Folsom 25). This makes TREEHOUSE OF HORROR an archive of deconstructed narratives. Accordingly, the series does not only blow the dust off almost forgotten texts; at the same time it offers a virtual archival space for ani-

---

74 The discursive formations of Homer Simpson's masculinity will receive detailed attention in my analytical chapters on the American horror cinema (3.4) as well as on TREEHOUSE OF HORROR's TWILIGHT ZONE cycle (3.5).

mated re-enactments and re-mediations of these literary, filmic, and television texts (cf. Folsom 26).

So what kind of archive includes horror? Does the widening of the archival frame to a popular context bring with it a tension between 'popular-culture memory' and archival 'truth claims'? In her cross-disciplinary overview "Theories of the Archive" (2004), literary scholar Marlene Manoff sheds light onto the formerly purely academic discussion about the nature of the archive. Looking back on the archive from a contemporary perspective, she resumes that only when the conversation was widened from a purely academic one to include archivists and librarians have the different interests of those involved begun to enrich the concept of the 'archive' (cf. 2004: 9).

Michel Foucault and Jacques Derrida, for example, participated in the discussion of the archive and helped moving the archive out of the library. Foucault writes about the archive in *The Archaeology of Knowledge* from 1972 [1969]:

> Between the *language (langue)* that defines the system of constructing possible sentences, and the *corpus* that passively collects the words that are spoken, the *archive* defines a particular level: that of a practice that causes a multiplicity of statements to emerge as so many regular events, as so many things to be dealt with and manipulated. It does not have the weight of tradition; and it does not constitute the libraries of all libraries, outside time and place; nor is it the welcoming oblivion that opens up to all new speech the operational field of its freedom; between tradition and oblivion, it reveals the rules of a practice that enables statements both to survive and to undergo regular modification. It is *the general system of the formation and transformation of statements*.
> (130, ital. in orig.).

Based on Foucault's idea that the archive is an instrument of power revealing the rules of cultural practices, I started to read THE SIMPSONS' archive as a discursive system from which discourses of knowledge emerge and where they are transforming, and in which the conditions for the emergence of knowledge can be policed. For Foucault, the archive is not the sum of all texts – "the libraries of all libraries" – which a culture has preserved to sustain the memory of its identity formation processes or in which discourses are being recorded as traditions (cf. 1972: 128–129). Rather, Foucault sees the archive as "born in accordance with specific regularities" so that the archive sets "the law of what can be said" and becomes the system that governs "the appearance of statements" (1972: 129). Foucault has always been concerned with the power of language and the archive became his central method to think in new ways about the function of language within history.

In his 1996 essay "Archive Fever," Jacques Derrida further reworks the concept of the archive. The French philosopher does not see the archive as static like a library or a museum, but indicates that for him it is "something more theoretical and abstract," as Ed Folsom explains (2017: 23). Derrida supports Foucault's view that the archive is not just a static *place* where documents and artifacts are collected. Accordingly, Jacques Derrida thinks the archive as a public *space* where the new digital technologies at the dawn of the internet begin to organize knowledge and history in a new way.

Seen from this perspective, Treehouse of Horror as The Simpsons' horror archive is not only a place that statically preserves the history of popular arts; as a multimedial archive of American cultural history, it performs and thus frames history by digging more deeply into the texts' contexts by means of their animated re-enactment and re-mediation. Animation is its medium of choice to control the material in just the right way, horror the operational umbrella genre, parody the narrative mode.

The more I thought about Treehouse of Horror as The Simpsons' horror-media archive, the more I became convinced that the framing, genre, and adaptation practices are not static categories or closed systems that observe recurring narrative elements and canonize aesthetic conventions. Rather, the producers of Treehouse of Horror have a fairly open understanding of which examples from the past can become part of The Simpsons' "horror" archive; they include Gothic texts, science-fiction- and fantasy narratives, as well as all kinds of audiovisual horror stories. Treehouse's parodic way of approaching the mix of horror texts makes use of its genres in a dynamic cultural and media practice; the parodies' aim is to lead the audience outside the box of a traditional reading of a referenced text.

The British media scholar Jonathan Gray sees parody as an act of stepping into another text's or genre's space to threaten and eventually destabilize their former power (2005: 225). Jason Mittell further explains that parody in Treehouse of Horror helps viewers look beyond traditionally framed media texts themselves and thus asserts their power to re-interpret these texts in their new animated form. Mittell points out that "if our goal is to understand the cultural life […] of contemporary media culture, we must critically explore the shifts and implications of its genres as discursive processes found in interactions between these spheres of media practice" (2001: 26). I will explore how the shifts and implications offered by the genre archive of Treehouse of Horror help to understand the contextual relationship between the show and America's popular-culture history.

The Language of Treehouse of Horror: Reinventing American Halloween TV

Between the carnivalesque revelry of American Halloween and its fictional manifestation, Treehouse presents a very special discursive system. Halloween-inspired episodes as used in Treehouse of Horror are concerned with the darker side and broader scope of entertainment than everyday shows. The popularity of horror, says Stephen King in his non-fiction book *Danse Macabre* from 1981, increases whenever economics and politics lose the trust of citizens and become increasingly untrustworthy.

For a long time, television was not considered trustworthy or sincere. But in contrast to the easily digestible, traditional television formats such as game shows, soap operas, or reality tv, TREEHOUSE continues an American tradition of the dark Gothic genre. With a special focus on its predecessor of Gothic literature, the animated show stands in a long tradition of foregrounding dark and oppressive aspects of American culture and history and revealing the costs of its myths.

At this point let me to explain how the meaning of horror changed in the 1930s from the way it had been defined in the sublime aesthetics of the late 18th- and early 19th century. Philosopher Edmund Burke differentiated between horror and terror as two possible reactions to sublime aesthetic experiences. According to Burke, 'horror' describes the spontaneous, paralyzing shock that ambushes the intellectual reader, listener, or viewer of a fictional setting and forecloses their understanding when confronted with a monster or a corpse, for example. 'Terror' is the second stage of the reaction to the sublime onslaught. It slowly sets free the consciousness of one's own secure position as part of the audience, creates an awareness of one's distance to an endangered protagonist and her or his world. The distance gained through reaching the stage of terror then could serve as the beginning of intellectually understanding, mastering, and thus emotionally enjoying the portrayed horrible situation.[75]

The sensationalist triggers of Hollywood's popular pre-Code horror movies during the Depression no longer aimed at reactions of 'horror.' Rather, as the advertising language on promotional posters shows (see Fig. 8), they tried to draw a less intellectual, less philosophically schooled audience than Gothic texts around 1800 did. The horror films aimed for sudden moments of shock, they relied on film's power to make things visible rather than on the power of darkness. Movie horror was deflated to a visual spectacle for a new mass audience. Whereas texts by Brown, Poe, or Hawthorne were influenced by Burke's aesthetics and offered an exercise in masculine self-control and -empowerment, audiences of the 20th century were exposed to easily consumable, fleeting moments of spectacular horror.

In his recent book *A Place of Darkness* from 2018, Kendall R. Phillips, an expert in rhetorical theory and the horror film, argues that the visual medium of cinema first had to develop its own language before it could create horror in the sense of 18th-century narrative aesthetics. He writes that prior to 1931 "there were

---

75 Klaus Poenicke's *Dark Sublime: Raum und Selbst in der amerikanischen Romantik* from 1972 offers insightful approaches for a distinction between horror and terror.

9 Theater Promotion for Universal's FRANKENSTEIN illustrates how the language of horror was introduced through advertising language in 1931, which had a decisive influence on the definition of 'horror' as a genre.

no horror films – the language of horror had not yet solidified into a definable genre," although the elements that constitute much of what we call 'horror' today were already present in Gothic literature (e.g. ghosts, monsters, haunted houses, etc.) (2018: 3). According to Phillips, the movie-theater release of FRANKENSTEIN and DRACULA in 1931 demonstrates that the publicity writers at Universal Studios clearly struggled with finding a language to describe the filmic adaptation of Bram Stoker's and Mary Shelley's popular novel (cf. 2018: 2). Although entertaining promotional phrases such as "Chilling horrors of the Night" or simply "Horrors!" (mind the exclamation mark) worked well enough at first, Universal began to settle for something more ambiguous later. Consequently, DRACULA was announced as "The story of the strangest passion the world has ever known!"; the promotional material for FRANKENSTEIN announced the movie as being "the original horror show," and movie theaters declared Shelley's *Frankenstein* to be "The Chilling Horror and icy mystery of a hundred thrilling tales frozen into a superb epic of terror" (see Fig. 9) (Phillips 2018: 2–3).

Kendall R. Phillips emphasizes that the language introduced during the early period of horror film became typical for many movies that followed – after all, American show magazines such as *Variety* soon began to adopt the terminology of horror for the new genre cycle. The early movies also shaped the creative visions of directors and even influenced the transgressive genre parameters of, for example, visual monstrosity (cf. 2018: 3). Similarly to the literary Gothic, film horror created its own visual, aural, and visceral corporealities. Film horror has a long history of aiming at a physically tangible visual and acoustic experience which often utilizes sensationalist triggers in order to evoke viewers' reactions between fascination and disgust.

Besides melodrama, pornography, and also comedy, horror is one of the body genres celebrated by Linda Williams in her acclaimed essay "Film Bodies: Gender, Genre, and Excess" (1991). Horror film has quite distinct strategies to arouse fear and test their viewers' emotional stability in the face of the unexpected 'other.' TREEHOUSE OF HORROR has ways of confronting audiences with the unexpected too. THE SIMPSONS' horror special makes use of old films by presenting their monsters as 'other.' But it also presents old monsters as 'same,' namely in the shape of Homer, a massive man-eating Blob gobbling its way through Springfield by devouring everyone who crosses its/his way.[76] The Blob can only be stopped when it/he fears the loss of his beloved wife Marge. Obviously viewers are invited to read him not only as a rampaging Blob with an insatiable appetite, but also as a creature full of love.

Homer eats promiscuous teenagers, declaring to "savor them" and eats fat Germans at a local Oktoberfest, claiming "must eat more fat people, thank God I'm in America." Homer as the Blob challenges audiences' expectations. For the sake of keeping the family intact, Homer "vows to use his insatiable appetite for more constructive purposes" (*Simpsons Wiki.com*). Eventually, Springfield's mayor Quimby makes good use of Homer, the Blob. Along with other city officials, he makes the Blob turn his anti-social behavior into an asset for the community: He shall eat bothersome delinquents cornered behind the door of a fake refuge. This development proves that Homer, the Blob, impersonates a conservative moral concept and that his platitudes were implemented in the anti-Communist Cold-War movie THE BLOB from 1958 the TREEHOUSE segment is based on. Also in many other TREEHOUSE moments, Homer's monstrosity as shown in "Married to The Blob" as well as in the black-and-white GODZILLA parody "Homerzilla"[77] illustrates that TREEHOUSE OF HORROR turns monstrosity into what German media scholar Oliver Fahle describes as a "wandelbare Kontaktzone" (2010: 233), i.e. a mutable contact zone between otherness (the Blob) and sameness (Homer). In such a threshold space the relationship between disorder and order can be tested. Horror as portrayed in TREEHOUSE OF HORROR does not imitate THE BLOB's sensationalist Cold-War propaganda, but instead addresses an already educated audience to present them with a language they intellectually understand as a power imbalance between normality and the other.

TREEHOUSE OF HORROR works within the field of the horror genre which focuses on monsters as mutable contact zones. Through the mutable body of Homer, horror can initiate an intellectual process in the audience and help them understand which moral implications are inscribed in the representation of a monster.

---

76 TREEHOUSE OF HORROR XVII, "Married to the Blob," s18e04s01, dir. David 'Tubatron' Silverman / Malicious Matthew C. Faughnan, Fox 2006.
77 TREEHOUSE OF HORROR XXVI, "Homerzilla," s27e05s02, dir. Steven Dean Moore, Fox 2015.

This way, TREEHOUSE distances itself from the familiar patterns of Halloween seasonal television. On Halloween, TREEHOUSE doesn't simply make us of the sensationalist triggers from early 20th-century Hollywood movies. Rather, TREEHOUSE's cartoon horror makes determined statements about U. S.-culture's symptoms and dark feelings because it is not a cartoon archive that simply employs horror; it is a horror archive that makes productive use of the cartoon framing. Staying in the domain of medical metaphors, Stephen King says horror "is talking to us, like a patient on a psychoanalyst's couch, about one thing while it means another" (32). With respect to TREEHOUSE OF HORROR, King's quote translates to the freedom of animation to intellectually frame the terror and transform it into comic horror narratives. The horror version of THE SIMPSONS isn't a horror sitcom rattling with its chains once a year. Rather, TREEHOUSE is a comic confrontation with the serious world behind its horror-story adaptations.

As contemporary discussions about the archive showed, the quality of texts from the past that are worth becoming part of an archive was commonly questioned after World War II. This led me to thinking about what texts are included in TREEHOUSE OF HORROR's archive and why. Unlike television sitcoms, in which the return to normality is part of the comedy formula and of its episodic continuity, horror plots hardly ever end happily or restore normality. Instead, horror plots tend to take an anticlimactic course. Due to this, TREEHOUSE OF HORROR's archive frames horror texts comedically and lets them end in a serio-comic cesura.

A quick look at the endings of the majority of TREEHOUSE segments shows that they are usually left open or end badly for their protagonists. Homer gets frazzled by Werewolf Ned while the rest of the family escapes in ToH X;[78] he ends up as the last man on earth, the "Hômega Man" in ToH VIII, after having survived a neutron-bomb attack;[79] and Homer engages in intercourse with two satanic demons in "UNnormal Activity" in ToH XXIII.[80] At the end of the ToH VIII's "Night of the Dolphins"[81] the final take uses a written 'The End?' made up of the drowned bodies of those who did not survive the ultimate battle against the revolting dolphins which have defeated 'mankind.' Endings in the TREEHOUSE series don't offer the same comic relief and good feelings as those in THE SIMPSONS. THE SIMPSONS' holiday special is distinctly different from other Halloween-sitcom specials in that it refuses to oscillate between formulaic party-piece plots and haunted-house stories known from traditional television sitcoms produced between the 1950s and

---

78 TREEHOUSE OF HORROR X, "I Know What You Diddily-Iddily-Did," s11e04s01, dir. Pete Michels, Fox 1999.
79 TREEHOUSE OF HORROR VIII, "The HΩmega Man," s09e05s02, dir. Mark Kirkland, Fox 1997.
80 TREEHOUSE OF HORROR VIII, "UNnormal Activity," s24e02s02, dir. Steven Dean Moore, Fox 2012.
81 TREEHOUSE OF HORROR VIII, "Night of the Dolphins," s12e01s03, dir. Matthew Nastuk, Fox 2000.

1990s. TREEHOUSE obviously is setting up new laws for what kinds of texts can be included in the animated archive of a Halloween TV show.

TREEHOUSE's refusal of using traditional comedy formulas can be seen, for example, in the closing sequence (as part of the wraparound) of ToH V, when a mysterious fog turns the bodies of the Simpson family inside-out. Unexpectedly, the dark setting turns into a bright vaudeville stage and the family breaks into a blood-spattering chorus line, dancing to a macabre version of "One" from the musical *A Chorus Line*. If the tradition of the literary Gothic initiated a "writing of excess" (Botting 1996: 1), TREEHOUSE now retells old stories by means of excessive imagery to exercise not only comic irony on, but also exerts entirely unironic critique of popular horror. TREEHOUSE's monstrous bodies, anticlimactic endings, and excessive imagery can signal "the disturbing return of pasts upon presents and evoke emotions of terror and laughter," as Fred Botting writes with respect to the traditional Gothic (1996: 1). After all, the end of THE DAY OF THE DOLPHIN shows Springfield's population being ruled by a mob of angry dolphins and doomed to living in the ocean while many of them are already dead and drifting on the water. Krusty the Clown's dead body floats by and joins the final "the end?" made up of corpses that leave the question open whether this is truly 'the end.'

Remediation makes a New Archive: Repurposing Practices in TREEHOUSE OF HORROR

According to Henry Jenkins' *Convergence Culture* (2006), the decision which historical sources become part of a cultural archive nowadays heavily depends on consumers; when consumers become cultural agents they can make good use of and interact with those sources. The cultural archive then becomes a space, as Jenkins explains, of a media convergence that occurs in the brains of individual consumers and through their social interactions with others (cf. 2006: 3). Remediation, thus, becomes an important instrument for constructing "our own personal mythology from bits and fragments of information extracted from the media flow and transformed into resources through which we make sense of our everyday lives" (Jenkins 2006: 3 f.). In the following paragraphs I will explore whether the concept of remediation can help to understand the archival work of TREEHOUSE OF HORROR as an open-ended project. I wonder whether the show's strategy of repurposing older media can be seen as establishing a way of re-membering older media content even before digital media were introduced.

It has already been noted that Foucault and Derrida no longer saw the archive as static. The two scholars changed the way people were thinking about the archive, about the relations between texts, and about the possibility of telling stories with them. I see TREEHOUSE OF HORROR as an example of a new, dynamic archive which became typical in the digital age with new digital media and new relationships between media and texts. In the digital archival space the links between texts and media were established in a new way because these archives include the technique of "repurposing."[82]

In 2000, Jay Bolter and Richard Grusin coined and introduced the concept of "remediation" to explain how the contemporary entertainment industry makes use of "repurposing: to take a 'property' from one medium and reuse it in another" (45).[83] Bolter and Grusin foreground that, although their focus lies on digital media, the process of remediation by means of repurposing can be identified "throughout the last several hundred years of Western visual representation" (2000: 11). Moreover, the authors observe that the processes of remediation are not hierarchical, but reciprocal processes between old and new media: "Remediation operates in both directions: users of older media such as film and television can seek to appropriate and refashion digital graphics, just as digital graphics can refashion film and television" (48). According to my understanding, the gap between old and new media content becomes Fahle's 'wandelbare Kontaktzone,' a 'mutable contact zone' "where", to say it with the subtitle of Henry Jenkins' *Convergence Culture*, "old and new media collide" and where the interplay between media and consumer turns into a culture of convergence (see Jenkins 2006a; Blog "Confessions of an ACA Fan" 2006). The collision between old and new media can be seen at various moments in TREEHOUSE OF HORROR too.

How today's consumers make sense of their everyday life can be seen in how they produce and use 'new media' (the Internet, smart phones, social media, mobile communication, etc.) as a means of collective intelligence. Jenkins explains that "consumption has become a collective process" which teaches us how "we can put the pieces together" by using this collective intelligence in day-to-day interactions within convergence culture as "an alternate source of power" (2006a: 4). This also explains why the implementation of new media has changed the material and the reciprocal relationships between those materials. In this context and as was said with Huhtamo and Parikka earlier, repurposing means to go beyond the confines of older media such as film and television and use them as an alternate source of power, enabling the user to deconstruct and redefine the historical fragments and pieces in a radically different order.

---

82   Writing about parody, Grusin and Bolter state in their preface that remediation is a way to "complicate the notion of repurposing other media" (45) and call parody "a strategy of remediation" (142). In terms of textual repurposing, parody has similar objectives as remediation. According to Bolter and Grusin, remediation can be read with a focus on the intertwining of different media, as, for them, remediation and parody as forms of remediation emphasize "a conscious interplay between media" (142).

83   As a classical example of such media transfer, Bolter and Grusin use literary screen adaptations which recycle and at the same time re-define the media content "to spread the content over as many markets as possible" (2000: 68). Along with the repurposing and re-membering of previous media content Bolter and Grusin remind us that the strategy also includes an economic dimension.

To borrow from Jenkins' terminology, the authors of TREEHOUSE OF HORROR "take historical media into their own hands" (2006a: 17) and redefine old assumptions about what it meant to consume media in the pre-digital age – from written to aural and audiovisual media – and how digital media have significantly changed the way of consumption (cf. Jenkins 18).[84] In a move comparable to digital media, TREEHOUSE OF HORROR has been remediating prior texts via techniques stressing the performance's immediacy. But the animation has also remediated older media content while drawing the audience's attention to animation as a method and thus inviting to be seen as a means of self-referential hypermediation. According to Bolter and Grusin, the refashioning process of remediation is defined by a double logic. Firstly, "new media" such as the World Wide Web share with older technologies such as television the claim for "immediacy," i.e. to become, for the user, invisible as a medium. Secondly, new media also foreground "hypermediacy," a term that defines the exact opposite of immediacy, namely the visibility and self-referentiality of the medium. The 'couch gag' is a productive example of how this double logic of remediation became a common practice. In the regular SIMPSONS series, the couch gag uses animation to give its viewers a parodic take on the steady image of the traditional family in their usual domestic sitcom opening. TREEHOUSE OF HORROR's opening couch gags, however, are often animated by guest animators who remediate SIMPSONS' characters as claymation figures in stop motion, puppets, or translate them to other media contexts, and thus shift the viewers' attention from the action back to different kinds of animation techniques.[85]

Another productive example to illustrate the connection between immediacy and hypermediacy is "The Raven" from ToH I (1990). In this segment the characters act in varying roles and redirect the viewer's attention away from the poem's content towards the remediation process of a 19th-century literary text through diverse channels of reception. The cartoon adaptation uses visual cues as well as

---

84   To take media into our own hands and push the limits of media content's mediality are two aspects which Jay Bolter and Richard Grusin consider part of "our culture's contradictory imperatives for immediacy and hypermediacy" (2000: 5). Taking this as their point of departure in *Remediation: Understanding New Media* (2000), the media scholars examine how media at the turn of the millennium began to "refashion" and "improve on the limits" of prior media forms (Cantoni et al. 2011: 200).

85   Comic scholar Mark Bould refers to the graphic novel adaptation of Frank Miller's film SIN CITY (2005) which consciously uses computer-generated imagery (CGI) to create an analogue effect (e.g. avoids deep focus; comic panel framing leads from one scene to another), reminding viewers that the film adaptation is based on a graphic novel that is based on noir films which are based on pulp fiction novels. By raising viewers' attention to a whole repertoire of already existing techniques, media clichés, and animation aesthetics, Bould explains that as the SIN CITY film uses digital tools to give its viewers the immediacy of the comic book image, it "remediates" the comic book "so that the immediacy on offer is the product of hypermediation" (2005: 112).

different sound- and aural-storytelling techniques to translate the immediacy of Poe's narrative poem to its viewers. But as the cartoon remediates the 19th-century poem, the medium of animation self-reflexively draws attention to itself. Many examples for this double-sided strategy in TREEHOUSE can be found; over and again this "specific style of visual representation" reminds the viewer of the referenced texts' mediality the same way Bolter and Grusin claim for the digital refashioning of texts (2000: 272).

For THE SIMPSONS, however, the opposite can be observed. Jason Mittell has claimed that this animated mimicry of American everyday life makes productive use of "cartoon realism," an aesthetic device to which Mittell dedicated an entire article in 2001, "Cartoon Realism: Genre Mixing and the Cultural Life of THE SIMPSONS". In his opinion, cartoon realism is often employed to achieve a 'documentary look' which evokes the impression of immediacy and hides the show's mediality. But for me the documentary look also includes various moments of hypermediacy that offer the audience a look at the Simpsons' workshop of filthy creation. SIMPSONS episodes which illustrate the series' simultaneous staging of immediacy and hypermediacy are "Behind the Laughter" (2000) and "Springfield Up" (2007) whose style transcends the boundaries of genres and media, visual styles, and narrative techniques.

As is portrayed in the framing of "Behind the Laughter" (2000), THE SIMPSONS' episode remediates the TV show BEHIND THE MUSIC which was running on the cable network VH1 (1997–2014). Here THE SIMPSONS repurposes formulaic conventions from live-action tv in order to direct viewers' attention to the cartoon shows' conscious use of realism. The episode stages the Simpson characters as a crew of unrelated actors performing as the Simpsons in a TV show named THE SIMPSONS. "Springfield Up" (2007) remediates THE UP SERIES, a British documentary show following the lives of 14 children in eight subsequent seasons (ITV *et al.*,1964–1972). "Springfield Up" draws attention to the immediacy of the documentary look of the source material. Through the staging of its own documentary capabilities, the medium refers to itself as an animated social-experiment documentary that looks back on the coming-of-age stories of different Springfield characters, from childhood to adulthood.

Hypermediacy is also offered when viewers 'look at' the Simpsons watching television as a reflections of themselves in the regular opening sequence; and just 'look at' THE ITCHY & SCRATCHY SHOW as a cartoon-in-the-cartoon spoof of ultraviolent cat-and-mouse cartoons like the short films TOM & JERRY from the 1940s. 'Looking at' the family reconvening on the domestic couch or 'looking at' THE ITCHY & SCRATCHY SHOW means watching the small screen from the same position as the Simpson's children in the regular canon series: boxed-in by television. But in TREEHOUSE OF HORROR, Itchy & Scratchy can appear as figures that allow the audience to 'look through' the pictures to their cultural function. In the

TREEHOUSE episode "The Terror of Tiny Toon"[86] the Simpsons' children become part of THE ITCHY & SCRATCHY SHOW. The hypermediacy of the animation can direct the viewers' gaze not only to the remediating animation style in the present, but also shift their attention to how previous media already made use of remediation processes. Obviously this form of hypermediacy is not only concerned with TREEHOUSE's own medium as it is in the examples of "Behind the Laughter" or "Springfield Up". Rather the Halloween special uses animation to transcend today's televisual frame and remind viewers of prior medialities such as popular Gothic fiction (see chapter 3.3), spectacular film attractions (see chapter 3.4), and early innovative television storytelling (see chapter 3.5).

By borrowing from the definition of "remediation" offered by the Fandom Wiki of "Writing Across Media" (WAM) remediation in THE SIMPSONS has two purposes: Firstly, it is a practice inviting viewers to think about or criticize a prior medium or text, and secondly, remediation can "revise something into another medium and deepen its meaning" (*WAM.Fandom*.com, undated). Critical satires and parodies are popular devices for repurposing not only a story or genre, but also change the face of older media to renegotiate and re-member the whole repertoire of conventions and aesthetics of different capabilities previous media had on offer. By doing so, THE SIMPSONS as well as TREEHOUSE OF HORROR follow the double logic of remediation, creating a new media archive that engages in different forms of immediacy and hypermediacy.

THE SIMPSONS, A Funhouse Mirror: A Conclusion

In the beginning of this chapter, I was interested in exploring whose minds the show has embiggened in the past thirty years and what we can learn about postmodernism when looking at the period's theories through THE SIMPSONS. While reading my way through research on THE SIMPSONS as a prototypical example of postmodern popular culture, I became increasingly more intrigued by the question how the longest-running scripted animated-television primetime show in American television looks back on and re-members its own history in thirty years of critical thinking about and through popular-culture representations.

So far we have learned that THE SIMPSONS has turned TV consumption into a practice of active participation, that it created narratively complex television with mass appeal before HBO released high-budget and complex quality dramas for small-screen audiences, and that it validated the academic study of popular culture by challenging the division of high art and popular entertainment. From a contem-

---

86 TREEHOUSE OF HORROR IX, "The Terror of Tiny Toon," s10e04s2, dir. Steven Dean Moore, Fox 1998.

porary perspective, THE SIMPSONS not only helped to have the 'popular' factor added to Western cultural studies. The show of America's yellowest family moreover established itself as an intellectual site where collective social understandings about American everyday life have been renegotiated. In return, TREEHOUSE OF HORROR introduced a space where U.S.-American culture and its myths are re-membered by way of popular media and a space that engages viewers in the question how past media have tried to win American audiences over to particular ways of seeing the world.

The theoretical instruments introduced by Umberto Eco, Angela McRobbie, Linda Hutcheon, and Michel Foucault have influenced my understanding of postmodern Western culture as re-membered through an animated comedy show in the 21st century. To clarify the meaning of memory once again, I want to return to Siegfried J. Schmidt's definition from 1991. In his essay "Gedächtnis – Erzählen – Identität," the German philosopher argued that "re-membering produces a sense that is necessitated by the present and conditioned by the past" with which a coherent order can be re-established in the light of present interests, as Gunzenhäuser appended (Schmidt qtd. in Gunzenhäuser 1998: 76–77).

I used Umberto Eco's approach to Kitsch, fake, and clichés as means to re-evaluate and reconcile high art and mass culture in order to analyze whether THE SIMPSONS has what Eco termed 'Homeric profundity' and thus can be read as complex art between originality and plagiarism. Whereas Angela McRobbie in the mid-1990s re-formulated popular culture as a radical political project by reconsidering earlier postmodern theory, I used her notions of the 'surface' to explore THE SIMPSONS' characters as discursive practices concerning gender, education, and class. Before I discussed how Linda Hutcheon used parody as a theoretical tool to show the functions of postmodern metafiction, I did a comparative analysis of Walt Disney's and Matt Groening's animation traditions. In my detailed analysis of the men's animation styles I showed that parody is fundamentally important for the framing, not for the aesthetics of animation. Lastly, I introduced Michel Foucault's redefinition of the archive as a space to re-organize 'historical knowledge' and made a point of including different media into my thoughts. For me, the archive of TREEHOUSE OF HORROR is a multimedia site, a site of media archaeology to re-member popular-culture history in the digital age.

How, then, can THE SIMPSONS and TREEHOUSE OF HORROR be combined under the umbrella label of "the most complete piece of postmodern art" that Diederichsen suggested (cf. 2013: 15)? I think that both series helped raise the generation of Western millennials, those born around the year 2000, to an intimate understanding of self-reflexive irony, postmodern parody, and rich intertextuality. For the millennials, THE SIMPSONS has been that part of reality that embiggened their "perfectly cromulent" worlds. However, the time has come to continue questioning what exactly TREEHOUSE OF HORROR has contributed to the embiggening of minds through Western popular culture?

In his dictionary entry "Archive," Ed Folsom cuts right to the heart of the matter: "[T]o control the archive is to control the past and, in some sense, to control what can be made of it" (2016: 25). The question how THE SIMPSONS' TREEHOUSE OF HORROR controls the archive of popular culture Gothic- and horror texts and how the show controls what can be made of them, will be central to the following chapters. My initial assumption that TREEHOUSE OF HORROR makes different use of postmodern popular-culture theory than THE SIMPSONS will be an essential aspect of the next sections.

In an article about THE SIMPSONS' satirical depiction of religion and science, Wm. Curtis Holtzen, Professor of Philosophy and Theology at Hope International University, CA, concludes that, after thirty years, TREEHOUSE OF HORROR is a "funhouse mirror" (2018: 130) whose reflections, subjects, motifs, and discourses are too manifold to be addressed all at once. Holtzen's "funhouse mirror" can be linked to the early postmodern writer John Barth's 1968 short story "Lost in the Funhouse." The story introduces its protagonist as someone for whom the funhouse actually is no fun but "a place of fear and confusion," as Barth writes (72). However, at the end of the short story, Barth's narrator-protagonist, thirteen-year-old Ambrose, is an unreliable narrator whom readers shouldn't believe when he says that there is nothing to be afraid of in the funhouse as long as there is a "secret operator" who controls it "from a great central switchboard like the console of a pipe organ" (Barth 97). Following the postmodern lead, Ambrose is certainly wrong when he indulges in the fascist belief that the control of a single instance over the funhouse would be the solution. With "Lost in the Funhouse" Barth challenged the postmodern reader to become an active "prosumer," i. e. someone who actively consumes and produces his or her own readings, thus, controls his or her practice of creating meaning. The quote from Barth's story gives reason to assume that to control the funhouse would instill the same confidence in some minds as an individual's control over popular culture. Applied to THE SIMPSONS and TREEHOUSE OF HORROR, however, the shows' creators might control the input, but they can't control the intake. We are encouraged to take the intake in our own hands and are confronted with the choice of either framing our experience or just getting lost in the funhouse.

3 Analysis | TREEHOUSE OF HORROR: Lessons to Remember

Opening Credits | THE SIMPSONS' TREEHOUSE OF HORROR Teaches Lessons to Remember

For executive producer of THE SIMPSONS, Matt Selman, the promotional poster to the 2019 TREEHOUSE OF HORROR was the evidence that "we are living in a simulation," as he posted on Twitter on the day of the episode's television premiere (2019).[1] As I understand the concept, a simulation is a procedure for the analysis of specific systems as in THE TRUMAN SHOW (USA 1998), a formal interrogation of the real as in THE MATRIX (USA 1999), or as Baudrillard believed in *Simulacra and Simulation* (1994), a virtual representation of reality which, in the context of THE SIMPSONS, uses the means of animation to 're-animate' the 'real.' What does that mean?

Generally speaking, "simulation" is "a model of a set of problems or events that can be used to teach someone how to do something, or the process of making such a model" (*Cambridge Dictionary.org*, undated). Well-known examples are digital flight-, tank- or boat simulators. Accordingly, in 2003 game-studies scholar Espen J. Aarseth discusses computer simulation in video games and celebrates the "rich and varied world" (1) of game simulations. Aarseth's states that digital simulation is able "to portray, in principle, any phenomenon we could care to think about" (2003: 1). If everything can be simulated, then every medium can be simulated, too, as has been discussed with Jay David Bolter and Richard Grusin's *Remedi-*

---

[1] For a better understanding, see Matt Selman's tweed posted on 20 Oct. 2019 on the occasion of THE SIMPSONS' episode 666 promoted on Twitter under URL: https://bit.ly/3uQkbn1.

ation: *Understanding New Media* (2000) in the previous chapter. Their title explicitly takes up Marshall McLuhan's 1964 book title *Understanding Media: The Extensions of Man* where McLuhan insists that the power of a communication medium itself is one of the central messages of every (and he meant every non-digital) medium (1994: 8 ff.). Bolter and Grusin explain that media, by which they mean digital media as well as non-digital ones, remediate and thus transform older, often non-digital media by retaining some of their features and discarding others in order to charge their own medial power.

Especially when looking at animated and narrative video games with the notion of remediation in mind, it becomes obvious that their power derives not only from the omni-potency of digital technologies, but also from the rich and varied art of animation. Much of video games' simulation- and remediation work is done by way of animation, a relatively old, albeit today mostly digitalized artistic practice. Medial simulation or remediation is, then, not merely a digital phenomenon, but also an artistic practice, that in the case of its TV presence, THE SIMPSONS have heavily influenced.

The simulation of a medium means that one can make use of its medial power, or, as Winfried Fluck[2] would say, of the "reality effects" of this medium. In other words, video games can profit from all reality effects other media have established before them. Accordingly, they simulate not the world, but rather the reality effects already established by a medium to create interpretations of the world certain groups of readers have learnt to read and accept as 'authentic,' as 'real' (e. g. as the viewers of the reality show in THE TRUMAN SHOW). And these reality effects can also be realized by the remediation of one medium, by animation. In the following paragraphs, I want to further explain this statement.

The simulation comment given by THE SIMPSONS' executive producer Selman cannot be understood unless one recognizes that the readers of the billboard have to be familiar with the poster's visual cues such as the iconic details from the Netflix fantasy hit series STRANGER THINGS (USA 2016-present) and the movie THE SHAPE OF WATER (USA 2017). In the poster, THE SIMPSONS' Police Chief Wiggum impersonates Chief Jim Hopper from STRANGER THINGS and Milhouse's mom is shown as Will's mother Joyce Byers from the Netflix series. But the poster makes us focus on Lisa Simpson at the center of the billboard's left picture. She is shown with a shaved head much like the medium Eleven, STRANGER

---

2   In his essay collection *Romance with America?* from 2009, the German American Studies scholar Winfried Fluck uses the term "reality effect" as one concept to define systemic elements that constitute "the system's power in an 'invisible', yet highly effective way" (see "Cultural Radicalism", 55–56). He writes: "On the level of representation, there exists indeed a continuity between realism and naturalism, because both aim at the creation of a credible illusion in their depiction of the 'real' world". He continues to argue that "such a 'reality effect' can be used for entirely different purposes and can therefore also have entirely different functions" (2009: 203).

Things' central heroine, whose nose also starts to bleed when she uses her supernatural powers.

On the right side of the billboard, one can recognize a strong aesthetic resemblance with Guillermo del Toro's Cold-War fantasy drama THE SHAPE OF WATER because of the characteristic underwater coloring one might know from the fantasy film's original poster. Based on the key sequence at the end of Guillermo del Toro's film, when the characters of the fish man and the mute human Elisa embrace under water, a romantic love scene is shown between the SIMPSONS' characters Kang (or Kodos) and Selma Bouvier.

If today we are living in a simulation, as Selman's comment indicates, convergence culture, the culture of media transformation, has opened new opportunities for media and fans. As media scholar Henry Jenkins explains in his numerous books, today's fans can engage in participatory practices and in the culture of remediation of the 21st century. But Jenkins also points out in his texts that today's media practices didn't begin in the digital age. Rather, their origins can be found in non-digital media, especially in TV fan culture. Jenkins shows in a book like *Textual Poachers: Television Fans and Visual Culture* as early as in 1992 that fans learned to read today's state-of-the-art simulation practices with TV texts like STAR TREK. Accordingly, THE SIMPSONS and TREEHOUSE OF HORROR already made use of animation to revisit, transpose, and remember the complex reality effects their viewers had internalized via American popular-culture texts.

But to come back to the billboard celebrating THE SIMPSONS' 666th episode. Here a small tagline informs us: "Episode 666 – As We Planned From The Beginning." This was meant to be a joke as longtime writer and showrunner Al Jean had already revealed on Twitter in 2017 that everything was just a lucky coincidence. But the line on the billboard shows that the creators of THE SIMPSONS made use of the reality effects that previous traditions in other mediums had established before them, long before fans, critics, or academics were ready to understand and theorize them. Intended or not, the simple fact that THE SIMPSONS celebrated its 30th anniversary in 2019 with the 666th overall episode makes it all the more interesting to look back on the show's formula and how it revisits the traditions of other, earlier mediums. Simulation in this context is also a form of remembering how, for example, generations of viewers learned to question constructions of reality in other media and eventually changed their reading approach.

In their book *THE SIMPSONS in the Classroom* (2010), the authors Carma Waltonen and Denise Du Vernay document many lessons 'we' learned from THE SIMPSONS. Yet the education scholars only trace how THE SIMPSONS have improved our knowledge about language learning, linguistics, literature, and cultural literacy. They leave out TREEHOUSE OF HORROR and what viewers can learn about reading in the digital age when looking back at the history of other media. THE SIMPSONS' Halloween Special offers not only exercises in nostalgia for classic

Hollywood movies or Gothic literature. We can also learn a lot about the history of American broadcasting, about genre traditions, comic book culture and about their historical reality effects. After all, TREEHOUSE OF HORROR remediates more than one hundred years of media history.

What is TREEHOUSE OF HORROR? – The Boom of the 'Danse Macabre'

Currently, the horror genre undergoes an unprecedented boom in writing, cinema, and on television. This can be proven not only by the ongoing popularity of Stephen King's novels, but also by the manifold recent big-screen adaptations of his books PET SEMATARY (2019) or IT (2017) as well as by THE SHINING's sequel DOCTOR SLEEP (2019) both in written and filmed form. Recent supernatural-horror series on the streaming service Netflix such as the already mentioned STRANGER THINGS, but also the comic-book adaptation CHILLING ADVENTURES OF SABRINA (2018-present) or Sho Miyake's JU-ON: ORIGINS (2020), based on the Japanese cult-horror film franchise JU-ON: THE GRUDGE by Takashi Shimizu, attest to the globality of the trend as well. Horror-film specialists such as Robin Wood (*Hollywood from Vietnam to Reagan*, 1986), Stephen Prince (*The Horror Film*, 2004), or Peter Hutchings (*The Horror Film*, 2004) would certainly agree that the popularity of horror has always occurred in waves, depending on the market value of certain film cycles and horror trends since the 1930s' golden age of Hollywood horror. But the present wave is still going strong. Today's wave can also be explained by crises like the terrorist attacks on September 11, the 2007/2008 breakdown of the U.S. mortgage market culminating in the global financial crisis of 2015/2016, and the rising power of the Alt-Right which has had a lasting influence on how the horror genre evolved. Already in the late 1980s, TREEHOUSE OF HORROR showed a deep understanding of horror as a genre dealing with what concerned Americans and what aroused their cultural fears.

So TREEHOUSE OF HORROR was there before director Andrès Muschietti helped Stephen King's IT become the most successful horror movie of all times in 2017, and before the Duffer Brothers' STRANGER THINGS 'flashed' audiences back to a purely nostalgic Spielberg version of 1980s' Americana. In an interview with *Entertainment Weekly*, Stephen King said that the 2017 IT "was the right movie at the right time" because it helped revisit some of the audience's worst experiences with creepy clowns since the novel became a miniseries in 1990 (qtd. in Breznican 2017). The same can be said for TREEHOUSE OF HORROR: Its thirty episodes helped revisit some of their audiences' most thrilling, but also chilling experiences with the horror genre. Journalist Joshua Kurp writes on the online-media platform *Vulture.com*:

> The last year without a new 'TREEHOUSE OF HORROR' episode was 1989, when PET SEMATARY, PUPPET MASTER, and HALLOWEEN 5 were playing in theaters. Nearly 30 years later, PET SEMATARY is getting a bigger-budget remake,

Puppet Master is up to the 13th film in the franchise, and Halloween 5 isn't canon anymore, but Treehouse of Horror is still going strong. *(2018)*

Treehouse of Horror emerged during the decade that executive producer Mike Reiss calls "the golden age of horror," when the genre went through a sea change that primed America for its first Treehouse of Horror episode; and "when the Simpsons' core-creative team was a group of unmarried men in their twenties who shared a universal love for horror" (Reiss qtd. in Horner 2018). Al Jean, the second executive producer of The Simpsons beside Reiss, remembers:

> Horror movies used to be known as B-movies, the kind of things you would watch on Friday nights when you were sleeping over at friends' house or whatever. But movies like The Exorcist in 1973 – one of the finest movies ever made, period – and Halloween in 1978 launched a whole new era of horrors that were higher budget and scarier and made by A-list directors. The 1980s were very different for the genre. *(qtd. in Horner 2018)*

Beginning their success story, so-to-speak, at the end of horror's second "golden age" in cinema and fiction writing, the core-creative team of Treehouse had a shared passion for the genre. The series' adventurous horror narratives rifle through pop-culture references at such a ferocious pace that it takes real fervor to understand all homages.[3] For thirty years, the show's "barrage of riffs," as Horner calls them (2018), of horror texts from across literary, television, and cinema history has not only been a lesson on the proliferation of adaptation in the digital age. The show keeps instructing and inspiring new generations of viewers to learn how to read the genre of horror across time. I want to start my discussion of historical-horror reading practices with the radio.

American Broadcasting Traditions: In the Beginning there was the Radio

The Treehouse segment "The Day The Earth Looked Stupid" (ToH XVII, 2006) re-members the tradition of the radio play with Orson Welles' War of the Worlds from 1938. After watching the segment over and over again, I realized that the segment doesn't parody Welles' infamous Halloween audio play alone, but uses the piece to pay homage to media practices of a whole historical period, the time of the Great Depression.

---

3   In this context, David Silverman mentions fans scratching their heads over the David Cronenberg parody "The Ned Zone" (i. e. a film adaptation of Stephen King's *The Dead Zone* from 1983) or the opening of ToH IV that parodies Rod Serling's TV anthology Night Gallery. He argues: "The rule was, even if the audience don't notice it or understand, they'll feel it." (qtd. in Horner 2018).

3 Analysis | TREEHOUSE OF HORROR: Lessons to Remember

10 Orson Welles performs his radio play WAR OF THE WORLDS: Scene shows him speaking about the Martian invasion with the Foley artist on his right side who is doing the sound effects

The episode is set in the Depression-ridden Springfield of the year 1938, where unemployed Carl Carlsson ironically wonders "what's so 'great' about this Depression?," while lining up at the Salvation Army to get his food supply. In this ToH segment, the past is bathed in sepia colors – a reality effect pointing to today's media experience of the time – and Homer and Marge are shown dancing to the music aired on their radio. The radio dominates their living room just as characteristically as the television set does in THE SIMPSONS' contemporary mise-en-scène.

Homer and Marge are interrupted by a male voice which announces that "reports are coming in of giant metal cylinders [from Mars] landing on the outskirts of major American cities." A different voice begins to describe what the Martians look like ("a tentacle is emerging") and that they start "firing a beam of pure energy" and "burning people alive." The audience also hears the background noises of screaming people and shooting sounds that represent to this day the metallic sound of lasers. The series shows Springfieldians getting nervous. The scene changes to an establishing shot of the radio station of KBBL where a young Orson Welles reads out his script of the Martian invasion. The viewers also see how the impression of the "incredible devastation" and the "human bodies [which] are grinded up" is created: The Foley artist, i.e. the person who creates the sound art, uses a mixer on wet corn flakes to stimulate the listeners' imagination (cf. Fig. 10).

Whereas the Springfieldians fall prey to (and freak out about) the radio's illusionary power to fabricate aural landscapes of terror within the sterility of a recording studio, viewers of the TREEHOUSE episode learn how these illusions were created in former times that seem long forgotten. TREEHOUSE OF HORROR remembers the aural art of radio storytelling as an illusion, thus portraying it as an art creating convincing reality effects.

A similar moment occurs at the end of ToH V. Here, Marge makes use of an old radio-play convention when she verbally explains what would not have been visually obvious in a radio play, but is apparent now, on a visual medium. In the segment, Marge soothes Bart and Lisa who just woke up from a nightmare and says: "There is nothing to be afraid of… except that fog that turns people inside-out." Like the aural impression of the laser-gun firing and of bodies being ground up, Marge's announcement intervenes in the narrative and forestalls the tale of what will happen next, namely that the fog turns the Simpsons visually inside-out.[4] Some attentive viewers may have wondered why Marge comments in detail on what we are visually shown in the animation. In fact, Marge hints at the aural medium's dependence on persistent verbal intervention to keep the story moving. Narrating voices had to feed the listeners' imagination by making horror more 'visual.'

Although I used to believe that the inside-out fog of ToH V was a reference to John Carpenter's 1980 horror film THE FOG, it indeed honors famous radio playwright Arch Oboler's "The Dark," an episode from the radio program LIGHTS OUT.[5] As can be read in John Dunning's *Encyclopedia of Old-Time Radio* from 1998, LIGHTS OUT was billed as "the ultimate in horror" (399). After its premiere in 1935, LIGHTS OUT was one of the earliest radio formats that were entirely dedicated to horror drama and the supernatural, and Arch Oboler was one of the first radio auteurs who understood the radio play as an art form. TREEHOUSE pays tribute to Oboler's inside-out fog also because no recordings of the original broadcast have survived (Dunning 1998: 399). When massive pressure from television programs such as CBS's successful sitcom I LOVE LUCY contributed to the death of radio, Oboler's pioneering efforts to define the radio play as an art form practically got lost. In cases like this, it is necessary for TREEHOUSE OF HORROR's creators to encourage us to collectively remember and learn where medial conventions have their origins.

The TREEHOUSE series also reminds us of Welles' and Oboler's radio plays to highlight that adaptations of successful texts from the horror genre have always been part of American pop culture. To 'remember' horror also means to 'rethink' it by the help of various different medial languages: the American Gothic confronted readers with the language of horror in written form; in early public broadcasting horror dominated the radio play, while cinema and television had to develop their own audiovisual vocabulary to put horror on display and bring it to their own audiences until TREEHOUSE OF HORROR created a cartoon language to continue this ongoing dialectical process.

---

4   I already mentioned the scene from ToH V (Fox 1994) in Chapter 2 in the context of the show's sometimes "excessive imagery" of the corporeal (cf. Ch. 2).
5   LIGHTS OUT was broadcast on NBC Radio between 1935 and 1947 after which NBC turned it into a TV show. (cf. Dunning 1998: 399 f.).

Treehouse of Horror Exclusives: Title Cards & Wraparound

In the course of the 20th century, it became increasingly clear that Halloween belonged to American culture and Halloween TV specials to seasonal television programming. Seasonal television seems to conceive of itself as the treat for audiences who stay home and in front of the screen instead of tricking their neighbors. U.S.-America is the nation which has cultivated seasonal-television horror like no other country. The average American 'habit viewer' traditionally gets in the mood for Christmas when he or she feels the warming glow of Frank Capra's all-time favorite It's a Wonderful Life (1941). On Halloween, people chuckle on their couches at the familiar dialogues of the timeless classic It's the Great Pumpkin, Charlie Brown (1966).

These habits coincide with those leading fans to The Simpsons' Halloween Special which audiences wait for an entire year to see. Put differently, Treehouse of Horror perfected the format and idea of the American Halloween Special on TV. With thirty years, The Simpsons' annual cycle has the longest continuity and undoubtedly the greatest density of complexly layered narratives. Every episode is usually divided into three three-to-five minute segments plus an opening. In comparison to the production of the remaining 20 Simpsons episodes in one season (the number varies between 19 and 25 episodes), the Halloween Special claims more production time and demands higher efforts.[6] Therefore it is not surprising when Al Jeans informs that the Treehouse of Horror series was almost cancelled after ToH III in 1992. But after some discussion, the creators changed their mind again and until today, the show runners hold on to the annual format.[7] For this reason, audiences usually have high hopes when the character-centered continuity of The Simpsons gets disrupted by Treehouse of Horror.

As I document in my "Treehouse of Horror Episode Guide" (see App. in 6.1), The Simpsons' Halloween Special was changed into Treehouse of Horror in the premiering episode of season 14 (ToH XIII, 2002). Practically unnoticed by the general public, the Halloween cycle emancipated itself from The Simpsons due to its immense success with critics and audiences. When Treehouse of Horror became its own marketing category, an anthology series with its own continuity and aesthetic, the show's creators started to complement the Halloween episode with further mini-stories.

To begin with, Treehouse of Horror episodes started to use Roman numerals, just like the Super Bowl, but often written in blood red, from ToH I in 1990 to ToH XXXI in 2020 (cf. Fig. 11). In addition, each of the usually three-story segments bore

---

6   Jean, Al. The Simpsons season 2 DVD commentary for the episode Treehouse of Horror, 20th Century Fox, 2002.
7   As Al Jeans informs on the DVD audio commentary of season four, the high efforts almost resulted in the cancelling of the Treehouse of Horror series after ToH III in 1992 (s04e05). But after some discussion, the creators changed their mind again (Fox 1992).

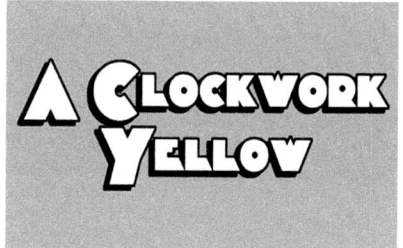

11 Exemplary title card from ToH XVII (2006) shows the typical Roman numerals usually written in blood to underline the seasonal disruption for Halloween

12 Exemplary title card of the ToH segment "A Clockwork Yellow" as a visual reference to the parody's original source, in this case Stanley Kubrick's A CLOCKWORK ORANGE (UK 1971)

pun-based titles reminding of films or TV series. ToH V's segment "The Shinning," for example, is only complemented with an additional 'n' because Groundskeeper Willie fears he will be sued for a copyright violation of Stephen King's title *The Shining* and Stanley Kubrick's film adaptation of the same name as he self-reflexively explains in the respective segment. David Cronenberg's THE DEAD ZONE (1983) is parodied as "The Ned Zone" in ToH XV, Stanley Kubrick's A CLOCKWORK ORANGE (1971) becomes "A Clockwork Yellow" in ToH XXV (cf. Fig. 12), and Alfred Hitchcock's suspense thriller DIAL 'M' FOR MURDER (1954) is lengthened to "Dial 'M' For Murder Or Press '#' to Return to Main Menu" (ToH XX). The title cards often adapt or consciously hint at the original layout of film posters or iconic imagery and typography probably to re-member the visual aesthetic of the original source. Many of the episodes' titles make obvious reference to popular songs and idioms too. Frank Sinatra's 1973 song "Send in the Clowns" becomes "Send in the Clones" in ToH XIII (2002) and in ToH XVI (2005) Charles Darwin's phrase describing the mechanism of evolution, "Survival of the Fittest," is turned into "Survival of the Fattest" – and the list continues. The title cards usually give basic information concerning the 'original' horror text or theme the following segment will focus on.

Looking at the period between 1990 and 2001, in which the special episodes were still announced under the title 'THE SIMPSONS Halloween Special,' each segment consisted of five parts: The segment starts with opening- and title sequence and is followed by the establishing of the story set up by means of a wraparound that provides the subsequent short segments with their narrative frame. The wraparound of the first TREEHOUSE episode is the only one that uses the eponymous 'treehouse' to introduce each segment with Lisa and Bart who tell each other horror stories while sitting in their treehouse.

In the second Halloween Special from 1991, the segments are framed by dreams which introduce us to three nightmarish stories as dreamt by Homer, Bart, and Lisa respectively. In ToH III, each of the three scary stories is told at a SIMPSONS'

Halloween party in the style of *Scary Stories to Tell in the Dark*, a series of collections consisting of illustrated short horror stories for children. Even the 1993 episode TREEHOUSE OF HORROR IV still makes use of the wraparound because here the opening framework is the guiding principle to which the three stories-within-the-story return, a framing device to organize the three subsequent mini-movies. In this case, the guiding-framework technique was borrowed from Rod Serling's supernatural anthology series NIGHT GALLERY (CBS 1970–1973). In the tradition of Serling's fantasy shows hosted by him, the wraparound has become a form of interstitial structuring which has a long tradition in U.S. television. Such narrative bridges can potentially fill air time or serve as commentary before and after the presented content. The TV host Rod Serling most prominently cultivated the wraparound technique with his famous lead-ins and lead-outs in the science-fiction anthology series THE TWILIGHT ZONE (see Chapter 3.5).

Only two years later, the opening of ToH VI (1995) shows that the creators obviously cut their ties with the wraparound and no longer used it as the narrative glue of the three stories. The sixth TREEHOUSE episode is introduced by the Headless Horseman holding up Krusty-the-Clown's head. The re-animated Headless Horseman refers to the literary figure known from Washington Irving's 1809 novella "The Legend of Sleepy Hollow," and may have inspired Tim Burton to re-imagine the character according to the TREEHOUSE interpretation in his own film adaptation SLEEPY HOLLOW that was released four years later, in 1999. From this time on in 1995, the opening turned into an additional popular-genre reference; it pointed not only to American Gothic fiction, but sometimes also to other television programs such as THE MUNSTERS in 2000 (ToH XI), TALES FROM THE CRYPT in 2006 (ToH XVII), or the monstrous version of THE OFFICE U.S. in 2010 (ToH XXI).

In other episodes, the opening is also used to create a seasonal atmosphere that ends on a negative note, directly confronting the viewers with the seasonal disruption by physical violence known from some Warner Bros' and Hanna-Barbera cartoons. This becomes visible, for example, in ToH XX (2009). Here, the Simpsons celebrate a Halloween party at home where Homer's head gets cut off and eventually lands in the punchbowl. His eyes show a common motif known from the LOONEY TUNES or TOM & JERRY: a double X replaces the character's eyes to signify its death and, in case of TREEHOUSE, the Roman numeral crediting the 20th episode of the cycle. Another example is ToH XII from 2001 which shows the Simpsons while trick-or-treating in the neighborhood. Mr. Burns lets the dogs out and the Simpsons keep running even after Mr. Burns' razor-sharp entrance gate has cut them into slices.

As of 2013, TREEHOUSE's popularity is also palpable when looking at the manifold contributions from guest animators like the Mexican filmmaker Guillermo del Toro, who made fantasy films like HELLBOY (USA 2004) or THE SHAPE OF WATER (USA 2017), and who created the opening sequence to ToH XXIV (2013); or cartoon artist John Kricfalusi who created the REN & STIMPY show for Nickelodeon and worked on the opening of ToH XXVI (2015). Both artists will receive detailed attention in chapter 3.2 in which I ask in how far these artists can be labeled as 'cartoon auteurs' who helped to elevate Treehouse of Horror's opening sequence to a new art form of participatory culture.

Because the series is a cycle of so-called one-off seasonal specials and not a part of The Simpsons' regular canon and continuity, there exists no stock of images, but for every new episode many new designs have to be created.[8] According to *The Atlantic* staff writer David Sims, the audacity of Treehouse of Horror's annual horror spoofs serves "as a reminder of the creative freedom The Simpsons pioneered for years and years" (2015). Sims considers The Simpsons first and foremost a family sitcom that developed the larger world of Springfield; but he regards Treehouse of Horror episodes as particularly avant-garde in their lack of emphasis on laughs, their thrill of telling a story 'out of canon,' and their daring of killing characters off or turning them into monsters (cf. Sims 2015). When comparing The Simpsons' with Treehouse of Horror's opening sequence, Treehouse's greater freedom becomes evident. In comparison to The Simpsons' regular opening, that of Treehouse of Horror has several sections that have changed over the course of time. Whereas the 'funny tombstones' were characteristic of the show's early years, the typical green lettering of the credits was kept to mark the seasonal disruption. But there are further notable features and exclusives which were created to help distinguish Treehouse of Horror from The Simpsons.

Serial Memory & Simulated Continuity: Recurring Elements

As indicated above, the wraparound was one of the first elements abandoned to increase air time. More structural features underwent change in the course of the cycle's development, but other things have become a fixed essential and recurring tradition.

Considering change, Allie Goertz and Julia Prescott note in *100 Things The Simpsons Fans Should Know & Do Before They Die* from 2018 that the creative team of The Simpsons stopped using different writers and multiple directors for several segments at a time (cf. 68); starting in 2002 (ToH XIII), they passed on creative control over individual segments of Treehouse of Horror instead. Although the segments are traditionally created independently from each other, ToH V forms an exception. The episode which has entered TV history as the goriest, most violent episode within the Treehouse cycle also had an effect on the adventuresome freedom which Groening's team was still experiencing in the mid-1990s. Groundskeeper Willie has an appearance and is being ax murdered the same way in each of the unrelated three parodies of The Shining from 1980,

---

[8] For more information, listen to David Mirkin's audio commentary on The Simpsons' season 5 DVD commentary for the episode "Treehouse of Horror VI" (DVD), 20th Century Fox, 2004.

Raymond Bradbury's short-story "A Sound of Thunder" from 1952, and Richard Fleischer's dystopian thriller SOYLENT GREEN from 1973. By breaking with the narrative conventions of both the sitcom and the TV anthology, viewers were reminded of the format's freedom and overall complexity. No other network-cartoon show has ever shown the self-referential killing of a character or presented a comparable approach to avant-garde storytelling by avoiding to play for laughs. Only TREEHOUSE has been using such unconventional cartoon storytelling.

Recurring Elements 1: **Kang & Kodos**

Considering the features which became fixed essentials on TREEHOUSE OF HORROR, one recurring element hints at the cycle's innovative approach to serial memory and simulated continuity. Over the years, the Halloween special has gained increasing autonomy from the main series through a variety of more exclusively recurring characteristics which audiences anticipate every year. It is an unwritten law that Kang and Kodos, the two aliens from planet Rigel-7, exclusively appear in each of the Halloween episodes.

Kang and his sister Kodos as the show's Halloween exclusives are portrayed as two green, constantly drooling cyclops in a space helmet and with tentacles. Their design is a mix of two EC Comics issues of *Weird Science* from the 1950s as executive Mike Reiss informs on the DVD commentary to ToH II (2003). The recurring appearance of the aliens evokes nostalgia for the early days of American popular science-fiction imagery the creators lovingly ripped from the comics' covers, for example, of the *Weird Science* series. When comparing the two EC Comics covers of issue No. 6 (1951)[9] and No. 16 (1951)[10] with the cover of THE SIMPSONS' special comic book *Bart Simpsons Horror Show* published by Bongo Comics in 2010, the *Weird Science* issues demonstrate that Kang and Kodos amalgamate stereotypical features of aliens as green reptiles with tentacles and big-headed automatons in glass helmets. The extraterrestrials Kang and Kodos became staple features of TREEHOUSE OF HORROR in 1990. In the 2015 regular SIMPSONS' episode "The Man Who Came to be Dinner,"[11] Homer even admonishes the aliens' 'irregular' appearance with his comment "It's not Halloween!" Kang and Kodos are named after the STAR TREK characters Kang, the Klingon captain in "Day of the Dove" (THE ORIGINAL SERIES 1968), and Kodos who plays the bad-guy executioner in the episode "The Conscience of the King" (THE ORIGINAL SERIES 1966).

9   See the EC Comics' cover of *Weird Science*, No. 6 by artist Al Feldstein from 1951 under URL: https://bit.ly/2Q6aIJe.
10 See the collage of the EC Comics' cover of *Weird Science*, No. 16 by artist Wally Wood from 1952 next to the cover of Bongo Comics' *Bart Simpsons Horror Show*, No. 14 co-illustrated by Matt Groening & Bill Morrison from 2010 under URL: https://bit.ly/3rUhi2B.
11 Cf. THE SIMPSONS, creat. Matt Groening, s10e26, Fox 2015.

Beside their sometimes tangential function as time-filling sidekicks in Treehouse, there are also several segments in which they take up center stage, for example, in the already mentioned Treehouse XVII segment "The Day The Earth Looked Stupid" (cf. Ch. 3.5). Three years after Kang and Kodos' successfully subjugated Springfield, the aliens look down on the town in ruins and wonder: "Why are we not greeted as liberators?" in what they call their "Operation: Enduring Occupation," a reference online critics read as a macabre mockery of the U.S. occupation in Iraq. So did Roger Cormier write on the online-media platform Mental Floss in 2014 that in the version that was sent to TV critics before broadcast, Kang had the final commentary of the scene: "This sure is a lot like Iraq will be." And although even Fox would have been fine with it, Al Jean decided to cut the line from the final version. Like the cartoon-in-cartoon characters Itchy and Scratchy, the Iraq-joke exemplifies that Kang and Kodos can also serve as bearers of something which the show's writers want to satirize, but which could not possibly be articulated by a 'real' character, namely one who represents a human.

The segment with the title "Citizen Kang," another homage to Orson Welles, here to his film Citizen Kane from 1941, shows how Kang and Kodos attempt to enslave humanity in Springfield once more. The episode was aired one week before the real U.S.-presidential election in 1996. It shows how the aliens kidnap the competing candidates, the Republican Bob Dole and the Democrat Bill Clinton, take on their physical appearance and, while looking like them, agree on leading the country together. Homer eventually investigates who is behind the masks of Dole and Clinton, but accidentally kills the original presidential competitors by pushing the wrong button. In the ensuing election, Kang and Kodos in the guise of Bob Dole and Bill Clinton are the potential candidates. Although Homer uncovers the fraud at a public event, Kang wins the election and becomes President of the United States. Although Homer can realize the aliens' plan and tries to perform damage control by unmasking the fake presidents in the public, it is too late: Kang and Kodos enslave the country and force it to build them a giant laser cannon.

This Treehouse episode was not only the lead-in to The Simpsons' eighth season in 1996. The segment "Citizen Kang" is unique in that it was the first one to be aired close to the presidential-election campaigns between President Bill Clinton and Senator Bob Dole. In the audio commentary of season eight, writer David X. Cohen mentions that "Citizen Kang" violated every rule of Treehouse of Horror because the episode is locked in a specific time and names specific candidates. Nevertheless, by breaking these conventions the segment fulfills the Treehouse of Horror formula as a simulation machinery.

There are more exclusives which give Treehouse of Horror its recognition value. They include the tracking shot over Springfield's cemetery, a part of the credit sequence that only the Treehouse cycle used to introduce the annual "The Simpsons' Halloween Special" between 1990 and 2002 before it was changed to

TREEHOUSE OF HORROR. Even the so-called 'couch gag' is adapted to the horror format and has become a well-received format itself. While the animation auteur receives an individual examination in chapter 3.2 with readings committed to several opening contributions from outside the SIMPSONS' creative team, I want to say a few words on the evolution of the couch gag.

Recurring Elements 2: **The Couch Gag and its History**

Any of the more recent SIMPSONS episodes from the past twenty years is introduced in the same recognizable way, always accompanied by the characteristic theme melody. The newer episodes continue with a tracking shot that includes more visual cues than in the early years, e. g. of a black crow that crosses the screen or of Ralph Wiggum eating ice cream until the head of the statue presenting town founder Jebediah Springfield falls on his head – but after that we still see the camera moving down to follow the action. Although specific details are changed in each episode, the stock of background images remains the same. Compared with this, the TREEHOUSE openings are always new and always different to signal that the regular order is suspended on Halloween.

But let us start at the beginning. The term 'couch gag' should not off-handedly be conflated with the 'opening sequence' in general. In the regular series, the couch gag itself has become institutionalized as the last instance of the opening sequence, when the Simpson family has finally converged on their famous couch to signal to the audience: Now you are watching the Simpsons watching television. Music journalist and self-proclaimed biographer of THE SIMPSONS, Chris Turner, writes that the couch gag is "a twist of events that befalls the Simpsons family" (2004: 71). Turner's "twist of events" includes the changing saxophone solo by Lisa along with different portrayals of how the family gathers on their couch, but altogether, the TREEHOUSE openings are full of twisted events alongside a stock of innovative background images.

In the first twenty years of THE SIMPSONS, the opening sequence was established as consisting of six stable parts. First, the show introduces its title card in the 'cumulus clouds,' followed by an establishing crane shot that shows Springfield from above while the camera zooms in on the town (complete with the 'Billboard gag' as of 2009). The camera pans over to Bart standing at the board of Springfield Elementary, writing ever changing chalk messages while being on detention. The so-called 'board gag' is followed by various cuts, first to Homer's workplace of the nuclear power plant's 'assembly line,' then to Lisa's 'saxophone solo' during band practice, and finally to Marge and Maggie's checking out at the 'grocery store.' The opening concludes with the 'couch gag' after every Simpson family member has made their way home to Evergreen Terrace 742. The opening belongs to a whole sequence of events which underwent crucial revisions since the series began to be produced in 720p high definition with the episode "Take my Life, Please" (2009).

13 Exemplary couch gag from one of altogether seven classic TREEHOUSE openings between 1992 and 2000, here showing the Simpsons dangling on nooses in ToH VI (1995)

Although the new permanent opening since 2009 features diverse visual changes such as an increased amount of visual cues and characters (e.g. headless God), the sequence of the 'twist of events' nevertheless remains considerably stable.[12]

Compared to the standard series, opening changes 'befall' the Simpsons even more often in the Halloween Special. The cycle offers special one-shot openings such as Marge's early stage warnings, homages to classic TV shows such as ALFRED HITCHCOCK PRESENTS, or guest-directed mini movies such as director del Toro's couch gag from 2013 which has a length of almost three minutes. There can also be found cross-over short films which use alternative animation techniques to portray the Simpsons as stop-motion characters as, for example, in the SAUSAGE PARTY (i.e. a R-rated CGI comedy from 2016) opening "The Sweets Hereafter" from ToH XXVIII (2017). Another well-known tradition from the early years is the 'funny tombstones' (as part of the Springfield-cemetery tracking shot) which were cancelled in 1994 and resurfaced after twenty-three years in 2017.

Nowadays, the couch gag has become almost synonymous with the opening in general, although in TREEHOUSE OF HORROR the literal couch appeared only between 1992 and 2000. The seven examples in which the couch became part of TREEHOUSE's opening show the Simpsons in horrible situations. In ToH III they are skeletons, in ToH IV they break through the floor as a group of zombies, and they appear assembled from body parts like Frankenstein's creature in ToH V. ToH VI shows them dangling on nooses from the ceiling (cf. Fig. 13); in ToH VII, Death himself is sitting on the couch, waiting for the Simpsons who instantly collapse in front of his scythe; and in ToH VIII, metal caps fall from the ceiling and electrocute them all.[13] After 1998, the horror-inspired TREEHOUSE 'couch gag' was

---

12 See a collage of the two different opening sequences juxtaposing every little detail that occurs in the "Original Version (1989) compared with the "High Definition Version (2009)" in the Wikipedia article "*THE SIMPSONS* opening sequence" (undated) under URL: https://bit.ly/3cR0PrE.
13 In the final TREEHOUSE opening that includes the couch, which I left out for matters of space, the Simpsons themselves don't show up while the popular serial-killer icons Freddy Krueger,

entirely banned and became renewed as an open tangent for all sorts of avant-garde- and fan-art productions (cf. 3.2).

On the occasion of THE SIMPSONS' 600th anniversary, for example, which coincided with the 27th TREEHOUSE episode, Google made a request for an unprecedented innovation: They commissioned the creation of a virtual-reality (VR) experience to which viewers were directed via an URL included in the original 45-second clip. This up to that point unused couch gag "Planet of the Couches," a riff on PLANET OF THE APES (USA 1968), portrays how the couch itself becomes the subject matter of the opening.[14] The title card for the opening "Planet of the Couches" shows an additional insertion that reads: "If you don't have VR glasses you miss everything."[15] The audience's involvement in this couch gag thus culminates in a form of media convergence that was unprecedented in the history of THE SIMPSONS and probably U.S.-American television in general: The television medium intersected with digital media, smartphone applications, and the technology of virtual reality.[16] Besides such promotional purposes, a concerted close reading of the couch gag and the larger dialectics of its more recent production will be provided in chapter 3.2.

TREEHOUSE OF HORROR's Major Influences: EC Comics' Scary Names & "The New Trend"

So far, I have only brushed some of the major influences on TREEHOUSE OF HORROR. I used some influences – from EC Comics' cover design to Serling's narrative lead-ins and -outs in CBS' NIGHT GALLERY – to introduce several of the show's 'exclusives,' gave insight into the narrative framing of the wraparound, and shed light on the opening sequence with a special focus on the couch gag. But there is

---

the one with the striped pullover from the slasher franchise NIGHTMARE ON ELM STREET, and Jason Voorhees, the one with the ice hockey mask from the slasher franchise FRIDAY THE 13TH, wait on their couch to presumably kill them.

14 According to an iconic scene from PLANET OF THE APES, the Simpsons flee from a group of persecuting couches that ride on horses (as stand-ins of the empowered apes). After having captured the Simpsons, the couches take them to a rural town and imprison them in a "Homo Reclinus" cell (as stand-ins of the enslaved humans), a cell for the species of the reclining man. But in the end, their own loyal couch comes to free them.

15 In order to fully see the 360° rotation in the animation, viewers of the VR experience needed an iOS or Android compatible smartphone, the app "Google Spotlight Stories" as well as Knoxlabs "Google Cardboard Viewer", the actual virtual reality glasses which Fox promoted in the announcement of the special couch gag.

16 *Entertainment Weekly* reported that if users didn't have the Google Cardboard Viewer, a limited version of the couch gag was available online that provided not 360°, but at least six different views on the scene, as executive Al Jean told EW (cf. Snierson 2016).In the interview, Al Jean explains that the VR allowed users to look at the ceiling and see what was going on behind or below characters (cf. *ibid.*: 2016).

14 The slimy green lettered scary names have become an exclusive element in TREEHOUSE OF HORROR

certainly more to say about the impact EC Comics and Rod Serling has had on the show's creation history. Whereas EC Comics inspired the idea of TREEHOUSE's 'generic clustering,' Rod Serling's impetus becomes visible in the show's narrative structure of the 'anthology arrangement.' Both influences can be considered as touchstones for developing the TREEHOUSE formula.

Only few horror enthusiasts know that the so-called 'scary names' from the opening- and the end credits of TREEHOUSE OF HORROR are a gag taken over from EC Comics too (cf. Fig. 14). These scary names play with the team's original names and add some scary details.[17] In these horror credits, executive producer James L. Brooks becomes "James Hell Brooks," Simpsons inventor Matt Groening turns into "Bat Groening," and showrunner Sam Simon, who died in 2015, has since been credited as "Sam 'Sayonara' Simon." The idea is credited to longtime writer and show runner Al Jean who adapted them from EC Comics. But what else can be said about the influence of a graphic print medium on the animation style of TREEHOUSE OF HORROR?

On the DVD audio commentary of TREEHOUSE OF HORROR II, former SIMPSONS showrunner David Silverman remembers that later show runner Sam Simon had a collection of EC comic books in his office, featuring anthologies of strange and sinister horror vignettes. Although with slightly different effect, EC Comics also followed the self-contained anthology trend within their different illustrated comic books. In the 1950s, the EC Comics company stood for "Educational Comics" or "Entertaining Comics Group" and was famous for the horror

---

17 In the section "Scary Names / Selected Credits" of my first Appendix (6.1), I have collected some examples of the scary names crediting the episodes' writers, directors, creators, show runners etc.

franchises *Tales From The Crypt* (27 issues) and *The Vault Of Horror* (29 issues), but also featured science-fiction anthologies such as *Weird Science* or *Weird Fantasy* (both: 22 issues), and is still known for the satirical magazine quarterly *MAD* (more than 550 issues) which first appeared in 1952 and stayed for over 67 years. A vertical signature caption on the top left side of the comic covers usually informs about the genre fans are about to expect: *Tales From The Crypt* commonly offers "Terror," *Weird Science* expands across the vast range of "Fantasy," and *The Vault of Horror* nominally includes stories credited as "Horror" – the genre the EC Comics' company was most famous for. EC Comics was nonetheless open towards a variety of genres including comedy which might explain to what extent EC's openness had inspired THE SIMPSONS' creative team – an openness the team aimed to transplant into TREEHOUSE OF HORROR.

The Tales From The Crypt series, for example, was a bi-monthly horror-comic anthology published between 1950 and 1955 with a circulation of 27 issues. Each edition issued a different horror tale with the famous Cryptkeeper making his debut in 1950 (*Crime Patrol* #15), delivering an irreverent but wacky final statement to lighten the scary atmosphere he had introduced. HBO adapted the horror stories for its half-hour TV adaptation TALES FROM THE CRYPT which ran between 1989 and 1996. All HBO TV adaptations from EC Comics consisted of self-contained suspense narratives and horror tales which were drawn to a conclusion by their respective hosts. The iconic opening not only gave EVIL DEAD (1981) cinematographer Tim Philo's Shaky-Cam horror-film effect a new home on '80s television; the chasing style of the camera has also been adapted to the opening sequence of ToH XVII in which Mr. Burns as the Crypt-Keeper welcomes his horror-genre savvy fans in an animated version of the Victorian mansion's eery basement.

In contrast to the satirical tone of the *MAD* magazine which influenced the style of humor in THE SIMPSONS,[18] the cover of EC's horror comics envisioned

---

18 Whereas TREEHOUSE OF HORROR has taken a lot from EC's horror comics, THE SIMPSONS shares a lot with *MAD*, the EC Comics' magazine which was not focused on horror and suspense, but inherited its irreverent undertone from earlier EC Comics. This becomes evident when American cartoon artist Harvey Kurtzman describes *MAD* as lampooning-comics culture itself (qtd. in Fink 2019: 13). Moritz Fink, the author of *The Simpsons: A Cultural History* (2019) argues: "Using parody, *MAD* became a forum for satirizing the culture and aesthetic conventions that dominated the comics industry." (13) The interest in paying tribute to each other finds particular resonance in the characters of Bart Simpson and Alfred E. Neumann. The comic cover from an Australian "XL Super Special" issue of *MAD* shows Bart's head as merged with the magazine's official mascot, Alfred E. Neuman. 'Bart E. Neuman' is surrounded by his family whose members all resemble typical characters from *MAD*, i. e. Marge and Homer as envisioned by *MAD*'s cartoonist Don Martin, or Maggie and Lisa who are lookalikes of *MAD*'s arch enemies black Spy and white Spy. In The Simpsons, however, over the years there were multiple occasions the show payed tribute to *MAD*, for example, in the episode "Marge in Chains" (1993) in which Marge is arrested for shoplifting and becomes friends with Tattoo Annie who wears a huge Alfred E. Neuman fold-in tattoo over her shoulder blades; or in "The

Opening Credits | THE SIMPSONS' TREEHOUSE OF HORROR Teaches Lessons to Remember

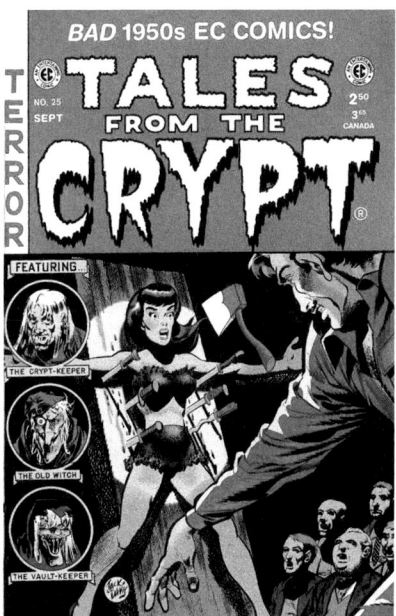

15 Cover from EC Comics' *Tales From The Crypt* issue No. 41 (1950)

16 Cover from Bongo Comics' *Bart Simpsons' Treehouse of Horror* issue No. 11 (2005) makes direct reference to EC Comics cover design

a less satirical, but far more sinister and graphic imagery to criticize the culture industry which inspired the kind of horror in TREEHOUSE. This can be seen in a comparison with the *Tales From The Crypt* cover from 1954,[19] exhibiting a show girl besieged by the knives and axe of a knife thrower (see Fig. 15) with another Bongo issue of "Bart Simpson's TREEHOUSE OF HORROR" from 2005 which illustrates the close aesthetic ties with EC's horror comics (see Fig. 16).[20] Any of these comic series from EC Comics are decisive graphic and conceptual sources not only for THE SIMPSONS, but also for TREEHOUSE OF HORROR's use of subject mat-

City of New York vs. Homer Simpson" from 1998 in which Bart sneaks into the New York headquarter of *MAD* and meets Alfred E. Neuman together with the white Spy and the Don Martin character Fonebone on a pogo stick.

19   The entire issue can be read online as part of the comic archive *Zipcomic.com* under URL: https://www.zipcomic.com/tales-from-the-crypt-1950-issue-41.
20   The open fan platform Wikisimpsons has archived the entire collection of "Bart Simpsons Treehouse of Horror" of Bongo's special comics issues, first published in 1995 with the final issue No. 23 published in 2017. The example of No. 11 that shows Marge on a rotating platform of a knife thrower was published in 2005, cf. *Simpsonswiki* under URL: https://bit.ly/3dbHhhK.

123

ter and formal architecture. In a video contribution on "Screen Rant," a YouTube vlog with a special focus on movie reviews, the commentator explains: "It's from these comics that the writers of the show [TREEHOUSE] became inspired to go all out for Halloween" (*YouTube.com*, undated). According to producer James L. Brooks, the idea for TREEHOUSE was to create a format that was "original and kind of shocking for a cartoon network program" (qtd. in Cormier 2014). The commentator on "Screen Rant" further writes: "these comic books were so out there and over the top and unafraid to be scary […] They were the perfect creepy source material for the Simpsons to parody" (undated).[21]

According to show runner Sam Simon, EC's comics were a product of market research suggesting that ex-soldiers who had served in WWII no longer wanted their reading material to boast caped crusaders, sex, and violence, but rather something that emulated those comics instead (qtd. in Horner 2018). Horner points out that the creators working on TREEHOUSE simply started "pairing the outlandish tales of EC with the otherworldliness and irony of the TWILIGHT ZONE and Stephen King" (2018). Much like the television-anthology auteur Rod Serling, EC publishing-company owner William (Bill) Gaines saw great potential in adapting the "New Trend" of rather intelligent entertainment, unexpected twists, and ironic humor for his short title stories and graphic adaptations of popular American science-fiction writers such as Ray Bradbury, Charles Beaumont, or Richard Matheson.

What came to be known as the "New Trend" is referred to as the golden era of EC Comics between 1950 and 1955 when their creators were experimenting with new styles and concepts. Comic scholar Qiana Whitted tells in her 2019 EC Comics study *Race, Shock, and Social Protest* how EC's compliance with the New Trend also led to the invention of a new trend in the comic genre: EC comics coined the so-called "preachies,"[22] i. e. "socially conscious stories that boldly challenged the conservatism and conformity of Eisenhower-era America" (2019: 4). EC Comics brought together current issues of the time such as civil rights struggles and anti-Semitism with EC's frequently offensive horror stories. In other words, the comics included stories with "some sort of plea to improve our social standards" (Feldstein qtd. in Whitted 2019: 3–4). On the science-fiction newsfeed SyFy Wire, journalist Sara Century points out: "In retrospect, these stories are considered classics but, while they were popular in their time, the '50s was a strange time for America

21 For more information, see "Screen Rant"'s "15 Dark Facts About THE SIMPSONS TREEHOUSE OF HORROR" posted on *YouTube.com*, undated under URL: https://www.youtube.com/watch?v=ULt7BJPL7pw.
22 Whitted quotes from an interview with EC Comics' former lead editor and writer Al Feldstein who explained that in the postwar era, they did "a little proselytizing in terms of social conscience," and annotates that the "'preachy' stories" had been their own invention (Feldstein qtd. in Whitted 2019: 3).

[…] the crackdown on 'subversives' covered most mediums of art, and EC Comics became a target for censors." (2008)[23] In the *Time* article "The Glory and Horror of EC Comics," journalist Richard Corliss confirms that the horror-comic industry was shut down by state committees and moral lawmakers (cf. 2004). Still under the influence of Eisenhower's Cold-War politics, the authorities enforced an interdiction of graphic violence in comics and censored trigger terms such as "terror" and "horror" (cf. Corliss 2004) as well as covers which featured dismembered women and bloody axes. Fans relished the new blend of horror, science fiction, and fantasy with moral tales which only ten years later led to the trend of experimenting with genre in other media, too, especially pronounced in the television formula of Rod Serling's supernatural anthology series.

Treehouse of Horror: Anthology Structure & Portmanteau Films

In television's formative period of the 1950s, the anthology format was a way of popularizing visual equivalents to the radio play on TV-network broadcasting. The self-contained storytelling aesthetic was well received by creators and consumers of radio plays and later on also of television-drama series. Accordingly, the 25th 'thing' which the comedy writers Goertz and Prescott list in their *100 Things* book (2018) is Treehouse's portmanteau structure. Goertz and Prescott write that the anthology style was popularized by portmanteau films in the late 1960s and 1970s, for example, by Amicus productions such as The House That Dripped Blood (1971) or the Tales from the Crypt anthology film by director Freddie Francis (1972) and its far more popular half-hour TV adaptation by HBO I've mentioned before. In linguistics, 'portmanteau' refers to a blending or contamination of parts of words to create a new word (smoke + fog = smog), in film studies it means the blending of genres. Goertz and Prescott suggest that the idea to use the anthology structure as a framing for its scary horror stories is based on the portmanteau aesthetic in order to create "one cohesive piece of art" (Goertz/Prescott 2018: 67–68). Along this line of thought, Treehouse of Horror blended the subversive aesthetics of EC's comic illustrations with the narrative structure of television's most popular programs to create a new home on primetime TV for these blended practices.[24]

---

23 For more information, see Sara Century's article "The Strange History of Anthology Horror" on *SyFy Wire.com*, posted under URL: https://www.syfy.com/syfywire/the-strange-history-of-anthology-horror.

24 Nowadays there exist many so-called 'seasonal anthology series.' They are, for instance, organized as series with eight to ten episodes arranged as self-contained seasons with different themes of a popular mythology. In case of the horror anthology American Horror Story (FX 2011-present) the popular mythology is subject to change while the cast remains the same. Each of the nine seasons of American Horror Story to date is part of a different popular my-

I have already mentioned that anthologies are self-contained narratives which, while favoring serious content, are not bound to a serial continuity. In television history, anthology series have always been an experimental terrain on which new ideas and concepts could be tested. They meant a low risk for networks and producers because without continuity a rather poor episode could easily be succeeded by a better. Like short-story collections, anthology series are closed stories which are unified under a common subject. Treehouse's three segments are usually bound to three different genre anchors: horror, science fiction, and fantasy. Apart from having the same length (the running time for most of these programs is limited to half an hour), episodes in anthology series nevertheless share an overall thematic thread in order to be generically pigeonholed in a, as Rod Serling suggested, "popular mythology" of science fiction, horror, or fantasy (qtd. in Hill 114). The stories are then subsumed under the popular mythology of 'horror,' as the title Treehouse of Horror indicates.

In contrast to what media historian Eric Barnouw defines as the "formula-bound episodic series," "the anthology series emphasized diversity" (154) and thus meant "carte-blanche invitations to writers" (Barnouw 156). Treehouse of Horror is known for employing a large creative team of writers who pitch ideas, create new designs and material, and match gags anew for each episode. Since the 14th season, each segment has its own director to organize the team of writers (cf. Geortz/Prescott 68). Barnouw goes on to explain: "Although episodic series had come to television from the radio world (and were taken over by film makers) another kind of drama was largely the creation of theater people [...] This was the anthology series." (154) The blending of the different performative environments of radio, theater, film, and television contributed to the emergence of a new, genuine format in 1950s television. Moreover, the television anthology offered jobs to different and changing scriptwriters from diverse creative directions, even from the literary domain.

During the first era of Serling's Twilight Zone on CBS between 1959 and 1964, the grey-flannelled play-wright developed not only his own scripts. In the five seasons, he made ample use of scripts from Charles Beaumont, Richard Matheson,

> thology as expressed in the season's individual title. In 2012, the series premiered with "Murder House"; the second season from 2012 was titled "Asylum," and the fourth season from 2014 is called "Freak Show." The respective title does not only prescribe the central setting in which the seasonal anthology is going to be situated; it also foreshadows that the concept's popular mythology is that of a horror-inspired mystery mash-up. There also exist seasonal anthologies with a different cast but a recurring environment. The Coen Brothers' anthology series Fargo, for example, makes North Dakota's Fargo its background location, but uses different temporal arrangements (i.e. story times) in which different criminal cases take place. Both American Horror Story and Fargo are booming horror-anthology examples which offer viewers a television experience in blockbuster quality. The rise of big-budget anthology dramas on Netflix, HULU, or Amazon Prime Video displaced traditional anthologies on the networks.

or Jerome Bixby, who, at that time, had already been established American horror- and science-fiction authors. Resembling a blank sheet, a script just needed to be filled with content of the writer's choice. Serling's formula found increasingly more support in the 1960s. Accordingly, 1960s television was full of anthology series and Treehouse includes some of them in its stories; Alfred Hitchcock Presents, The Twilight Zone, The Outer Limits, and Night Gallery were inspiring sources for some of its most frightening stories.

Although the decline of classic network-anthology series like The Twilight Zone already began in the 1970s and can be attributed to the rising popularity of cinema, Treehouse sticks to its anthology structure. The Halloween show holds on to the popular mythology as envisioned by those who translated the American horror genre into tales for a larger audience. Accordingly, Treehouse of Horror offers "carte blanche" to scriptwriters and animators, blends an often cinephile experience with television's short narratives, and adheres to its creative diversity of including funny and serious content in order to stay the "cohesive piece of art" that Goertz and Prescott see in it.

In an interview with the Deutschlandfunk, the German seriality scholar Andreas Jahn-Sudmann points out that the anthology format's attraction lies in its capability to permanently reinvent itself (qtd. in Efert 2014, my transl.).[25] As will be shown in the following subchapter, Treehouse's ability to reinvent itself is based on the inventiveness and experimental spirit of the horror genre's former master minds. Fans constantly are invited to watch out for their traces in the Treehouse of Horror archive.

From Radio to Comics to TV to Cinema:
Adaptation & Genre Mixing in Treehouse of Horror

The show's narrative structure and its intrepid use of parody are based on the practice of adaptation and the mixing or layering of genres. What was considered too gory for comics and their readers in the 1950s was welcome to The Simpsons' cartoon horror in the early 1990s. Treehouse's adaptation practice transforms texts from different media and genres to fit its own cartoon genre. The Simpsons' former show runner David Silverman assesses that because the language of Treehouse of Horror builds on the principles of parody, the audience will find it hard to understand but "they'll feel it" as Silverman is quoted to say in Horner (2018). In the following paragraphs, I aim to discuss the adaptation practices of

---

[25] "Diese Möglichkeit komplett, sich neu zu erfinden, darin liegt meines Erachtens der Reiz des Anthologieformats." Andreas Jahn-Sudmann qtd. in Efert, Hendrik. "Serien-Anthologie: Neueinstieg ohne Vorkenntnisse," *Deutschlandfunk Nova.de*, 24 Mar. 2014. Accessed on 18 Sept. 2019 under URL: https://www.deutschlandfunknova.de/beitrag/serien-anthologie-tv-erfolg-trotz-wechselnden-schauspieler-und-orte.

the TREEHOUSE formula which critics mainly see as being defined by the mode of parody. I will show that in the context of THE SIMPSONS' Halloween Special, parody, i.e. the referencing of other texts, is not used to make fun of a forerunner, but to direct the audience's attention to its importance for the genre of American horror – a technique I will continue to explore in the following four subchapters.

Adapting written stories to stage plays, translating historical texts into visual form, devising film versions of novels are long-standing practices which have become central to digital culture. In *A Theory of Adaptation* (2006), Linda Hutcheon captures the pleasure and appeal of adaptation as a popular global phenomenon by suggesting: "Adaptation has run amok" (xi). Cultural-studies scholars Siobhan O'Flynn and Linda Hutcheon regret that there are still critical voices that reduce adaptation to a "lesser, more simplistic mode of reworking content" (O'Flynn/Hutcheon 2006: xxvii). Especially TREEHOUSE OF HORROR's persistent referencing of other texts and media has often been read as a commercial trend of pastiche production or a simple postmodern fashion of citation. O'Flynn and Hutcheon criticize that adaptation and parody were long understood as a "commoditization and commercialization of franchise storytelling" (2006: xxvii). Adaptations used to be seen as "derivatives" that reduce a story to the status of a 'copy' and to "secondary productions," narratives of second degree (2006: 3). But how does TREEHOUSE OF HORROR make use of adaptation and genre mixing?

According to film semiotician Christian Metz, cinema "tells us continuous stories; it 'says' things that could be conveyed also in the language of words; yet it says them differently" (1974: 44). The same can be said for the medium of animation which makes visual reference to the use of other texts in order to, as O'Flynn and Hutcheon suggested for parody, "actualize or concretize their ideas" (O'Flynn/Hutcheon 2006: 3). TREEHOUSE OF HORROR is widely labeled as cartoon parody. But the show is frequently also a cartoon adaptation of stories "which are taken from elsewhere, not invented anew" (*ibid.*: 3).

It is clear that for a TREEHOUSE segment such as "The Shinning" from 1995, the segment's writers have to make "simplifying selections" when reducing a 140-minute feature film like Kubrick's THE SHINING to an animated three-to-five minutes TREEHOUSE story. But critics tend to overlook that the director of "The Shinning," David Mirkin, "makes analogies to show respect" both to Stanley Kubrick's feature film and to the underlying novel's writer, Stephen King.[26] As I see it, David Mirkin takes it even one step further and references King's well-known reluctance towards the medium of television (the author frequently talked about in the 1980s) by satirizing it in Homer's rampage being soothed by a portable

---

26 That being said, Siobhan O'Flynn and Linda Hutcheon refer to the appreciative, investigative rather than the degrading, ridiculing function of parodic adaptation as a form of re-membering the past. For more information, read *A Theory of Adaptation* from 2006, here on page 3.

TV. "The Shinning" is emblematic to how Treehouse makes use of adaptation practices not simply to parody, but also to raise an awareness for the fact that its adapted sources are in themselves already adapted from other sources as is the case with Kubrick's film adaptation of King's eponymous novel.

This strategy has a long tradition. In his 2004 monograph *The Horror Film*, Peter Hutchings wonders: "Given that horror production in the genre's initial formative period during the 1930s was based almost entirely in the United States, it is striking that the work of American Gothic writers did not feature at all in 1930s American horror films" (2004: 11). In the year 1931, the first filmic examples of the American horror genre were released in U.S.-American cinemas. Dracula and Frankenstein are based on the European Gothic rather than on Gothic texts by American writers because Bram Stoker's and Mary Shelley's novels were already adapted for the stage. It is interesting to observe that the Treehouse episodes mostly deal with visually adapted, Americanized interpretations of previously written content. But in 1931, the global medium of film gave audiences the world over their first version of vampire and monster prototypes. The Simpsons' creators are, however, not only interested in the visual prototype, they also look back to the original literary sources behind the previous Americanized versions. That's why I will thoroughly analyze Treehouse of Horror's horror-movie-adaptation strategy to layer rather than blend previous material in chapter 3.4.

The show partly owes its success to the practice of reducing live-action genre masterpieces to their constituent parts and translating them into Treehouse segments that combine scary tales with the aesthetic sensibilities of animation and witty humor. Treehouse of Horror makes use of the huge visual repertoire from other homages and adaptations to shed a critical light on, for example, how a specific cinematic iconography such as that of Boris Karloff's Frankenstein monster serves as the pattern for our imagination and memory throughout visual media history.[27] O'Flynn and Hutcheon write: "Like parodies, adaptations have an overt and defining relationship to prior texts, usually revealingly called 'sources.'

---

27 In the context of adaptation practices and integrity, James Whale's Frankenstein meant a radical shift away from the source novel. It transformed the monster from a well-spoken, sensitive, and murdering monster to a near-mute animal killer. Mary Shelley's novel described the creature as an eight-foot tall and hideously ugly, but sensitive and emotional being. Universal's hideous monster exhibits a certain outlandishness and non-American foreignness in order to distance the excited audience from the film's terror. Since it was law in the 1930s that nefarious characters had to be destroyed in the end, director James Whale decided to change the outcome and make the angry mob of concerned villagers burn down the old mill containing Frankenstein's laboratory which buries the creature under its ruins. Although the filmic creature threatened current morality concepts when it killed a little girl simply because it did not know any better, the monster became the star that led America into a golden age of horror films. The film's make-up artist, Jack P. Peirce, created a film icon when he turned Boris Karloff into the tall and slightly greenish creature with its edgy head and screws in its neck which everybody familiar with Western popular culture knows.

Unlike parodies, however, adaptations usually openly announce this relationship" (2006: 3). Hutcheon revisits the significance of adaptations for the digital age by claiming that today's adaptations announce themselves as "deliberate, announced, and extended revisitations of prior texts" because they are "acknowledged transpositions of a recognizable other work", a "creative and an interpretive act of appropriation/salvaging" as well as an "extended engagement with an adapted work" in which "strong parodic elements may be present" (*ibid.*: xiv, 6). She argues that the relationship of the adapted text to the 'original' should be described as a recasting, a transformation, a remediation or a rewriting that has interpretive, intertextual, and palimpsestic aspects (cf. 2006: 8–9). Seen within a historical framework, Hutcheon and O'Flynn argue, the intertextuality of texts poses a challenge "to dominant post-Romantic notions of originality, uniqueness, and autonomy" in favor of an "ongoing dialogic process" (2006: 21).

TREEHOUSE OF HORROR accepts this challenge for instance in "The Raven" segment from 1990. This segment both calls attention to how contemporary American pop culture continues the "ongoing dialogic process" of adapting Poe's stories and accommodates strong parodic and interpretive elements. Lisa, for example, mentions the relationship to the original source when she introduces Poe's poem and informs Bart that he is about to hear a "classic tale of terror." In turn, Bart's character transforms into an irreverent Raven figure who drives Homer, the personification of the 'nameless narrator,' into madness; both can be described as a "recasting, a transformation, a remediation" of the original figures. The narrative poem is adapted in its entirety, so its background images also take on parodic, interpretive, and intertextual functions. By way of these elements the segment asserts its relationship to the prior source both aurally and visually. The sound design of "The Raven" bursts with Halloween spirit with its score, voice-over, and concomitant sounds. A Gothic-style organ and a sinister voice-over establish the mood, followed by a spherical violin and harp sounds. Genre-typical elements of spooky creaking, eerie tapping, and alarming knocking underline the segment's dark atmosphere. Visually, the scene opens towards a meta-referential parody and shows a bookshelf with multiple titles by Poe such as *The Tell-Tale Heart*, *The Pit and the Pendulum*, and *The Purloined Letter*, all of which were written before *The Raven* was published in 1845. As a visual joke not interrupting the retelling of Poe's source text, Bart, the Raven, pulls the books out of the shelf to drop them on Homer's head which encourages Homer to throttle Bart for his disrespect, a running gag which viewers know from THE SIMPSONS.

TREEHOUSE's "The Raven" is one of the most complex segments of the entire cycle. Due to its complexity that ranges between adaptation and parody, "The Raven" has found its way into my analysis at various points of this project but receives detailed attention in my investigation of the show's literary parodies in chapter 3.3. But at this point I am trying to illustrate with the 'parodic adaptation' of Poe's classic Gothic text and of Kubrick's adaptation of THE SHINING that TREEHOUSE, as Metz suggested, "tells us continuous stories," which "are taken from elsewhere," "yet it says them differently" (1974: 44). Sometimes the references are obvious, while at other times the sheer density of popular-culture layers may not only challenge "post-Romantic notions of originality," but also the audience's media literacy. In the digital age, these moments function as simulations; they demonstrate the significance and proliferation of adaptation practices in Postmodernism.

To draw a line between adaptation and parody in TREEHOUSE OF HORROR is often impossible. I will show how the Halloween Special parodies texts and operates with adaptation to show its "overt and defining relationship to prior texts" (O'Flynn/Hutcheon 2006: 3). In the digital age, adaptations rarely stay within one genre or medium. After my discussion of how TREEHOUSE deals with adaptation, I will next discuss another aspect Jason Mittell used to define by way of genre-mixing, a technique with high prominence in TREEHOUSE OF HORROR's adaptations and parodies. The Halloween Special not merely 'steals' from the visual repertoire of popular media; the show also consolidates various genres under one TREEHOUSE roof.

The blending or mixing of genres has always played a major role in the creation of innovative television programs. THE SIMPSONS' predecessor THE FLINTSTONES had proven that a sitcom could be transposed into a cartoon. TREEHOUSE OF HORROR showed that cinematic horror and the literary Gothic could be transformed into an animated anthology program. In his book *Genre and Television*, television expert Mittell suggests: "One key effect of THE SIMPSONS' use of generic blending was to broaden its target audience" (2004: 185). The TV industry, writes Mittell, defines genres according to an assumed audience segment (cf. 2004: 185) and sure enough, both THE SIMPSONS and its Halloween special explicitly link genres and target audiences. Whereas sitcom viewers have commonly been defined as a mass audience and the domestic sitcom addresses the whole family, TREEHOUSE OF HORROR rather appeals to genre enthusiasts and horror aficionados and potentially reaches out to wider demographics. But how does the show accomplish this?

Mittell argues that there exists a commonplace but erroneous assumption that generic practices are dependent on distinct, singular categories (cf. 2004: 153). But, he goes on to say, "[g]enre analysis must be able to account for the common practice of mixing genres, to be broadly applicable to how genres operate in television today." (2004: 153) For Mittell, genre mixing indicates the ongoing dialogic process of generic combination and interplay in contemporary culture. According to him, parody has often been characterized by postmodern theory as a denigrating mockery of a referenced genre and as a signal that the genre was on its decline (cf. 2004: 159). In opposition to this opinion, Mittell suggests not to think of genres as having "distinct boundaries," but to imagine them with "permeable borders" which parody pervades or even transgresses without causing generic dissolution (cf. *ibid.*: 154). Read in such a way, the adaptations and parodies in TREEHOUSE OF HORROR take up a conversation with different genres as cultural categories. TREEHOUSE's cartoon-horror archive can show how related genres operate because "generic boundaries are permeable, fluid, historically contingent, and subject to change, while still offering categorical coherence at any given moment" (*ibid.*: 154).

TREEHOUSE OF HORROR is a comprehensive guide to what Mittell in the same text terms "generic mixology" (154). By following this guide, we learn how parody and genre fusion go hand in hand. The eleventh Halloween Special's opening parody of THE MUNSTERS (2000), for example, shows the Simpsons as black-and-white versions of the classic Munster family from CBS's 1960s afternoon programming and adds a cartoon layer to sitcom and horror. Another telling example is the ToH IX segment "The Terror of Tiny Toon" (1998). Here, Hanna-Barbera's cat-and-mouse aesthetics are used as a palimpsest layer to expose THE SIMPSONS' technique of cartoon realism; but then, the divergent worlds are blended into one in order to eventually "bring generic practices to the surface," says Mittell (2004: 157). It is important to remember that here 'blending' does not mean that one source is superimposed on the other so it extinguishes the older one, but that the older level stays recognizable.

The blending/layering of the genres horror and animation has led to an entirely new genre mix. SIMPSONS' critic Al Horner points out: "The way TREEHOUSE abandoned the rules, logic and style that normally governed over Springfield allowed the show to lay references on even thicker and faster than usual, occasionally getting impressively obscure with these nods" (2018). Already the title of my last example, "The Terror of Tiny Toon," is a word play that obscures its intertextual references, leading to the expectation of a parody on Warner Brothers' LOONEY TUNES with Bugs Bunny and Daffy Duck. On the contrary the segment adapts TOM & JERRY, the Hanna-Barbera show which serves as an inspirational source of THE ITCHY & SCRATCHY SHOW, the cartoon-in-cartoon of the regular SIMPSONS series. The course of events demonstrates a layering of different cartoon traditions exposing the mixing of styles and making it explicit: "The conventions and assumptions [are] clustered within individual categories through the juxtaposition of conflicting genres," as Mittell puts it (2004: 154). While the Warner Brothers' LOONEY TUNES and Hanna-Barbera's TOM & JERRY both employ exaggerated forms of violence (remember the double-X-eyes marking dead characters I mentioned earlier) which can exclusively coexist in THE ITCHY & SCRATCHY SHOW, THE SIMPSONS' aesthetic sensibility is "conflicting" because it is generally committed to a form of cartoon realism. According to Mittell, "genre parodies rely upon and activate generic definitions, interpretations, and evaluations much more explicitly than 'pure' cases of the genre being lampooned" (*ibid.*: 159).

Following the insights of Jason Mittell in his text "The Politics of Parody," TREEHOUSE OF HORROR cannot simply be attributed to the horror genre. The show rather is a site of generic operations that takes genres seriously and makes diverse horror categories explicit and culturally active (cf. Mittell 159). Accordingly, the blending or rather layering of horror and animation looks back on a long tradition of anthology film- and television productions. Because when the film industry continued to breathe life into the EC-Comics tradition, they also served as the predecessor for TREEHOUSE OF HORROR's genre mixology.

How, then, are parody and comedy related? Historically, parody enabled comedy to absorb material from a diversity of different forms and repurpose it in various ways. In other words, parody operates as a comedic mode that reminds audiences of a prior text's success. In cooperation with the horror genre, however, parody has a brightening effect – it offers viewers the exit of comic relief. Both ways proved popular in the portmanteau horror films of the 1960s and 1970s.

Between 1962 and 1977, the British Amicus Production company was famous for its film adaptations of a series of EC Comics such as THE HOUSE THAT DRIPPED BLOOD (1971), TALES FROM THE CRYPT (1972), and VAULT OF HORROR (1973). Although online-journalist Sara Century writes on the website SyFy Wire (2018) that what seemed far too gory for comics in the 1950s was welcome in movies of the early 1970s, when strong parodic aspects were either used for intertextual revisitation or served as comic relief (cf. Century 2018).

These 'portmanteau films' featured four to five different horror shorts and starred a whole range of notable movie actors such as Joan Collins, Christopher Lee, or Peter Cushing who played the villainous evildoers. In the Amicus films, the Gothic castles and sinister noblemen of earlier times were replaced by contemporary middle-class ordinariness revolving around present-day settings of common homes with normal families. THE VAULT OF HORROR film episodes, for example, make use of dissociating shock elements a mainstream audience wasn't used to yet.[28] THE NEAT JOB (UK 1973) shows how the abusive character Arthur

---

28 Stylistic influence on the British portmanteau films by Amicus can be seen in the Italian Giallo films by auteur Mario Bava which had their heyday in the 1960s and 1970s. The Giallo creates a subgenre to the thriller genre. Films like SEI DONNE PER L'ASSASSINO / BLOOD AND BLACK LACE (1964) by Bava and Argento's L'UCCELLO DALE PIUME DI CRISTALLO / THE BIRD WITH THE CRYSTAL PLUMAGE (1970) established a remarkably brutal staging of murders as well as other motifs (psychosexual serial murders, phallic murder weapons of knives or axes and fetishistic objects such as black leather gloves) and characteristic aesthetic cinematography which served not only various other filmmakers for their creative output (e.g. Dario Argento, Lucio Fulci), but can also be viewed as paving the way for the Slasher horror film of the 1980s. For more insights into the Giallo genre, see Michael Flintrop and Marcus Stiglegger's *Dario Argento: Anatomie der Angst* from 2013, Peter Scheinpflug's *Formelkino: Medienwissenschaftliche Perspektiven auf Genre Theorie und den Giallo* from 2014, and Alexia Kannas' recent publication *Giallo!: Genre, Modernity, and Detection in Italian Horror Cinema* from 2020.

Critchit is overpowered with a hammer in the laundry room of his home that remains stuck in the frontal cortex of his head. Although viewers are confronted with graphic violence in the first place, acting, cinematography, and the irony behind the phallic murder weapon of the hammer introduce a brutality including an element of comic relief and often unintentional humor; an element which TREEHOUSE makes conscious use of when the graphic gore tends to abound, e.g. in "The Shinning" or "Nightmare Cafeteria." Moments of comic relief are commonly featured in THE HOUSE THAT DRIPPED BLOOD and VAULT OF HORROR when the respective evildoers are punished in such a kinky way critics started to describe close to the Italian Giallo genre. In their revisitations, Amicus films adopted the brutal imagery of the Giallo from Mario Bava or Dario Argento and mixed it with the grotesque comicality of EC Comics to brighten the portrayed terror underneath the surface of ordinariness. The producers recognized that the mixing of horror and comedy appealed to larger audience segments. Amicus Productions and American International Pictures (AIP) as well as the British Hammer Studios were production companies which began to enhance their eerie Gothic and horror scenarios with a considerable amount of grotesque imagery and exaggerated violence that complemented Peter Cushing's or Christopher Lee's performances with irony and gross humor as is the case in the films THE HOUSE THAT BLED TO DEATH (1980) and MADHOUSE (1974). In a 2012 interview with the *L.A. Times*, Matt Groening remarked that "in animation you create your own universe" where the limits of reality "can be improbable but not physically impossible" because, he concludes, "[t]here's got to be blood" (qtd. in Lloyd 2012). After thirty years of TREEHOUSE OF HORROR, the series' universe keeps growing.

The show's generic mixing of live-action horror and animated cartoon as well as the 'cart blanche' offered to artists to create their own universe has always guaranteed unique horror-related themes reflecting the zeitgeist, socio-political subtexts, and inner workings of American society. EC-Comics scholar Sara Century observes that horror anthologies continued to thrive in other media which took the layout of EC Comics and Amicus's film adaptations to new directions (cf. 2018). And, Century argues, "[i]n all their many forms, a shared element across the board of horror anthologies is their political commentary" (2018). TREEHOUSE OF HORROR's genre-mixing parodies are so popular because the show is also "able to push relevant subject matter while delivering scares" (Century 2018). Following Jason Mittell's line of argument, THE SIMPSONS' denigration as 'just a cartoon' is further problematized by TREEHOUSE OF HORROR's horror and its claim to incorporate all kinds of different genre texts into an anthology program.

As a site of generic operation, TREEHOUSE's horror-anthology archive abandoned the rules, logic, and style of a single genre like the conventional sitcom and favored an innovative form of instructive genre parody on prime-time TV by means of adaptation. In my discussion of how TREEHOUSE OF HORROR became an early exemplar of what Jason Mittell later called television's complex storytelling, I will offer analyses of the sources which TREEHOUSE layers, transposes, blends, and references to revisit the cultural history of the horror genre in the digital age. Inspired by Mittell, I intended to demonstrate that TREEHOUSE's adapted archive does not suggest "the declining importance of genres" (2004: 195). Rather I favor Mittell's idea to read TREEHOUSE as a show which puts emphasis on genres as cultural categories and on the role they play within larger historical contexts (cf. 2004: 195).

What We've Learned So Far...

In this analytical introduction I was concerned with the question how TREEHOUSE OF HORROR fulfills Matt Selman's notion that "we are living in a simulation." I revisited the various sources which make up the building blocks of the Halloween series including aspects from different broadcasting traditions, the salvaging of other media such as the illustrated comic, and the repurposing of parody as a means to remember historically relevant texts and genres.

TREEHOUSE was, even in 1990s' terms, an experiment that added another dimension to the New Trend of EC Comics and Rod Serling's TV anthologies. Therefore it is not surprising that the creators initially worried about the audience's response. In order not to face the same censorship consequences as the EC Comics company had in the mid-1950s, the special's writers had Marge break the fourth wall to warn parents against problematic content. In this early stage of TREEHOUSE production, the creators made Marge appear two more times, in an upfront disclaimer of ToH II and ToH V because they feared otherwise concerned parents would write them angry letters instead of sending their kids to bed (cf. Marge's prologue in ToH I).

The 'trigger warnings' between 1990 and 1994 were born of insecurity about the reactions of the show's large audience of children to the disturbing moments of, for example, bleeding walls in "Bad Dream House" or Zombies and cannibalistic teachers at Springfield Elementary in "Nightmare Cafeteria" (cf. 2nd-5th season's DVD audio commentary). The disclaimers were later taken off the show, not only to increase air time, but also because the producers felt they were not taken seriously. The message was clear: The Simpsons had left their sitcom home, climbed up the ladder to the 'treehouse,' left behind Saturday-morning cartoons to conquer primetime programming to (re-)define the domain of adult animation television. The show runners revived the trigger warning in the 28th TREEHOUSE edition (Fox 2017), but only to have Lisa warn the audience of the disturbing quality of the segment "Mmm Homer" that shows Homer cannibalizing himself (cf. chapter 3.4). The comeback of the disclaimer might evidence that the times have definitely changed. Lisa's warning demonstrates that horror anthologies have gradually become more graphic. Especially the television medium is longing for more intense tales and graphic styles which follow the demands of contemporary audiences and commercial imperatives. The industry's conditions and the audience's viewing habits have changed since 1930s Hollywood horror, 1950s horror comics, and their 1960s TV- and 1970s film adaptations. Horror's current boom seems the right moment to test new directions of horror storytelling.

In the next chapter, I will analyze exemplary scenes from TREEHOUSE OF HORROR in order to come closer to an answer to the question: What can TREEHOUSE's simulation of former styles teach us about America's media culture and genre history, about its techniques of genre mixing, parody, and adaptations? I will inquire in detail how TREEHOUSE has taught us lessons by which to remember American popular culture.

17 The famous Simpsons' couch marks the show's center of convergence culture

History Lesson No. 1 | Animation Auteurs and Auteur Television: Analyzing THE SIMPSONS' Couch Gag as Means of Participatory Culture

After the clouds reveal the familiar yellow logo "The Simpsons" and the camera zooms in on Springfield's different locations, the show's main characters are introduced during their everyday routines in school, at band practice, at work, and at the supermarket. The opening to almost every episode leads our attention to where the Simpson family ultimately comes together, hastily gathering in their living room on Evergreen Terrace to meet on their famous brown couch in front of the TV set (see Fig. 17).

It is debatable whether THE SIMPSONS' opening sequence and familiar theme tune introduce the episode or should rather be seen as a lead-in to the 'couch gag' which has received much more attention by itself than the whole of THE SIMPSONS' opening. In recent years, the Simpsons present to viewers ever new versions of quirky and abnormal worlds in transition to THE SIMPSONS' conventional family reality. The comediennes and devoted SIMPSONS fans Allie Goertz and Julia Prescott explain: "[…] similar to THE SIMPSONS opening chalkboard gag, the couch gag would become its own means of artistic expression for the show's creators" (2018: 33).

The couch in the gag refers to a piece of furniture which has become a cultural icon. In the "encyclopedia of the people" *American Icons*, cultural-studies critic Dennis Hall writes: "[N]o other cultural sign so efficiently communicates the concept of 'family' as does the couch as the sets of television soap operas and sitcoms demonstrate." (2006: 161) In American popular-culture production, the couch is an ubiquitous motif that throughout the decades maintained its centrality to the life of the Brady family in THE BRADY BUNCH (ABC 1969–1974), the Bundys in MARRIED… WITH CHILDREN (Fox 1987–1997) or the Cosbys in COSBY SHOW (NBC 1984–1992). In THE SIMPSONS, however, the couch gag unexceptionally opens with an exception, a variation on the sitcom motif of familiar lead-in uniformity.

The authors suggest that each couch gag is different and detached from the episode. The opening couch often functions as what Goertz and Prescott describe as a "signature meta-commentary" (2018: 33) when the Simpsons have trans- or intermedial encounters with other famous popular-culture families such as the Flintstones, film icons such as Freddy Krueger, or cartoon duos such as Rick and Morty (from the show of the same name on Adult Swim, since 2013) who crash into their living room with their flying saucer. As the series evolved over the decades, the couch gag has become its own experimental media space in which different kinds of animation techniques can be tested. Here, readers may feel reminded of ROBOT CHICKEN's stop-motion clay animation (Adult Swim, since 2005) or SOUTH PARK's paper cut-out cartoon aesthetic (Comedy Central, since 1997); the mixing of different animation styles need to be read as a form of meta-referential homage, by which THE SIMPSONS' creators express their appreciation of the art of animation.

First in the 2000s, THE SIMPSONS' producers began to open the couch gag to guest animators who contributed their individualistic cartoon art, transforming the Simpson family to their own interpretation. The following chapter will be concerned with how the variation of the couch gag has been realized by what I define as the 'animation auteur.' Since the couch gag has always been a site of exception to the television norm and invites guest animators ranging from A-level artists to fans, I contend that THE SIMPSONS is a unique form of auteur television. More precisely, the animation auteur adds a new dimension to the often problematically discussed notion of the "auteur," who usually is a film artist with a central position within a collaborative production and who is at once author (transl. from French 'auteur'), 'composer', and 'interpreter'. In recent years, the comically framed art as showcased in the opening sequence has perpetually confirmed my wish to analyze the concept of the animation auteur through the couch gag in particular. Goertz and Prescott ascertain that the couch gag's transition from a simple visual joke across absurdist gag to sometimes highly complex short films indicates that THE SIMPSONS has reinvented the TV show opening as an experimental genre standing by itself. I would even go so far as to claim that the couch gag exhibits THE SIMPSONS' singularity through the show's collaboration with its contemporaries.

As a symbol of both media production as well as consumption on the one hand and domestic togetherness[29] on the other, the couch turned the pre-episodic opening into a site and symbol of participatory culture. My first subchapter will try to

---

29 In *'THE SIMPSONS': A Cultural History*, author Dennis Fink examines the different locations in Springfield. He conceives of the couch in THE SIMPSONS as representing "the furniture's actual function in late twentieth-century Western culture as a place that invites people to collectively watch television" (95).

reconcile the two paradoxical concepts of the exclusive auteur, who has major subjective control over the creative production, and the more inclusive approach of participatory culture that considers the consumer as an actively engaged agent who is invited to participate in the creative process. I will begin with the auteur.

Television: A Producer's Medium

In the golden age of the Hollywood studio system – i. e. an oligopolistic production economy which had its heyday between the 1920s and 1950s – film was a producer's medium. So did it happen that more and more filmmakers, but also cinematographers, script writers, and editors sought for a greater independence from Hollywood's studio system to have more creative control in the realization of their art.

Theories concerning the cinema auteur emerged in the late 1940s when the French art-film movement of the Nouvelle Vague was still embryonic. Influenced by the bohemian filmmakers Jean-Luc Godard and Claude Chabrol, the French film critic Alexandre Astruc coined the term in his famous article "La camérastylo" (Engl. 'camera stick') to distinguish a film's artistic visionary 'brainware' from the film as a producers' medium and commercial product. Beyond the intellectual environment of mid-century French film critics who wrote for the renowned film magazine *Cahièrs du Cinéma* – among them Alxandre Astruc, André Bazin, and François Truffaut – the auteur determinant consequently extended its vision. In his polemic article "A Certain Tendency of French Cinema" (orig. *"Une certain tendance du cinema français"*), published in *Cahièrs* in 1954, the filmmaker and critic Truffaut emphasized the meaning of the director as the actual creator, the true author, in French translation 'auteur,' of a film. He saw that directors such as Alfred Hitchcock, Howard Hawks, or Fritz Lang remained stylistically independent, although they contractually adhered to the commercial treadmill of Hollywood's studio system with its oligopolistic economy that reached far into the 1950s.

Animation scholar Paul Wells remarks: "An auteurist director was recognized as having a unique signatory imprimatur across a canon of work, that marked out an aesthetic and thematic terrain, and offered a coherent view of the discourses fundamental to its understanding and 'art'." (72) Even under the strict conditions of the classical Hollywood era, filmmakers like Howard Hawks, who worked in virtually every conceivable American genre, the Austrian Fritz Lang, whose films are known for their outright expressionist realism, or the inventor of the suspense thriller, Alfred Hitchcock, all had the 'unique imprimatur' that made their films into outstanding examples of stylistic coherence.

Film historian William D. Routt (1990) defined imprimatur as "auteurprints," i. e. as directors' personal stylistic signatures, the distinct artistic diction by which they created new genres (qtd. in Nelmes 150). Routt pushed this notion even further when he suggested that these auteurs embodied the shaping power of an individual auteur sensibility in popular art because he believed that "auteurism was, indeed, a way of looking rather than a theory of any kind" (Routt 1992, qtd. in Ritzer 311). French Nouvelle Vague filmmakers and critics laid the foundation for the auteur's propositional 'way of looking,' which positioned the director as a film's central creative force. Film historian Jill Nelmes concludes: "In this way, then, auteurism's first provocative move was to locate the author and creative center of a film not as its writer (auteur translates as 'author') but as its director insofar as it is the director who orchestrates the visual aspects of cinema" (150). Film critics like Alxandre Astruc, William D. Routt, but also the film semiotician André Bazin focused their attention exclusively on the medium of film; they denied that television as a producer's medium had any auteur qualities. Next I will look at the opportunities producers, creators, and writers working for television may in fact have to develop their own artistic signature of 'auteurprints' and orchestrate the visual aspects in a television series.

The Contemporary Television Auteur

When flicking through TV-series history of the past three or four decades, one finds proof of an equally inventive spirit and artistic independence in the art and development of television series production. Increasingly more cinema auteurs picked up on the trail of alternative mediums and discovered the creative potential in television too. Striking examples that come to mind are Alfred Hitchcock's anthology mystery program ALFRED HITCHCOCK PRESENTS and THE ALFRED HITCHCOCK HOUR of the 1960s or David Lynch's travels in absurdity in the TWIN PEAKS series of the 1990s.[30]

Additionally, recent television drama series have become more and more infused with the creative vision of television auteurs such as MAD MEN's creator Matthew Weiner or BREAKING BAD's Vince Gilligan each of whom combines the roles of writer, director, and producer. The detailed design of the 1950s' urbanite work-life in MAD MEN (AMC 2007–2015) as well as the panoramic vision of BREAKING BAD (AMC 2008–2013) that keeps closing in on itself are examples that indicate how for the first time television's creative minds could realize their individual imprimatur in the construction of the characters and mise-en-scène in recent complex TV.

---

30 On account of Alfred Hitchcock's television career, however, German film scholar Ivo Ritzer explains that such developments are nothing new. It is almost forgotten that the transposition of the cinephile auteur from film to TV was common at the very end of many filmmakers' careers. Alfred Hitchcock, for instance, belongs to the generation of directors who in the 1950s were handed over to U.S.-broadcasters when double features disappeared and B-movie-production units were liquidated (cf. 105).

For a long time, television was unquestionably a product of a corporat industry with producers managing the money and thus having major creative control "over the look and life of a series" (Falero 85). In 1985, media scholars Horace Newcomb and Robert Alley published an entire book on the idea that, in contrast to film, television is *The Producer's Medium*, and not a medium of directors. But recently, the new creative freedom given to the creators of television series caused a shift in the perception of script writers, directors, and, of course, producers.

The three groups of writers, directors, and producers which formerly were thoroughly separated and hierarchically organized were blended into one group, the so-called 'show runners.' The show-runner category has not just replaced hierarchies, but also turned the work of each group into a common, collaborative process. A new form of directing for television was born. The show runner has come to serve as an umbrella category for the all-in-one talent who develops ideas, writes teleplays, and produces as well as directs entire episodes. In an interview with the LATE NIGHT ACTION host Alex Falcone,[31] former SIMPSONS co-show runner Bill Oakley explains that "a show runner is akin to a director of a movie who is also the film's writer and producer. You make every decision about everything" (qtd. in Goertz/Prescott 121).

In this context, the job specification of television as a producer's medium experienced a redefinition when the show runner suddenly became the new shining star on the U.S.-television sky. Matt Groening, Sam Simon, and James L. Brooks are THE SIMPSONS' show runners of the first hour. They were suddenly equipped with as much creative freedom as they wished. They could freely decide what was created by whom, who wrote an episode, and how to direct the voice actors, animators, and sound editors regardless of what the Fox network suggested (cf. Goertz/Prescott 121). This shift gave birth to the new television auteur.

Of course, the concept of the television auteur had found entrance via another field of cinephile television before and had led to an early form of complex-TV series. David Lynch, for example, was far ahead of his time when he made his series TWIN PEAKS that ran on ABC network, but for only two seasons between 1990 and 1991. Film scholar Peter Wollen discussed the filmmaker's artistic integrity in *Signs and Meaning in the Cinema*: "The meaning of the film of an auteur is constructed *a posteriori*; the meaning – semantic, rather than stylistic or expressive – of the films of a *metteur en scène* exists *a priori*." (1972: 78, *ital. in orig.*) This might explain why Lynch's TV-customized auteur techniques of slow-burn and static storytelling rallied a highly selective group of film geeks in front of the TV and received only much later the desired fame of a mainstream audience. However, tel-

---

31 The full episode of the already discontinued live and Portland-focused late night show LATE NIGHT ACTION W/ ALEX FALCONE starring interview guest Bill Oakley can be accessed on Alex Falcone's YouTube channel, posted 05 May 2014 under URL: https://bit.ly/31kJFvO.

evision network's syndication and the shift from broad- to narrowcasting in the digital age of internet-based smart television attracted ever more cine auteurs to TV projects. These show runners helped to reinvent TV and to trigger a new age of continuity storytelling as they started to spend their creative energy on made-for-TV art programs. The fame of established filmmakers such as David Fincher helped to promote a continuity format such as his political drama series HOUSE OF CARDS (2013–2018) or the Coen Brother's serialized film sequel FARGO (2014–2018) addressing new generations of audiences.

During the American Depression and throughout WWII, the audacity of Hollywood film auteurs like Alfred Hitchcock, Howard Hawks, and Fritz Lang had a great influence on the early invention of the writer-director-producer in the U.S.. This kind of artistic will to break fresh ground for mainstream media is already palpable in the auteurprints of Orson Welles' radio adaptations (e.g. WAR OF THE WORLDS) as well as in Rod Serling's television anthology THE TWILIGHT ZONE. Accordingly, the auteur concept should not be limited to the medium of film. I will further demonstrate that THE SIMPSONS' show runners must be seen as animation auteurs since they have established a 'new way of looking' at the visual and narrative aspects of American popular culture.

I already indicated that the French cinema-auteur concept[32] carries the notion of cinephile artistry which is reserved for a highly selective community of free spirits who let their audience catch a glimpse of their way of looking at the world. Since the 1980s such a conservative avant-garde understanding of the television auteur has become central particularly to the perception of television drama as a genre. Media critic Robin Nelson argues:

> In respect of textual production, the distinctive vision of a special individual – a film auteur or playwright – has been seen in critical discourse, as noted, to guarantee authenticity and independence of viewpoint in a liberal romantic tradition that carried over through high modernism into early television.
> *(Nelson qtd. in McCabe/Akass 2007: 40)*

TV researcher Janet McCabe concludes that not only early pioneers such as David Lynch, but also later television auteurs like David Chase, known from HBO's ma-

---

32 It should be noted that the auteur theory has never been a theory at all, but should rather be considered a policy defining the approach of certain film critics who, in recent years, have come to use the label to any director they see fit in. For this reasons it has often been questioned whether directors such as David Lynch or the Peter Greenaway should be defined as auteurs as their material is 'art' and pursue their personal vision without the intention to pander the tastes of the masses. For more discussion, see Robert C. Cumbow's exploration of John Carpenter's auteur in *Order in the Universe* from 2000, pp. 1–6; or take a look at Michelle Le Blanc's & Colin Odell's critical approaches to the auteur concept in *John Carpenter* from 2011, pp. 11–26.

fia drama THE SOPRANOS (1999–2007), or W. G. Walden from NBC's THE WEST WING (1999–2006) can be considered special individuals in the American television business. As TV auteurs who write, direct, and produce, the multitalented Chase and Walden were seen for a long time as a guarantee for, above anything else, profitability through "primetime quality" (cf. 2007: 10). According to McCabe's and Falero's observations, back in the 1980s and 1990s networks often used famous names to establish marketable "brand-new programming" as a brand (cf. Falero 2016: 85). By the end of the 1990s, the new "writer-producer" (Falero 2016: 86) had initialized an era of 'quality television' (see R. J. Thompson 1996, K. Thompson 2003). THE SIMPSONS' early stages as a brand-new program fall into a period when cultural and media studies began to pay serious attention to innovative television texts because of their unusual form, not necessarily because of the fame of their 'authors.'

THE SIMPSONS' Auteurs: Fans, Filmmakers, Freaks

When the central roles in TV production amalgamated as the show runner in the early 2000s, the new form of television storytelling also fed the understanding of what Jason Mittell theorizes as contemporary serial complexity (2006, 2013). As Falero observes, during the 1990s "we start to see an emphasis on particular creators or 'show runners' (formerly called 'producers') as notable and distinctive artists, a kind of 'television auteurs'" (*ibid*.: 85) who provided audiences with ever new serial artworks. As a result, the concept of the auteur has obviously shifted the meaning of authorship to well-known executives who write, direct, and produce all at once.

As the stratospheric popularity of THE SIMPSONS already evidenced in the early 1990s, younger audiences were longing for TV series that carried 'authenticity,' brought innovation, and had an experimental attitude. New generations of viewers is the reason why, in recent years, Netflix and other on-demand streaming services have become so tremendously popular. Only through the cultivation of the "'writer-producer' function," Falero argues, "the critical praises of these television auteurs validated television as an art form and elevated the seriousness with which critics (both popular and academic) approached the medium" (86). His statement is not only relevant for TV drama, but has validity for other areas of television production as well. These areas include weekly sitcoms, daily soaps, and self-contained anthologies which are, of course, continued as well as commercial narratives. Through the commercial looking glass, sitcoms, soaps, and anthology series do not per se qualify as auteur art. Quite the opposite – these formats were traditionally seen as fully commercialized. As branded products, these formats depend on the premises of the American copyright law and traditionally make use of targeted advertising tools such as product placement and pre-edited slots for commercial breaks.

3 Analysis | TREEHOUSE OF HORROR: Lessons to Remember

18-19 Screenshots from the ToH XVIII opening show Marge's reaction to Fox's interventionist marketing

Traditionally, the TV viewer enters into a commercial contract with a program as soon as s/he decides to follow a particular episode. The conditions of the contract are made visible when a disclaimer tells audiences that the following program contains product placement and when the program is interrupted by commercial breaks, or when the screen is split for some program announcement or note from the sponsor.

In the opening to TREEHOUSE OF HORROR XVIII, Marge reacts to such interventionists marketing. By breaking the fourth wall, Marge welcomes the audience to Halloween at the Simpsons in her kitchen, but is constantly being interrupted by inserted pop-up banners of other Fox-related formats such as AMERICAN IDOL (since 2002), DR. HOUSE (2004–2012), and FOOTBALL ON FOX which are not just visible for the viewer, but also part of THE SIMPSONS' intradiegetic world. Marge is so annoyed by the pop-up ads that she puts them all into a meatloaf for dinner that promises to be filling due to the ads' letters (see Fig. 18–19).

The names of famous Hollywood directors operate as a creative force behind auteur television series in quite the same way. Filmmakers such as David Fincher or Joel and Ethan Coen advertise their series – HOUSE OF CARDS or FARGO – as potentially being authentic and valuable.[33] The name of a cine auteur is a marketing tool itself. THE SIMPSONS, however, proved early on that famous names can be commissioned to upstage the commercial interests of a TV series and, at the same

---

33 Similar to the original feature film from 1996, the Netflix series FARGO by the Coen Brothers, for example, prefaces each episode with the text: "This is a true story. The events depicted in this film took place in Minnesota in [the year in which the respective narrative is set]. At the request of the survivors, the names have been changed. Out of respect for the dead, the rest has been told exactly as it occurred." What was so special about this is that the Coen Brothers commented this strategy as a genre technique: "We wanted to make a movie just in the genre of a true story movie […]; you don't have to have a true story to make a true story movie." (Qtd. in Hooton, *The Independent*, 2016) Based on their their intricate aesthetics, Joel and Ethan Coen became acclaimed cine auteurs.

time, foreground the pleasure of creating a unique form of auteur animation. The following analyses of some of the show's most outstanding examples of auteur animation aim to demonstrate that auteurs are not only marketing tools, but that they also refer to themselves as life-long consumers and fans of THE SIMPSONS. Some well-known auteurs have willingly taken a seat on THE SIMPSONS' couch in order to put their own auteurprint into the service of THE SIMPSONS couch gag. In the case of THE SIMPSONS, the medium of animation could evolve into a site of participatory culture.

Media researcher and inventor of the concept 'participatory culture,' Henry Jenkins, argues that participatory culture runs counter the principles of consumer culture in which viewers are seen as passive consumers (cf. 2013: x). When Marge stuffs her meatloaf with TV commercials in the TREEHOUSE couch gag from 2007 (Fig. 16), she testifies to the fact that THE SIMPSONS' show runners address their audience as active readers. Jenkins observed a shift in audience's and academic foci when people became interested in "the complex interactions between fans and production [...] at a time when a logic of 'engagement' shapes many of their policies and promotions" (2013: xxii). Jenkins suggests: "A focus on participation shifts what questions we ask." (*ibid.*: xxii)

Marge's opening example shows how pop-up ads commonly try to lure viewers' attention astray and how we should react. The opening mirrors Jenkins' idea that we can *resist* the commercial imperative of advertisement and *participate in* something. This is how THE SIMPSONS teaches us a more nuanced look at "the social, legal, and economic relationships within which media consumption now occurs" (Jenkins 2013: xxiii). In contemporary participatory culture as imagined by THE SIMPSONS, the television auteur is both consumer and producer and thus can make use of the medium of animation with different effect than traditional producer-directors. The following three analyses open up to three different ways of engaging an auteur. I will examine how the complex interaction between fans and production reveals different nuances of resistance and participation.

In the next section I will parade different artists who contributed as guest-animators to THE SIMPSONS couch gag such as John Kricfalusi, Sylvain Chomet, and Bill Plympton. Furthermore, I will explore THE SIMPSONS' couch gag as a crossover space, so-to-speak, an experimental playground for different adult-animation formats and their heroes to meet and 'mash-up' with the Simpsons. After having reconsidered some notable examples from THE SIMPSONS' guest-animated couch gags and the creative influence on the show by artists from other creative fields, I will continue my couch-gag analysis with the infamous British street artist and urban activist, who is known for hiding his (presumably) identity behind the pseudonym 'Banksy.' Banksy's pre-episodic opening couch gag immediately went viral on the internet because he stylized the Simpsons through the looking glass of a 20th Century Fox sweat shop located in some dystopian Asian country. The short film serves as the basis for thinking about the animation auteur as an agent of resistance and the practice of culture jamming.

My second close reading is dedicated to fan art. I will concentrate on claymation artist Lee Hardcastle and his disturbingly unconventional SIMPSONS' couch gag. It is a stop-motion revisitation of the familiar SIMPSONS couch-gag scenario translated into a home-invasion crime scene like the one in Adam Wingard's horror film YOU'RE NEXT from 2013. Hardcastle's film is a piece of fan art which is available on his YouTube channel. The short film not only credits Hardcastle for being a hard-boiled fan of the exploitation genre and claymated torture porn. The piece of the British artist further illustrates the factors limiting the access to participatory culture; in this it may have struck a wrong note with the SIMPSONS' show runners but also with the viewers' sense of humor. In contrast to this, the pixel artists Paul Robertson and Ivan Dixon exemplify what factors allow access to participatory culture. The two Australians are artists on the internet which provides access to successful fan art as auteur animation.

My third and final example for auteur art will be the opening couch gag of the 2013 TREEHOUSE OF HORROR XXIV created by fantasy-film auteur Guillermo del Toro. The short film that is over three minutes long will be used to illustrate what creative potential cine auteurs see in animation as a means of setting up a popculture archive and, at the same time, a self-referential source of inspiration. It is a commonly known fact that del Toro refers to himself as a big fan of the TREEHOUSE OF HORROR episodes in particular. His couch gag is an outstanding piece of mixed-media art that encouraged the filmmaker to participate in auteur practices by discovering the medium of animation for himself.

Television comedy – just like the genre of comedy in general – has suffered from its low prestige at least since the late 18th century due to what the sociologists Sam Friedman and Giselinde Kuipers call "High Cultural Capital Boundary-Drawing (HCC)" (2013: 183). While popular television comedy was largely ignored and excluded from the academic debate surrounding complex TV, THE SIMPSONS began fashioning their own strategy to reach out to their intended audience instead of attempting to catch the interest of conservative film critics. Reaching out to a potential audience paving the way for what in 2013 Henry Jenkins theorizes as participatory culture. Whereas Sandra Falero sees the auteur as disregarding the "very important element of collaboration" (85), THE SIMPSONS' creators insist from the beginning on a grassroots approach of co-production. Their success proves them right: THE SIMPSONS is one of the longest-running scripted primetime series ever made. Although the collaborative aspect has been discussed in the context of the (re)liability of fan criticism elsewhere, the following analysis will first look at the couch gag as a site of solidarity that encourages the contribution of animation auteurs.

History Lesson No. 1 | Animation Auteurs and Auteur Television:

20-21 The two guest-animated couch gags for THE SIMPSONS (2011) and TREEHOUSE OF HORROR XXVI (2015) by REN & STIMPY artist John Kricfalusi

The 'Real' Animation Auteurs:
Revisiting THE SIMPSONS with Kricfalusi, Chomet, Plympton

The Canadian comic artist John Kricfalusi is credited for the first couch gag in 2011 that was guest-animated by someone who already had made a name for himself as cartoon artist. The quirky and often surreal cartoon adventures of the psychotic Chihuahua Ren and the simpleton cat Stimpy manifest what critics acknowledge as John K.'s memorable retro-style in THE REN & STIMPY SHOW (Nickelodeon 1991–1996). Kricfalusi's couch gag is accompanied by a classical big-band score and depicts the Simpsons as wobbling and pulsating characters (see Fig. 20–21), whose bizarre movements and coloring are accurately orchestrated by the sound technique known as 'Mickey Mousing,' i.e. funny musical elements are edited to the movement or speech of characters.

Shortly after, a whole variety of couch-gag submissions followed both in animation style and content matter.[34] In this regard, THE SIMPSONS' couch gag can

---

34 The list of couch gags reveals that more than twenty openings have been guest-animated by artists-as-fans across the full range of animation art (see App. 6.3). Among them are the Simpsonized versions of the "Plymptoons," i.e. the six contributions by above-mentioned

147

22–23 For a 2018 SIMPSONS' opening, Bill Plympton's visually translated his 1987 Oscar-nominated hand-drawn short film YOUR FACE into "Homer's Face" for which Homer's voice-actor Dan Castellaneta sings a hymn on facial beauty

be subdivided into individual auteur styles with which guest animators transform and reinterpret the Simpson characters. This becomes particularly visible in the distinct couch gags of French comic artist and film director Sylvain Chomet or in those by American indie-cartoon artist Bill Plympton. The auteur couch gags deliberately undercut the usual cartoon realism of THE SIMPSONS' opening by creating highly abstract 'looks' at the Simpsons from other artistic points of view.

Sylvain Chomet's 2014 couch gag,[35] for example, shows an "enticingly bizarre take" on the Simpson family which he translates "into his unique visual vortex" (Harrington 2016). Chomet's vortex envisions the Simpsons as undergoing a cultural shift. In his couch gag, the artist employs an American gaze on the Simpsons as a clichéd Frenchized family with a father who indulges in eating escargots and Lisa who has exchanged her saxophone for an accordion. In addition, Bill Plympton's sixth couch-gag contribution is a variation, a repurposing of his Oscar-nominated short film "Your Face" from 1987 (see Fig. 22). Consequently, the short "Homer's Face" portrays Homer as replacing the original short film's man and singing "Your Face" while his head transforms into various shapes similarly to the original (cf. Fig. 23).

In his detailed analysis of the "Animation Auteur," Paul Wells, expert in the field of animation studies, raises attention to the fact that while cinematic practice generally rules out the prominence of a god-like,[36] genuine author-

American Academy Award winning indie-animator Bill Plympton. Additionally, Polish artist Michal Socha received considerable attention for his simplistic "Ikea Coüch Gag" and then again for his complex surreal journey into Homer's brain in red and black, each unique pieces of art. These examples demonstrate that the couch gag has been a site for unique styles of auteur animators.

35   Watch Sylvain Chomet's "French SIMPSONS couch gag" posted on 13 Oct. 2014 on YouTube under URL: https://bit.ly/3a8S5LD.

36   In his famous essay from 1968, "Death of the Author" (French orig. *"La mort de l'auteur"*), French philosopher Roland Barthes speaks about the *"auteur-dieu,"* the 'author god', which he

ship, this is completely different in animation. Wells argues: "[A]nimation may be viewed as the most auteurist of film practices which, even at its most collaborative moments, insists upon the cohesive intervention of an authorial presence." (73) He suggests that the film industry has mostly belittled the role of the cohesive intervention of the *metteurs en scène* (see Wollen 1972: 78). Literally translated from French, *metteurs en scène* are the "scene setters" a group which includes not only writers, but also editors and sound designers engaged in filmmaking who notably contribute to a film as 'commercial verifiers'[37] (i. e. film director).

The guest auteurs of THE SIMPSONS can be read as participating in a collaborative process because they re-imagine the Simpsons' characteristic aesthetics and employ their own authorial presence in re-animating the Simpson characters. In Wells' definition, artists like Kricfalusi, Chomet, or Plympton contribute to THE SIMPSONS' "commercial, cultural, and critical construction of coherence and consistency […] where none may exist" (74). Altogether, Wells refers to the animation auteur as the central creative force rethinking the collaborative aspects behind animation authorship as a participatory practice.[38]

Auteurs' Crossover Sphere of THE SIMPSONS' Couch Gag

The focus on shared labor within auteur practices is further foregrounded in my second category consisting of couch gags by guest-directors who integrate the Simpsons into another artistic cartoon universe (cf. *VICE* 2014). In these crossover sequences, the Simpson family is interacting with other characters and animation techniques (i. e. claymation, CGI) from a range of popular formats, foremost from cable-television cartoon shows. THE SIMPSONS' "institutional structure" of a domestic setting operates as a pre-condition to implement other, already familiar cartoon characters (cf. Wells 75).

The adventures of characters from, for example, SOUTH PARK, ROBOT CHICKEN, and THE RICK & MORTY SHOW address an adult audience and are known to range beyond the TV-PG rating line. In THE SIMPSONS, however, they are transferred to the crossover sphere of the couch gag. In such a way, the different adult-oriented formats enter the sphere of public-network television and reach a far bigger audience than on their niche-market channels of Adult Swim or Comedy

---

replaces with the "*écrivain*", the writer. For more information, get access to the full essay on *Google Docs.com* under URL: https://bit.ly/3jMJqlz.

37 Paul Wells traces the pre-eminence of the director back to the Romanticist conception of the author which is at the heart of an industry that still 'sells' auteurs as commercial verifiers of a work. The notion is similarly valorized by audiences that favor a "coherent view of a style" (cf. Wells 73).

38 For a better overview, see also App. 6.3: "List of Guest-Animated Couch Gags"

3 Analysis | TREEHOUSE OF HORROR: Lessons to Remember

24–25 THE SIMPSONS' couch gag as a crossover space for auteur animation, here with a reference to Cartoon Network's ADVENTURE TIME

Central where those adult-animation shows are usually aired. In the experimental media space of THE SIMPSONS' couch gag, the alcoholic scientist Rick and his grandson Morty can, for example, accidentally kill the Simpsons in their living room and leave them as spilled dabs of yellow color.

A second experimental instance occurs when the couch gag becomes a site of transmedia crossover. In the "Simcraft" opening, for example, the Simpsons appear in form of the cube-headed video-game avatars from Mojang Studios' sandbox video game MINECRAFT (which is called the best video game of all times by many). Thirdly, the couch gag can set up a completely altered environment as in the opening in which a tracking shot zooms in on an ADVENTURE TIME version of Springfield with Homer as Jake the Dog and Bart as Finn the Human (Cartoon Network 2010–2018) (cf. Fig. 24–25).

But how to read those couch gags which can neither be categorized by their authorial presence nor by their cross-over aesthetic? As will be shown in the following subchapter on Banksy, one possible way is to consider them as examples for reclaiming authorship in order to make a subversive impact on public network television.

Banksy: Street-Art Auteur for the Masses

Banksy's couch gag introducing the 2010 episode "MoneyBART" is entirely different from any of the previous couch gags.[39] After the Simpsons have settled on the couch, the camera zooms out of the scene, revealing the living-room scenario as being only a static print which hundreds of seemingly excruciated female Asian workers mechanically replicate. By changing our familiar perspective to an alienated one, the scenario of the Simpsons on the couch turns into a meta-reflexive

---

39 See the full couch gag by Banksy on YouTube, posted on 08 Nov. 2015 under URL: https://www.youtube.com/watch?v=sSU1IJk70i4.

History Lesson No. 1 | Animation Auteurs and Auteur Television:

26-27 Banksy imagines 20ᵗʰ Century Fox as a maximum-security prison that contains a SIMPSONS' sweat shop full of Asian workers

symbol for the exploitation of exhausted workers who craft the cel animation, i. e. the coloring of single panels, for THE SIMPSONS (cf. Fig. 26).

As this couch gag makes instantly clear, viewers are consciously torn out of their comfort zone. Banksy's couch gag turns into an anti-capitalist critique as the camera pans over to another section of the factory. We see a thrashed unicorn poking holes into SIMPSONS DVDs next to little kittens which are shredded to serve as stuffing for little Bart toy dolls. The camera ultimately gives the larger picture by zooming out to show the factory's surroundings. The sweat shop is boxed in by the familiar 20ᵗʰ Century Fox building which is presented as a gritty, inhospitable place surrounded by barbed wire with searchlights like those of a maximum-security prison (cf. Fig. 27).

Accompanied by a dismal score of sinister sounds, Banksy primarily works within the color panoply of black and brown so that the bright colors of THE SIMPSONS' merchandise are even more salient. Banksy's opening gives an insight into the dystopian, post-apocalyptic vision behind the SIMPSONS' couch arrangement that sharpens our eye for the outsourcing of THE SIMPSONS' animation and merchandise to low-wage countries.[40]

---

40 THE SIMPSONS' admins were massively criticized after relocating the final stages of animation to AKOM, a studio in South Korea, in 1996. On *The Verge.com*, Chris Plante (2015) gives a re-

On the occasion of THE SIMPSONS' 500th episode in 2012, show runner Al Jean gave an interview to the *L. A. Times*. The interviewer Patrick Day asked Jean how they had managed to get in touch with Banksy, whose notorious policy of anonymity has strengthened his popularity worldwide. Al Jean replied that it was bizarre to never speak to or meet Banksy, so he could not even tell whether Banksy is a man or a woman (cf. Day 2012). In the interview with the *L. A. Times*, Jean explains that Banksy had submitted the storyboards in his style which, except for "some even sadder parts", were subsequently processed by the animation studios.[41] In a different interview, Al Jean further stated elsewhere that "95 percent of [the couch gag] is just the way Banksy wanted" since "almost all of [the content] stayed in" and did not fall prey to Fox's censorship (Itzkoff 2010). Although the somewhat awestruck public-media critique labeled Banksy's opening a provocation, describing it as controversial and subversive, Jean's comment testifies to a different response. According to him, THE SIMPSONS' showrunners reacted to Banksy's concept with composure because they welcomed Banksy's unique signature and his recognizable auteurprint combining social critique and creative participation.

Urban-media critic Robert Neu writes on the streetart platform *Stencilrevolution.com* that Banksy is a "legend" whose name "ignites controversy, starts conversations and piques curiosity" (2017). Banksy's thought-provoking art performances have gained him world fame. Especially notable are his subversive urban stencil creations which keep making the point that one of the world's most obscure characters promotes an artistic subculture. This has made him one of the most-wanted artists in the world.

In the same *L. A Times* interview with Al Jean, Patrick Day expresses his concern that the couch gag "seemed to have pushed things to a different level" compared to anything THE SIMPSONS had exposed its audience to before. The 'things' which the couch gag seems to have pushed can be related to what Henry Jenkins brought up in his discussions about participatory culture: Banksy visualizes Jenkins's notion of the contexts turning the viewers' eye toward the 'social, legal, and economic relationships' within which media production and consumption operate these days. As I read it, THE SIMPSONS makes productive use of an auteur who, much like the show itself, exemplifies the compatibility as well as the necessity of mainstream popularity and a consumer-critical attitude of culture jamming.

Banksy's critics claim that his fame pushed the development of subversive street art going mainstream.[42] Robert Neu insists instead that "as an unrivaled

fined step-by-step insight into "How an episode of THE SIMPSONS is made" by meticulously looking at the creative processes involved in developing one single SIMPSONS production.
41 For more 'unofficial' imagery drafted for THE SIMPSONS' couch gag, see *Banksyunofficial.com* under https://bit.ly/37c9th3.
42 Critics leave open whether Banksy's mass appeal is positive or negative. Similarly to how THE SIMPSONS became a merchandise phenomenon in the 1990s, Banksy products prove being pop-

phenomenon, Banksy's irreverent, socio-political style is paving the way for future street artists and perhaps changing the way graffiti is seen" (2017). In my opinion, Bansky's sweat-shop couch gag has moreover challenged the way THE SIMPSONS is seen. His broad influence on street art – an art which conceives of itself as a "movement" – has already been termed the "Banksy effect."[43] This individuated effect can be called the artistic mantra of participatory culture. According to this mantra, Banksy encourages to make use of previous ideas – the so-called copycat-style – and thus inspires the art of other recent "talented as well as not-so-talented street artists" (Gilbride 2018), who are thus enabled both to consume and produce.

Blogger Paige Gilbride further writes in "The Movement: The Banksy Effect" that Banksy has created a "new brainwave" which has become the entry point to accepting art as a part of everyday culture and daily life (cf. 2018). In this context it is amusing that Banksy identifies with the character of the irreverent Bart Simpson. In the 2010 episode "MoneyBART," Bart's 'board gag' that precedes Banksy's couch gag shows Bart writing beyond the board's limits "I must not write over the walls," a meta-referential link at using street art and graffiti as a means to visually express public indignation. Over the years, Bart Simpson's subversive board gags often pointed beyond the show itself and obviously played into Banksy's 'brainwave' too.

Unsurprisingly, Banksy's close up of the supposedly exploitative corporate empire behind THE SIMPSONS provoked much public outcry. According to Wells' various definitions of auteur practices, Banksy as an auteur is, paradoxically, a "challenger to corporate, institutional and systemic oppression and coercion" (75). Hence, critics and journalists had problems accepting how Fox and the SIMPSONS' showrunners could allow such harsh self-mockery. Despite the fact that Al Jean felt the need to stress the clip's deviousness and lack of realism, he equally emphasized that "[Fox] is a place where comedy can really thrive, as long as it's funny" (qtd. in Itzkoff 2010).

Whether Banksy's couch gag is funny is certainly debatable, although, in *Topographies of Popular Culture* (2016), cultural-studies researcher Markku Salmela reminds his readers that the sequence appears within THE SIMPSONS' long history of satire and self-referentiality; this satirical context connects the consumption of popular culture and "a world of nauseating albeit comfortingly fantastic exploitation" (Salmela 2016: 70). As a temporal television auteur on THE SIMPSONS, Banksy has definitely reinforced the satirical impact of the cartoon show. By di-

---

ular. Besides all kinds of paper art and prints, the internet is packed with Banksy-inspired duvet covers, coffee mugs, spread shirts, and shower curtains.
43   See Paige Gilbride's full article "The Movement: The Banksy Effect" on *Medium.com*, posted on 13 May 2018 under https://bit.ly/39fXKPI.

recting his satire against exploitive capitalism at large, Salmela argues, Banksy has a point when arguing that "the suburban living room [here symbolized by THE SIMPSONS couch] has become a location in which sinister discoveries are made – a place (or non-place) of anxiety, apathy, and alienation that carefully hides but ultimately reveals its dark side" (2016: 71).

In a comment on the educational online repository of user-generated media *Critical Commons*, the "very dark portrayal" of the SIMPSONS production line is said to have been widely hailed as marking a return to the glory days of the show. The review reads:

> [W]hile there is much serious commentary to be made about the realities of outsourcing and exploitative labor practices in the U.S. and abroad, the criticism implied by the Banksy opening is significantly blunted by the impossible extremes to which the gag is carried. A bedraggled unicorn being used to poke holes in DVDs and a giant panda being whipped like a draft animal undermines any potential seriousness of the critique. *(Criticalcommons.org, undated)*

Where the author sees Banksy's critique as blunted by the show's absurdity and thus freed from any serious criticism, it should be questioned whether Banksy really dedicated himself to sell out THE SIMPSONS. After all, THE SIMPSONS has largely been acknowledged for their subtle criticism and seriocomic branding – why not reminding them that one can push the critical frame even farther? At the same time, I doubt that the "impossible extremes" of the unicorn and the panda prevent the couch gag from being a serious anti-corporate statement framed by the sinister atmosphere of Banksy's auteurist animation style.

Ultimately, Banksy addresses satire's alleged paradox of both evoking laughter while at the same time raising an awareness for social injustice. In his article "The State of Satire, the Satire of State," comedy scholar Jonathan Gray concludes: "Satire is ultimately a negative form (albeit with positive intentions) and therefore runs the risk of alienating the audience through its negative properties." (14) Although 'alienating the audience' seems a little far-fetched in the context of Banksy's couch-gag satire, its "negative properties," for example of the exploited, fantastic animals, has definitely positively irritated the SIMPSONS fans.

Today, many people recognize Banksy's distinct style as well as auteurprint aesthetic; after all, his overarching sense of subversion is tangible in all of his artworks. Through animation, Banksy forces us to think about the exploitative conditions of Asian workers behind the barbed-wired 20th Century Fox building and puts his finger on the dark side of U.S.-America's entertainment industry of which Banksy himself, his art, and THE SIMPSONS have become a crucial part.

The following close reading departs from the world of artistic fame and subversive celebrities. I aim to shed further light on different forms of fan art and its relation to exclusive auteur art as well as inclusive participatory culture. Over the years, THE SIMPSONS have become known for their active inclusion of fan auteurs. Due to the open space of the couch gag, fans have obviously felt invited to produce their own pre-episodic short-film ideas. But although some fan auteurs were given the opportunity to have their ideas realized, other examples demonstrate how THE SIMPSONS block fan accesses the show. Thus I will investigate which distinct factors enable and which factors limit participation. My comparative reading of the couch gags of the fan artists Lee Hardcastle and Paul Robertson will illustrate how fan participation comes to an end.

Fan Art, Lee Hardcastle, and the Limits of Participation

We have seen how the couch gag created and animated by guest animators established a trend which has become increasingly visible in recent years. Since 2010, the couch gag has been farmed out to acclaimed animation auteurs. In Patrick Day's 2012 *L. A. Times* interview with Al Jean, the show runner explains that the creative team puts names of artists on a wish list of whom the writers and creators themselves often are fans.

Pixel-art animator, art director, and fan Ivan Dixon states that fan art born out of mutual inspiration has only come to the fore in recent years of THE SIMPSONS, namely since among the "animation community" the guest-directed couch gags have become the series' most eagerly awaited highlights (qtd. in Polson/Kalina 2015).

Potential candidates like Ivan Dixon are asked to draft their own ideas for an auteur-inspired couch gag, others are invited to appear as guest voices on the show, such as the publicity-shy writer Thomas Pynchon. According to a comment on *The A. V. Club*, the famously reclusive American author so far had two appearances in the show in both of which he is depicted with a bag over his head. However, as it turned out, Pynchon contributed more than just this little in-joke about his reclusiveness. According to tweets from former show runner Matt Selman, Thomas Pynchon also edited his own dialogue and added his own jokes to the script (cf. Vago 2014). Yet, a fan doesn't have to be an acclaimed genius in order to have their jokes realized in a couch gag. Regular, but committed SIMPSONS viewers have been offered to become part of the 'auteur community' and get involved in the process of couch-gag production too.

In 2012, Fox organized "THE SIMPSONS Couch Gag Contest" in which fans living on the North American continent could submit their own ideas consisting of "100 words or less" to become animated as a real SIMPSONS opening in the final episode of the show's 24th season (2013) (cf. *SIMPSONS Wiki by Fandom.com*). *TV Guide*'s online journalist Kate Stanhope subsequently reported that more than 30,000 SIMPSONS fans submitted entries of which only three were selected as finalists. THE SIMPSONS' creative team also included fans in the decision about the best idea. Finally, Cheryl Brown's storyboard for "Dandelions" won the competition and was consequently made into an animated couch gag. The second and third finalists received crafted drafts, i.e. drawn illustrations of what their ideas could have looked like if they had won. In Canada, THE SIMPSONS' Contest crew further awarded the submission of Ray Savaya, whose plain black-outlines-on-white-background couch gag portrays typical Canadian characters such as a loon, an ice-hockey player, Canada's first prime minister Sir John A. MacDonald, and a beaver who replace the Simpsons on the couch.

Similar forms of audience interaction had already happened earlier, for example, when fans were invited to vote for or against "Nedna," a campaign which was promoted in the "2011 Fox Fan Initiative" on THE SIMPSONS homepage. The initiative emerged from a cliffhanger between the seasons of 2010 and 2011 and fans were invited to decide whether the incipient erotic relationship between the pious widower Ned Flanders and the elementary-school teacher and notorious single Edna Krabappel would be continued in the following 23rd season (2011). As can be read on related sites of *THE SIMPSONS Wiki*: "Also wallpapers, videos, Twitter badges, and Facebook profile pictures of each vote were available for download and use" (undated). With the premiering episode the result revealed to be "Pro Nedna" which meant that near the episode's end Edna broke the fourth wall to thank the social-media voters by directly winking into the camera. To extend on Janet McCabe's observation from 2007, in this moment the process of edging closer "to a shift from analogue to digital" seems complete because my examples prove consumers' (or users') pleasure of having "more control over content, with more choice about what to watch" (McCabe 2007: 10). Such shifts invite SIMPSONS fans to go on a journey and participate in the process of edging closer within this animated worlds. This collaborative auteur practice has further affected other talented fans to become artists such as the British 'claymator' Lee Hardcastle and his 'fan art' couch-gag projects, which will receive detailed attention in the following paragraphs.

Inspired by Adam Wingard's home-invasion slasher film YOU'RE NEXT from 2013, the British indie artist Lee Hardcastle literally opened a new door into the Simpsons' living room.[44] As online editor Joseph Sheldon writes on *1428Elm.com*, a horror-movie news site: "Hardcastle has found another way to ultimately desecrate our childhoods by literally axing through THE SIMPSONS." (2015) The hor-

---

44 Besides Hardcastle's YOU'RE NEXT couch gag, he also released a SIMPSONS homage read through the lens of Quentin Tarantino's first feature film, RESERVOIR DOGS (1992). Here we see a range of Springfieldians reenacting the film's crucial momentum of the bank robbery, during which everyone dies. In comparison, both shorts are partly nostalgic for THE SIMPSONS, partly paying homage to the horror-film genre, and partly a reflection of Hardcastle's distinct sense of humor. See the entire series of Lee Hardcastle's "100 % Unofficial" on YouTube under URL: https://bit.ly/3da1sN3.

ror-film fan Hardcastle was already known for other stop-motion productions that had 'axed' through people's childhoods such as his widely praised independent film T IS FOR TOILET, part of the horror anthology THE ABCS OF DEATH (2012), the MINIONS spoof "Minion Ways to Die" (2015) or his series "60 seconds with clay," including parodies of popular horror film remakes such as THE THING (2011) and EVIL DEAD (2012). He once more raised his fans' attention when he released the by now fourth edition of his "100 % Unofficial SIMPSONS Couch Gag[s] 'The Joker'" in June 2020.[45] On his website, Lee Hardcastle informs that he generally creates claymation "that's not for children" (cf. *Leehardcastle.com*).

His translation of THE SIMPSONS' couch gag into 'claysploitation' evidences that his "taste for gore" is inappropriate for a younger audience which explains why such couch gags will probably not be aired as a pre-episodic act of getting-into-the-mood for THE SIMPSONS and not even for TREEHOUSE OF HORROR. The short film tells the following story: While the Simpson family sits quietly on their couch, spellbound by the light of the television screen, Springfield's three teenage hooligans invade their home. Hardcastle stays close to Adam Wingard's post-slasher and its original cinematography of twisted camera angles, costume design, as well as low-key lighting and flat coloring. By these means viewers are forced to join the side of the killers and share their outside perspective on the doomed family that does not see it coming. The sad classic of Beethoven's "Piano Sonata No. 14" replaces dialogues and diegetic sounds and dominates the action when the armed young men go on their sadist rampage.

First, Bart gets head-shot with something that looks like a handcrafted arrow. When Homer wants to dial 911, Jimbo Jones brutally chops through the flesh of his lower arm with a machete. Jimbo is accompanied by the other bullies of Springfield, Dolph Starbeam and Kearney Zzyzwicz, and all three wear the same animal masks as the killers in Wingard's YOU'RE NEXT. Homer's last tears are stopped by his head bursting so that his brain is dispersed all over the living room's walls. Marge is scalped and while we see blood running down her face, she is forced to watch Jimbo slaughter baby Maggie with his machete. In a final act of blind rage, Marge gets a grip on Dolph's axe with which she attacks the three assailants, Jimbo, Dolph, and Kearney. Suddenly Jimbo surges and kills Marge at last. Lisa, the only survivor, waves dismissively when an awstruck Chief Wiggum

---

45 The altogether four claymation installments of Hardcastle's "100 % Unofficial Simpsons Couch Gag" series all situate characters from THE SIMPSONS into popular (horror) film settings. Whereas the first is based on Adam Wingard's YOU'RE NEXT, the second, "THE SIMPSONS Couch Gag – part II" (2018), is a reference to Quentin Tarantino's RESERVOIR DOGS (1992), "part III" is subtitled with "FABULOUS SECRET POWERS" (2019), an homage to the '80s' MASTERS OF THE UNIVERSE mixed with elements from the films of cine auteur Gaspar Noé, and "THE SIMPSONS Couch Gag – part IV" (2020) puts Krusty the Clown into the role of Arthur Fleck / The Joker of Todd Phillips recent film success JOKER starring Joaquin Phoenix from 2019.

3 Analysis | TREEHOUSE OF HORROR: Lessons to Remember

28–29 Lee Hardcastle's "Banned Play-doh couch gag: YOU'RE NEXT meets THE SIMPSONS" ends in a blood bath

recognizes her as the remaining offender and shoots her in the head from outside the broken window (see Fig. 28–29).[46]

Hardcastle modeled his plot after Wingard's film, but decided that no one but the police chief would survive his couch gag. The cynicism and gross comedy of this anti-climactic ending exceeds the boundaries which stay in effect even in the series' most disturbing couch gags when, for example, the Simpsons are all killed off in one way or another. While there is a surviving girl in Wingard's YOU'RE NEXT, no final girl is left amidst the bleak carnage of Hardcastle's film.

After my first screening of the short, I tried to align it with Hardcastle's definition of SIMPSONS' fan art. I started to read through some comments by the over ten million viewers who had clicked on Hardcastle's couch gag on his YouTube channel. The majority of statements listed below the video upload proved the users' outright bafflement. Most fans comment on their sadness and on feeling sick. In an article on "the world's leading progressive business media brand," *Fast Company.com*, editor Joe Berkowitz writes about Hardcastle's claymation style: "[A]nyone who might be on the fence about watching non-Aardman [creator of

---

46   Chief Wiggum's final shooting of Lisa can be read as a metareference to George A. Romero's NIGHT OF THE LIVING DEAD from 1968 in which the black protagonist Ben (Duane Jones) is accidentally mistaken as a zombie by the Caucasian police chief who shoots him at last.

30 The fan couch gag "Simpsons Pixels" by Paul Robertson and Ivan Dixon use familiar elements from the original in a surreal homage to 8-bit arcade games from the 1980s

WALLACE AND GROMIT, ann. SD] claymation should know that these videos have a vitality, dark humor, and a sense of homage well outside the boundaries of what might be expected of the medium." (2012)

In the context of Hardcastle's SIMPSONS couch gag spin-off, however, the artist not only alters the medium of animation, but also translates the couch gag into a genre piece that operates within the genre of 'torture porn'.[47] One YouTube user, for example, explains that he doesn't understand that the mutilation of the Simpsons supposedly affected him more than if he had seen similar acts of violence in reality (the fan doesn't make clear whether he talks about the everyday news or live-action films). Reasons for such a pronounced empathy may lie in the sympathies the fan feels for the dysfunctional yellow family. The Simpsons may be artificial cartoon characters, but most of today's fans have grown up with them. THE SIMPSONS has been accompanying the lives of many for the past thirty years and thus may seem more real than most live-action sitcom characters.

Most critics agree that Hardcastle's stop-motion productions stand out with their dedication to detail and the well-placed music that underscores the visual excesses. Hardcastle's underdog status becomes evident when his film is compared, for example, to another, more accepted fan-art couch gag as the one by the Australian animators Ivan Dixon and Paul Robertson called "SIMPSONS Pixels" from 2015 (cf. Fig. 30). The artists entered on a "local success story" (Polson/Kalina 2015) when they, for fun, translated cel animation into the pixel aesthetics of early video-console, so-called arcade games from the 1980s – a graphic style

---

47 Based on a cycle of films that showcased "explicit scenes of torture and mutilation," "inherent sadism," "visceral impact," and a "viciously nihilistic" attitude, *New York Magazine* film critic David Edelstein coined the label "torture porn" in 2006 to discuss Eli Roth's HOSTEL (USA 2005), Greg McLean's WOLF CREEK (AUS 2005), Rob Zombie's THE DEVIL'S REJECTS (USA 2005), or Gaspar Noé's IRRÉVERSIBLE (F 2002) – films which, in the mid-2000s, were subsumed under the umbrella term 'New Extremity.' For further information, see David Edelstein's article "Now Playing at Your Local Multiplex: Torture Porn," posted in *New York Magazin.com*, 26 Jan. 2016 under URL: https://nymag.com/movies/features/15622/.

which today is often used in pixel art and by hobbyists. Dixon and Robertson reworked the classic opening of the Simpsons' coming home, but added further pixelated references from earlier episodes (e.g. "King-Size Homer," Fox 1995) and placed recurring exclusive characters such as Kang & Kodos into the opening's almost surreal ending. The Australians also make meta-ironical jokes at their art because in the 'board gag' they make Bart write "Pixel Art is not Real Art." As an online article of *The Sydney Morning Herald* (2015) informs, a video was uploaded on YouTube which combined THE SIMPSONS' new pixelated retro-style with an arcade-sound version of the show's musical theme. The article's journalist Laura Polson writes that the clip not only received more than one million clicks within two days; Dixon told *The Sydney Morning Herald* that less than twelve hours after its publication, he also received an email from one of the SIMPSONS' creators, asking him "to call them straightaway" (Polson 2015).

The sequence of "SIMPSONS Pixels" was streamed in its entirety of nearly two minutes, introducing season 26th episode "My Fair Lady" (Fox 2006). Dixon explains in an interview: "'SIMPSONS Pixels' is part nostalgia for the show, part homage to video games of the '80s and '90s and part a reflection of [my] and Robertson's humour." (Qtd. in Polson 2015) Judging by Dixon's comment, a mixture of SIMPSONS nostalgia, 1980s 8-bit video game fancy seems to be the crucial intersection where old and new forms of media production can successfully collide.

When I compared THE SIMPSONS' artists' reactions to the two fan productions, I started to wonder whether Lee Hardcastle had received an invitation to have his couch gag included as well. After all, his couch-gag short is also part transmedia homage, part nostalgia for THE SIMPSONS with an obvious admiration for genre horror and clay animation, with some humor thrown in. I began an email correspondence with Hardcastle. He instantly replied: "no response no. it's just a fan film." (Private e-mail correspondence)

Hardcastle raised public attention to his couch gag by engaging in the same YouTube strategy of DIY social-media self-marketing as Dixon and Robertson, but his couch gag obviously follows the premise 'the more gore the merrier.' Hardcastle claims in an interview with Joe Berkowitz that he tries his best to make his films as gross as possible – until the set is completely covered by red (Hardcastle qtd. in Berkowitz 2015). Due to the massive amount of blood and guts, Hardcastle's couch gag cannot ever pass even the most flexible censorship board at the Fox network.

Hardcastle's filming practice and his self-description remind me of how film theorist Peter Wollen once described the director as auteur: "The director does not subordinate himself to another author; his source is only a pretext, which provides catalysts, scenes which use his own preoccupations to produce a radically new work" (Wollen 1972: 113, also qtd. in Hutcheon 2013: 82). Hardcastle definitely used THE SIMPSONS' couch gag as a catalyst in order to create "just a fan film," but his fan film transforms the couch gag into a newly framed piece of genre work that culminates in a different representation of horror-film reality.

This new "100 % Unofficial" horror-film reality has its home on the internet which enables a more radical artistic independence from commercial cooptation than other media do. Hardcastle desires complete control over the full creation process from script and storyboard across character crafting and set design to the shooting and, consequently, the post-production process including editing as well as sound design (cf. 2015). In his case, Wells is literally right when claiming that animation is the most auteurist of film practices (cf. 73). At the same time, Hardcastle's claymation art speaks for an animation auteur who extends the boundaries of participatory culture to the utmost bringing him extremely close to previous notions of the film auteur. His experimental productions open up spaces where no animation auteur and no audience went before.

Hardcastle's YOU'RE NEXT homage shows on which grounds different kinds of fan art are permitted to be medially consumed and distributed. Returning to Jenkins' question about what factors enable or limit cultural participation, the interaction between fan auteurs and THE SIMPSONS as part of a corporate industry is defined by a continuum of nuances within contemporary pop culture. Along this continuum, the Pixel artists Dixon and Robertson can be seen as shining examples for how Jenkins' liberating notions of participatory culture work at their best, even on Fox network. Hardcastle's fan art, on the other hand, runs up against the limits of public attention and critical acclaim and thus is restricted to the internet as its platform.

So far, I discussed two different understandings of the animation auteur. In the following paragraphs I will introduce my third and last category of the horror-film auteur. While a variety of Hollywood filmmakers used the potential of THE SIMPSONS' continuity format which provided them with more creative freedom than the medium of film, other equally acclaimed filmmakers began to explore the creative opportunities TREEHOUSE OF HORROR offered them and experimented with the specific Halloween look of this show's couch gag. The specific visual translations of the Halloween couch gags are invitations to seeing the world of the Simpsons with new eyes. At the same time, the concept of the animation auteur opens up new perspectives on America's popular genre-horror.

Guillermo del Toro made himself a name with his nightmarish fantasy tales PAN'S LABYRINTH (2006) and, more recently, THE SHAPE OF WATER (2017)[48] for

---

48   Subsequently, del Toro was offered to submit his idea as well as produce, and direct an entire segment in the 2019 Halloween jubilee episode TREEHOUSE OF HORROR XXX. In the segment "When Hairy Met Slimy," del Toro pays tribute to his own film A SHAPE OF WATER and features Selma as Elisa falls in love with the alien Kang as the Amphibian Man.

which the Argentinian filmmaker received an Oscar in 2018. Del Toro is further known as being an admirer of THE SIMPSONS which he proved in his extended 2013 couch gag of TREEHOUSE OF HORROR XXIV. His deep-felt admiration for the TREEHOUSE OF HORROR special series seemed to him the ideal basis for a successful blend of genre horror and auteur animation. Already in the first seconds of his couch-gag short film, I felt instantly invited by del Toro to participate in his love letter to the horror film. My final analysis therefore widens my text's scope to well-known and successful film director such as Guillermo del Toro who has found ways to translate his auteur inclinations into animation practice and into the television medium while being able to follow his own rules and visual language. Hence, the couch gag by Guillermo del Toro will be used to apply the auteur concept to the creation of a comprehensive popular-media history archive within a film of only three minutes.

The Collaborative Space of the Animated Archive:
TREEHOUSE OF HORROR, Guillermo del Toro, and Genre Memorabilia

Ominous clouds slowly fade to reveal the sinister background to del Toro's 2013 episode of THE SIMPSONS' TREEHOUSE OF HORROR. The camera tracks down on soldiers firing machine guns at groaning zombies who crave for the remaining brains behind the fence sealing off the "Human Resources Dept." A long shot subsequently opens onto a bleak and burning Springfield with shattered windows and barricaded buildings (cf. Fig. 31). The camera zooms in on a bedeviled Lard Lad, the 50 ft advertising figure in front of Springfield's donut store that gets attacked by an even more gigantic cyclops. The beast is inspired by the cyclops from the 1958 movie THE 7TH VOYAGE OF SINDBAD created by visual effects artist Ray Harryhausen and bears some similarity to Chief Wiggum from Springfield's PD. In front of Springfield Elementary, Edna Krabappel reminds viewers of actress Tippi Hedren in her debut role as Melanie Daniels when she was sitting outside the school of Bodega Bay in Hitchcock's suspense classic THE BIRDS from 1963. As a reference to Alfred Hitchcock's regular cameo appearances in his movies, we see him sitting next to the school teacher Krabappel. Del Toro depicts him as feeding the birds that already wait on the monkey bars until they can attack the school teacher just like they attacked Melanie Daniels in the original thriller.

After an extended, detailed tracking shot that shows us Bart at the board being joined by Stephen King and that continues with Homer in the nuclear power plant, mutating into a big-mouthed creature as in del Toro's BLADE II (2002), viewers are confronted with a fireworks of popular culture references (e.g. Carl Carlson as Blade from del Toro's 1998 BLADE I; Mr. Burns as the Pale Man from

History Lesson No. 1 | Animation Auteurs and Auteur Television:

31-32 Del Toro's couch gag: a "creature feature" of genre memorabilia

del Toro's 2006 PAN'S LABYRINTH). Some of which need further summary and explanation in the following.

On his way home, we see Bart on his skateboard to escape from zombies along Springfield's main street. Unlike in the regular SIMPSONS' opening, the asphalt under his wheels suddenly is broken by del Toro's interpretation of Cthulhu which is not only referring to the H. P. Lovecraft creature in the novella *At the Mountains of Madness* from 1931, but is one of del Toro's much desired, enthusiastic future projects planned to be released in 2022 (cf. Lambie 2010). The camera now directs the viewers' attention to the shopping street where we normally meet a range of permanent supporting characters of THE SIMPSONS. But instead of showing Moe, the Comic Book Guy, Apu Nahassapemapetilon, and the Crazy Cat Lady, del Toro sets the stage for a different cast of characters. Next to Lovecraft, who is touching tea cups with one tentacular end of Cthulhu, stands a Simpsonized version of Edgar Allen Poe with a three-eyed raven on his shoulder. Science-fiction writer Ray Bradbury stands next to Poe inking something on the arm of his framing device "the illustrated man" who as narrator 'wears,' i.e. holds together the 18 unrelated stories of Bradbury's short-story collection *The Illustrated Man* from 1951. Richard Matheson, another well-known member of 'the Southern California

Sorcerers,' a group of fantastic-fiction writers, is shown turning his back on the protagonist of THE OMEGA MAN (1971), the film adaptation of his post-apocalyptic novel *I Am Legend* from 1954.[49]

Del Toro's opening sequence ends with the familiar couch scenario in the Simpsons' living room, but offers a slight extension to another fantastic dimension. The mise-en-scène of the Simpsons' home on Evergreen Terrace remains recognizable, although the neighborhood appears being characterized by abandoned houses. Homer arrives and the family members meet on the couch as usual – except for the fact that Homer is shown as del Toro's version of a zombie in THE DEVIL'S BACKBONE (2001). Marge appears in the shape of a life-size blue cockroach from MIMIC (1997) after having finished her grocery shopping, during which she bought some bizarre 'eggs' from del Toro's science fiction drama CRONOS (1993). Bart has transformed into the goat-legged and horned Pan from PAN'S LABYRINTH (2006), who welcomes his sister Lisa as Ofelia, who, just a second ago, looked like Alice in her light-blue dress in 20th-century illustrations of Lewis Carroll's *Alice's Adventures in Wonderland*[50] when she fell into the magic couch hole (cf. Fig. 32).

What I intend to say with this lengthy summary from above is what film critic Glenn Ward sums up in the title of his essay from 2014: "There is no such thing" titles Ward's detailed exploration of del Toro's opening sequence in the volume of essays edited by Ann Davies, *The Transnational Fantasies of Guillermo del Toro*

---

49 For matters of length, the opening's following course of events is put here: What follows is that Bart is run over by a horde of SIMPSONS' side characters escaping from a mob of Universal classic monsters from the golden age of Hollywood horror. The mob is led by Boris Karloff's FRANKENSTEIN creature and Bela Lugosi's Dracula from 1931. The mob carries forks and torches (e.g. Frankenstein's creature and his bride carry the torches which were used against them in the films) turning tables with the townsfolk that made attempts on their existences in the respective films. THE WOLF MAN (1941), THE MUMMY (1932), THE CREATURE FROM THE BLACK LAGOON (1954) as well as THE BRIDE OF FRANKENSTEIN (1935), THE INVISIBLE MAN (1933), and the alien creature from the science-fiction film THIS ISLAND EARTH (1955) join the group of avengers. Once more, this scenery is followed by a tracking shot across, as del Toro explained, a hail of "guilty pleasure" references from all kinds of mid-20th century science-fiction horror B-movies also known as "creature features." Under the threatening sky painted red and black, Rod Serling is shown smoking a cigarette, Count Orloff from Robert Wiene's silent vampire film NOSFERATU (1922) stands, somewhat lost, on a hill, looking down on the scientist-turning-fly from Kurt Neumann's THE FLY (1958). Schlitzie, the mentally disabled sideshow attraction of Tod Browning's FREAKS (1932) is surrounded by a group of science-fiction creatures such as for example the green mutant from Christian Nyby's THE THING FROM ANOTHER WORLD (1951) and the laser-eyed robot Klaatu from Robert Wise's THE DAY THE EARTH STOOD STILL (1951).

50 Although Carroll makes no reference as to which color Alice's dress has, one illustration in Macmillan's 1903 "Little Folks" edition showed Alice in a blue dress for the first time which became the most iconic version until today. See Wikipedia's related article "Alice in Wonderland dress" under URL: https://bit.ly/3rylepo (undated).

from 2014. Ward salvages del Toro's three-minute opening as a "creature feature" calling it a "master class of playful pastiche, quotation, and self-reference" (11). Glenn Ward concludes that "Treehouse demonstrates the ease with which del Toro crosses media" (12). In my opinion, del Toro's ease can be explained with animation's discursive freedom. Ward celebrates

> [t]he sheer diversity of genre sources and discursive constructions... where science fiction meets supernatural fantasy, horror meets fairy tale, children's fiction meets adult fiction, vampires meet cyborgs... the marvelous meets the uncanny, gothic historicism meets digital hypermodernity, skepticism collides with belief, metacinematic smartness runs headlong into childlike wonder, and history and fiction crash into each other. *(2014: 12)*

What the critic calls "diversity" gets to the core of The Simpsons' animation auteur. First of all, del Toro's "masterclass" pastiche is employed in a constructive rather than a demystifying way. Del Toro adds a new historical meaning to the embedded source texts, repurposes the "sheer diversity of genre sources and different constructions" (Ward 12) and thus puts them into a different text and context. Secondly, in del Toro's "masterclass," quotation becomes a device to honor other well-known literary authors and cine auteurs who are considered to be innovators. For example, del Toro includes animated versions of Stephen King[51] and Hitchcock to acknowledge their influence on horror writing and suspense thrillers[52] which have become substantial sources for his own creative work. The portrayal of del Toro's other spiritual mentors, the American science-fiction writers Richard Matheson and Ray Bradbury, gives evidence of how relevant their authorial presence still is for today's creative productions. The presence of the two mid-century members of the Southern California Sorcerers evidences how relevant they are for popular culture even today. This becomes especially visible in the "sheer diversity" of film projects to which Richard Matheson and Ray Bradbury

---

51 Stephen King's role as writer of approximately sixty novels between 1974 and 2020 is certainly comparable to his role as inspiration for filmmakers. While the novel and the film adaptation of The Shining show family man Jack Torrence going mad and filling the hotel lobby's walls with the famous 'dull boy' quote, del Toro chooses King himself to leave his message on the walls of Bart's school classroom.

52 Hitchcock's The Birds, for example, was the first sound film in film history which completely forwent an extradiegetic score. The American fantasy-horror author H. P. Lovecraft invented a whole legend around Cthulhu, which subsequently also inspired other fantasy-fiction writers such as Robert Bloch, August Derleth, or Robert E. Howard to perpetuate and extend the Cthulhu mythology long after Lovecraft's death. To say nothing of Edgar Allen Poe, who can confidently be defined as a driving force in accelerating the genre of the American Gothic during the 19th century. In his attempt to sensually affect his readers, Poe emancipated the genre from its European heritage, which he most significantly did with his narrative poem *The Raven*.

have contributed their scripts and ideas throughout American popular history; a list which is far too long to be adequately appreciated here.⁵³ The writers lining up along Springfield's main street form a gallery of animated ancestral portraits of some of the most notable American horror-genre pioneers. The animated Lovecraft, Poe, Matheson, and Bradbury stand in for the many small- and big-screen adaptations of their texts.

Finally, del Toro's "masterclass" makes use of the postmodern device of self-referentiality by re-visualizing multiple of his own films. The Argentinian filmmaker inscribes himself as an auteur into TREEHOUSE's cultural history by presenting to the audience an amalgamation of his monsters with the leading characters of THE SIMPSONS, for example in Homer as the black-eyed zombie from THE DEVIL'S BACKBONE (1993) and Marge as the giant cockroach from MIMIC (1997). Unlike the animation auteurs in the examples before, del Toro translates the relation between texts, their intertextuality into a transmedia framework and thereby creates yet a new layer in the dialogical relationship between texts, their creators, and their original media.

In the context of THE SIMPSONS' couch gag, del Toro's artistic practice strongly reminds of how *Cahiers du Cinéma* film critic Andrew Sarris thought about the institution of the auteur, namely as a "reminder of movies to be resurrected, of genres to be redeemed, of directors to be rediscovered" (qtd. in Caughie 61). Within 1960s film theories on authorship, Andrew Sarris' revisionist idea led the auteur away from the French avant-garde and straight into American popular-culture consciousness. I see a similar strategy in del Toro's project. By quoting some of his "guilty pleasures," examples from the early days of horror-film art which haunt him, he resurrects their directors' status – after all, many of them were marginalized by the oppressive Hollywood industry following them. After the MGM release of FREAKS (1932), for instance, Tod Browning's career as a thriving Hollywood director came to an abrupt end. Many of del Toro's references re-animate examples from a period of film production prior to the introduction of the Hays'

---

53   This adaptation practice concerns a multiplicity of American writers. For example, since its publication in 1954, Richard Matheson's original novel *I Am Legend* has been made into four films. But unlike OMEGA MAN's rather unknown director Boris Sagal, Richard Matheson's sujet still seems to be attractive, for example, when looking at its latest adaptation from 2007, the post-apocalyptic science-fiction horror I AM LEGEND, starring Will Smith. Whereas Ray Bradbury was an incredibly industrious author and screenwriter not only in all kinds of genres (mainly fantasy, science fiction, and horror) and across all sorts of media (television, radio, film, theater), del Toro depicts him while painting his stories onto the body of an animated version of the Illustrated Man. Bradbury's original, *The Illustrated Man* from 1951, is a collection of eighteen short stories, literally drawing the picture of eighteen uncertain futures which are all tattooed onto the body of a former member of a carnival freak show, who serves as the narrator framing the stories. Like many of his other stories, this was made into a film, but was far less successful than Bradbury's collection.

Code that forced a standard view of morally acceptable behavior on Hollywood films produced after 1934.

Del Toro's opening is unique in his usage of archival space and in the way he realized the carnivalesque potential of animation. In bringing together the core influences on his personal development as an auteur filmmaker, del Toro imprints himself on the collaborative effort of creating Treehouse. The filmmaker is the auteur of his own fantastic film worlds, but his Treehouse opening testifies to the influences he owes to all those who came before him. Del Toro clearly fulfills Andrew Sarris' criteria for the artist-as-auteur-as-archivist.

Del Toro's couch gag establishes a distinguishable personal meaning that emerges "from the tension between his personality and the material" (qtd. in Nelmes 137). In his conversation with Snierson, del Toro explains that to take credit for the entire titles in the couch gag had been a "unique opportunity" for him as "all of this stuff" interconnects and unites in itself (qtd. in Snierson 2013). Del Toro's opening testifies to his own role within participatory culture; after all, the Argentinian filmmaker is a consumer of popular culture that serves as his inspiration and in return inspires others with his own films.

In a conversation with *USA Today*, del Toro confirms that he deliberately mixed his own movie references with those creatures and monsters that inspired his work most (cf. Nateog 2013). Genre aficionados can practice their literacy while swimming in a vast pool of shared genre knowledge. An insertion before the explanatory video uploaded by Moviepilot on YouTube reads: "Hey Guillermo, we think we found all the references in your Simpsons Intro! Let's see …." (*YouTube.com* 2015) Del Toro created a genre-related site of participatory culture, engaged in his role as consumer and as a producer who challenges his viewers to indulge in recognizing the vast flood of genre references. I agree with Glenn Ward who suggests that del Toro gives voice to his childlike fascination with a "discursive heterogeneity" (12). The filmmaker's fascination oscillates between The Simpsons and his own movies, generically jumps back and forth between horror, fantasy, and science fiction, and offers the same amount of space to today's famous directors as to almost forgotten auteurs, e. g. film directors, screenwriters, or literary authors. Del Toro's heterogenous approach stresses American horror history as a collaborative site within a huge participatory culture.

As I aimed to show within my analysis of Guillermo del Toro's couch-gag opening, his practice as filmmaker devalues the bias of the unique gaze of a film auteur. Although del Toro's first animation is perhaps only a footnote to his Oscar-winning career, his vision as auteur in animation shows how Treehouse's Halloween format is itself an art form that functions as a cultural history of the digital age. There are two reasons for this. Firstly, del Toro manifests how the medium of animation within the medium of television can become a collaborative site for diverse authorial presences across time and at the present moment. Within this context, del Toro has set a standard by preserving the auteur tradition in the protected space of THE SIMPSONS as cartoon television. Secondly, del Toro as animation auteur is privileged in that he could fully unfold his authorial agency within the realm of THE SIMPSONS couch-gag tradition. Whereas my other auteur analyses focused on the auteur as method, del Toro's couch gag foregrounds the significance of a popular-culture history archive of horror texts from across the full range of the Western media landscape.

Conclusion: Animation Auteurs, Auteur Television, And Participatory Culture

The era of Astruc's avant-garde and Truffaut's 'Auteur-Dieu,' the elitist author-as-artist with a 'caméra stylo' is long gone. Visible authorial presence, creative control, and a personal imprimatur have lost the war against a neoliberal mass-producing entertainment industry in which Disney's CGI-spectacles and Marvel's mainstream franchises reach the largest audiences possible in order to maximize profits.[54] As my close readings illustrated, the fan auteurs I examined were mostly offered the chance to preserve their status as signature artists and, at the same time, participate in the collaborative arena of THE SIMPSONS couch gag.

It may not be surprising that not only filmmakers look for new ways to step out of the shadow of major film studios such as the Walt Disney Corporation. In recent years, animation artists attest to the fact that television is the medium of the moment which offers auteurs stylistic individuality, but also a space for creative experiments, rewards aesthetic audacity, and promotes booming genres like horror.

What Andrew Sarris claimed for independent movies of the late 1960s and 1970s such as EASY RIDER (1969) is also applicable to cartoon series such as THE SIMPSONS: Both represent a specific understanding of authorship and creative collaboration. Considering the 'culture jamming,' street-art protest aesthetic of Banksy, the unconventional, transgressive claymation fan art of Lee Hardcastle, or the archival style of del Toro, more conservative auteur critics may claim that their fan art is a lukewarm mimicry of American independent film towards the end of the 20th century. But from such copycat mimicry there emerged not only a

---

54   The independent movie and TV news website Screenrant titles in 2017, Disney's major purchase of crucial Film and TV assets from 20th Century Fox increased their market value to a twenty-seven percent share of the entire film industry (Mithaiwala 2017). Together, the Walt Disney Studios, primarily consisting of Lucasfilm (STAR WARS), the Marvel Studios (AVENGERS), and Pixar Animation (TOY STORY), has now complemented its imperial entertainment power with some of the highest grossing movie franchises ever produced, including ALIEN VS. PREDATOR, James Cameron's AVATAR (grossed $3 billion in global box office), DIE HARD I-VI, Marvel's FANTASTIC FOUR, among many others. For more information see Mansoor Mithaiwala's "Disney Now Owns 27 Percent of the Film Industry," posted on *Screenrant.com*, 14 Dec 2017. Accessed on 14 Jan 2019 under URL: https://bit.ly/3pksOTv.

repurposing concept, but also highly personal styles which have become particularly visible in the various examples of THE SIMPSONS' couch gag. All of my examples can be called 'cinemacraft' which highlights the specific quality of auteur animation within THE SIMPSONS.

To conclude, the couch gag developed from a signature meta-commentary to a short film. In *100 Things THE SIMPSONS Fans Should Know & Do Before They Die* (2016), Allie Goertz and Julia Prescott claim that the transition from a simple visual joke to complete short films indicates that THE SIMPSONS was reinventing itself, searching for new visual styles, and finding out how to collaborate with contemporary artists (cf. 35). My detailed analyses aimed to show how the concept of the animation auteur can be rethought in connection with the art of animation. Banksy, Hardcastle, and del Toro came from completely different visual media – street art, independent claymation, and film – but proved useful in order to exemplify how my idea of the fan auteur could be opened up in the direction of participatory culture and of contemporary production methods of television. As a television pioneer, THE SIMPSONS is a role model for implementing the auteur into their collaborative practices and production processes. The couch gag was used to illustrate that animated meta-commentary and creative subversion can be established within one of the most mass-appealing and longest-running scripted primetime cartoon shows in television history. THE SIMPSONS' contemporary experimental auteur practices have helped to rediscover television not only as a space for committed consumption, but also for active fan participation.

History Lesson No. 2 | The Literary Legacy of American Gothic Fiction: Complex Television & TREEHOUSE OF HORROR

When I watched TREEHOUSE OF HORROR's "The Raven" parody for the first time, I was speechless considering the tremendous complexity of this small Halloween-special segment. I had never encountered a text like this before. A cartoon show that obviously acknowledges the difficulty of making 19th-century Gothic poetry not only scary, but also relevant to contemporary viewers, was something of a curiosity by 1990s' TV standards.

Up to this point, I firmly believed that television would either entertain *or* educate, but the TREEHOUSE segment "The Raven" felt to me like the paragon of what would later be summarized under the designation of "edutainment." By now, I have watched "The Raven" probably more often than even the truest SIMPSONS fan. What still strikes me most about the faithful adaptation of Edgar Allen Poe's Gothic poetry is that each time I re-visited the segment, I discovered new interesting details adding up to my performative literacy (i.e. the ability to decode and contextualize all the details) and equally to the complexity of TREEHOUSE's Gothic reworking. This chapter will be dedicated to read TREEHOUSE OF HORROR's literary adaptations as an early form of "Complex TV" – a concept which American television scholar Jason Mittell first introduced in 2015.

In the course of my research in the field of TREEHOUSE OF HORROR, I not only realized that the show drew a popular-culture history of the digital age. In addition, to a greater extent than THE SIMPSONS, TREEHOUSE can be considered as a review or reworking of what can be subsumed under the 'supergenre' of Gothic, i.e. a genre which condenses a range of different traditions. In addition, the literary parodies in particular illustrate to what extent the critical discourses surrounding television narratives have increased in complexity in order to meet audience's higher expectations and the commercial demands of the TV industry. "The Raven," for example, proved highly effective to start thinking about TREEHOUSE as a complex-television media archive.

In their article about THE SIMPSONS' seriality concept, "Rücke vor bis auf 'Los:' Die Serialität der SIMPSONS," the German media scholars Thomas Klein and Christian Hißnauer, for example, remarked that THE SIMPSONS' "structural unit" of the TREEHOUSE OF HORROR episodes are mostly parodies. But Hißnauer and Klein also regret that the term parody often falls too short to fully grasp how these stories function in many instances (cf. 2014: 24). Along with the authors, I suggest to exchange the term 'parody' for the term 'generic irritations' situating the audience's between familiarity and difference. Klein and Hißnauer explain,

> Es geht also nicht mehr so sehr darum, etwas über die Familie der Simpsons oder andere Figuren zu erzählen und davon ausgehend auch Aussagen über

die Gesellschaft und die Populärkultur zu treffen, sondern diese Figuren und unser Wissen darum, wie sie funktionieren, zu verwenden, um zu Aspekten des Fantasy-Genres eine neue Interpretation zu liefern. *(2014: 24)*

The interpretational statements referring to society and popular culture take a detour to indirectly say something about American culture and history. Its focus, accordingly, doesn't lie on storytelling, but rather on testing its viewers' literacy. The show aims at irritating audiences and at taking up an antithetical relation to conventional TV formats.

The Russian formalist Viktor Shklovsky saw the artistic process as the "liberation of the object from the automatism[55] of perception;" this liberation leads to a form of complex alienation (qtd. in Marcuse 2007: 117). In our case, the viewer is alienated or irritated because what he gets to see in the TREEHOUSE segments is not too different from the re-animated 'originals,' but different enough to challenge the viewers' familiarity with genre conventions and formula. The genres used in TREEHOUSE's anthological storytelling often point back at the specific historical period during which they emerged. Therefore it does not suffice to conceive of TREEHOUSE's reworkings of Gothic literature as mere 'parodies;' rather they have to be understood as complex dialogues between past and present, between familiarity and difference as was mentioned in 3.1. TREEHOUSE's creators challenges the audience's knowledge' to invite the attentive and TREEHOUSE-literate viewer to what Jason Mittell calls an aesthetically conscious viewing experience (cf. 2012: 113). To evoke this viewing experience, the series employs a specific form of complex storytelling and seriality that help with hinting at a great variety of discourses and feeding the audience with bite-sized genre packages (cf. Klein/ Hißnauer 25).

If my project had been realized in the early 2000s, I probably would have interpreted TREEHOUSE's animated "Raven" as attesting to a new form of 'quality TV.' When the television industry began to expand and capitalize on its narrative possibilities by the mid-1990s, quality TV used to define the predetermined

---

55 In Herbert Marcuse's *Art and Liberation*, the German American philosopher and sociologist quotes Victor Shklovsky who used the term "automatism" as a distorting and restricting obstacle of people's perception to really see, in the words of Marcuse, "what things are and what things can be" (2007: 117). Victor Shklovsky, the founder of the Society for the Study of Poetic Language helped to develop the methods of linguistics technique and style of Russian Formalism, as editor Douglas Kellner writes in the editor's note about the Russian Formalist (cf. 117). At the time of the Bolshevik Revolution, Marcuse refers to Shklovsky by translating his statement: "Art is a means of experiencing the becoming of the object" by assuming that "art discovers and creates new immediacy, which emerges only with the destruction of the old" (117). In short, Shklovsky believed that "the essence of art consisted in the 'de-automation' of seeing" (243), for example, through irritation. For further information, get full access to the e-book on the cloud service *Amazon Aws.com* under URL: https://bit.ly/394BhoG.

breaking point between audience's sophisticated entertainment by high-budget television-drama series and quality-television's 'Other' of fast-food TV formats like sitcoms, cartoons, and other, more 'conventional' TV formats. But I wrote this book with enough historical distance to the early quality-TV discussions. The discipline of television studies emancipated itself but finally overlooked that not only THE SIMPSONS,[56] but also TREEHOUSE OF HORROR had development "its own vocabulary on its own medium terms" (Mittell 2015: 18).

The most vital impulses to read a television phenomenon like THE SIMPSONS and its 'related' annual Halloween series TREEHOUSE OF HORROR as "a new model of storytelling on American TV" (2015: 17) were provided by American television scholar Jason Mittell. He convincingly extended previous assumptions when he argued that complex series like THE X-FILES (Fox 1994–2002) had begun to redefine "episodic storytelling," which was considered a closed narrative form, as an open format that he called "serial narration" (cf. 18 f.). Mittell took this argument even further when he claimed that narrative complexity is a "distinct narrational mode" (2006: 26; 2012: 17). In their article "Rücke vor bis auf Los," German media critics Thomas Klein and Christian Hißnauer confirm Mittell's idea:

> Wenn es um Komplexität geht, finden sich […] 'narrative Spezialeffekte', […] u. a. Formen der Selbstreflexivität, die jedoch nicht wie im Autorenkino der 1960er und 1970er Jahre die Fiktionalität des Films ausstellen oder in Frage stellen, sondern das Spiel mit der Fiktion als bewusste Steigerung des Unterhaltungswerts zelebrieren. *(2014: 24)*

On the one side, TREEHOUSE OF HORROR is an anthology series and thus depends on the format of episodic storytelling, while the show characteristically draws from the continuity storytelling which is understood as working in 'cycles.' The latter becomes visible when looking at the cycle of TWILIGHT ZONE parodies or the various examples where TREEHOUSE OF HORROR adapted from the literary Gothic. Either way, Hißnauer und Klein were convinced by Mittell's notion that THE SIMPSONS was the first sitcom that encouraged viewers to engage in an "aesthetically conscious reception" (cf. 2014: 24, Mittell 2012: 113).

But how did TREEHOUSE distinguish itself from more conventional TV episodic series and how could it do so within the television medium? In order to answer these questions, I will first look at TREEHOUSE's "own vocabulary" to bring together the format of episodic television and specific genre continuities. In a sec-

---

56 In each of his publications about "genre mixing" (2001), the "politics of parody" (2004), "narrative complexity" (2006), "television in American culture" (2010), and "complex tv" (2015), THE SIMPSONS play a crucial role in Jason Mittell's explorations by which he has furthered our understanding of contemporary television and pushed the academic discipline of TV Studies.

ond step, however, I will apply Mittell's medium-specific conditions for production, reception, and content and consider their manifestation in three literary parodies from Treehouse of Horror's horror archive.

In order to read the Treehouse segment "The Raven" as complex television, I first have to first clarify how the 'supergenre' of the American Gothic contributes to Treehouse's overall complexity. In other words, what are the credentials of Treehouse of Horror for complexity in general? In most basic terms, Mittell conceives of complex TV as "a storytelling mode and set of associated production and reception practices that span a wide range of programs across an array of genres" (2015: 233). The genre of the American literary Gothic is, accordingly, only the starting point for Treehouse's journey through an array of Gothic-inspired genres which offer the starting point for the operational aesthetics or, as Hißnauer and Klein say, "narrative Spezialeffeke" which transform the cartoon series into a visual spectacle, or as the Russian Formalist Shklovsky believed, "a sensation of the object" (qtd. in Marcuse 2007: 117). Mittell explains:

> Television genres are cultural categories that bundle texts together within particular contexts and cultural circulations, not simply sets of textual conventions. This is not to suggest that questions of genre are irrelevant to understanding complex television – to the contrary, looking at genre as part of its growth and circulation highlights how the mode has grown to pervade and influence a wide-range of types of television fiction, including both comedic and dramatic genres. Complex television is a site of tremendous genre mixing, where conventions and assumptions from a range of programming categories come together and are interwoven, merged, and reformed. *(2015: 233)*

Along these lines, "The Raven" parody mixes, first of all, 19th-century Gothic poetry and The Simpsons Halloween-cartoon special. The more I thought about this, the clearer it became that The Simpsons became complex TV on the day in later October 1990 when Fox aired the first "The Simpsons Halloween Special."

The Simpsons was the first animated series that mixed many previous programming categories on Halloween, thus offering a new experience of watching a genre such as horror interwoven with a comedy program. Compared to Mittell's analysis of the live-action sitcoms Seinfeld (NBC 1989–1998) and Arrested Development (Fox 2003–2006) as complex series, The Simpsons is not only the single cartoon which has the qualifications for carrying the label 'complex comedy.' Mittell also remarks that his live-action examples are complex because they only "selectively engage in serial norms" (21) – just like Treehouse. To him, the two analyzed situation comedies are examples that highlight "why we should conceive of contemporary television seriality not as a simple marker of continuity but as a multifaceted variable, with a range of potential storytelling possibilities"

(22). Mittell's reading can certainly be transferred to THE SIMPSONS' variable. But the cycle of TREEHOUSE OF HORROR adds an important aspect concerning its new form of serial continuity: the Gothic. How, then, does the Halloween special link the aesthetics of the literary Gothic with its own visual vocabulary of animation, both historically and aesthetically?

The Modern Horror Story and its Literary Touchstones

What do the following texts have in common? Mary Wollstonecraft Shelley's 1818 novel *Frankenstein*, Robert Louis Stevenson's *Strange Case of Dr. Jekyll and Mr. Hyde* from 1886, Bram Stoker's 1897 *Dracula*, H.G. Wells's 1898 *The Island of Dr. Moreau*, the dark poetry of Edgar Allen Poe, and the short fiction of H.P. Lovecraft as well as Washington Irving are all outstanding examples of Gothic literature both from the European and the American tradition. Stephen King celebrated their authors in his non-fiction 'world of horror' book *Danse Macabre* from 1980. According to King, these writers have always influenced him as one of 20th-century America's most proficient and commercially successful horror-fiction writers. According to Stephen King, any of their fictional works stand "at the foundation of a huge skyscraper of those twentieth century gothics which have become known as 'the modern horror story'" (King 37).

In other words, the modern horror genre as we know it would not exist without the creative imagination of those 19th-century Gothic-fiction writers. The first three examples in particular, *Frankenstein*, *Dr. Jekyll and Mr. Hyde*, and *Dracula*, still are extremely popular; these literary classics have "embiggened" (to use a SIMPSONS' inspired nonce word) the popular-culture pool of myths of the Gothic's literary bequest. Audiences the world over know them even if they haven't read any of the original source texts. Accordingly, TREEHOUSE OF HORROR emphasizes the significance of 19th-century Gothic fiction as the bedrock of contemporary horror. TREEHOUSE OF HORROR has additionally broadened people's horizon of American Gothic classics by reviving almost forgotten texts such as Steven Vincent Benét's 1936 short story "The Devil and Daniel Webster" which would only have been recognized by the most attentive readers of American literature among the TREEHOUSE fans. In the thirty years of its existence, TREEHOUSE OF HORROR already reworked a considerable number of Gothic texts.

Critical viewers may argue that actually these parodies are not referencing the literary texts themselves but rather their film adaptations. The Hollywood horror film ISLAND OF LOST SOULS by director Erle C. Kenton from 1932, for example, can be seen as a loose adaptation of the late-19th century Gothic novel *The Island of Dr. Moreau* by H.G. Wells. In fact the following chapter illustrates how TREEHOUSE OF HORROR made use of these earlier visual translations not solely to develop its own visual vocabulary, but also to broaden the critical scope of their parody. By way of different literary examples I will demonstrated how TREEHOUSE OF HORROR has become what Mittell considers the "site of tremendous genre mixing, where conventions and assumptions from a range of programming categories come together and are interwoven, merged, and reformed" (cf. Mittell 2015: 233).

TREEHOUSE OF HORROR's literary archive consists of Gothic fiction imported from 19th century Europe but it also takes texts from the American Gothic of the late-19th and early-20th centuries. The European imports include Mary Shelley's *Frankenstein* (1818),[57] Robert Louis Stevenson's novella *Strange Case of Dr. Jekyll and Mr. Hyde* (1886) inspired by Jack the Ripper,[58] H. G. Wells's novel *The Island of Dr. Moreau* (1896),[59] Bram Stoker's *Dracula* (1897),[60] as well as "The Monkey's Paw,"[61] a supernatural short story by W. W. Jacobs (1902). Shelley's, Stevenson's, and Stoker's novel are certainly the best known as there is a myriad of adaptations in a variety of different media. Sweeney Todd,[62] the fictitious "demon barber from Fleet Street," is the main character of a Victorian Gothic tale which is taken up by THE SIMPSONS' musical segment "There is No Business Like Moe Business."[63] Among 19th-century American Gothic texts, TREEHOUSE OF HORROR pays homage to E. A. Poe's narrative poem *The Raven*[64] from 1845,[65] but also includes some Gothic texts from 20th-century writers such as short stories like H. P. Lovecraft's "Call of Cthulhu" (1928)[66] or Stephen Vincent Benét's "The Devil and Daniel Webster" (1936)[67], but also the famous Gothic drama *The Crucible* (1953) by Arthur Miller.[68]

---

57   In "If I Only Had A Brain." TREEHOUSE OF HORROR II, s03e07, Fox 1991; and in "Frinkenstein." TREEHOUSE OF HORROR XIV, s15e01, Fox 2003.
58   In "Four Beheadings and A Funeral." TREEHOUSE OF HORROR XV, s16e01, Fox 2004.
59   In "The Island of Dr. Hibbert." TREEHOUSE OF HORROR XIII, s14e01, Fox 2002.
60   In "Bart Simpson's Dracula." TREEHOUSE OF HORROR IV, s15e05, Fox 1993.
61   In "The Monkey's Paw." TREEHOUSE OF HORROR II, s03e07, Fox 1991.
62   The character of Sweeney Todd first appeared in a penny dreadful of 1846 entitled "The String of Pearls: A Romance;" but the old serial-killer barber from Fleet Street received considerable attention when Johnny Depp and Helena Bonham Carter performed in the recreation by Tim Burton with the title SWEENEY TODD (2007).
63   TREEHOUSE OF HORROR XX, s21e04, Fox 2009.
64   In "The Raven." TREEHOUSE OF HORROR I, s02e16, Fox 1990.
65   Although "The Raven" is the only SIMPSONS episode which credits E. A. Poe as writer of the ToH I segment, Poe's influence on TREEHOUSE OF HORROR shines through in various episodes. Poe is not only mentioned by name in diverse episodes; his tombstone also stands on the grounds of Springfield cemetery; the plot of the episode "Lisa's Rival," basically follows Poe's "The Tell-Tale Heart;" Guillermo del Toro portrayed Poe with a three-eyed raven on his arm, standing side by side other influential horror-fiction writers such as Richard Matheson and H. P. Lovecraft in del Toro's opening sequence of ToH from 2016; "Bad Dream House" has an imploding house which according to fans resembles the *House of Usher*.
66   In the pre-episodic opening to TREEHOUSE OF HORROR XXIX, s30e04, Fox 2018.
67   In "The Devil and Homer Simpson." TREEHOUSE OF HORROR IV, s15e05, Fox 1993.
68   In "Easy-Bake Coven." TREEHOUSE OF HORROR VIII, s09e04, Fox 1997.

Stephen King argues that Gothic narratives share a basic agreement about their genre: They force secrets on us that would best remain undisclosed and say things that would best remain untold. Gothic storytellers like Shelley, Stevenson, Stoker, Wells, or Poe, among many others, are famous for how they reveal the secrets or subtexts at the heart of their stories and their mastery sets the standards for future writers. In a comparable context, literary critic Pat Berman says about *The Island of Dr. Moreau*: "Wells cut a memorable swath in his time, leaving a legacy new generations continually revisit and mine" (*Local Journalism.com* 2006). When journalist Scott Meslow reviews the bequest of Edgar Allen Poe in *The Atlantic* magazine, he calls him "pop culture's undying obsession" (2012), while Stephen King emphasizes the fact that "*Frankenstein* has probably been subject of more films than any other literary work, including the Bible" (37). King considers the many representations of *Frankenstein* proof of how dynamic today's pop-cultural matrix is and continues: "this modest gothic tale became caught in a kind of cultural echo chamber" (cf. 40).

Keeping such considerations in mind, Gothic stories brought not only some of popular-culture's most iconic monsters into the world (i.e. the vampire, the undead, and the doppelganger), but are also echoing or 'rewinding' the secret fears and social anxieties these monsters represent. As I see it, these Gothic lessons stand at the beginning of what Mittell defines as complex seriality, creating "multifaceted variable[s] with a range of potential storytelling possibilities" (22).

Developing its Own Language – The Gothic of Treehouse of Horror

Although Treehouse is tied to Halloween season and bears horror in its title, the question remains what is Gothic about this series. One of the first lessons we learned from Treehouse is that the show's parodies and adaptations can be distinguished by either making use of the Gothic as mode or of the Gothic as genre. Early texts on the aesthetics of the Gothic sublime for example by Edmund Burke, foreground the effects the practice of Gothic storytelling creates in the recipients. Literary critic Alastair Fowler suggests instead that the Gothic romance began as a fixed genre with a recognizable set of recurring features such as archetypal characters, themes, motifs, and other story elements (cf. Spooner 2006: 26). In addition to this, Helen Wheatley reads the Gothic-television narrative in her monograph *Gothic TV* through the filter of a whole range of stylistic devices.[69] I pay heed to all

---

[69] In her book *Gothic TV* (2006), Helen Wheatley isolates characteristics which she considers prototypical of Gothic television's topography, including "the presence of highly stereotyped characters and plots, often derived from Gothic literary fiction;" "representations of the supernatural" (either overtly present or suggestively implied);" "a proclivity towards the structures and images of the uncanny" (doppelgangers, returns, déjà-vues, animated inanimate objects, severed body parts etc.), and, most importantly, homes and families which are troubled in some way (cf. 3).

of these definitions of the Gothic by assuming that the way the Gothic's features are bundled and the stylistic devices of literature are interwoven with the animation techniques of Treehouse of Horror's artists creates the particular "mood of dread and/or terror inclined to evoke fear and disgust in the viewer" (2006: 3). For contemporary audiences, it perhaps goes without saying that "Gothic television is usually visually dark, with a mise-en-scène dominated by drab and dismal colors, shadows and closed-in spaces," as Wheatley suggests (3). Wheatley postulates that, due to specific camera aesthetics and sound stylistics, Gothic television can at times be "highly impressionistic." Going by Treehouse's impressionistic style for instance in "The Raven" with its twisted angles, spectral sounds, distinct silences, and impressionistic voice-acting, Treehouse has created its own distinct way of translating the Gothic romance and the newer horror story into complex animation for the domestic medium of television.

Helen Wheatley considers the television the ideal medium for keeping the iconic Gothic spirit alive. After all, the TV scholar understands the concept of Gothic television "as a domestic version of a genre which is deeply concerned with the domestic, writing stories of unspeakable family secrets and homely trauma" (2006: 1). In her topography of Gothic formats across the television landscape, Wheatley is fast to assume that Gothic television is not a programming category, nor does it serve as shorthand to label a new series or a film. Rather, she follows the same line of argument as Jason Mittell and assumes that *Gothic TV*'s development of an on its own medium terms (cf. Mittell 2015: 18).

The Gothic genre exists as television formats' *modus operandi*, persisting as a cultural practice and as a critical term. Treehouse of Horror's parodies re-animate Gothic stories, engaging at the same time in a dialogue with the Gothic as a genre tradition. But they do so on their own terms. Treehouse for example re-imagines Victor Frankenstein's creature, originally assembled from dead-body parts, both as a lazy robot worker[70] as well as a self-made zombie collecting body parts.[71] In the course of the series' history, recurring Gothic motifs such as split personalities, human hubris, and various forms of madness came to life in Mr. Burns,[72] Sideshow Bob,[73] Dr. Hibbert,[74] and even Lisa Simpson.[75] The vampire has found several incarnations in Mr. Burns,[76] but also in the archival ride through the vampire's iconography in the Treehouse segment "Tweenlight."[77] Secret ex-

70 "If I Only Had A Brain," Treehouse of Horror II, s03e07, Fox 1991.
71 "Frinkenstein," Treehouse of Horror XIV, s15e01, Fox 2003.
72 "Survival of the Fattest," Treehouse of Horror XVI, s17e04, Fox 2005.
73 "Wanted: Dead, Then Alive," Treehouse of Horror XXVI, s27e05, Fox 2015.
74 "The Island of Dr. Hibbert," Treehouse of Horror XIII, s14e01, Fox 2003.
75 "MultipLisa-ty," Treehouse of Horror XXIX, s30e04, Fox 2018.
76 "Bart Simpson's Dracula," Treehouse of Horror IV, s05e05, Fox 1993.
77 "Tweenlight," Treehouse of Horror XXI, s22e04, Fox 2010.

periments, secret identities, and secret family traumata are further motifs which have complemented the Gothic archive of Treehouse of Horror.

As will be examined in greater detail in the following three subchapters of critically thinking about the Gothic, the recognizable conventions of the Gothic genre support Treehouse of Horror in its critical activity to dig ever more deeply into narratives' subtexts in order to expose the stories' underlying complexity. What remains to be seen, however, is how Treehouse translates the literary Gothic into something completely new, "aesthetically and morally" (cf. Gunzenhäuser/Laemmerhirt about the Gothic as mode 2017: 34) re-framing an older text and becoming what I call a pop-culture Gothic cartoon. Next I will approach the Gothic as a mode from three different perspectives.

Initial Thoughts: The 'Gothic Mode' as Critical Activity

Mittell defines complex TV as "a distinct narrational mode." So is the Gothic with its specific practice of narration, its distinct method and style of making sense of reality. As a mode of narration, the Gothic romance invites readers to focus on its distinct style of writing and to acknowledge its particular way of looking at the world, of constructing reality, and of framing it by way of a specific mise-en-scène (cf. Gunzenhäuser/Laemmerhirt 1; Fowler 100). In their article "Romance and Gothic,"[78] the American-studies scholars Gunzenhäuser and Laemmerhirt point out that at the same time as the Gothic as genre is constantly changing, the Gothic as mode keeps adapting to an even wider range of changes because it can participate in different genres (cf. 2017: 34). This is why the Gothic might be understood as a 'supergenre,' subsuming a range of other genre variants such as horror, science-fiction, and fantasy to name but a few.

In other words, the Gothic romance is essentially concerned with the dialectic between an historical event (which is usually 'uncanny', i.e. deliberately made uncanny, de-familiarized, un-homely) on the one hand and its re-inscription into a contemporary cultural order (which is usually 'canny', i.e. familiar) on the other. Along this dialectic, Treehouse of Horror tends to emphasize the relation between the seemingly orderly surface of today and the uncanny history underneath. In good Gothic tradition, the show revisits the horrors which are part of American culture. This concerns, for example, the horrors of the inherent racism in early Hollywood's film production when thinking of Schoedsack's King Kong (1931) or Kenton's Island of Lost Souls (1932) as well as the essential injustice of America's legal system shown in Steven Vincent Benét's short story "The Devil and Daniel Webster" (1936).

---

78 For more insights into the American Gothic, see the *Handbook of the American Novel of the Nineteenth Century* edited by Christine Gerhardt and published in 2018.

Treehouse makes productive use of its viewers' knowledge concerning those horrors.

The Treehouse segment "Four Beheadings and A Funeral" references the legend of Jack the Ripper meshed with other stories located in Victorian London. Included in this category are the Sherlock Holmes tales or William Hughes' 2001 period slasher and comic adaptation[79] From Hell and its portrayal of a 19th-century opium den, called "den of inequity" in Treehouse's take on the story: A series of stabbed prostitutes mystifies the police mysterious so they first accuse a man with suspicious side whiskers, but ultimately lock up "the mysterious Hindu" impersonated by Apu "until we've found someone darker," as Inspector Wiggum explains. The overt racism of this scene makes explicit how Gothic storytelling is often based on implicit racial othering. In the Treehouse segment, inspector Wiggum tries to divert attention from himself by pointing to a racial Other only to be revealed as the true serial killer at the end – the seemingly trustworthy officer turning out to be the malefic monster himself.

The visual vocabulary of this segment paints a telling picture. It consists of a dismal coloring that indulges in the visual cues we have come to understand from popular media as fiction-over-fact representations of 19th-century Victorian England (e.g. shady streets covered with thin layers of mist and the sound of carriages and horseshoes on cobbled pavement). On the one hand, the Treehouse segment clearly engages in the movie's atmospheric mice-en-scène and period set design. But on the other hand, "Four Beheadings and A Funeral" further takes up on the graphic novel's highlighting of social issues such as racism, class distinctions, and existential cries Alan Moore and Eddie Campbell foregrounded within their visually rather purist design of a black-and-white imagery in their graphic novel *From Hell* from 1989. In order to successfully implement the real-life horror of racism into other popular mediums, literary Gothic devices have been remediated across cartoon aesthetics and live-action film-horror techniques through the visual repertory of animation.

Second Set of Thoughts: A Mode is not a Genre – Treehouse Of Horror's Gothic Ways of Making Us Look at the World

As becomes obvious in the example "Four Beheadings and a Funeral," Treehouse of Horror uses a recognizable set of characters which are already familiar from The Simpsons' regular cast. But when Lisa Simpson takes over the role of master detective Eliza Simpson and Bart the role of her "easily amazed assistant Dr. Bartley,"

---

[79] William Hughes' script of From Hell starring Johnny Depp is a loose adaptation of Alan Moore (author) and Eddie Campbell's (illustrator) graphic novel adaptation of the Jack the Ripper murder case, *From Hell* from 1989. Hughes' departed from the protagonist's existential questions and the society's political concerns and created rather a cliché-ridden whodunnit detective movie.

TREEHOUSE OF HORROR distances itself from THE SIMPSONS' continuity by giving the regular characters different roles and incorporating them into an infinitely flexible Gothic mode. This practice often means turning the Simpsons characters into something completely new, "aesthetically and morally" (cf. Gunzenhäuser/ Laemmerhirt about the Gothic as mode 2017: 34). It may mean to show Reverend Lovejoy burning witches on the town's cemetery and Bart operating the guillotine in the opening sequence of the fifth TREEHOUSE installment which introduces an imagery that is considerably darker than usual. Fans may also remember Maggie's frequent appearances as "Terrible Child"[80] in the style of Linda Blair from THE EXORCIST (USA 1973), or recall del Toro's versions of Homer as the monstrous Reaper from the fantasy-film auteur's BLADE II (USA/D 2002).

TREEHOUSE's color palette, sound design, and cinematography largely work within the style of Gothic and horror and sets the mood for the annual Halloween experience. In the early cemetery openings of THE SIMPSONS' Halloween Special between 1990 and 1994, the setting always included a *tristesse* that set the tone for the following segments. Graphic violence can be expected, beheadings, gore, and blood galore, while THE SIMPSONS' opening-theme melody usually intonated by brass and alto saxophones becomes a horror-movie arrangement in which flutes and organ sounds dominate.

Literary-studies scholar Emma McEvoy calls the "Gothicization" of popular culture in the 20th century a form of "Gothic tourism" (2012: 113). In her book of the same title, McEvoy claims: "Gothic tourism is not merely restricted to those areas that have already received Gothicization in literature, film and television; it can be found almost anywhere" (113). British-Gothic scholar Catherine Spooner compares Gothic tourism as coined by McEvoy to a "malevolent virus" that has "escaped the confines of literature and spread across disciplinary boundaries to infect all kinds of media, from fashion and advertising to the way contemporary events are constructed in mass culture" (2006: 8).

The 'viral persistence' of the Gothic expresses characteristics that Mittell makes out in the television spectacle. On television, the horror genre stages visual spectacle as an addition to its "narrative special effects" (2015: 43) that are supposed to impress the viewer. While live-action horror scores with jump scares and other "narrative pyrotechnics" (Mittell 2015: 43), TREEHOUSE's anthology pieces bank on the harmonic interplay between narrative construction, textual layering, and artful animation. "Four Beheadings and a Funeral," for example, softly blends different texts of European descent, draws its comedy largely from

---

80 In his book chapter "Introduction to the American Horror Film" (1979), film historian Robin Wood lists a set of five thematic motifs for the American horror film of the time. Beside "the monster as human psychotic," "revenge of nature," "Satanism and diabolic possession," and "Cannibalism," another popular trope was the "Terrible Child" (1979: 16–17). For more information, see Robin Wood's *American Nightmare: Essays on the Horror Film* from 1979.

the use of the Cockney accent in its dialogues, and creates a distinctive look by working with gruesome chiaroscuro effects.[81]

Fan critic Joshua Kurp discredited "Four Beheadings and a Funeral" on the ground of the segment's failure "to tell a convincing detective story in seven minutes […] that also makes you laugh" (*Vulture.com* 2019). But this is not the point. The segment from ToH XV is a convincing example for a complex amalgamation of different Gothic modi. Due to its systematic use of standard Gothic devices, the segment's particular look helped me to understand TREEHOUSE's fundamental aesthetic strategy. When McEvoy suggests in 2012 that the "Gothic has become a dominant way of looking at the history of twentieth century popular entertainment itself" (165) – he points to both the genre's easy recognition value and the plurality of its representations. Concerning the diversity of Gothic guises, TREEHOUSE's artists have certainly done their homework. They know many historically and medially specific ways of emotionally arousing an audience, evoking fear, and creating suspense. While sitcoms of the 1960s were likely to playfully apply the made-for-television Gothic genre conventions, TREEHOUSE segments such as "The Raven" and "Four Beheadings and a Funeral" completely draw their audience into the Gothic diegesis (cf. Mittell 2015: 52). Traditional Gothic sitcoms of the 1960s such as THE ADDAMS FAMILY or THE MUNSTERS usually employ uncanny devices and objects to arouse cheap laughs and instantaneous effects. In TREEHOUSE's sequences, however, the more thoroughly disturbing quality of the careful atmospheric interplay between lighting, colors, music, sounds, and subjects cannot be overridden by the characters' bright colors or the funny details of Halloween napkins or sweets.

TREEHOUSE's "The Raven" shows Marge only on a wall painting which preserves her deceased beauty as the "Lost Lenore;" Maggie and Lisa act as scent-spreading seraphim angels, i. e. the Hebrew category of burning angels which Poe mentions in his tale; and Bart transforms into the tantalizing 'mockingbird' or, more precisely, the mocking raven who causes the nameless narrator's ultimate madness. In terms of camera angles, the point of view the audience takes up mostly privileges the perspectives of dead Lenore, the seraphim angels, and the raven. All of them hover over the nameless narrator impersonated by Homer and put him under pressure (e. g. cf. Fig. 33). On the narrative level, the narrator's love relation was torn apart, on the level of the Simpsons, their 'normal' family unit is destroyed; both can be read as part of the "narrative special effects" that are visible in various sections of the segment. They are also contributing to the aesthetic 'pyrotechniqes' that set TREEHOUSE OF HORROR apart from more conventional forms of THE SIMPSONS' continuity.

In the previous chapter 3.1 I discussed how the early SIMPSONS' Halloween episodes include a range of horror variants of how during the opening couch gag the

---

81   Chiaroscuro – meaning 'light-dark' in Italian – describes the effect of contrasting light and shadow in the arts.

3 Analysis | TREEHOUSE OF HORROR: Lessons to Remember

33 Homer, the nameless narrator & Bart, the raven, in "The Raven", a segment of first Halloween Special episode from 1990

family is dismembered, hung, reduced to zombies, to skeletons, or other monsters, for example in "Frankenstein's Bride" meets "The Fly." Mittell reminds us that most episodic storytelling begins with "some crucial markers" of framing material to demarcate individual episodes and locate within a specific continuity (2015: 27). Gothic markers of TREEHOUSE OF HORROR signal to viewers that the Simpsons' idyllic environment is replaced by the disturbing reality of an edgy animation. Compared to the classic family idyll, TREEHOUSE's portrayals feel like a sacrilege against the family. In its Gothic version, the show invites its audience to critically inspect television's white-washed version of American family ideology. John Hartley suggests that Gothic sitcoms offer a darker version of the suburban family, exposing the less pleasant realities of life which their idealizing precursors 'glossed over:' He writes: "These programs tended to suggest that, like modernity, progress, science and reason themselves, the modern suburban family was shadowed by darker and mostly unspoken 'others' from pre-modern and irrational traditions" (Hartley 2001: 66).

While THE SIMPSONS already invites its viewers to critically look back at contemporary myths, TREEHOUSE takes a closer look. It goes back to how literary sources like Mary Shelley's *Frankenstein* or Bram Stoker's *Dracula* introduced their dark versions of the world. Then the literary monsters are embodied by familiar, yet transformed characters, e.g. Homer who transforms into the Blob, or is shown as Homerzilla, as the giant ape King Homer, or as death himself aka the Grim Reaper. In most of these segments the monster eventually evokes our pity because it reveals itself as being the victim of exploitation by Springfield's spiteful town leaders,[82] greedy industrials,[83] or inhuman freak show owners.[84]

---

82 "Married To The Blob," TREEHOUSE OF HORROR XVII, s25e10, Fox 2014.
83 "King Homer," TREEHOUSE OF HORROR III, s04e05, Fox 1992.
84 "Freaks, No Geeks," TREEHOUSE OF HORROR XXIV, s25e02, Fox 2013.

Third Set of Thoughts:
History 'Revives' Itself – The Gothic's Mode of Genre Participation

A third feature of the Gothic in TREEHOUSE OF HORROR not only brings us back to Mittell's emphasis on the relevance of genre. British-Gothic scholar Catherine Spooner also makes an interesting observation in her book *Contemporary Gothic* (2006): "[T]here is no 'original' Gothic; it is always already the revival of something else" (10). French philosopher Jacques Derrida's statement that texts do not 'belong,' but rather 'participate' in genres may illustrate why, in Spooner's words, the Gothic "has spawned other genres like science fiction [...]; has interacted with literary movements, social pressures and historical conditions to become a more diverse, loosely defined set of narrative conventions, and literary tropes" (26). In that sense, TREEHOUSE OF HORROR participates in the Gothic genre by reinstalling, i. e. 'reviving' familiar techniques and horror aesthetics from popular horror, science fiction, and fantasy narratives, and (re-)frames them as animated cartoon Gothic. Accordingly, the series defines itself as standing in a dialogical relation to other media and earlier narratives; its literary Gothic imports demonstrate that the past is more important for TREEHOUSE's storytelling than the present (cf. King 2010: 154).

My discussion aimed to prove that the art of horror storytelling in TREEHOUSE is complex. Its horror narratives have a distinct style and a – for TV – unconventional form of narration; it rearranges carefully selected content and chooses to show telling details from the original. The Halloween Special re-animates Gothic stories from literature by transforming them into visual eyecatchers for a contemporary audience. Today's audiences expect to be blown away by today's TV shows. The Showtime series PENNY DREADFUL (2014–2016), for example, impresses viewers with the full range of Gothic iconography, from Dracula across vampires to werewolves and Frankenstein's creature, which together produce an excessive spectacle. TREEHOUSE OF HORROR fulfills its audience's high expectations by way of complex-television narratives which re-animate Gothic texts on its own medial terms. The question is how TREEHOUSE OF HORROR reinvented the art of Gothic storytelling specifically for the television medium.

TREEHOUSE OF HORROR and Narrative Complexity on the Series' Own Medium Terms

In the course of studying Mittell's insights into TV narratives' contemporary complexity, I asked myself about TREEHOUSE's potential credentials for being called complex TV. The last sections demonstrate how TREEHOUSE created its own vocabulary in order to translate generic horror into an animated-cartoon Gothic. The following paragraphs concentrate on how TREEHOUSE manifests its complexity in relation to the medially specific demands of television. Mittell relates the criteria for complex-television storytelling to the medium's three relevant sites: production, reception, and content. Accordingly, I will discuss three of Treehouse's 'genre irritations,' i.e. three homages to Gothic literature which operate between the viewers' familiarity with the tradition and their irritation.

On the side of production, the show is a cornucopia of pop-culture sources profiting from its episodic anthology structure. I will elaborate on this by way of "The Island of Dr. Hibbert" from ToH XIII which is based on H. G. Wells' Victorian Gothic-horror novel of *The Island of Dr. Moreau* from 1896. With respect to content, I will turn toward "If I Only Had A Brain" which serves as the cultural "echo chamber" for Mary Shelley's *Frankenstein* and demonstrates how Treehouse of Horror contributes to the persistence of Gothic fiction in all its narrative variability and thematic flexibility. Finally, The Simpsons' "The Raven" serves as the example of how the double-coded parody of a series-within-the-series speaks back to the its audience's everyday world. For his viewers, the series sets up an exchange between Poe's concept of the literary "unity of effect" and Mittell's narrative special effects and "operational aesthetics" of complex TV. In both cases authors are aiming at their audience's active engagement.

Before I will examine Treehouse of Horror's particular way to formally engage audiences in my their close reading of "The Raven," I will first focus on content. To reflect on Shelley's *Frankenstein* means to point to its traces left in popular culture, where according to Stephen King the narrative "became caught in a kind of cultural echo chamber" (40). Jason Mittell defines such traces as techniques to guide, manipulate, deceive, and misdirect viewers (2015: 42), in short, these traces challenge the viewers' literacy. At the same time, the traces allow the pleasure of unraveling the operations of narrative mechanisms and their cultural implications (Mittell 2015: 42), challenging the viewers to rethink their own norms as opposed to TV's conventional sitcom standards (cf. Mittell 2004: 32).

Treehouse makes intensive use, for example, of misdirection (cf. Rabin 2010). In the literary adaptation of W. W. Jacob's short story "The Monkey's Paw,"[85] the Simpsons are strolling on a Moroccan souq, i.e. an open-air marketplace where supposedly strange-looking folk sell even stranger-looking goods such as the monkey's paw which turns out to be a mummified talisman. Marge asks Homer where he bought "that ugly thing." He first points to a mysterious cloud of stirred sand, indicating that strange things can happen in such an exotic place. Instead of remembering Jacob's short story, viewers may feel reminded of Hollywood clichés such as apparent in the souq scene of Raiders of the Lost Ark from 1981. In 1980's Hollywood terms, such Middle-Eastern markets are hurly-burly places full of mysterious turbaned vendors, serpents, camel, dates, and handcrafted products.

---

85   Treehouse of Horror II, s03202s01, dir. Jim Reardon, Fox 1991.

The segment reveals that cultural appropriation has been a popular strategy in the Hollywood film industry. The original English story is not located in Morocco at all, but uses the British colony of India as the origin of the monkey's paw. Misguiding audience attention is not only a crucial part of THE SIMPSONS' humor, but also an essential element of TREEHOUSE's approach to scaring and entertaining its audience too. *A. V. Club* editor Nathan Rabin states that a thirty-year SIMPSONS diet trained fans to instantly recognize that whenever a joke goes in one direction, the story will right away steer off course and reveal that the joke's direction had nothing to do with the story at hand (cf. 2011). The mysterious cloud of sand in "The Monkey's Paw" is a rather minor detail, the joke indirectly scoffs at the film industry's cheap tricks by which films like RAIDERS OF THE LOST ARK have vilified the Arabic Other. Rabin defines gags like this as "half-red herrings and half-sequitur" by which he means gags that are partly feinting and partly illogical so it helps to foreground that the audience is literate enough to look behind the show's twists, clichés, and irritation strategies.

The original 19th-century short story "The Monkey's Paw" is used as the narrative framework rendering Homer's misfortune as an allegory for the desire of the American middle class to become rich and famous at whatever costs (cf. Rabin 2011). By playing on the popular 'be careful what you wish for' theme, the narrative makes use of Homer's ignorance as an American tourist on a family trip to Marrakech. The merchant advises Homer not to purchase the wish-fulfilling monkey's paw because "behind every wish lurks grave misfortune," but Homer muzzles the old man with a sharp retort. By exaggerating the familiar cliché of the mysterious Arabic Other (which, for example, finds excessive use in Disney's 1992 animated feature ALADDIN), Homer's behavior deliberately helps to turn around traditional TV's subject-object relation by evoking laughter about the stereotypical ugly American rather than about Arabic culture.

The parody "If I Only Had A Brain," the third segment of the TREEHOUSE II episode, introduces Homer who dreams of being fired from his job. He starts working as a grave digger, but, exhausted from the hard work, takes a nap in the open pit. Mr. Burns and his assistant Waylon Smithers come along on a quest to desecrate a body for a robot experiment and take Homer with them to surgically remove his brain. Robot Homer comes to life and calls Burns "Daddy," but immediately is seen as an "abomination" by Burns because he spends his time in sleep mode and uses his X-ray vision only to uncover hidden donuts. After Burns contritely complains about "the mysteries of life," he returns Homer's brain to his body. But while he subsequently incriminates the huge machine, it ironically crushes and kills Montgomery Burns from the neck down.

The parody seems only loosely inspired by Shelley's *Frankenstein* plot and the TREEHOUSE OF HORROR segment formally negotiates various framings: In contrast to the offensive behavior of Boris Karloff's monster in Frankenstein's Hollywood adaptation from 1932, Homer's cognitive limitedness rather reminds viewers of the pitiful destiny of Shelley's modern Prometheus. Also, Victor Frankenstein's 'enlightened' endeavors to explore the "sweet mystery of life" (a direct quote from Mel Brooks' 1974 comedy-horror movie Young Frankenstein which already parodies the film version from 1931) were not heroized in Shelley's novel, only in the Hollywood pre-Code horror movie. In contrast to the whimsical character of Victor, Universal's first sound feature Frankenstein portrays "Henry" Frankenstein as a genius who is equipped with the farsightedness of an early-20th-century scientist. In the Treehouse segment, Henry's persona is taken over by the evil Mr. Burns who is sick and tired of his lazy workers in the nuclear power plant. Burns' belief that "weak flesh" just has to be replaced by "strong steel" pushes him to playing God for which he is immediately punished. In the Treehouse interpretation, the inanimate heap of steel takes revenge on its flawed creator and also on James Whale's horror adaptation which kills off not Frankenstein, but his tragic, speechless monster in the end.

As I read it, Treehouse of Horror re-animates Shelley's anti-Enlightenment tale by mocking its Hollywood movie version. The movie's ideological re-reading that completely alters the novel's moral, is turned around again, in a move of double negation. The fact that the Halloween cycle's cinematography is returning to Universal's film original only strengthens the segment's criticism. After all, Homer's fate raises the viewers' pity and invites a critical reading of dehumanization in the labor sector until machines replace the human workforce altogether. Homer, on the other hand, continues to behave like his usual affect-ridden self who, even as a supposedly dehumanized robot, is only interested in donuts.

Film auteur Guillermo del Toro considers *Frankenstein* the "pinnacle of everything" (qtd. in Douglas 2016), pointing to the mythological quality of the novel and its symbolic ramifications which are still ripping through popular culture.[86] Or, repeating the words Henry Frankenstein uses in Whale's film: "It's alive! It's alive!" Treehouse's homage invites viewers to take a close and critical look at the contradictory traces the Frankenstein myth left in popular culture. Mr. Burns is eventually rescued by his assistant Waylon Smithers who sews his head onto Homer's body. The Halloween show mixes Frankenstein with Lee Frost's Blaxploitation B-movie The Thing With Two Heads from 1972, daring viewers to follow up on this connection "in that giddy lost age of 1991" (Rabin 2011), the year in which the Treehouse of Horror episode was aired. The Thing With Two Heads shows how the white and racist but terminally ill head of Dr. Maxwell

---

86   Already in the 1980s, Stephen King assumed in *Danse Macabre* (1980) that "Frankenstein has probably been the subject of more films than any other literary work in history, including the Bible" (38). See, for example, Harvard historian and editor at *The New Yorker* Jill Lepore's article "It's Still Alive: Two Hundred Years of Frankenstein," published February 12, 2018, that consists of various selected sources from the full range of research on Shelley's novel.

Kirshner is sewn onto Jack Moss' body, a black prisoner on death-row who receives the chance to live a prison-free second life. The loosely *Frankenstein*-inspired B-movie was released in 1972 and played with the grotesque idea of creating a mixed-racial monstrous "thing" consisting of a white man's head implanted on a black man's body. Although THE THING WITH TWO HEADS was almost forgotten upon its direct-to-video release, "If I Only Had A Brain" uses the B-movie in its final twist of the animated FRANKENSTEIN-movie version.

In Whales' classic, Henry is saved from the creature's threat by an angry mob setting fire to the old windmill to trap the monster inside. After this spectacular climax, James Whale sets his finale at Castle Frankenstein, where Henry Frankenstein celebrates his wedding party. The movie ends in a predictable Hollywood ending, a decision that I read as being thwarted in TREEHOUSE's final twist of mixing in a Blaxploitation B-movie from the 1970s. The pleasure to experiment with content is directed against Hollywood's perpetuation of standard endings which, upon the introduction of the Hays' production code in 1934, had to be 'happy' in one way or another. "If I Only Had A Brain" offers literate viewers a choice of historical narratives and endings stirring their irritation on the one hand; a choice, which on the other hand, challenges the audience to re-evaluate them.

Transgressing Genre Boundaries: TREEHOUSE OF HORROR'S "The Island of Dr. Hibbert" & the Production of TV Horror

British writer H.G. Wells was still alive when his novel *The Island of Doctor Moreau* from 1896 was first captured on celluloid under the title THE ISLAND OF LOST SOULS, the book's first sound adaptation from 1932. According to film historian Richard Scheib, Herbert George Wells strongly disapproved of Erle C. Kenton's horror film; whereas Wells had written a cautionary parable about vivisection and experiments with human bodies, highly controversial subject matter at the end of the 19th century, Kenton's ISLAND OF LOST SOULS is a mad-scientist movie with an exceptionally bold tone. H.G. Wells is said to have been pleased when the movie was banned in Britain,[87] considering ISLAND OF LOST SOULS "a vulgarization of his novel, which had been intended as a serious investigation of the moral hazards that might accompany the accelerating advancement of modern science" (Ashlin undated). Scheib notes: "He [Wells] wrote *The Island of Dr.*

---

[87] According to a BBC article, the British Board of Film Classification (BBFC) rejected ISLAND OF LOST SOULS twice, in 1933 and again in 1957. In 1958, the BBFC gave Kenton's movie an X rating after several cuts. As late as in 1996, cut-out sequences were restored and re-edited into the movie, and the film received a PG-12 rating. The BBC calls ISLAND OF LOST SOULS a film which has taken "the remarkable journey towards respectability." See Tim Masters: "BBFC anniversary: How banned horror film ISLAND OF LOST SOULS got a PG rating." *BBC.com*, 28 Mar. 2012. 20 Dec 2019. URL: https://bbc.in/3shGArX.

Moreau as a Frankensteinian take on the Garden-Eden myth, one where the creations take revenge on their flawed creator" (2017). In opposition to this, the first full-length sound film adaptation of Wells' novel from 1932 spectacularly sets the creatures on fire in the end. Its studio, Paramount Pictures, even shifts the focus from the mad scientist towards the sensational effects of Moreau's creations themselves, the "lost souls" of the film which consequently figure in the film's title, THE ISLAND OF LOST SOULS. The new name highlights Hollywood's sensationalizing practice and is an indicator of the industry's commercial orientation.

Kenton's ISLAND OF LOST SOULS belongs to the period of "pre-Code" Hollywood films. The time between 1930 and 1934 marks a short period of American studio-film productions situated between the introduction of the sound film – the so-called "talkies" – and the enforcement of the Hays' Code in 1934. During the Great Depression, pre-Code films offered to their audience an overt sexuality and violence that remains unparalleled ever since. As part of the pre-Code era, THE ISLAND OF LOST SOULS aimed to translate a well-known literary Gothic novel into a pulp movie with a sensational appeal.

Film scholar Jeff Stafford explains that Wells hated the film adaptation because "it changed Moreau from a well-intentioned visionary to a sadistic tyrant" (TCM Classics). In his blog Twenty Four Frames, film critic John Greco introduces the adaptation as "bizarre, daring; a sadistic […] sideshow of strange creatures" (2012). Next to James Whale's FRANKENSTEIN and Rouben Mamoulian's DR. JEKYLL AND MR. HYDE (1931), the Paramount production was the third film in a series of films with the topic "man playing God and trying to alter the course of nature" (Stafford 2017). Audiences were shocked by the morally controversial portrayal of the Panther Woman as an exotic temptress, by the mistreatment of animals, the mentioning of human mating, and the blasphemic cannibalism shown in the movie. Until the late 1960s, the film was banned in the UK and wore the label "especially worthless" which may have inspired Matt Groening to re-animate the text with a parody in the 13th edition of TREEHOUSE OF HORROR.

"The Island of Dr. Hibbert" pays homage to H. G. Wells' fantastic novel and shows contempt for the novel's first screen adaptation. The Simpson family is invited to spend their vacation in Dr. Hibbert's skull-shaped island resort. But there the family experiences Hibbert's experiments with humans in the "House of Pain." After having discovered the mixed-species community of so-called "manimals," Homer prompts the other Springfieldians to fight against the person who turned them into "human guinea pigs" and "invertebrates." But "in the name of progress," Hibbert reminds his "hideous children" that they are better off than they were as humans. When Homer finds out that all they have to do is "eat, and sleep, and mate, and roll around in [their] own filth, and mate, and eat …," he asks: "Where do I sign up?"

The episode aims at evoking laughter while indeed addressing several critical issues: The parody is a spillover of late-19th-century anxieties concerning vivisection and scientific megalomania transferred from the novel to the cartoon format by way of Kenton's horror-movie frame. Post-Enlightenment anxieties concerning social Darwinism, Galvanism, and other scientific progress found new, more spectacular directions in the pre-Code monster-horror films of Hollywood's 1930s. But TREEHOUSE further translates them into a late-20th-century context. Thus, the TREEHOUSE episode reframes both the written original and its filmic adaptation: In the case of Dr. Hibbert's island men are transformed into animals and not vice versa as in the film.

In Hibbert's camp full of manimals, viewers encounter most of the Springfield citizens who are partially or entirely vivisected to animals, but all of them keep their iconographic characteristics. Although Patty and Selma are elephant and mountain lion, they still chain-smoke and have unshaven legs. Apu carries his octuplets as a possum on his back, Chief Wiggum resembles a pig in a police uniform, Hans Moleman is a tortoise as usual, and Waylon Smithers a flamingo, probably referring to his secret homosexuality. Unlike Kenton's "Beast Men" who are just a group of animal creatures that lack distinct personalities (cf. Scheib 2017), the TREEHOUSE segment shows that no character equals one another. By this, it critically recalls that Dr. Moreau in Kenton's ISLAND OF LOST SOULS indifferently calls his 'lost souls' "Beasts" with a mixed pool of genetic origins, who appear as creatures part owl, part ape, and part boar. But in contrast to the pitiful creatures who long for Moreau's respect, Comic Book Guy, half man half ram, advises his "cursed brethren" to throw their tattered pants into the bonfire in order to fully embrace their animal essence.

In this context, the TREEHOUSE segment is inspired by the ethical questions raised in Wells' "Frankensteinian take on the Garden Eden myth" rather than by Kenton's staging of the outrage of the insurgent beast people against their flawed creator (cf. Scheib 2017). Unlike the film's wretched mutations who scant "Are we not men?," the Springfield citizens embrace their metamorphosis and eventually relax at the pool. Gothic scholar Fred Botting observes that in any of Hollywood's credited and uncredited Dr. Moreau tales[88] "humanity is left in question by the nightmare vision of other and future worlds" (106).

But in most of its 1930s monster movies, Hollywood conceived of 'humanity' in terms of cautionary tales about interracial romances. Film critic James A.

---

[88] In his related movie review, Richard Scheib writes "THE ISLAND OF LOST SOULS was the first of three screen adaptations of H. G. Wells's novel *The Island of Dr Moreau* (1896). It has since been remade twice – as the dull THE ISLAND OF DR MOREAU (1977) featuring Michael York as the castaway and Burt Lancaster as Dr. Moreau, and the underrated THE ISLAND OF DR MOREAU (1996) featuring David Thewlis as the castaway and Marlon Brando as the good doctor. There have also been several uncredited adaptations – THE ISLAND OF TERROR (1913), the Filipino-shot films TERROR IS A MAN (1959) and THE TWILIGHT PEOPLE (1972), and the cheap DR MOREAU'S HOUSE OF PAIN (2004)." For more information, see *Moira Reviews.com*, 2017, URL: https://bit.ly/2Nr4e6s.

Snead reads the protagonist of RKO's KING KONG from 1933 as an encoded form of blackness: "[T]he carrier of blackness is an ape" (30). Snead's reading also allows to conceive of Dr. Moreau's ape-like creatures as 'white' Hollywood's representation of 'black' America on an island out in the sea "in order to repress elements of 'blackness' inside" (30). By "blackness inside," Snead refers not only to African American actors who start to appear in Hollywood films, but to the African American population in the USA *per se*.

Keeping that in mind, the TREEHOUSE segment reframes the role of the archetypal mad scientist to critically reflect on Hollywood practices during the 1930s' pre-Code era. At the time, monsters served as "markers of racial difference"[89] while sexualized advances of both men and women "encode[d the] racist American discourse of the 1930s on masculinity, femininity, rape, and lynching" (Young 1991: 431, 404). In this context, I would even argue that Dr. Hibbert's human experiments trigger another dark memory by not only reminding of American lynchings, but also of Nazis' medical experiments on concentration-camp prisoners during the Third Reich.[90] American film scholar Elizabeth Grant speaks in this context about the emergence of "scientific racism" which enjoyed popularity during 19th- and 20th-century portrayals of people with a different skin color. She notes that people of African descent were commonly portrayed as unnatural – monsters – or too natural – primates – in representations of racist and sexist stereotypes, an image which can be exemplified in the character of Dr. Hibbert.

Springfield's physician Dr. Hibbert is the only upper middle-class African American of the town and appears as the exotic Other of his mostly yellow – white – small-town community.[91] In terms of the "scientific racism" motif, it seems quite ironic to make him (and not the even crazier, but Hispanic physician Dr. Nick Riviera) embody the mad Caucasian scientist whom Hollywood once imagined. Dressed in the white suit of a medical pseudo-deity, the suit which his role model Charles Laughton wore in Kenton's film, Dr. Hibbert appears like a satirical twist on Hollywood's "whiteness" and thus its often criticized as a racist representation.

89   See also Elizabeth Young's full essay "Here Comes the Bride: Wedding Gender and Race in Bride of Frankenstein," published in *Feminist Studies*, Vol. 17, No. 3 (Autumn 1991): 403–437. Accessible via Jstor under URL: https://www.jstor.org/stable/pdf/3178280.pdf.

90   On *Medium.com*, online critic Adam Bat reads Island as a commentary on the bourgeoning Hollywood culture of the time. He writes that it's "rather amusing that many of the acts being committed by Dr. Moreau (plastic surgery et al) [*sic*!] are the sort of things celebrated by modern Hollywood culture". See the full article "Thoughts On Kenton's ISLAND OF LOST SOULS", posted on 31 May 2012 on URL: https://bit.ly/3aIGvrh.

91   Readers may feel reminded of the 2017 documentary THE PROBLEM WITH APU by comedian Ari Kondabolu in which he discusses the convenience store owner Apu as a prototypical example for inherent racism as practiced in the U.S. entertainment industry. See the official trailer on the YouTube channel of *truTV*, posted 27 Jul. 2017, URL: https://bit.ly/3tWZ5Tk.

In front of the background of Treehouse's complex remediation of motifs from the pre-Code horror film, the segment remains remarkably faithful to Wells' Gothic novel. "The Island of Dr. Hibbert" testifies to the Gothic cartoon's freedom to contribute to and comment on Hollywood's communication practices. The Treehouse segment clearly highlights the sensationalist quality of Kenton's Hollywood adaptation that ends in a sensational mess when the beast people re-transform back into their animal shape, rise up to stab Dr. Moreau while shouting "Law no more!," and set the island on fire. Wells' novel instead ends with Wells' narrator Prendick rather silently returning to civilized London which makes him realize that his contemporaries are equally pitiful as the island's beast people.

Partly traumatized, partly disenchanted, the experiences on the island alienate Prendick from his surroundings in the novel. Treehouse of Horror takes up this idea, but transforms Wells' fear of human degradation into the Springfieldians' cheerful pleasure at the end of "The Island of Dr. Hibbert." Like in a holiday resort, the Springfield manimals fully assimilate to their new degenerated existence while lazily relaxing by the pool. Treehouse of Horror turns Prendick's horrific future vision into an American middle-class heterotopia. Treehouse's complex interweaving of different narratives and its re-formation of Wells' Gothic text demonstrates that the show fully engages in a Gothic gaze at the past of America's popular productions, while forging a new take on Hollywood's serializing practices that turned literary originals into pre-Code horror flicks for the masses.

Popular Gothic Fiction, Form, and Forensic Fandom:
Treehouse of Horror's "The Raven"

My final close reading is concerned with the American Gothic-fiction writer Edgar Allen Poe. It was mentioned before that Poe's *The Raven* is certainly the best-known literary adaptation of The Simpsons' Treehouse which premiered in 1990 in the show's very first Halloween Special. It was also mentioned earlier that a large part of its complexity builds on the layering of multiple dimensions of voice. According to the categories of narratologist Gérard Genette, Lisa's extra-diegetic voice is replaced by the sonorous sound of actor James Earl Jones' extra-diegetic voice-over. That changes the level on which the act of narration takes place which is further suspended by Homer's intra-diegetic voice. In the course of the storytelling process, the extra-diegetic narration by Jones means that Lisa's voice takes over a meta-diegetic, explanatory function when responding to Bart's critical comments. A second aspect of the segment's complexity is how the writers anticipated audience reception. Both aspects deserve more detailed investigation.

Before I talk about including the viewer, I first want to ask: What or who is the audience? As I initially explained, the segment demands "forensic fandom." It is almost impossible to watch Treehouse's "The Raven" without noting the formal complexity of the adaptation. The strategic use of genre mixing and transtextual referencing as well as the layering of different diegeses (i.e. storyworlds) oscillating between extra-, intra-, and meta-textual narration, have influenced my way of watching the show in general and awakened my forensic interest in the generic framing of the Halloween Special. I have already stated in previous chapters that The Simpsons' creators define 'audience' not simply as the people who occasionally watch the show. Rather, the series' audience is understood to consist of actively engaged, highly committed, and media-literate fans.

In his article "Making Fun of Genres," Jason Mittell suggests in 2004 that genre television invites viewers to activate, construct, draw upon, or revise generic categories (cf. 99). Such audience activity clearly goes beyond critics' sometimes cursory inspection of the Treehouse series as "annual spook spoofs" (cf. Ashley 379) that are just "dusting off creaky old tales" (cf. Rabin 2011). Treehouse's "The Raven" evidences that even if the segment is a straight reenactment of Poe's original text, there are various visual and aural components that complement and increase the segment's narrative complexity. The decoding of the dialogical relation between cartoon parody and Gothic poetry unravels the complex cultural practices operating within the different genre categories. Because of those practices it does not suffice to confine "The Raven" to a narrow genre box. Whereas some critics considered the segment a "trashy camp" version, spreading "the deadening air of the classroom" (cf. Rabin 2010), the parody of Poe's poem set the generic standards for the coming years of Treehouse of Horror. Jason Mittell suggests:

> You cannot simply watch these programs as an unmediated window to a storyworld into which you might escape; rather complex television demands you to pay attention to the window frames, asking you to reflect in how it provides partial access to the diegesis and how the panes of glass distort your vision on the unfolding [...] – complex television at its best employs all of these elements while adding the operational possibilities of formal engagement.
>
> *(2015: 53)*

As an example of Treehouse's complexity, its "Raven" version invites us to pay attention to various "window frames" which open onto ever new ways to analyze the segment. My close reading of Treehouse's adaptation will show how its "panes of glass" have distorted, i.e. irritated at least my own "vision on the unfolding." After every visit to the segment, I felt more and more engaged both in the segment's textual as well as formal storytelling.

Readers of *The Raven* celebrate Poe's best-known poem for its musicality, atmospheric density, its supernatural intensity, and, most notably, for its composition. All of these features were essential in Poe's poetic construct with which he aimed at "dénouement" and "unity of effect" (Poe 163–164).[92] According to Poe's seminal essay "The Philosophy of Composition," emotional excitement depends on a work's length, but 'keeping it short' does not foreclose complexity.[93] How this resonates on various levels with Treehouse's animated interpretation will soon become visible.

Lisa announces to read a "classic tale of terror" when she presents to her siblings Maggie and Bart a bound copy of E. A. Poe's *The Raven*. Lisa's plan is attacked by her brother Bart, who disparages Poe's poetry collection as "schoolbook" material. His statement does not only express his contempt for Poe's work as belonging to the literary canon of the North-American education system. Bart's pre-pubescent defiance also hints at a seeming incompatibility between a classic Gothic tale and his own consumerist Halloween habitus. Through Bart's character, the show acknowledges the difficulty of making 19th-century Gothic poetry scary and thus relevant to contemporary audiences raised on slasher movies like Wes Craven's A Nightmare on Elm Street from 1984 (cf. Rabin 2010). Bart's rejection continues as he intermittently disrupts Lisa's exposition with "Are we scared yet?" or a remark that anything else would be scarier than the poem. Lisa admonishes him to stop because Poe is "establishing mood." 'Mood' is a crucial component of Poe's unity of effect which is necessary for the reader's sensual delights when indulging in the poem's horror.

In his novel *The Narrative of Arthur Gordon Pym* (1838), Poe wrote that "words have no power to impress the mind without the exquisite horror of their reality" (105). Lisa's hint at the necessity of mood allows for second thoughts concerning the importance of the question whether a 19th-century text can still terrify an audience living within the reality of 1990. So she points to what a story needs to produce a lasting psychological effect. Besides the adequate framing of telling a horror story on Halloween, "establishing mood" can be related to the scary tenor of James Earl Jones[94] which adds depth to the scary gravitas that perfectly re-

92 For more information, see Edgar Allan Poe's essay "The Philosophy of Composition" first published in *Graham's Magazine*, Vol. 28, Nr. 4, (1846): 163–167.
93 Although (or perhaps because) Poe dismisses the necessity to write poems in order to "suit at once the popular and the critical taste" ("PoC" 163), he claims that prose is only the sum of brief poetical effects, or, in other words, of intense, and therefore necessarily brief, excitements (cf. "PoC" 164). He writes: "It appears evident, then, that there is a distinct limit, as regards length, to all works of literary art – the limit of a single sitting – and that […] it can never properly be overpassed in a poem. Within this limit, the extent of a poem may be made to bear mathematical relation to its merit – in other words, to the excitement or elevation – again in other words, to the degree of the true poetical effect which is capable of inducing; for it is clear that the brevity must be in direct ratio of the intensity of the intended effect: – this, with one proviso – that a certain degree of duration is absolutely requisite for the production of any effect at all" (Poe, "PoC" 164).
94 James Earl Jones is also known for his voice acting of the villain Mufasa in Disney's The Lion King (1994).

34–35 The Raven sits on the bust of Pallas, the goddess of wisdom, who turns her head in horror in the Treehouse version.

flects Poe's psychological strategy of "dénouement." Jones becomes the actual narrating voice of Poe's poem, while Lisa and Bart control the meta-diegetic level outside the narration and perform as intra-diegetic figures within the story, too.

The background scenery largely reminds of Gustave Doré's steel-plate engravings from 1883, visually capturing the Gothic feel.[95] Doré's illustrations are mirrored in an animated setting that includes high ceilings, heavy curtains, the wooden chamber door, the halo around the raven, the velvet armchair, and the winged seraphim angels. In addition, Poe created the raven as an unbearable threat to the poem's narrator. When the raven flies into the room and lands on the bust of Pallas, the Greek goddess of wisdom, Poe's as well as Bart's raven both symbolize a menace to the nameless narrator's reason.

The comparison between Doré's and Treehouse of Horror's depiction of the raven sitting on the bust of Pallas (cf. Fig. 34) shows that in opposition to Doré's version the animated goddess of wisdom averts her gaze from the scene below her as if she could no longer bear to look down on the narrator Homer. The growing tension between the raven and the narrator is remediated as a metaphor for the father-son conflict between Homer and Bart in the Treehouse version. Raven Bart infuriates the desperate Homer and causes his ultimate madness by dropping other Poe-related books onto his head, thus defying Homer's reason and 'wisdom' (as represented by the bust of Pallas who turns her head in horror) (cf. Fig. 35).

After the last "Nevermore," the terror unfolds in the ultimate climactic moment: Voice over, dramatic off score, and twisted angles culminate in a scene that can be read as the illustration of Homer's 'real' dread. The viewers return to the framing narrative which is situated in the treehouse where they have been introduced to Lisa's Halloween reading. The camera zooms out to show how father

---

95 For a better illustration, see the complete set of "Gustave Doré's Beautiful 1883 Illustrations for EdgarAllen Poe's 'The Raven'" on *Brainpickings.org*, illustrated and discussed by Maria Popova, posted on 05 Aug. 2015 under URL: https://bit.ly/3abT4ux.

Homer is sitting outside on the treehouse's ladder obviously scared to death as he trembles with terror.

The parody of "The Raven" sets high standards with respect to the other Gothic translations within the Treehouse corpus. Reanimating a 19th-century Gothic poem means that it has to be modernized and given a new look to reach out to younger audiences. The operational aesthetics of the segment's so-called Easter Eggs are thoroughly embedded in the cartoon translation and tailored to the specific demands of audiences who first had to learn how to watch such a Gothic cartoon.

The Gothic décor and Halloween framing enhances The Simpsons' representation of psychological terror and graphic scare remediated in a cartoon-sitcom format that aims to be both scary and educationally relevant. The jumping back and forth between (Gothic) horror and (cartoon) comedy becomes a complex transmedial circuit between Poe, Doré, and Groening which redefines the rules for pop-cultural continuity. Cultural-studies scholar Linda Hutcheon described this continuity as a double process of installing and ironizing by which "the parody signals how present representations come from past ones and what ideological consequences derive from both continuity and difference" (*Politics* 1986: 93). The parody weaves the sinister mood of Poe's 19th-century text into the visual representations of Gustave Doré's steel-plate engravings each of which are again translated into Treehouse's complex language playing with continuity (for the sake of a coherent reception) and difference (for the sake of disruptive humor).

It has been illustrated that to filter what Hutcheon calls the "ideological consequences" from Treehouse's "Raven" requires a quite literate form of fandom. To return to Mittell's notion of complex TV, viewers of the Treehouse-specific processing "find themselves both drawn into a compelling diegesis (as with all effective stories) and focused on the discursive processes of storytelling needed to achieve each show's complexity and mystery" (2015: 52). By renegotiating practices of a 19th-century reading (Lisa, Homer) by way of those of a 20th-century viewer (Bart), the "Raven" parody delivers the satirical attitude of how the show engages with its contemporary 'forensic fans.'

Between my first rather clueless watching of The Simpsons Halloween Special and my present, more advanced status lies a long period of practicing and learning how to become part of an active audience who is capable of creatively reading genre. Mittell explains that in a time when genres transcend the bounds of media texts, audience practices are becoming more than just reception, consumption, or textual decoding (cf. 2004: 100). Genres, according to Mittell, rather "include discourses of definition and evaluation, as well as interpretation" (2004: 100). Any of these discourses are based on what I have defined as generic irritation. Viewers re-view how a 19th-century Gothic text was re-formed to merge into something entirely new; something which has definitely shaped my own – but certainly also many others' – way of defining, assessing, and interpreting the complexity of TREEHOUSE OF HORROR within the past thirty years.

Conclusion: The Complexity of Cartoon Storytelling in TREEHOUSE OF HORROR

All my readings prove that THE SIMPSONS has invented a form of complex TV which highlights the popular original texts as potent and persistent cultural discourses. Based on Mittell's complexity approach, I first explored what specific vocabulary TREEHOUSE OF HORROR has developed. The show's literary adaptations are trans-medial translations working largely within the supergenre of the Gothic. In a second step, I examined how the show's particular visual and aural techniques were realized on television's own medium terms.

In this context, Stephen King's allegory of Gothic texts acting as "cultural echo chamber[s]" has proven helpful as the TREEHOUSE series presents to its viewers' how American popular culture can literally be captured within the small echo chambers of the television apparatus, in form of three-to-five minute long genre irritations. Here, Mittell's premises of alternative television storytelling are realized in terms of production and content as well as in viewers' invitation to become an active part of the content and of the formal operations of the story. Preparing the ground for my subsequent analyses of cinematic horror portrayed in the TREEHOUSE cycle and of Rod Serling's 1960s THE TWILIGHT ZONE anthology series, my investigation aimed to outline the following arguments.

THE SIMPSONS' creator Matt Groening not only set up a whole new vocabulary predicated on specific facets of the sitcom format; he moreover revolutionized the conventional TV formula with TREEHOUSE OF HORROR, a Gothic cartoon that is worth bearing the label of complex TV. After all, Matt Groening says in a 2009 interview that his "goal from the very beginning was to invade pop culture."[96] With TREEHOUSE OF HORROR's Gothic genre irritations, Groening has not only forced his way into untrodden spaces for television storytelling. He moreover persistently trampled on older viewing habits. He taught us that 19th-century Gothic literature can be relevant and scary by opening up new ways of looking at American culture and of developing practices suited to watching complex television in the digital age. Thus, even if TREEHOUSE OF HORROR is "trashy camp" or at times "spreads the deadening air of the classroom," this doesn't mean the show forecloses narrative complexity.

---

96 The quote is taken from Morgan Spurlock's THE SIMPSONS 20TH ANNIVERSARY SPECIAL. IN 3D! ON ICE! (Fox 2009).

History Lesson No. 3 | Exotic Islands, Haunted Houses, and Home Invasions: TREEHOUSE OF HORROR's Cinematic Archive

> "Sometimes a mysterious invisible being from hell waits for a family to go to sleep and then kills them."
> – Homer Simpson.

> "We really heard a lot of people saying they wanted something that was scary – and this one's scary."
> – Al Jean

In 2018, I couldn't wait to watch the syndicated 28th edition of the TREEHOUSE series on German television together with my 10-year-old who, at that point, had become slightly infected with my excitement over, especially, the horror show of THE SIMPSONS. I had already seen the American version of ToH XXVIII aired on Fox one year earlier in the week before Halloween 2017,[97] but I was particularly eager to see my son's reaction to something that was unique up to this point even on German television. Besides the first segment which presents Maggie as the possessed incarnation of Linda Blair from William Friedkin's possession tale THE EXORCIST from 1973, and the second adapted horror tale, "Coralisa," an homage to Henry Selick's stop-motion dark fantasy-horror film CORALINE[98] from 2009, the third segment "Mmm ... Homer" was a novelty. For the first time in twenty-seven years, the segment is introduced with a message to the audience by Lisa who is ironically warning us: "What you're about to see is so disgusting, you'll watch GAME OF THRONES to calm down!" And right she was. What my son was about to see definitely taught him a lesson in cinematic horror. The segment is packed with a form of violence which has a long history in cinema, but certainly not on television.

"Mmm ... Homer" is a straightforward body-horror cartoon which shows what happens when Homer Simpson is left alone at home over the weekend and runs out of food. While barbecuing the last remaining frozen hot dog, Homer accidentally cuts off his finger which consequently lands on the grill. Enchanted by the delicate smell, Homer eats his finger and begins to gain increasing pleasure from cutting off ever more parts of his body to cook "asseroles" and make "pastra-me" of himself (see Fig. 36). When Marge and the children return home, Homer first tries to hide his dismembered body from his family by wearing oven mitts that hide his incomplete hands. Homer's self-cannibalism eventually ends when the American star chef and restaurant owner Mario Batali arrives. On his quest to

---

[97] TREEHOUSE OF HORROR XXVIII, s29e04. Dir. Timothy Bailey. Fox, orig. air date 22 Oct. 2017.
[98] Neil Gaiman, who wrote the modern Alice-in-Wonderland fantasy-horror novella CORALINE (2002) Selick's stop-motion movie is based on, also lends his voice to the cat Snowball V.

3 Analysis | TREEHOUSE OF HORROR: Lessons to Remember

36 Homer makes "asseroles and "pastra-me" from his respective body parts in "Mmm... Homer" from ToH XXVIII (Fox 2017)

find new ingredients, Batali finds Homer who invites him to cook his remaining body and brain to be served to other Springfield cannibalistic gourmets for the restaurant opening of "Chez Homer." Marge and the children seem almost proud that Homer has literally "made something of himself," indicating that Homer's body for once fulfills a purpose. In "Mmm... Homer" the Simpsons' home is turned into a place for the breaking of a major taboo.

My son's visible irritation confirmed my premonitions. His inability to quickly forget his new horror experience ties in with the initial quote from executive show runner Al Jean who suggests that TREEHOUSE OF HORROR XXVIII just gave fans what they had wanted (remember "The Monkey's Paw" pattern of "Be careful what you wish for!"). Clicking through the critical commentaries on web platforms such as The Internet Movie Database, IGN, or *The A. V. Club*, I found reviews that shared a common language. Apparently, Homer's self-inflicted body horror had irritated many viewers. Self-cannibalism is usually not thought to be funny and you don't expect to see it during primetime on network television. Among fan reviews, "Mmm... Homer" is the most "disturbing segment" and carries the label "unsettling and scary." Beside the collective disgust, reviews also reveal perplex appreciation. One fan describes the segment as "gross and weird" and then concludes: "It was amazing!" Another review comments that the segment is "certainly not for the faint-hearted, but I really admire how far they went this season" (cf. *IMDB.com*). "How far they went" indicates that the idea of graphic horror in TREEHOUSE can become taboo-breaking which has obviously taken the format to new scary heights (cf. Snierson 2017).

Such horrifying extravaganza usually belongs to the critical circles of cinephile shop talks, but is rarely heard when it comes to network-television content. Al Jean tells *Entertainment Weekly* that they wanted "to turn up the horror factor

[to] surprise those fans who wanted the horror back in Treehouse of Horror" (Snierson 2017). The gross, unsettling humor which the audiences witnessed in this 2017 Treehouse of Horror demonstrates how (cinematic) horror can be remediated for new purposes. The segment "Mmm … Homer" attests to Lorna Jowett and Stacey Abbott's statement at the beginning of their book-length exploration of TV Horror, namely that "horror begins at home" (2013: xi).

In Treehouse's annual 'trilogy of terror,' each act deals with a different form of domestic horror. Maggie's possession in the "The Exor-Cis," the parental misconduct in "Coralisa," and the self-cannibalism in "Mmm … Homer" question the compatibility of the horror genre with commercial network television. The episode is replete with references which may challenge fans' knowledge of cinematic genre-horror. In this chapter, I therefore examine how film horror has found a new home in Treehouse of Horror. I will ask what kind of genre-horror films The Simpsons' Halloween show has adapted and translated into its own animated language and explore the concrete functions of remediation for the televisual context.

My aim is to discuss how Treehouse of Horror has remediated a range of horror films in order to generically, aesthetically, and formally oscillate between different forms of remembering genre texts that have almost been forgotten. The British horror scholars Jowett and Abbott assume that "the relationship between horror and television is fraught with tension and potential" (2013: xiii) and it is my aim to reveal how these tensions and potentials have been made use of in the reimagining of filmic horror in the Treehouse cycle.

Objects for Cinematic Horror: Television / Monsters / Abnormal Homes

The Simpsons' horror show has given its audiences an insight into how to give a new animated home to various horror sub-genres, such as the 1930s radio play[99] or the Gothic sitcoms of the 1960s.[100] However, the following anaylsis suggests a different path. In contrast to The Simpsons, Treehouse of Horror has a keen interest in cinematic horror. Following the idea that "horror begins at home" hence

---

99 The ToH episode such as "The Day The Earth Looked Stupid" (s18e04, Fox 2006) is not so much a parody of Robert Wise's black-and-white science-fiction feature The Day The Earth Stood Still from 1951 or its radio broadcast of the same name from 1954, but instead a love letter to Orson Welles' Halloween radio play and H. G. Wells' novel adaptation War Of The Worlds from 1938. The Halloween segment is reminiscent of the tradition of the radio play by portraying an imagery of how the people consumed radio, how Foley artists created sound effects of the Martian invasion, and how committed Orson Welles was in the interpretation of H. G. Wells' classic science-fiction tale from 1898. For more information, see John Dunning's *On The Air: The Encyclopedia of Old-Time Radio* from 1998.
100 In terms of its sustainable success as a Gothic horror comedy, Treehouse of Horror both shares a lot with and, similarly, owes a lot to the black-and-white television sitcoms The Munsters on CBS (1964–1966) and The Addams Family on ABC (1964–1966).

requires an investigation of how the Halloween Special paved the way for cinema to enter our living rooms and expose us to all kinds of different genre horror.

In 1919, Sigmund Freud's study of E. T. A. Hoffmann's short story "Der Sandmann" / "The Sandman" (1816) ascertains that the uncanny cannot be found without the presence of the familiar.[101] *The Sandman* is a dark Romantic tale in which the main characters Nathanael and Coppola compete for the love of Spalanzani's mysterious yet beautiful daughter Olimpia. The woman whose attractive appearance first seems so appealing to the two men, ultimately reveals being an automaton that only looks like a human. Olimpia is uncanny because her mechanical movements are familiar, but almost too perfect to be human. In other words, as this and other examples from the Gothic and the German *Schauerroman* prove, the supposed homelyness of the home, the familiarity of characters and plots, as well as of recurring traditions can suddenly lead to an antithetical reaction in readers and make them feel eerie, strange, and haunting.

The German word for 'homely' is '*heimlich*' which has two divergent meanings (cf. Freud 1919: 2). On the one hand, '*heimlich*' equals '*heimisch*' which refers to the domestic and the family as an intimate, familiar comfort zone; on the other hand, '*heimlich*' means that within the home there exists something repressed, hidden, or traumatic. Watching a horror story like "Mmm … Homer" on your television at home thus leads to an uncanny experience when the television set amidst the intimate sanctuary of the home suddenly turns into a site of estrangement.

The author of *Gothic TV*, Helen Wheatley, claimed television to be the ideal medium for horror. She argues that there is a synergy between horror and television because certain events are made more frightening by being broadcast on TV and thus watched within the domestic space (cf. 2006: xi). In my first analysis, I will take a glance at those animated movie reworkings in which the television is itself the object of horror as a 'haunted medium' that unsettles the familiarity of the family's protected home. The double entendre of television's 'home invasion' motif is not about the 'boob tube' indispensability for American households, but rather about the terrors television itself can hold. In this context, I will employ the TREEHOUSE segments "The Terror of Tiny Toon," "UNnormal Activity," and "The Others" to reflect about the meaning of TV as a popular source of uncanniness in the horror movie.

Secondly, thanks to the changing landscape of television within the past thirty years, especially American (but also British) film horror has had a somewhat positive influence on the prominence and popularity of horror themes and motifs on television. Around Halloween time in particular, American audiences are used to the cozy 'pastness' (cf. Hills 123) of classic black-and-white horror films such as RKO's KING KONG (1933) and Hammer's Gothic mysteries starring Vincent Price

---

101 Get full access to Sigmund Freud's "The Uncanny" from 1919 on URL: https://web.mit.edu/allanmc/www/freud1.pdf.

and Christopher Lee, F. W. Murnau's expressionistic Nosferatu: Eine Symphonie des Grauens (1922) or Bela Lugosi's Dracula performance (1931).

While rummaging through the list of Treehouse episodes that show a clear affiliation to cinematic classics, film-horror adaptations begin with texts from the early 1930s which have a significant influence on our perception of horror and the monster on television to this day. The rediscovery of classical horror movies on television began in the 1950s when program makers needed to fill their expanding schedules. Jowett and Abbott explain that at that time, the Hollywood studios saw an opportunity to sell their back catalogue to television, thus developing a new strand of income (cf. 2013: 5). By taking a closer look at how Treehouse of Horror has re-discovered classical pre-Code movies to fill its own back-catalogue archive of movie references, I will reconsider how certain motifs of monstrosity and Gothic-horror aesthetics have been renegotiated in television's contemporary horror animation.

Treehouse's pre-Code horror archive includes two versions linked to James Whale's first sound feature of Shelley's Frankenstein (Universal 1931); the first is "If I Only Had A Brain" and the second "Frinkenstein" in which Prof. Frink reanimates his longtime shock-frozen father. In addition, the archive includes "Freaks, No Geeks," featuring Tod Browning's controversial body horror film Freaks (MGM 1932), the black-and-white animation "King Homer" which is an homage to Ernest B. Schoedsack's landmark sensational monster horror King Kong (RKO 1933), as well as the retranslation of Erle C. Kenton's The Island of Lost Souls (Paramount 1932), a film which I have already examined for its literary antics in the previous chapter. Most movies are likely known either on the basis of hearsay, for example, because a film's infamous iconicity has gone beyond the actual prominence of the film itself; or because they show a resurgence of the mad-scientist motif or of famous monsters such as King Kong.

With this in mind, the next paragraphs will be concerned with the special relation of the Treehouse series to the monsters of pre-Code Hollywood cinema. I will look at whether the black-and-white segments "King Homer" and "Freaks, No Geeks" are just (unfaithful) parodies, animated spoofs of the original films, or whether they are rather adaptations in cartoon form, attempting to translate, reimagine, or point to what the Hollywood films carefully tried to avoid showing, namely that audiences feel pity for the respective monsters and become critical about the status of the monster.

In addition to the Hollywood horror that is now restricted to TV's late-night Halloween slots, the anthology concept of the fifties and sixties by Hitchcock and Serling not only helped the medium to keep booming. Those landmark horror- and science-fiction anthologies further enabled the genre of horror to fuse into most other TV-relevant formats, from real-crime programs to Gothic soaps, to horror comedies and cartoon horror shows like the series at hand. Boris Karloff's

3 Analysis | TREEHOUSE OF HORROR: Lessons to Remember

THRILLER (NBC 1960–1962), Rex Marhall's SUSPENSE (CBS 1949–1954), and Rod Serling's THE TWILIGHT ZONE (CBS 1959–1964) terrified audiences by filling the home with oftentimes rather human monsters that haunted American homes.

Despite the fact that the anthology series will be closely scrutinized in the next chapter, which is fully dedicated to science-fiction television and the 1960s TWILIGHT ZONE series, these programs had a remarkable effect on the broader acceptance of horror in Western culture. When the censorship board of the Motion Picture Association of America (MPAA) lowered the regulations for graphic violence in 1970s movie productions, television's equivalent agency, Federal Communications Commission (FCC), also allowed more and more made-for-TV horror films and serials to become coated in the technicolored red of blood. Jowett and Abbott argue that the relaxation of censorship regulation "have changed how we come to understand it on television, requiring us to rethink what we mean by horror with a televisual context" (2013: xiii). Let us start to rethink horror by means of TREEHOUSE OF HORROR and within a television context.

Although horror has been at an all-time peak, the 1970s can certainly be read as the second golden age of the horror movie. In my third close-reading, I will shed light on the animated homages from TREEHOUSE OF HORROR's horror collection from the 1970s and 1980s. First, I am interested in exploring how the films' themes, motifs, and aesthetics have been rethought by creators of THE SIMPSONS and reworked for the televisual context. For example, can be postulated that the social and political climate of the '70s and '80s had an influence on the portrayal of the American family in relation to the unhomely horrors which the family members had to experience in AMITYVILLE HORROR (1979), POLTERGEIST (1982), or THE EXORCIST (1973). What kind of monsters had become the current threat to families during the Reagan era? How did the haunting of American homes manifest itself in the popular slasher and body-horror movies of the time? A prominent genre motif of '80s horror was built around the American family and their life that turns out to be a foremost economic nightmare which the TREEHOUSE segment "Bad Dream House" (Fox 1990) will demonstrate. By renegotiating what is behind many of the troubled-family-in-a-haunted-home horror films, I will explore what lessons the cartoon retrospective teaches about that not ghosts, but quite real social and political anxieties unsettled American families in the 1980s.

I will further pay attention to those famous horror films which helped some rather unknown Hollywood directors to become world-known cinematic auteurs with an unmistakable imprimatur (see chapter 3.1). It is exciting to explore how the TREEHOUSE horror archive presents to us different American horror traditions, storytelling aesthetics, and recurring motifs that have shaped our image of monsters, of television as the object of evil, and of haunted houses. Since I am essentially interested in investigating where precisely the horror begins in the home of the Simpsons during TREEHOUSE times, I chose an example that can be categorized as psychological horror, ascending from the (under)ground of familial normality. "The Shinning," a film homage to Stanley Kubrick's 1980 movie THE SHINING, evidences that TREEHOUSE OF HORROR stands out from the average attempts to produce television horror by reimagining auteur films. Without Kubrick's THE SHINING our perception of psychological terror amidst the American family would certainly not be the same.

Since the television medium was given a new domestic companion with the VCR,[102] a home video system that invaded the American households most prominently in the 1980s, watching television at home was certainly the first contact zone to familiarize children and adolescents with the defamiliarizing moments of the horror genre. Since I have started to watch TREEHOUSE OF HORROR together with my 10-year-old son, I have come to understand how the horror stories have trained his media literacy and improved his textual skills of dealing with horror of the past from a present-day perspective. The following analyses will demonstrate that horror begins at home in many different regards. I will take you on a cinematic journey through different periods of American horror-film production. This journey begins with my son and me sitting in front of the television screen and watching hours of TREEHOUSE OF HORROR that taught us how to enjoy a plethora of memorable film-horror moments.

TREEHOUSE OF HORROR and the Strange Site of Television

In a regular opening of a SIMPSONS' episode, each family member comes from a different direction to eventually meet on the couch in the living room and switch on the TV. From a meta-reflexive position, the Simpson family meets our gaze at the screen. They simulate how we are sitting in front of our television sets, observing how the Simpsons switch on the television. The introduction to TREEHOUSE OF HORROR episodes functions, however, completely differently. I have explained earlier that the Simpsons sometimes make their way into the living room while breaking through the floor as zombies or by falling down from the ceiling with a noose around their neck. The Simpsons' unconventional appearances demonstrate that the home in the horror episodes does not depend on doors, but has permeable borders, is haunted and can easily be invaded by killers who just wait on the couch for the family's return.

When we watch the Simpsons in the opening of TREEHOUSE episodes, the family often mirrors and acknowledges our media literacy. In my chapter on the cartoon auteur my assumption was that couch-gag openings can be sites where the

---

102 The first analogue home video-cassette-recording system, short VCR-system, was invented by Grundig and Philips already in 1971, but only became a commercial success when the film industry started to market their products also on VHS tapes for the home use.

Simpsons meet all kinds of different cartoon characters from other media contexts (e. g. Rick and his grandson Morty from Rick & Morty or the Belcher family from Bob's Burgers).[103] The Simpsons virtually seem to invade our television screens and become incarnations of how we allow "unwholesome intrusions into the home through the permeable membrane of its screen" (Stephens 2014). Instead of invading the Simpsons' home, which The Simpsons invites us to do in the regular series, we allow the Simpsons to enter our homes through the screen in a way specific to the Treehouse of Horror series as the following paragraphs will show.

German film scholar Arno Meteling writes on the mediality of monstrosity in his book-length study *Monster* from 2006. He observes that particularly in horror films of the 1980s and the New-Gothic films of the 1990s, audiovisual technology becomes a representational marker of the medium film. By not only presenting bodies, but also audiovisual media as spaces of terror and sensation, Meteling sees as clear linkage to the literary tradition of the Gothic horror stories and their ill-fated use of Galvanism, mad scientists, man machines, hubris and perdition (cf. 2006: 11–12). Television's mediality of being not only an object, but a dynamic point to actively transform the home into a space for horror, invites to look into those Treehouse moments in which the horror derives from the television itself.

Treehouse of Horror extensively worked its way through the classics of literature, horror cinema, and television, but in its eighth edition (1997) it responds to the ambiguous censorship regulations for animation on network TV in a cold opening, i. e. a sequence that precedes the opening theme and credits in sitcoms. Stephen King has argued that it is very difficult to write a successful horror story for a televisual context in a world which is so full of real horrors (cf. 133). Besides or perhaps because of the 'real horrors,' in the period of Reaganomics and during the Bush era, sensitive interest groups pushed censorship to ban graphic violence and controversial horror from cartoon television. I will illustrate how Treehouse of Horror addressed this conflict in the cold opening to ToH VIII, introducing the episode's "commendably nasty flair for nihilism," as a critic writes on the Internet Movie Database (*IMDB.com* 2004). This nihilism was obviously directed at the networks' standards and practices.

A static camera presents a Fox censor reading through the episode's script. He disparagingly laughs while crossing out the script's dialogues before he introduces himself to the audience. "Hi, as the Fox censor it is my job to protect you from re-

---

103 Rick and Morty from Rick & Morty crash into the Simpsons' living room in the opening to "Mathlete's Feat" (s26e22, Fox 2015). On his quest to find the missing sail-boat painting that has disappeared in the Simpsons' living room, Homer meets (and kills) the South Park children in the opening to "The Cad and the Hat" (s28e11, Fox 2017). In the opening to "My Way or the Highway to Heaven" (s30e03, Fox 2019) Homer is not pushed into the living room at the end of the family's rush home as usual, but lands in the burger restaurant of Bob Belcher, the father figure of Fox's other prime time cartoon hit Bob's Burger (since 2011).

ality." Thanks to his self-attested prudence, he rates the Halloween Special "TV-G" and promises that there will be "no raunchy NBC-style sex or senseless CBS-style violence." Suddenly, the "TV-G" sign morphs into a hand holding a sword and stabbing the censor from behind. With every stab, the label changes from "TV-G" (unrestricted) across "TV-PG" (with parental guidance) and "TV-14" (viewers aged 14 and older) as well as "TV-MA" (inappropriate) to "TV-21" (non-existent). The sword only stops slaughtering the censor when he collapses dead on his desk. The last sign reads "TV-666" perhaps for content which is only suitable for the devil.

The opening shows TREEHOUSE OF HORROR complementing its annual presentations of animated 'horror on television' with its own 'television horror' cartoon. In a related review, TV editor Erik Adams writes on *The A. V. Club*, with this cold opening TREEHOUSE stabs its way to a "TV-MA," leaving a telling report about the state of the network's Department of Standards and Practices, but also of the culture in the late nineties (cf. Adams 2015). According to Adams, American culture in the late 1990s was driven by public statements and complaints of Congress members, claiming that THE SIMPSONS was too violent. But Adams also addresses the fact that THE SIMPSONS at that time had already become one of the strongest forces in television's 'cartoon wars' era, leaving a clear statement that the world of the 1990s was different than the world of the 1980s (cf. Adams 2015).

Before horror on television could overcome one of its major obstacles in the 1980s, censorship regulations and parental organizations were diligent to prohibit graphic depictions of body horror and violence (cf. Jowett/Abbott 2013: 131). In 1997, the same year ToH VIII was aired, more primetime animations began to invade the small screen with the even raunchier series BEAVIS AND BUTTHEAD (MTV 1993–1997, 2011), KING OF THE HILL (Fox 1997–2010), and most prominently the premiere of SOUTH PARK on Comedy Central (since 1997). These shows' vulgar language, overt portrayal of body horror and graphic violence significantly changed television's animated horror landscape. For the first time in network-television history, the changing scope of animated horror encouraged TREEHOUSE's creators to claim their freedom to further push visual boundaries.

In the context of pushing boundaries, horror scholar Matt Hills' remarks in his seminal book *The Pleasures of Horror* (2005) that television has long been a "para-site" for horror (iii) which the "relative invisibility of horror on television" proved especially in the 1990s. In contrast to the 'real horror' shown on the daily news, program makers obviously still relied on L-O-Ps ('Least Objectionable Programs')[104] and feel-good programming which, at the very most, included nostalgic black-and-white period horror featuring Boris Karloff or Peter Cushing.

---

104 Least Objectionable Program production is a broadcasting paradigm that was developed in the 1960s by former NBC vice president Paul Klein and was influenced by Marshall McLuhan's *Understanding Media* (1964). In the *TV Guide* interview from 1971 "Why You Watch What You

This trend was only countered by the fact that, since the 1990s, TREEHOUSE OF HORROR had rediscovered the marginalized genre so that it literally developed into a medium-infesting 'parasite' itself that above all influenced the generic hybridity between graphic horror and cartoon comedy. Because animators proved in TREEHOUSE for the first time that a horror comedy could not only play for laughs, but that it could be used in controversial and innovative ways. TREEHOUSE OF HORROR's meta-reflexive genre mixing of horror film and a television-comedy formula plays a prominent role when it comes to questioning the television industry, its modes of reception as well as its fixed discourses (see Hills 2005; Carroll 1990; Leffler 2000; Tudor 1997; Dresser 1989; Waller 1986).

Considering the changing modes of reception in the 1980s, Helen Wheatley inspired me to read the concept of television in TREEHOUSE OF HORROR in two different ways: the television set at the end of the episodes' opening is a metaphorical window that provides us a view to the outside of American (popular) culture and its history. But at the same time, the television in TREEHOUSE openings also functions as a mirror that reflects quite specific forms of domestic interiors in and in front of the screen (cf. Wheatley 106). When thinking of, for example, the many horror movies of the 1980s, we may remember those which featured the television set as a source of horror.

In POLTERGEIST (1982), the television set was neither a window nor a mirror, but a telekinetic portal leading to a family's eternal damnation. POLTERGEIST imagines the television as the central point of ghostly activity within a modern American home (cf. Jowett/Abbott 2013: 179). The same is true in the Japanese RINGU (1998) and its American adaptation THE RING (2002). In both movies, the audience is exposed to television's terror by way of a cursed video tape that proclaims death of those who watch it. Other film examples such as SHOCKER (1989) and NIGHTMARE ON ELM STREET III (1987) present the television as a magic way out of oppressive institutions, in these cases jail and psychiatry. In SHOCKER, television technician Horace Pinker loves his job because it enables him to pursue his hobby of murdering entire families in their homes, who called Horace to fix their television-technical problems. After several murders, the psychopathic Horace is send to death row and obviously cannot wait to be electrocuted. Because as soon as

---

Watch When You Watch," Paul Klein explains that producing L-O-P means to understand audience attraction not as a matter of "pleasing the greatest number of viewers but of offending the fewest" (qtd. in Grossberg et al. 125). In their joint publication *MediaMaking* from 2006, Lawrence Grossberg and other media scholars note that the L-O-P attitude is "hardly a strategy for innovative or novel products" but one that maximizes "the potential market by rethinking the product itself" (125). Rethinking the product itself meant to reproduce old formulae with few adaptations. Therefore the paradigm had a particular influence on the sameness of sitcoms. Klein was convinced that to be successful, television programs had to remain formulaic, cliché-ridden, instantly familiar, predictable, and monotonous in tone (cf. Grossberg et al. 125).

the surges reach his body, it seems as if electrical currents flow through his veins which increase his physical voltage to the point that he can zap himself into the television. Horace consequently can escape from his prison cell into the television to 'shock' the families' in their home, through their TV screens. The same form of the TV as the medium of home invasions is used in Dream Warrior (1987), the third edition of the Nightmare on Elm Street franchise.

Teenager Jennifer suffers from serious nightmares, auto-aggressive behavior, and sleep disorder which is the reason why she is a patient in the film's central location, the youth psychiatry. But since Freddy Krueger visits the adolescents in their dreams, the serial killer does not care what place his victims call their home. In order not to fall asleep, Jennifer zaps through the television in the clinic's TV room. As it is late at night, she falls asleep while watching a late-night show. Of course, Freddy Krueger takes his chance: His head and arms come out of the television, the killer grabs Jennifer, and slams her head into the TV while joking: "This is it, Jennifer. Your big break in TV. Welcome to prime time, bitch!" In this case, Jennifer's nightmare helps Freddy to cause her death by means of the television. In each of the last two examples, the TV inescapably channels the evil into families' living rooms. David Cronenberg's Videodrome (1983) unfolds its horror by presenting the TV screen as a semi-permeable membrane which turns into a corrupting gate to moral hell. Videodrome's concept of television turns viewers into passive-aggressive zombies, a recurring genre motif.

Currently, the Netflix hit Stranger Things (since 2016) returns to these films in its striking 1980s retromania. The series' creators, the Duffer brothers, highlight the television set as a telekinetic medium, portrayed as a liminal space in-between different worlds that literally widens the main character Eleven's psycho-kinetic and telepathic sight onto the upside-down world of Hawkins, where the lives of her friends are in serious danger. Hence the Duffer brothers, belonging to a young generation of directors, acknowledge television as a prosthetic device that enables Eleven to improve her ability as a seer.

Horror cinema frequently revolted against television's negative influence by essentializing cinema as the "genre's natural home" (Hills 2015: iii). Similar to Stranger Things, the Treehouse series often presents television as a point of access to the animated upside-down world that widens our view on American domestic consumption. In iconic horror films of the 1980s and 1990s such as Poltergeist and The Ring films, Shocker, and Nightmare's Dream Warrior, or Videodrome, television becomes "a symbol of anxiety over the insidious reach of outside influences into the domestic sphere, […] a medium for psychic pollution, physical corruption and deadly trespass," as *A. V. Club* blogger Emily Stephens argues (2014). In *TV Horror*, Jowett and Abbott explain that TV horror nevertheless continues to represent the television as a potentially malevolent portal, leaving aside the fact that its 'spectral' technology is indeed nothing new anymore. They define the homely television as "a gateway to another world" that transforms the domestic space into a site of defamiliarizing trauma, a sphere in which the television forces us to recognize ourselves. For a long time, the medium of television was criticized being the central disrupting force in horror movies. Stephens writes, "It's not just television's ubiquitousness that poses a threat, but the vacuum it fills" (2014). Stephens' rather negative notion on television's role as meaningful, integral part to fill the inner void in our living rooms somehow tunes in with Jowett and Abbott's more positive suggestion that television as the subject of horror is a means to express our changing relationship with domestic media technologies (cf. 2013: 181).

'Filling the Vacuum' I: ToH's "The Terror of Tiny Toon"

In the TREEHOUSE episode "The Terror of Tiny Toon" from ToH IX, the television fills Bart and Lisa's existential 'vacuum' of the home. The two Simpson children are even absorbed by television and become not only passive observers, but active targets of their beloved cat-and-mouse heroes in "The Itchy and Scratchy Show." Through a modified plutonium remote control, the children press a button to "enter" the apparatus and can only be rescued by Homer who zaps them back into the living room. The plutonium-energized remote control needs to be read as a prosthetic device to extend television's disruptive influence usually by empowering audiences to control their consumption from the living-room couch. According to Arno Meteling's suggestion, by using a modified remote, the television receives a 'demonic quality' visualizing the suburban terror through the transmissive medium of television (cf. 2006: 317).

Unlike in POLTERGEIST which shows the little girl just in front of the television set, "The Terror of Tiny Toon" converges the television not only into a mere threshold between worlds. Here television indeed serves as an interface between different medial practices (e.g. the Simpsons' realism as opposed to the cartoon 'unreality' of "The Itchy & Scratchy Show" or Lisa and Bart's short animated excursion into a live-action cook show). In short, the TV 'devours' Bart and Lisa's bodies and 'exhibits' the new content as a medium in itself (cf. Meteling 2006: 174). Homer is shown on the other side of the television glass screen, bored of watching Bart and Lisa in their attempt to survive. At the same time, this segment suggests that the screen is a permeable boundary that finally enables Itchy and Scratchy to follow Lisa and Bart into the reality of the Simpsons. The TREEHOUSE segment "The Terror of Tiny Toon" depicts television both as a window to other worlds and a mirror of our own consumption. Through the empowering means of the remote control, the segment hints at the first steps of the changing ways television content is received and manifests to what extent younger audiences begin to actively use and not passively consume television as an interactive media platform in the digital age.

37–38 "UNnormal Activity" transforms the Simpsons' home into a panopticon

'Filling the Vacuum' II: **ToH's "UNnormal Activity"**

"UNnormal Activity" from Treehouse of Horror XXIII comes entirely in the surveillance-camera style taking its inspiration from the Paranormal Activity movies filmed in the so-called 'found-footage style.' Director Oren Peli's[105] film that inspired an entire franchise[106] deals with nighttime hauntings manifested by the monitoring eye of surveillance cameras. The first take of "UNnormal Activity" shows Homer filming himself in the mirror noting that strange things are going on in the house at night (cf. Fig. 37). The strange things manifest in an unmotivated "hellfire" that ascends from the living room floor and a blood-written "Beware!" on the wall, prompting the Simpsons' to install CCTV all over the home. The CCTV-animation style (CCTV stands for "closed circuit television") first gives viewers the impression that there is an even greater cartoon realism involved. Due to a grainy animation as well as a camcorder framing, the animation operates with recognizable elements familiar from home-video and surveillance material (see Fig. 38).

---

105 Although Oren Peli only directed the first installment, he has been the producer of all of its sequels to date.
106 Starting the found-footage horror franchise in 2007, any of the subsequent movies, prequels, and spin-offs follow a similar narrative strategy and found-footage aesthetic. For more detailed information, see the official Paranormal Activity Wiki powered by Fandom website under URL:

My initial impression was that I am no longer watching, but observing, and thereby controlling the family through the camera eye. I felt like an eye-witness who controls the scene when the Simpsons are sleeping or weirdly standing in front of the bed for hours with eyes wide open. In his study *Surveillance and Film* (2016), film scholar Macgregor Wise suggests that in such cases our voyeurism becomes an act of power (cf. 1). In "UNnormal Activity" this voyeuristic power operates out of a need to extract information from the strange events in the Simpson home in order to control them and make sure nothing can escape our view (the red "REC" symbol confirms that the scene is documented on film). Wise continues to argue: "CCTV systems have come to be understood as meaning power, usually power to control. There is something we feel is sinister in such systems, though they are set up ostensibly for our protection." (2) In the bottom-right and top-left corners of the framed settings, a time stamp indicates the time and the room we are in. Additional insertions inform viewers about what day it is, similar to the camera footage in the Paranormal films. The split-screen further provides us with insights into four rooms at one time (cf. Fig. 27.2).

"UNnormal Activity," however, reveals the ultimate source of evil when the segment changes into, as police Chief Wiggum says, "a deal-with-the-devil-and-the-devil-wants-his-due" story. In the later course of the narrative, we are informed that thirty years ago, Marge's older sisters, Patty and Selma, summoned Satan when "there was nothing good on TV." Satan appeared and warned little Marge that he would return and take her favorite child. Obviously now the time has come to get Maggie. Unlike in "UNnormal Activity," in which the camera eventually reveals the source of evil as being Satan himself, the Paranormal films often leave their audience with grainy images that assume just a rough idea of a spectral phenomenon. Both the live-action horror of Paranormal Activity and the cartoon horror of "UNnormal Activity" build on the impression that the surveillance image is 'realistic' footage, putting the viewer in the position of an all-seeing, albeit powerless voyeur who uses CCTV as a prosthetic eye. The viewer passively witnesses, sometimes even in fast motion, how the families are plagued while peacefully sleeping in their respective rooms. Through the simultaneity and omnipresence of the surveillance image, viewers know more than the filmed characters. The master-bathroom camera shows how Homer stands in front of the toilet, not noticing that Marge stands in the door, staring at Homer for hours, as the time stamp tells, as if under hypnosis.

Film scholar Macgregor Wise suggests that many films that make use of the found-footage aesthetic are indeed horror films providing an opportunity to reflect on the aesthetic of the surveillance- or video image (cf. 2016: 132). On television, this 'reflexive cinema' aesthetic does not only increase the effect of suspense and horror for a home audience (cf. *ibid.*: 133), but also translates a cinematic experience into a new way of extrapolating footage horror for television.

In both live-action- and cartoon footage, however, the image becomes the surface of the demonic manifestation and source of the audience's unsettled feelings. Instead of assuring us that everything is safe in the house, and thus under control of the panoptic gaze, the horror evolves *because* of the remoteness of the camera to the events it films. Due to the changing ways of dealing actively with mediated images of a simulated reality, the surveilling aesthetics are a test to our need for control, a sinister test that unsettles our feeling of being protected in our own four walls. When, in the end, Homer and the devil agree upon a second deal of a 'threesome,' i. e. sexual intercourse between demon-demon-human, Homer immediately covers the camera eye that was supposed to capture the master bedroom. The final scene teaches us that it is not us, but the camera that controls our fears and scares. Hence, Homer's hidden demonic intercourse thwarts audience's compulsive desire and its credulity to still be the controlling gaze of the camera in this television horror cartoon. When Homer, for example, throws the blanket to cover the surveillance camera in order to prevent us viewers to join the demonic intercourse, our gaze is castrated, i. e. cut-off which makes 'the horror' even worse. We are suddenly unable to see, but instead forced to listen what is going on in the master's bedroom between demon-Homer-demon.

'Filling the Vacuum' III: ToH's "The Others"

In "The Others" from 2014's ToH XXV, Lisa wonders about a number of 1980s' references such as unexplained frosty chocolate milkshakes and bloody letters on the mirror saying "Help Me!." While zapping through the channels on television, the programs on Al Jazeera, BET, and others present alternate, ethnic spin-offs of MARRIED… WITH CHILDREN, a working-class live-action sitcom aired on Fox between 1987–1997 which ultimately confirm the existence of a ghostly presence. By way of syndication, one of Al Bundy's stale bedroom jokes is recycled on different TV channels and in five different languages. On the one hand, the TREEHOUSE segment evidences that paranormal activities are going on in the Simpson house. Following Meteling once again, "The Others" in this context inventories the uncanny systems of the home and transforms them into portals of otherworldly spaces, for example, to the Simpsons' own historical past in 1987 (cf. 282). The Simpsons are haunted by the family of Simpsons ghosts which now return to set the record straight because the TRACEY ULLMAN characters from 1987 who were murdered and buried under the house.

On the other hand, the MARRIED… WITH CHILDREN reference can also be read as a self-critical mockery of the broadcasting industry's preoccupation with syndication; a profitable practice which can be described as a form of comedy tourism which particularly concerned mass-marketable formats such as sitcoms. "The Others" hence jokes about the practice of recycling every past sitcom formula that has paid off, indicating that the network-TV industry is reluctant towards costly innovations, but rather generates profit primarily by syndication. Here, we can almost extract a certain horror from watching umpteen hours of syndicated sitcoms on television of the 1990s in which reruns of even the raunchiest humor of MARRIED … WITH CHILDREN had been the rule.[107]

TREEHOUSE OF HORROR's Kubrick/King parody "The Shinning" even privileges a portable TV as the final exit from Homer's deadly mission to kill his family. Although Homer doesn't kill them, all still die together by freezing to death while gathering around the little TV that Homer sanctifies as his "teacher, mother, secret lover." In the same TREEHOUSE episode from 1994, the science-fiction short story "A Sound of Thunder" (1952) by Ray Bradbury was adapted to "Time and Punishment" that shows Homer traveling through time by way of an ill-fixed toaster. In one of Homer's consequently changed realities, Ned Flanders rules over the world, lurking behind huge screens as an authoritarian dictator. As Springfield's new Big Brother, Ned is omnipotent as he is able to communicate via a big screen that suddenly ascends from the Simpson's kitchen floor, and heavily reminds of a life-size iPod.

My examples aimed to illustrate that TREEHOUSE creates its own cartoon-horror genre neatly tailored to the televisual context of media convergence, but also to our familiarity with the new transmission technology. By extrapolating the show's relation to the television, it seems a little clearer that while TV sitcoms may just be *watched* at home, TREEHOUSE OF HORROR indeed follows the cinematic thread that horror *begins* at home, ideally with us experiencing horror when sitting in front of the television.

Hollywood at Home: TREEHOUSE OF HORROR and Pre-Code Hollywood

In the previous chapter 3.3, I pointed out that the prominence of Gothic-fiction texts is primarily based on the fact that many of the best-known texts from Shelley, Wells, or Poe have been adapted to film. In Hollywood's pre-Code era, the big film studios of Universal, RKO, MGM, or Paramount Pictures were rewarded with considerable success. A whole range of films and sequels have reworked literary genre texts into horror- and crime films often adding explicit sexual content to them (e. g. Jacques Tourneur's CAT PEOPLE, 1942).

Universal's FRANKENSTEIN series is certainly the most prominent cash cow which best reflects Shelley's status as cultural echo chamber. The novel's first sound feature was followed by several sequels which, albeit rather being a repetition of the formula than a serial narrative (cf. Jowett/Abbott 2013: 58–59), can

---

[107] According to the related *Wikipedia* site, CBS opened MARRIED … WITH CHILDREN to off-network syndication in 1991. Since then the show has been aired in 46 countries. See *Wikipedia.org*.

nevertheless be seen as Hollywood's first movie franchise with THE BRIDE OF FRANKENSTEIN (1935), THE SON OF FRANKENSTEIN (1939), THE GHOST OF FRANKENSTEIN (1942) as well as Universal's monster rally between 1942 and 1948, featuring FRANKENSTEIN MEETS THE WOLF MAN (1943), HOUSE OF FRANKENSTEIN (1944), and ABBOTT AND COSTELLO MEET FRANKENSTEIN (1948). Hollywood's propensity to produce sequels is widely regarded as having contributed to the horror genre's booming period in the 1930s.[108]

Boris Karloff's performance as the creature vividly shaped our imagination of Shelley's monster.[109] Although James Whale's movie imported a whole range of archetypal Gothic motifs to film which later became familiar conventions of the horror genre on TV, nothing became as iconic as the creature itself. So while the Gothic sitcoms and period dramas of the 1950s and 1960s largely adapted features like the studio thunder and certain stock-character concepts such as the mad scientist, the sinister but loyal assistant creeping through eerie labs, or a beautifully vulnerable woman, the monster played a more significant role. In the decades following the 1960s, the monster became its own cultural echo chamber that, in one way or the other, threatened common attitudes towards North-America's idea of morality.

Hollywood's heritage of pre-Code horror films from the 1930s is addressed responsibly and taken seriously by the creators of TREEHOUSE OF HORROR. The great monsters from the Depression era received attention in a variety of different TREEHOUSE moments. But instead of playing them for laughs, the TREEHOUSE creators treated them with due respect. The creators filled the position of the Wolf Man with a triumphant Ned Flanders,[110] Count Dracula became an old-fashioned single-father of a pubescent teenage vampire,[111] and Frankenstein's creature became a pitiful, modern-day man-machine, created by Mr. Burns to realize his proto-Enlightenment plans and replace the useless human workforce in the nuclear power plant.[112] As monster scholar Jeffrey Jerome Cohen explains in his influential essay "Monster Culture (Seven Theses)" from 1996: "The monstrous is pure culture. A construct and a projection, the monster exists only to be read. […] [T]he monster

---

108 In the 1940s, however, the production of horror films and horror fiction stagnated. Stephen King writes: "The great Universal Studios monsters of the Depression days – Frankenstein's monster, the Wolf Man, the Mummy, and the Count – were dying in that particularly messy and embarrassing way that the movies seem to reserve for the terminally ill; instead of being retired with honors and decently interred in the mouldy soil of their European churchyards, Hollywood decided to play them for laughs, squeezing every last quarter and dime admission possible out of the poor old things before letting them go." (24)

109 Due to Universal's successful and iconic make-up for the monster, the production company obtained exclusive rights for its particular interpretation of the Gothic novel.

110 Cf. "I Know What You Diddily-Iddily-Did," TREEHOUSE OF HORROR X. Dir. Pete Michels, s11e04, Fox 1999.

111 Cf. "Tweenlight," TREEHOUSE OF HORROR XXI. Dir. Bob Anderson, s22e04, Fox 2010.

112 Cf. "If I Only Had A Brain," TREEHOUSE OF HORROR II. Dir. Jim Reardon, s03e07, Fox 1991.

signifies something other than itself: it is always a displacement, always inhabits the gap between the time of upheaval that created it and the moment into which it is received, to be born again." (4) Cohen's quote proves that TREEHOUSE not only reshaped the monsters of earlier days that evoked audience's sympathy, but paired them, for example, with other, more current horror-film monsters and motifs implying our familiarity with horror-genre conventions. THE SIMPSONS' TREEHOUSE has resurrected the traditional monsters, but gave them a new, animated appearance. In doing so, TREEHOUSE OF HORROR not only creates its own mixed-genre tradition of animated TV horror. The horror show also invites younger viewers to enter the genre of horror by way of a mash-up of older *and* more recent references.

As an obvious parody of the 1997 youth slasher I KNOW WHAT YOU DID LAST SUMMER the title "I Know What You Diddily-Iddily Did," for example, draws on the stylistic register of horror clichés from the respective film period, reactivating the dark stranger in a rain slicker or the well-known horror spaces where teenagers have met in former times such as the abandoned amusement park, the pet cemetery, the spooky roller disco, and, as Homer tells us, "the lake where sexy teens were killed a hundred years ago tonight." Similar to the stereotypical hit-and-run teenagers of Jim Gillespie's film, the Simpson family desperately attempts to cover up Ned Flander's death in a car accident. But unfortunately, the supposedly dead neighbor suddenly reappears, telling them "you can't kill the undead." The clouds release a full moon to appear and Ned mutates to Werewolf Ned who eventually kills Homer and triumphs as an immortal part of American cinema's monster history.

TREEHOUSE OF HORROR's "adaptation traffic," as Jowett and Abbott call it, mixes all kinds of different film texts. This strategy underlines that popular culture is characterized by diversion and mutual appreciation which the adaptation, the homage, but partly also parodies demonstrate. Helen Wheatley, for example, suggests that there are "precious few stories that have not been 'lovingly ripped off' from others" (2006: 177). Jowett and Abbott argue in the same vein that "genre itself is a process of adaptation, so it is hardly surprising that TV horror reworks horror classics" (2013: 57). The following examples will raise attention to how TREEHOUSE adaptations deliberately direct our attention to the show's basic idea, namely that horror-film classics are "lovingly ripped off" from all kinds of earlier films to dig deeper to their lurking secrets. In order to get to the heart of earlier horror films, the TREEHOUSE requires to have a special heart for the role of the monster. According to Cohen's fourth of seven monster theses: "History itself becomes a monster: defeaturing, self-deconstructive, always in danger of exposing the sutures that bind its disparate elements into a single, unnatural body." (7) TREEHOUSE OF HORROR's committed adaptations deliberately expose the sutures to unravel the interrelatedness of texts and genre as well as eventually create a new text.

Through the decades, newer film adaptations either have or have not 'lovingly ripped off' earlier films, have changed their backgrounds, changed their visual aesthetics from black and white to technicolor, and benefitted from the already existing toolbox of genre motifs and aesthetic conventions. What remains largely unchanged is the ideological reading of the monster as a mirror to common current morality concepts. James Whale created his creature as a sensational interpretation of Shelley's original that was assembled from dead body parts and remained unable to speak, but made audience's collapse because of his murderous instinct when he playfully throws little Maria into the lake. I have already argued in the previous chapter 3.3 that TREEHOUSE's FRANKENSTEIN version imagines the creature as a speechless robot, a man-machine animated by Homer's human brain which, similar to Victor's original creature, cannot live up to its creator's expectations, but becomes a self-parody of his creator. Obviously, it is worth taking a closer look at how TREEHOUSE OF HORROR's and its pre-Code Hollywood horror cartoons might have changed our perception of the monster in a television context.

Animating Hollywood Controversy I: FREAKS and ToH's "Freaks, No Geeks"

My first example is in many regards outstanding both in Hollywood's and TREEHOUSE's history. The segment "Freaks, No Geeks" from TREEHOUSE OF HORROR XXIV (2014) is a direct reworking of Tod Browning's highly controversial picture FREAKS from 1932. The animation's sepia-color palette instantly creates the impression that we are in the realm of art television drawing on Hollywood's pre-Code past of the 1930s. The animated mutilation of diverse characters furthermore make clear that this is going to be one more body-horror story like the "Mmm... Homer" (cf. Fig. 39). The segment may even challenge the audience's perception of whether it is politically correct to animate disabled people who perform as human absurdities due to their unconventional appearance.

"Freaks, No Geeks" shows Mr. Burnsum running a circus and freak show in Springfieldland in the 1930s. Among Mr. Burnsum's human curiosities there is Barney as the living torso, Principal Skinner as The Spineless Man, and Lenny and Carl as Pinheads. *A. V. Club* blogger Dennis Perkins suggests that the segment

39 "Freaks, No Geeks" from ToH XXIV (2014) and its re-enactment of Hollywood controversy

is a "tricky balancing act of being faithful to its source material" and a commentary on the still unsettling exhibition of human 'monstrosities' (2013). The basic plot revolves around Strongman Homer, who perceives himself "in the best shape anyone is in the 1930s." The able-bodied Homer schemes against Burnsum's most hideous creature, the freak-show attraction Moe (as himself) because he owns a valuable emerald ring which Homer wants to steel. In essence, Homer's plan for ill-gotten wealth is that his fiancée Marge (also a freak) marries Moe. Homer then plans to kill Moe so that Marge inherits the ring, Homer can marry Marge and thus ultimately possess the ring.

"Freaks, No Geeks" reflects on FREAKS' central argument that true monstrosity cannot be found on the outside of a person, but lurks on the inside. Apart from that, Browning's horror film was so different from anything that Hollywood produced in those days that it took the film more than eighty years to be rediscovered by a horror-cartoon special. Interestingly enough, it found a new audience in the same year with another appropriation, the TV anthology AMERICAN HORROR STORY which completely dedicated its fourth season, "Freak Show" (2014), to Browning's film. It seems that Browning's story concept to use real disabled people is still so out there that just very few dared to pay tribute to such a still controversial issue.

What makes FREAKS so outstanding is that Browning was not interested in re-imagining a ready-made screen version based on a Gothic-fiction tale as was common practice with Universal's FRANKENSTEIN[113] and DRACULA.[114] Following Stephen King's historical documentation in *Danse Macabre*, Metro-Goldwyn-Mayer commissioned Tod Browning to mix horror and the grotesque with an attempt at social criticism and some political correctness. So, Browning sought to sample real 'human offshoots' of carnivalesque freaks – a 'midget,' a strongman, a bearded woman, an armless wonder, and Siamese Twins – who starred in his pre-Code horror story about a circus in which the abled-body Cleo, the handsome trapeze artists, is the only monster and source of terror.

At the time FREAKS was released, people were so radically appalled that cinemas refused to screen it.[115] Already at its one preview (i. e. *before* the film was officially released in the cinema) in San Diego, "a woman ran screaming up the aisle,"

---

113 The first recorded stage version of Mary Shelley's *Frankenstein; or, The Modern Prometheus* is the three-act play PRESUMTPION; OR, THE FATE OF FRANKENSTEIN by Richard Brinsley Peake from 1823, and the only performance Shelley had seen during her lifetime. See *Wikipedia.org*, URL: https://bit.ly/3smyNsV.

114 The first authorized adaptation of Bram Stoker's novel *Dracula* (1897) is the stage play written by the Irish actor and playwright Hamilton Deane. After the American writer John L. Balderston had revised the stage version, DRACULA premiered in London in 1927. See *Wikipedia.org*, URL: https://bit.ly/2NXrLvC.

115 Stephen King remarks: "There is something so attractive about freaks, yet something so forbidden and appalling, that the one serious effort to use them as mainspring of a horror picture resulted in the film's quick shelving." (1980: 28)

which led to the film's banning in the UK for thirty years. To this day, FREAKS "remains a source of heated discussion, comment, and conjecture among horror fans," writes Stephen King in his review (29). Tod Browning's film may have been shocking and hotly debated, but only few have actually seen it. This may have changed after TREEHOUSE OF HORROR presented us with its animated version. The strategy of "Freaks, No Geeks" to mix horror and grotesquerie with an attempt at social criticism and frail political correctness becomes also visible in some of the most notable scenes from the film.

In one of FREAKS' famous sequences, the main characters sit around a huge table, heartwarmingly celebrating the wedding of the beautiful Cleo and the wealthy little man Hans. At this point, the viewer already knows that Cleo and strongman Hercules are scheming against Hans as the lovers plan to kill Hans because they are after his money. The freaks ultimately uncover the treachery and take revenge on the two able-bodied humans by killing Hercules and turning Cleo into a grotesque, legless "Bird Woman," thereby making her one of them. In this sequence, Browning particularly emphasizes the human side of the deformed characters and highlights the demonic, exploitative quality of Cleo's and Hercules' shadowy plans.

"Freaks, No Geeks" is committed to Browning's central act of horror, but confuses our moral judgement about monstrosity. Although strongman Homer receives his appropriate punishment too, as the freaks also turn him into one of them by taring and feathering him to turn him into the freak show's newest attraction, the viewer is certainly relieved to see that they keep Homer alive while killing the cruel circus owner Burnsum. Feathered as a Bird-Man and with amputated legs, the final take presents Homer in the present, who, in an obvious reference to the sitcom HOW I MET YOUR MOTHER, ends the story with the words: "And this is how I met your mother." Although the twist plays for laughs, Homer is shown as one of the freaks which he himself previously called "disgustos." Like they did with Cleopatra, the circus people also turn Homer into a legless and feathered curiosity; an imagery which invites viewers to reflect about Browning's original attempt to implement social criticism and a positive portrayal of challenged people.

Stephen King suggests that Browning's body-horror piece helped the horror genre to become "increasingly preoccupied with threats to the body" (27). Jowett and Abbott remark about FREAKS' legacy that the monstrous bodies of the supposed freaks are the "carny aberrations" in cinema which slowly but steadily ruled out the "threats to the soul," by which the authors mean all kinds of ghosts and Gothic hauntings that previously dominated high-grossing film productions (cf. Jowett/Abbott 2013: 136). Although the body-horror film has its roots in the depiction of the monster in early Gothic literature,[116] Browning's film was far ahead

---

116 Jack Halberstam uses the monster as a cultural object to review notions of the Gothic. In his book *Skin Shows: Gothic Horror and the Technology of Monsters* (1995), Halberstam reads con-

of its time. The body-horror genre with its visually intense, graphic violation done to the human body which is traditionally presented as 'whole,' first reached prominence in the late 1970s.[117] Ever since, the disabled, disfigured, and unconventional body has become characteristic for the horror genre which TREEHOUSE's cartoon horror further explores in "Freaks, No Geeks." The most recent example within the archive of TREEHOUSE episodes draws a thin line between monster exploitation and art horror.[118] "Freaks, No Geeks"' sepia-tinted portrayal of Springfield's beloved 'side characters' as *sideshow* characters' tenderly appeals to our sympathy for the freaks and makes us again ponder on who is the true monster after all.

Animating Hollywood Controversy II: KING KONG's Fever Dreams of the East and ToH's "King Homer"

My second pre-Code example is TREEHOUSE OF HORROR's "King Homer," a segment from ToH III (1992) which faithfully follows the storyline of Ernest B. Schoedsack's original picture KING KONG (MGM 1933). Schoedsack's film introduces a still well-known story: Together with his crew, a heartless Broadway stage owner (here Mr. Burns) travels to Skull Island (i.e. the same exotic island which KING KONG shares with Paramount's 1932 ISLAND OF LOST SOULS) to find and catch a giant ape that has become part of urban legends. On the island, the giant ape lives a proud life as a simian god, but the cruel businessmen manage to drug him, take him to America, and exhibit him as the eighth world-wonder sensation on Broadway.

But the sensation catches no public interest. When, in "King Homer," reporters ask impresario Burns what exactly the show is about, Burns stays close to the film's original shady message: "The ape's going to stand around for three hours or so. Then we'll close with the ethnic comedy of Dugan and Dershowitz." Similarly to the original, ape Homer eventually runs amok, but, due to the character's general physical shortcomings, he doesn't make it to the top of the Empire State Building as does the simian in the film's most memorable scenes. Instead, he plumps down to the street from the first floor. Mr. Burns declares his career as

    temporary horror films such as *Silence of the Lambs* or *Texas Chainsaw Massacre* through the Gothic as a versatile technology, a means to produce monsters as they did in the early Gothic fiction of Shelley, Stevenson, Stoker, and Wilde (cf. 1–2). (Durham/ London: Duke UP, 1995)

117 Peter Hutchings writes in *The A to Z of Horror Cinema* (2009), "the term *body horror* has been used by horror critics to describe a type of horror film that first emerged during the 1970s, one which offered graphic and sometimes clinical representations of human bodies [...]. In a sense, body horror describes the ultimate alienation—alienation from one's own body." (41) In: "Body Horror." Lanham, [et al.]: Scarecrow Press Inc., 2009, 41.

118 In her 2000 book *Cutting Edge: Art Horror and the Horrific Avant-Garde*, the horror scholar Joan Hawkins argues that due to Tod Browning's carnival setting and featuring of real sideshow artists, the film amply demonstrates the blurred line between exploitation and art horror (cf. Hawkins qtd. in Jowett/Abbott 2013: 158).

ended so that the beautiful heroine Marge ultimately promises to take care of ape Homer and becomes his wife.

The black-and-white animation film "King Homer" basically focuses on the love story between the blue-haired beauty Marge, a pure-hearted, indulgent woman, and Homer, who acts as the man-eating simian monster with problematic impulse control. *A. V. Club* blogger Nathan Rabin resumes the love story would end "in an agreeably perverse resolution [...] with King Homer marrying Marge in a ceremony that brings together the species in a bestiality-riffic ending" (2012). "King Homer"'s perverted resolution culminates in the bestialic crossing of species which can be understood as a satirical comment on the still prevalent social anxiety of the miscegenation between a black male and a white female in the 1930s.

Comparable to "The Island of Dr. Hibbert" and its re-interpretation of Paramount's ISLAND OF LOST SOULS (cf. chapter 3.3), this TREEHOUSE segment once more installs a harsh satirical commentary against the Hollywood studios' inherent racism. By reflecting on what online journalist Nathan Rabin defines as "the very racist tenor of the times," the vehicle of the segment's wedding resolution between the human Marge and ape Homer should be read as mockery of KING KONG's "fever dream of the East" (*Vanity Fair* 2017). Rabin argues that in this otherworldly dimension of the fictional Skull Island, located somewhere in the exotic realm of the Indian Ocean where the inhabitants were generally coded as African or sometimes Asian, King Kong himself would be the dark, mysterious East personified: "a brutal, vicious beast who destroys adventurers, dinosaurs, New Yorkers, and New York alike." (Rabin 2017) Ethnographic film scholar Thomas Wartenberg argues: "KING KONG initially presents its monstrous ape in terms that fit the racist stereotype dominant in Hollywood representations of Black males." (Qtd. in Schneider 76).

By making Homer perform as Kong, i.e. by representing supposedly black masculinity by an allegedly 'white' character, Homer passes into a black identity so that TREEHOUSE's "King Homer" allows the viewer to literally see the world through an indigenous perspective and thus foreground Hollywood's racist implications of portraying a noble savage existence. By consciously employing a white gaze in the animation, the message of TREEHOUSE's KING KONG movie homage is clear because a movie about a giant ape has never just been about a giant ape (cf. Rabin 2017).

Like in the original KING KONG, audiences of "King Homer" witness how the proud, indigenous ape is captured, kidnapped, and taken across the ocean in shackles to serve as a plaything for a wealthy white elite (cf. Rabin 2017). TREEHOUSE's "King Homer" almost confirms our assumption that, according to Rabin, "even in his savage original incarnation, [Kong] was already more sympathetic and, yes, human, than his captors and hunters, who complicate the film's colonialist and racist undertones by being so over the top in their boorish, ugly American awfulness" (2017). Homer is shown as a clumsy giant who instantly falls in love with Marge, the woman whom Mr. Burns willfully sacrificed to appease the island's ruler. For such boorishness, the crew members Lenny and Carl – in the logic of the Treehouse show – receive their well-deserved fate and are eaten by King Homer.

However, audiences know that the true source of evil usually lies in Springfield's cunning capitalist Mr. Burns as the satirical caricature which also Schoedsack's film imagined to mirror the "Yankee voraciousness and greed" (Rabin 2017). Treehouse's King Kong homage is close to the original cinematic fantasy, but one that confronts the contemporary viewer with the complex horror of racist stereotyping amidst 1930s' Hollywood representations of black masculinity (cf. Schneider 76). The segment points to King Kong's metaphorical portrayal of American slavery and raises attention to how monstrosity was produced in 1930s Hollywood.

As I have shown in the analyses above, Treehouse of Horror's reappraisal of some of Hollywood's pre-Code monsters follows an unmistakable path. Unexceptionally, Treehouse's 'monsters' represent a tragic heroism. In consideration of the pity state of Homer's mutated and mutilated personas in "Freaks, No Geeks" and "King Homer," we are invited to critically rethink the fact that especially the Hollywood movie frequently utilized the horror genre as a myth-making machine, aiming to express and compensate common cultural anxieties of a respective time in North-American history.

Treehouse stresses the cultural significance of 'monsters,' a strategy that once again reminds of Jeffrey Jerome Cohen's seminal essay "Monster Culture: Seven Theses" (1996). Cohen writes in his first thesis: "The monster is born as an embodiment of a certain cultural moment, incorporating fear, desire, anxiety, and fantasy in its body, which gives him life and an uncanny independence." (1996: 4) Treehouse's pre-Code homages exactly pay tribute to the monsters' "uncanny independence" and their freedom to echo American cultural fears and anxieties more than eighty years later in an animated television-horror show.

New Scares, Economic Nightmares, and Haunted Hotels: ToH's '80s-Horror Retrospectives

Horror-film production has always been a risky business. Stephen King argues that when a horror film becomes a financial fiasco, the most common reason is the film's painful absurdity and/or pornographic content. Mike Nichols' The Day of the Dolphin (1973), for example, was such a fiasco both at the box-office and with the critics. But the reason for this is that the film did not cause a public outcry. Film critic Roger Ebert explains that Nichols' movie, adapted from Robert Merle's 1967 French novel *Un Animal Doué de Raison*, lacks the novel's sociopolitical accuracy, its imagery of amoral Cold War activities of U. S. spies, as well as its sexual intrigues (cf. Ebert 1973). Ebert further comments that instead Nichols' film only gives us a "vast gray moral middle ground" of the original French novel (1973). TV-horror films also used to stick to the "vast gray moral middle ground" between censorship and L-O-Ps (cf. Hills 114). Accordingly, THE DAY OF THE DOLPHIN seemed perfect for television audiences in the 1970s. The film had all the ingredients to become a forgettable and "strategically exnominated" made-for-TV "eco drama," "science fiction thriller," or "spy action film" (Hills 119 f.). What happened? I suggest a retrospective of possible developments taking three different directions.

ToH's '80s-Horror Retrospective I: New Scares

In TREEHOUSE OF HORROR XI (2001), the third segment presents us with a reworking of Mike Nichols' film, tellingly renamed "Night of the Dolphin" After a family trip to Marine World, Lisa develops an animal-activist compassion for the conditions under which the star dolphin Snorky has to live in captivity together with his brothers and sisters. But Snorky turns out to be the King of the Dolphins, who, after being freed into the ocean by Lisa, incites a massive rebellion against Springfield, standing in as the epicenter of human existence. The dolphins finally team up against the humans and overthrow Springfield by waiting for the town's residents outside the church, silently watching the inhabitants like the birds in Hitchcock's 1963 eponymous film and forcing them to live (and die) in their unnatural habitat of the ocean.

The segment is psychologically thrilling and ensues much Hitchcockian suspense, eventually turning Lisa's moralizing attitude into a subversive move towards the doom of the entire humanity. When one of the dolphins face slaps Lisa, she also starts to drop her initially good intentions. Simultaneously, the drowned bodies of Springfieldians that compose the final "The End?" consequently question Nichols' unmotivated ending of Merle's dystopian fantasy, when the protagonists just head out to the sea and vanish into the horizon.

In his chapter "The Modern American Horror Movie" (1981: 80 ff.), Stephen King divides the modern horror film into "text" and "subtext" as well as divides between "artistic value" and "social value" (80). According to him, a horror film is a work of art if it provides more than it takes, hence, includes a subtext below its textual surface. If a horror film transgresses the limits of art, then it enters the realm of exploitation, goes past our claim for a subtext and ultimately remains pure text. King further suggests that the artistic value of a horror film is its ability to create a connection between our imagined fears and our real fears.

The eco-dystopian film THE DAY OF THE DOLPHIN obviously aimed at being seen as an art film, but was unable to tie in with any of the audience's fears, thus remaining a text without a subtext. The TREEHOUSE segment "Night of the Dolphin," however, makes use of people's more obvious fears which Hitchcock evoked in his suspense thriller THE BIRDS (1963). The segment is reminiscent of former horror techniques, rewriting them into an animation of new scares. THE BIRDS' acoustic atmosphere and aesthetic density spread the feeling that someday animals might go wild and take control of the American small town. "Night of the Dolphins" successfully makes use of Hitchcock's suspense strategy. In contrast to the original source adaptation, the segment turns the captive mammals into a horrible threat as the dolphins rise up against the Springfieldians and settle the score. By appealing to our familiarity with Hitchcock's THE BIRDS, the segment creates an alliance with the apprehensive feelings viewers had when watching Tippi Hedren in THE BIRDS fearfully navigate through masses of birds which occupy Bodega Bay. If Mike Nichols had invested in his audience's common anxieties and the film's subtext by e. g. more accurately translating Robert Merle's social criticism towards American Cold War espionage in his original novel, the film would have been equipped with a certain social and/or artistic value. According to Stephen King, a horror film has social value only when it accomplishes "to form a liaison between our fantasy and our real fears" (80). In this regard, the "liaison" between our unreal and real emotions invites us to access the supposed subtext of the horror film.

In the 1950s and then again in the 1970s, the liaison between imagined and real anxieties frequently revealed to be based on current sociopolitical issues. When television developed in terms of horror, a number of haunted family horror films such as THE EXORCIST (1973), THE OMEN (1976), and THE AMITYVILLE HORROR (1979) began to challenge the supposed security and peace of the home, progressing on the social anxieties of horror's intrusive, persuasive subtexts and their power over the individual, the family, and the home (cf. Stephen 2014).

The horror films adapted by TREEHOUSE OF HORROR all seem to be barometers for the phobic pressure points which, if triggered, prevent American citizens from sleeping at night. In many regards, TREEHOUSE's horror stories have both social and artistic value as they want to arouse fear by stepping over television's taboo limits. As the following analyses will prove, like the body of the monster, also horror stories often signify something other than just referring to themselves (cf. Cohen 1996: 4). TREEHOUSE's artistic value is concerned with helping us to better understand what kind of taboos and fears are embedded in the featured films.

In the examples "Bad Dream House" from the first TREEHOUSE OF HORROR (1990) and "The Shinning" from ToH V (1994), I am interested in the social value of horror. How does TREEHOUSE's animated TV-horror homages, for example, achieve "uncanny independence" and display the time's unease and shared fears, and fill the gap between the time when a film was created and the moment into which it is received as a cartoon-horror show (cf. Cohen 4).

History Lesson No. 3 | TREEHOUSE OF HORROR's Cinematic Archive

40 The repertoire of popular horror: The Simpsons move in a "Bad Dream House"

ToH's '80s-Horror Retrospective II:
Economic Nightmares and "Bad Dream House"

TREEHOUSE OF HORROR's "Bad Dream House" segment throws us into a scene in which the Simpsons have just moved into their new home (cf. Fig. 29). The architecture of the house immediately reminds of a whole range of horror-film houses across several periods, from PSYCHO (1960) across the Maitland's haunted house in BEETLEJUICE (1988) to the Victorian mansion of THE ADDAMS FAMILY (1964–1966, 1992). The Simpsons bought the house at a remarkably low price which, as they only find out later, is due to the fact that the house was built on an ancient Indian burial ground with evil spirits incarnating the walls that consequently bleed and speak.

The haunted-house motif further manifests in Maggie's twisting head, a vortex in the kitchen, and the fact that a bodiless voice convinces the family to attack and kill each other. The satirical pun is revealed in the basement where Lisa discovers the ancient Indian burial ground with the gravestones of "Pocahontas," "Tonto," "Geronimo," "Crazy Horse," and "Not So Crazy Horse". This scene speaks to the stereotyping practices of Hollywood (and Disney), producing movies which have lastingly influenced persistent misconceptions, the subtext about and social value of Native Americans on screen.

After "Bad Dream House" surprises the Simpsons with other specific horror-film motifs, Marge loses her temper and yells at the house to treat them with more respect. Eventually, the house decides rather to implode in on itself than to live with the Simpsons. In conventional haunted-house live-action horror films, most of the family members are usually dead as the house commonly reveals being more powerful than the family's cohesion to fight the evil (e. g. James Wan's INSIDIOUS 2011). In those movies, the house remains a memorable site of anticlimactic narratives which are slightly hampered by the fact that the protagonists just leave the site of danger, as Peter Hutchings argues (cf. 2004: 12).

The Simpsons lose their new home but stay alive, as they have unraveled the house's hocus-pocus. John Swartzwelder, the author of "Bad Dream House," rewrote the episode with a culture-critical distance. During that time, the '80s horror had already reached the deconstruction stage. *The A. V. Club* observes that whereas in most of these narratives the house torments a family until its members can no longer stand the situation and give up, the opposite happens here: "The Simpsons haunt the house instead of the other way around." (Rabin 2010)

The link between TREEHOUSE OF HORROR and its original film sources must be seen within the dynamics of a contemporary popular-culture matrix. In TREEHOUSE, this matrix is equipped with an uncanny independence, as it predominantly consists of numerous references of horror movies. These trigger audience's common fears and take them on an uncanny venture into horror cinema's past, opening the closed doors to our memory. "Bad Dream House," for example, unfolds as a collage of booming horror films from the seventies and eighties, giving them the larger frames of the segment's grotesque family haunting. The larger frames that captured America's past on celluloid are Tobe Hooper's POLTERGEIST (vortex, Indian burial ground), William Friedkin's THE EXORCIST (Maggie's turning head), Alfred Hitchcock's PSYCHO (architecture), Stuart Rosenberg's THE AMITYVILLE HORROR franchise (bleeding walls, economic breakdown), Mary Lambert's PET SEMATARY (Indian burial ground), Dario Argento's SUSPIRIA (use of primary colors), Roger Corman's HOUSE OF USHER (implosion) as well as the HAMMER HOUSE OF HORROR's fifth episode "The House that Bled to Death" (motif).

Yet, the collage or montage of former texts is not necessarily involved in the same amount of graphic horror and psychological thrill. Instead, the montage is woven around the quirks of American family life in times of collapsing real-estate bubbles when houses were sold at unbelievably low prices. Our laughter, however, seems in contrast pretty steep, regarding the implications of the used tropes which play with social anxieties, questions of guilt, ignorance, and racism, as well as issues of capitalism. The segment comprises the personal fears of American's surrounding the home in which the new house of the Simpson family becomes the place of unpleasure, excavating '80s horror films' subtext as an economic nightmare. The segment hence subscribes to the TREEHOUSE's actual premise of rather framing the moral dilemma of contemporary American living conditions.

The original AMITYVILLE HORROR was a big hit at the box-office in 1979 and TREEHOUSE's "Bad Dream House" examines the film (and its 'genre cousins') on how they managed to transform audience's real-life problems into a current social anxiety. Director Stuart Rosenberg created a classic haunted-house story that was deeply embedded in the collective memory and cultural heritage of American Gothic storytelling conventions. By using familiar, fictional conventions from the

Gothic-horror genre of bleeding walls and uncanny proceedings, the film touched upon people's economic and domestic nightmares. Hence, "Bad Dream House" settles for the quotidian element in 1980s' movie horror and its derby of economic fragility which often begins behind closed doors in the American middle-class home.

There is a reason why AMITYVILLE HORROR was a huge box-office success of its time since a whole series of sequels and remakes was produced for a new fan generation of horror until 2017. The film also succeeded because its underlying script, written by American author Jay Anson (1977), was marketed as "A True Story," thus automatically producing King's claimed liaison between the real and the unreal.

In Rosenberg's original film, the stairs to the basement collapse, the windows burst, and black glibber runs down the walls. These classic conventions of the 1980s' haunted-house horror film have been read as contemporary translations of the American Gothic. The collapsing of the borders between 1980s' horror cinema and the Gothic, however, is not only an observation that can be made in Rosenberg's AMITYVILLE HORROR. The film's prime concern with the quotidian, the threatening influence of the domestic, or the haunting of the American standard home by means of an Indian burial ground underneath the house; all three are aesthetics which will be analyzed in my next close reading. The fragility of the American family ideal, which any of these motifs portray, is also the central theme in Stanley Kubrick's novel adaptation THE SHINING (1980). The TREEHOUSE V homage "The Shinning" (1994) presents a five-minutes version of Kubrick's film. Due to the segment's poignant translation of one of the best-known American horror films, "The Shinning" is not only one of the most acclaimed TREEHOUSE adaptations, but is also worth a second look when it comes to the creation of animated TV horror.

ToH's '80s-Horror Retrospective III:
Made-for-TV Cartoon Horror and "The Shinning"

In his seminal study *The Pleasures of Horror* (2005), media scholar Matt Hills introduces his chapter on "TV Horror" with the question: "Where is horror *assumed* to exist on television?" (111, *ital. in orig.*) Hills holds television's subjugation through its limiting industry, its decision-makers, and L-O-P policies of the Standards and Practices departments responsible for the "relative invisibility of horror on TV" (*ibid.*: 111). According to Hills, broadcasters did what they could to keep horror a "para-site" on television by either displacing horror in the "showing less" category of Gothic TV (Hills 2005: 119, Davenport-Hines 1999: 376) or gave it a seal of cinephile auteur quality that allowed television at least to get acquainted with the "showing more" license of cinematic horror.[119]

---

119 Both categories of "showing less" and "showing more" prove being slippery categories. For the medium of television, historically speaking, Matt Hills only sees two categories. The first com-

Gothic TV, according to Hills, functioned as a "discursive other to TV horror" (119). But auteur horror, i. e. films that are credited to a distinct artistic value of a film director, has oftentimes been elevated to 'art horror.' Those kinds of art-horror films are usually bereft of any scare, but target a specifically committed fan audience which appreciates an aesthetic signature, an unmistakable recognition value that helps a film to stand out from conventional television (cf. Hills 125). Especially in cinema, the horror genre was, for a long time, associated with gore, splatter, and low culture, i. e. with graphic violations of the tolerable, visual limits. On television, however, the categories of Gothic- and art horror carried connotations of historical tradition and artistic value by either *implying* that there is a monster behind the door, but the door wouldn't be opened; or *hiding* graphic horror behind an obviously fictional art-house style, eliciting the original effect of horror's emotional response.[120] Hills is certainly right that in the 1970s and 1980s the recurrent Gothic genre motifs and story-loaded auteur-style art horror was a way to upgrade horror and associate television with sources of higher cultural value. Since the 1990s, however, television has evolved to prove that the medium remains the ideal site for horror; a horror which more often than not begins its traumatic journey in the bosom of the American family.

By means of animating cinematic horror and portraying graphic gore with the help of the cartoon medium, program makers have been offered a new slippage category to associate television with higher-valued horror stories made in Hollywood. The reworking of outstanding examples from the body-horror genre, including zombie apocalypse, intergalactic mutants, and disabled freak-show folk is thereby an important genre annex of the TREEHOUSE OF HORROR series. 'Showing more' than the average cartoon show or Gothic sitcom is, as I like to define it, the show's 'elastic freedom' which the creators have especially strained in TREEHOUSE OF HORROR's fifth edition (1994).

As I have repeatedly pointed out, to this day, TREEHOUSE OF HORROR V is widely regarded as one of the goriest of THE SIMPSONS' Halloween episodes. If Matt Hills had trouble to see where horror existed at the time of his book being published in 2005, he certainly was not aware that by then, TREEHOUSE had be-

prises television's Gothic period dramas and supernatural comedy programs allowed to show less, while television's rather auteur-driven horror films and series in the second category were usually allowed to show more. In contrast to the showing-less category, showing-more films in the latter category are often described as 'art horror' which have an artsy look and an impeccable concern to irritate the already small group of avid fans. The art-horror category instantly reminds of the made-for-TV mini-series and double features from the early 1990s including some successful Stephen King novels which were made into TV-tailored films of which IT (1990) with its papier-mâché clown Pennywise is certainly the best-known example.

120 As I see it, the latter is the case in the hyper-saturated visuals and deliberately unrealistic setting in Dario Argento's SUSPIRIA (1977, remake by Luca Guadagnino from 2018) and the first reminds of the slow-burn neo-noir narrative of David Lynch's TWIN PEAKS TV series (1990, 2017).

come the new TV-infesting (para)site that showed more horror than any other TV show. As mentioned at the beginning of this chapter, Horror as a generic ascription was mainly absent from television contexts. In his book *The Television Genre Book,* for example, TV scholar Glen Creeber defined Buffy the Vampire Slayer as "teen drama" (2001: 59) and considered The X-Files as a "paranormal sci-fi drama" (*ibid*.: 66). Treehouse of Horror was among the few, if not the only show that openly wore the 'horror' label in its title.

Treehouse of Horror V was developed in, what David Sims calls, "an act of aggression" (2013). Simpsons' show runner at that time was David Mirkin who came up with this three-some of gross horror and disturbing ideas as a deliberate protest against a Congressional outcry and the FCC's morose bleating about violence on television.[121] Since complaints had piled up from concerned parental interest groups who generally claimed to remove "Itchy and Scratchy" entirely from the show, David Mirkin decided to not only use the horror cycle to come up with an episode as violent as possible. He also made Marge enter the stage for one final time to directly inform the audience that Congress actually does not think that anyone should watch this episode.

For my analysis I chose the episode's first segment, which combines a mainstream appeal of animation with the oftentimes surreal 'showing more' attitude of auteur art horror. Although I must have been in my early tens when I first watched Stanley Kubrick's The Shining, already the first takes of the movie together with the cartoon's adapted uncanny score retrieved the uneasy feelings from that first viewing experience. The Simpson family sits in their car meandering along the empty roads that lead to their isolated destination of the remote hotel. Even in the animated version, I felt instantly introduced to the same feel of the solitary remoteness of the film's central location, the Overlook Hotel, as in Kubrick's original, where the hotel director Stuart Ullman (performed by Mr. Burns) welcomes the Torrances (performed by the Simpsons family) as the new caretakers to stay overwinter.[122]

When showing the afraid family around the major hall, Burns ironically presses several of Stephen King's horror plot buttons. He explains that the place has quite a long and colorful history involving mass murder.[123] "It was built on

---

121 The third segment "Nightmare Cafeteria," for instance, shows how the teachers at Springfield Elementary begin to brutally kill and eat their students; and in the second segment, "Time and Punishment," Ned Flanders is the Master of the World who lobotomizes his subjects and forces them to smile all the time.

122 The YouTube channel "World of References" has produced a compilation titled "The Simpsons Treehouse of Horror Movie References Part 1" juxtaposing some of the most memorable moments mostly from Treehouse of Horror's horror-film archive. A comparison of "Simpsons S06E06" and "The Shining (1980)" can be seen at 10"30' on *YouTube.com,* posted 14 Jul. 2018 under URL: https://www.youtube.com/watch?v=O7CWs1Tcjpc.

123 Whereas the hotel manager Ullman informs Jack in Kubrick's film that the hotel was built on an ancient Indian burial ground between 1907 and 1909, this isn't the case in Stephen King's

an ancient Indian burial ground" (as *Pet Cemetery*, 1983), "and was the setting of satanic rituals" (as King's 1978 short story inspired in Sometimes They Come Back… Again, 1996), "witch burnings" (as the title of King's novel Salem's Lot refers to, 1975), "and five John Denver Christmas Specials" (admittedly, Stephen King is unaffiliated to this sort of horrific irony).

Suddenly, the sound forestalls a moment of gore when the elevator's door gives way to a blood flood – one of Danny's channeled hallucinations in the film – which "usually gets over the second floor," as Burns informs his alarmed company.[124] The blood-from-the-elevator scene has reached an iconic status and is unmistakably attached to the visual repertory of Kubrick's adaptation of Stephen King's original novel. The blood flood serves as a device to hint at the cruel murders that were committed in hotel room 237. Apart from that, Burns cuts off the cable TV and confiscates the beer supply before leaving the place which Smithers assumes being the reason why all former caretakers may have gone crazy and slaughtered their families in the hotel.

In the following, the original course of events, as foreshadowed by Smithers, is faithfully 're-animated' from Kubrick's feature film. The imagined barkeeper-ghost Moe tells Homer, for example, that he will only get a beer after he has killed his family. In the film (but not in the novel), the ghostly bartender Lloyd is Jack's imagined friend, with whom he has several intimate conversations and who the dry alcoholic imagines to serve him drinks in the hotel's Gold Bar. The suspense further increases in the most famous of scenes, the original movie's ultimate watershed, in which Wendy makes the shocking discovery that Jack has pounded "REDRUM" a million times into his typewriter. The same shocking revelation is expected when Marge walks down the hall to uncover what Homer has typed. Playing a nerve-wrecking score mixed with the expectations of comic relief, the single sheet however just reads: "Feelin' fine". But as soon as the outside lightning bolts light up the walls, they are tagged all over with the "less encouraging" words: "NO TV AND NO BEER MAKE HOMER GO CRAZY."

Like Jack's wife Wendy, Marge succeeds to lock Homer inside the hotel's cooling house. Moe knocks on the door, uttering his concern that the "project is not going forward" when a number of classic horror characters suddenly enter, free Homer from his captivity, and remind us that this was supposed to be a haunted-hotel story. As film critic Roger Ebert so rightly observed: "The movie [The Shining] is not about ghosts but about madness and the energies it sets loose in an isolated

original novel where the hotel has no ethnic background, but is described as the ultimate bad place possessed by a demonic spirit from the past.
124 In the novel, the smart five-year-old character Danny has visions from early on when forestalling The Overlook, the snowstorm, REDRUM, an old woman in a tub (cf. 23 ff.), but the bloody elevator scene was an idea of Stanley Kubrick expanding on what King phrased as Danny's vision of "a slow trickle of blood… trickling down one of the fingers" in the original novel.

situation primed to magnify the psychic terror among the dysfunctional family" (2006). The appearance of the mummy, a werewolf, Count Dracula, Jason Voorhees, and Pinhead, a classical monster crew led by Moe, can hence be read as the adaptation's attempt to add some comic relief to the disturbing demons which influenced Jack's growing pains in THE SHINING. In order to emphasize the 'real' horror which is going on behind the walls of the Overlook Hotel, the irrational scares from the outside as represented by the Pinhead or Dracula are less horrific than the 'inner' demons that haunt Homer Simpson who is cut off from his addictions beer and TV.

On the way to surprise his family with an axe, Homer-as-Jack hatches through the splintered door and chases Marge and the children into the snowy labyrinth in front of the hotel's winter landscape. In the film, this is also when Jack chases his son Danny into the labyrinth, but Danny escapes, and Jack falls and is first seen the next day, dead, his face frozen into a ghastly grin (cf. Ebert 2006). Yet, Jack's violent pursuit of his wife and son ends a long abusive history; a history which the TREEHOUSE adaptation follows in a no less disturbing manner. Lisa discovers a little TV receiver on the snow-covered ground which, in the moment she makes Homer face it, extinguishes his mad obsession like lifting a curse from his beer- and TV-withdrawal symptoms. He shouts: "Television: teacher, mother, secret lover. Urge to kill: fading, fading, rising, fading, gone" until he lays down his wielding axe. In the end, the Simpson family freezes to death in front of the tiny TV screen while, as the deranged Homer ultimately suggests, "basking with daddy in television's warm, glowing, warming glow."

"The Shinning" is an auteur-inspired remake of Stanley Kubrick's 1980 big-budget art horror film THE SHINING that lines up with a whole range of Kubrick's key moments. The segment's sound designers harmoniously composed interfering sounds of scare to the mimicry of John Alcott's cinematography, a composition which becomes especially evident when comparing the lobby scene in the Colorado Lounge or the tracking shot that follows Danny/Bart riding on a trike through the hotel corridors. Even more so, the animated King/Kubrick parody is moreover an homage both to novel and film when it comes to the portrayal of the family's uncanny, truncated dynamic. Both families, the Torrances and the Simpsons, ostensibly suffer under a father figure that turns out being a child-abusing monster who began to destroy his family long before he enters the haunted Overlook Hotel.

Close to King's and Kubrick's original, the Simpson family's new home in "The Shinning" also becomes the Overlook Hotel which King imagined as the archetypal apotheosis of the "bad place" (159). To King, the "bad place" is a modern derivative of the haunted-house motif which he defines as "a psychic battery, absorbing the emotions that had been spent there" (159). Although the "bad place" of the shunned house with shady furniture and a "no trespassing" sign on the door is a pivotal element in many of King's novels, THE SHINING presents the bad place as a location in which we are not watching madness unfold from afar, but are pushed into it right in the middle of the family. King writes, "our homes are the places where we allow ourselves the ultimate vulnerability" and "horror is a cold touch in the midst of the familiar" (160). Although the Overlook Hotel is a public place, but without visitors, the seasonal break turns the hotel into a private sphere. The cold touch of the familiar haunts the family through a feeling of being lost in the vastness that disrupts familial cohesion. Consequently, THE SHINING's three members of the Torrance family have not come to a foreign "bad place" to lock out the trouble while staying for three months in isolation. They rather imprison us together with their vibrating unease; an unease that the TREEHOUSE episode delivers impressively.

What Kubrick's film accomplished is that the haunted house imported the psychic terror of the past into the growing madness and despair of its three characters. But also in TREEHOUSE's homage to the auteur art horror, the epilogue is infused with a horror which the online blogger Julia Alexander considers being "the saddest part of the episode." She argues: "The end is the first time Homer is truly happy" (2016). Homer's alcoholism and television addiction got the better of him, but his (classic monster movie) demons couldn't be silenced in his dry condition; an insight which also the Torrances should have had to recognize that an alcoholic, who has not had a drink in five months is not automatically a recovered alcoholic.

Stanley Kubrick's THE SHINING is one of film history's great moments of cinematic auteur art horror which, probably due to its devastating allusions to 1980s' dysfunctional family life, has been rare on television for a long time. Additionally, TREEHOUSE OF HORROR's animated version of THE SHINING should not just be seen as horror on television. Even more importantly, the segment has made it into the pantheon of memorable, strangely terrifying television horror. To answer Hills' question of where the horror genre is assumed to exist on television, I suggest to look into the cartoon-horror archive of a series which already carries the "horror" label in its title.

Conclusion: Horror (Begins) at Home

The chapter at hand aimed to shed light on TREEHOUSE OF HORROR's specific relationship to the American horror film. It was my plan to investigate how a nominally unique "horror" cartoon show accomplished to give a new home to a whole range of different genre-horror films most of today's audiences may have heard of but have never really seen. The animation medium has opened the possibility to rediscover genre artifacts from the 1930s pre-Code era within the digital age, rethinking their historical relevance with a present-day understanding. TREEHOUSE's reworkings of partly famous, partly infamous horror movies from America's historical movie vault were accumulated to a cartoon-horror archive that is especially tailored to the television context.

In my analysis of the Treehouse moments in which the television is in itself the source of 'evil,' I focused attention to how the technology has evolved. "Terror of Tiny Toon," "UNnormal Activity," and "The Others" are examples that tie in with audience's familiarity with the strange, unfamiliar quality behind the new technologies. The selection of Treehouse segments served to illustrate how CCTV, home-video cameras, and VCR have not consumed us, but rather opened our gaze against the notion of many of the 1980s' horror films. We grew up in an age of fast technological progress and were raised by the idea that horror cannot persist without the existence of the familiar TV screen at the center of our homes, where not we, but technologies seem to more and more have taken control over our gaze.

The close-reading of "King Homer" and "Freaks, No Geeks" as telling examples from Hollywood's pre-Code era of the 1930s presented their own means to widen our gaze, namely to take into account the historical dimension of Treehouse's horror archive. The animated adaptations offer a new way to access the ideological readings of earlier days. During the Great Depression, for example, the film monsters offered an outlet to common morality standards and had to stand in as incarnations of the nation's deeper anxieties.

My final analysis was primarily concerned with the modern horror film which experienced its second golden age in the 1970s and 1980s. The modern horror film has its own category within the Treehouse of Horror archive in which, yet again, the nation's common fears were shifting, adding a social subtext to the graphic surface. Movies showed haunting incidents amidst the families most secure place, the home, which in the 1970s and 1980s became the ultimate 'bad place' between the psychic terror of fathers who could not live up to their role as breadwinners anymore and the middle-class' economic nightmares of unpaid bills and terrifying mortgage loans. Not only does Treehouse's film-horror archive emphasize the significance of the genre for American culture. The series further puts special focus on the importance of television as an ideal site for horror. This is due to the fact that in the 1970s and 1980s the medium became an integral element of people's home the world over. While my son and I were watching Treehouse's "Mmm… Homer," I learned from him that it is in front of the television where most of us have a first contact with the horror genre. This cinematic-horror experience felt like an initiating event: while we were sitting in the supposed safety of our homes, I began to realize how strange and unfamiliar our domestic comfort zone can become.

In my final chapter, the gap in the cycle of horror's increased cultural visibility and popularity will be closed by looking at a remaining generic subdivision in Treehouse of Horror. In the following chapter, I will thus illustrate a detailed interest in the overall seven cartoon adaptations of Rod Serling's Twilight Zone which, taken together, compose the show's science-fiction anthology archive.

3 Analysis | TREEHOUSE OF HORROR: Lessons to Remember

41 Simpsonized fan-art "The Scary Door" of TWILIGHT ZONE-creator Rod Serling by Linda Fernandez illustrates the close ties between the two shows

History Lesson No. 4 | 'A Treehouse full of Twilight Zones' – The Legacy of 1960s' Anthology Storytelling, Science-Fiction TV, and TREEHOUSE OF HORROR's Love Letter to Rod Serling's THE TWILIGHT ZONE

American Comedienne and former SIMPSONS executive producer Dana Gould writes in her 'appreciation essay' "The House that Rod Built" about THE TWILIGHT ZONE that any program that came after it, such as THE SIMPSONS, STAR TREK, or THE SOPRANOS, all share a debt to THE TWILIGHT ZONE. According to her, they all are rooms "in the house that Rod built" (259) because all their doors lead back to him (cf. Fig. 30). Gould points out that during "the monster boom" that reactivated 1930s' horror films for TV audiences of the early 1970s, the one thing most creature features had in common was that they "were set far away, in some exotic, often mythic locale" (258): DRACULA was set in Transylvania, King Kong and Dr. Moreau were neighbors on Skull Island, and even FREAKS' nomadic circus didn't settle in some American small town, but kept on moving across the American countryside. But then, for the first time in American popular history, THE TWILIGHT ZONE brought the horror back to small-town America, to people's hometowns such as Binghampton (where Rod Serling was born), Hopedale (where Dana Gould was born), or Springfield (where the Simpsons live). In THE TWILIGHT ZONE, supposedly safe and sound homes were mobbed by angry villagers,[125] endangered by envious heirs,[126] intimidated by children,[127] or angry

---

125 Cf. "The Monsters Are Due on Maple Street," THE TWILIGHT ZONE. Dir. Ronald Winston, s01e22, CBS 1960.
126 Cf. "The Masks," THE TWILIGHT ZONE. Dir. Ida Lupino, s05e25, CBS 1964.
127 Cf. "It's A Good Life," THE TWILIGHT ZONE. Dir. James Sheldon / Tasos Giapoutzis, s03e08, CBS 1961.

stepfathers[128] who looked like average Americans. THE TWILIGHT ZONE made clear that every horror, every ghastly creation that stalked television already existed, albeit in a slightly different form, in America's small towns (cf. Gould 258).

Stephen King writes about THE TWILIGHT ZONE in his repeatedly referenced non-fiction book *Danse Macabre*: "[R]arely has any television program dared to present human nature in such an ugly, revealing light" (146). When tracing Rod Serling's legacy, A. V. Club editor Noel Murray observes,

> Even the worst TWILIGHT ZONES are rooted in Serling's understanding that it doesn't take much for the normal to shift just a bit and become abnormal. Serling turned small towns, suburban homes, and city streets into staging grounds for the nightmares his audience was already having, suggesting that the human capacity for superstition and paranoia could become more powerful than any magic spell or alien invasion.
> *(2013)*

According to Murray, 'the twilight zone' is the thin boundary between the normal and the abnormal. With this threshold space, Rod Serling coined an American idiom (cf. King 73) that became synonymous with the space in-between light and darkness which the Gothic had always inhabited. On a weekly basis, THE TWILIGHT ZONE presented stories that showcased "ordinary people in extraordinary situations" (King 148) – a concept which Serling introduced with his voice-over opening-theme narrative:

> There is a fifth dimension beyond that which is known to man. It is a dimension as vast as space and as timeless as infinity. It is the middle ground between light and shadow, between science and superstition, between the pit of man's fears and the summit of his knowledge. It is the dimension of the imagination. It is an area we call … The Twilight Zone.
> *(Rod Serling, opening narration, THE TWILIGHT ZONE, 1959;*
> *qtd. in Westfahl 2005: 93)*

THE TWILIGHT ZONE can be seen as the middle ground between good and bad. In this unexplored space Serling set his often cynical teleplays and adapted short stories to create rich, subtle cautionary tales that only at a first glance romanticized America's normality. Eventually it revealed the abnormality of institutions, of human nature, and normality itself (cf. Murray 2013). According to Gould, Rod Serling "took the horrors of Transylvania[129] and Planet X,[130] rewired them, and set them loose in a universal suburbia that still feels familiar half a century later" (258). 'Uni-

---

128 Cf. "Living Doll," THE TWILIGHT ZONE. Dir. Richard C. Sarafian, s05e06, CBS 1963.
129 Transsylvania is Count Dracula's home country as, for example, mentioned in Tod Browning's DRACULA (1931) from Universal studios.
130 Gould refers to THE MAN FROM PLANET X (1951), a black-and-white American science-fiction film by director Edgar G. Ulmer.

versal suburbia' entered popular broadcast television as a space where normal people, normal viewers, were confronted with the abnormal, dark sides of their homes.

In their practice of rewiring the American psyche to more homey terrors, THE TWILIGHT ZONE and TREEHOUSE OF HORROR have a lot in common. What both series share is not only that the executive writer-producers, the show runners in recent years, have full creative control over the content;[131] or the fact that each episode showcases a wide range of acting/voice-acting guest performers. More importantly, Gould claims, each show respects their audience's intelligence, talks up to them instead of down, and makes them feel better than before watching the show (cf. 258–259). In their *Critical History of THE TWILIGHT ZONE* (1998), authors Don Presnell and Marty McGee further confirm Gould's appreciation:

> Like any great work of art, THE TWILIGHT ZONE embodies and generates multiple layers of meaning, interpretation, and value. It is literary without being pretentious, commercial without being simple-minded or derivative. It entertains with substance, and it instructs without being over-bearing. *(1998: 8)*

It requires much creative ambition for a TV show to strike the balance between being relevant, offering intelligent storytelling, and, at the same time, appealing to a large audience and being commercially successful. In the same vein, TREEHOUSE OF HORROR abandoned the cartoon realism of the regular SIMPSONS show to be able to add an extra layer of meaning, complexity, and quality to the dysfunctional abnormality of family life in THE SIMPSONS. In this respect, TREEHOUSE OF HORROR has a lot in common with THE TWILIGHT ZONE because the horror stories are scary without being corny, reveal complexity behind commercial interest, and depict an American family whose arguing members rather chase each other with axes than with words.

Many committed fans share the critics' appreciation of both THE TWILIGHT ZONE and TREEHOUSE. Don Presnell argues that both shows appeal to adults and children alike (cf. 6). Former show runner for the remakes of THE TWILIGHT ZONE (2002), Pen Densham, is convinced that Rod Serling has changed television. Densham argues that Serling "had something that only few writers had, which was his ability to entertain through parables" (2007: 271). This ability can also be seen in TREEHOUSE for which Matt Groening and his team of writers drew much more from THE ZONE than its ability to entertain through parables, namely to teach "profound lessons that make you wrestle with your own comprehension of how society works" (*ibid*.: 271).

---

131 According to John Ortved's *SIMPSONS Confidential*, in 1986 Fox wanted James L. Brooks, director and producer and Hollywood's 'Dark Prince of Comedy,' to produce a series on board their still young network. Fox gave Matt Groening's team the official permission to 'run riot' and do whatever they wanted to without fearing censorship, as the former SIMPSONS writer Carolyn Omine said in an interview with Al Horner (Ortved 2009: 25 ff.; cf. Horner 2018).

Television's Unrelated Storytelling: the Anthology

It should not be forgotten that Rod Serling was the first who in the 1960s opened network television to horror and science fiction. Although Rod Serling's original TV series THE TWILIGHT ZONE was aired on CBS for only five seasons between 1959 and 1964, CBS's in-house production was later turned into a successful franchise which is currently running on the streaming service CBS All Access in its third revival since 2019.[132]

In terms of content, THE ZONE brought up many topics which found a new home in TREEHOUSE OF HORROR. These genre-formulaic aspects will be analyzed in the seven 'close readings' TREEHOUSE created to honor some of the most notable TWILIGHT ZONE episodes. Each of the seven TREEHOUSE segments receive my detailed attention in this chapter. In consideration of the form, however, I am first interested in how TREEHOUSE narration benefits from the anthology structure.[133] In the following paragraphs I will explore in what ways the show revived the narrational tradition of unrelated storytelling in its animated form.

The anthology structure allowed both shows to experiment within a variety of genres ranging from crime drama across supernatural horror to science-fiction mysteries. The narrative concept of unrelated storytelling engendered possibilities for experimentation and set the narrative framework for every one of the thirty TREEHOUSE OF HORROR Halloween episodes between 1990 and 2019. When the show premiered, the experiments resulted in a pairing of a science-fiction theme about an alien invasion of Kang & Kodos from the 1960s with a mash-up of 1980s' haunted-house horror movies and in ultimately traveling back in time to pay tribute to the tradition of 19th-century Gothic fiction with E. A. Poe. The trend to turn literary short stories into TV-tailored scripts stimulated television's adaptation practice.[134]

---

132 The original series THE TWILIGHT ZONE ran on CBS between 1959 and 1964 and had its first comeback with a new season produced in color between 1985 and 1989. The second resurgence of THE TWILIGHT ZONE goes back to the years 2002–2003, including several remakes of successful original scripts (e.g. "It's Still A Good Life" was a sequel to "It's A Good Life"). The one season produced between 2002 and '03 was hosted by Hollywood actor Forest Whitaker. The series' concept was renewed for a third revival hosted by the American horror-film director Jordan Peele in 2019 who also showrunner of the new CBS All Access format.

133 The anthology format proved particularly popular during the format's booming period of the 1950s and 1960s and was further deployed in ALFRED HITCHCOCK PRESENTS (CBS 1955–1962), TALES OF TOMORROW (ABC 1951–1953), and Boris Karloff's THRILLER (NBC 1960–1962). Most of television's serial anthologies extended the broadcasting traditions of radio horror and supernatural live-recorded dramas such as ONE STEP BEYOND (ABC 1959–1961), THE OUTER LIMITS (ABC 1963–1965), and NIGHT GALLERY (NBC 1969–1973) among many others.

134 Lorna Jowett and Stacey Abbott's explain in *TV Horror* from 2013 that, while printed short stories afford ready-made material, they were rather sold to the audience by way of THE TWILIGHT ZONE and not necessarily through the appeal of the 'original' text or the name of the writer (cf. 79). By acknowledging, however, the value and skill of writers such as Charles Beaumont, Rich-

Science-fiction-, horror-, and fantasy writers proved particularly helpful to visually transform the genre lineage from literature into proper television storytelling.

It is an advantage of the anthology formula that it can neglect matters of continuity. That left more freedom for Serling to kill off cast without consequences, transgress familiar formulae, and change the scope of television. By 'scope' I mean the narrow formulae which had been popularized during America in television's formative period by big-event shows such as THE ED SULLIVAN SHOW (CBS 1948–1971), Westerns like GUNSMOKE (CBS 1955–1975), quiz shows such as THE $ 64,000 QUESTION (CBS 1955–1958), medical drama like MEDIC (NBC 1954–1956), and radio adaptations such as the highly acclaimed comedy show I LOVE LUCY (CBS 1951–1957).

Unlike any of these, THE TWILIGHT ZONE and TREEHOUSE OF HORROR created a new formula. Both shows built a house with an open door for horror, the supernatural, and science fiction, and with a genre 'furnishing' each of which significantly differs in mood, style, and depth. Each show developed its own strategies to bring horror into the American home and people's everyday lives. One of Serling's early writers, Earl Hamner, Jr., comments that his interest lay not in writing horror that makes audiences feel sick. He was interested in writing "terror" which "needles your mind" (qtd. in Stanyard 2007: 168). Thus, the most compelling among the many aesthetic characteristics that TREEHOUSE shares with THE ZONE is certainly the daring attitude to unfold mind-needling terror behind the doors of seemingly safe American homes.

In the following analysis, I will concentrate on the inspirations TREEHOUSE OF HORROR took from THE TWILIGHT ZONE for its own anthology and horror formula. Although TREEHOUSE's writers have stopped paying attention to Rod Serling's early anthology dramas in recent years, the show's TWILIGHT ZONE archive includes seven direct (and two indirect)[135] homages to some of the most memorable TWILIGHT ZONE moments from the series' early history.[136] First, I will dis-

---

ard Matheson, or Jerome Bixby and their adapted short stories, THE TWILIGHT ZONE claimed priority to visually translate the written terrors for a television context.

135 The segment "I've Grown A Costume On Your Face" (ToH XVI, s17e04, Fox 2005) only indirectly takes up the idea of "The Masks" from THE TWILIGHT ZONE (s05e25, CBS 1963) and blends it with the teenage spook TV comedy film HALLOWEENTOWN II: KALABAR'S REVENGE (2001), which will not be part of my analysis. Whereas TREEHOUSE parodied the classic short story "The Monkey's Paw" (1902) by W. W. Jacobs, only the story's central morale – "Be careful what you wish for" – was taken up in several of THE TWILIGHT ZONE episodes.

136 THE TWILIGHT ZONE series continued after Serling's CBS career ended in 1964 after five seasons and 156 episodes. Ten years after Serling's death, CBS revived THE TWILIGHT ZONE for another three seasons between 1985 and 1989, in which renown horror and science writers (e.g. Stephen King & Richard Matheson) and later popular actors (e.g. Bruce Willis, Morgan Freeman) were hired. Besides the 1983 big-screen version TWILIGHT ZONE: THE MOVIE (directed by John Landis, Stephen Spielberg, Joe Dante, and George Miller) and the 1994 made-for-TV production THE TWILIGHT ZONE, CBS in 2002 tried once more to breathe new life into the established concept by giving Hollywood actor Forest Whitaker the role of the host of THE TWILIGHT ZONE

cuss Serling's aesthetics and subject matter, his psychology, and recurring story motifs TREEHOUSE OF HORROR translated into its animated versions of THE TWILIGHT ZONE. I argue that TREEHOUSE OF HORROR takes up that "twilighty show about that zone" (as Homer paraphrases THE TWILIGHT ZONE's title in "Homer³") because Rod Serling's concept withstands the test of time and the show has lost none of its relevance (cf. Gould 258). Secondly, my discussion will concentrate on the 'rewiring' of THE ZONE's domestic terrors in its cartoon version. The following list[137] gives an overview of my close readings (in chronological order):

"Hungry Are the Damned" (TREEHOUSE OF HORROR I, s02e03, Fox 1990)	"To Serve Man" (THE TWILIGHT ZONE, s03e24, CBS 1962) [based on Damon Knight's 1950 science-fiction short story of the same name]
"The Bart Zone" (TREEHOUSE OF HORROR II, s03e07, Fox 1991)	"It's a Good Life" (THE TWILIGHT ZONE, s02e08, CBS 1961) [based on the 1953 short story of the same name by the American writer Jerome Bixby]
"Clown Without Pity" (TREEHOUSE OF HORROR III, s04e05, Fox 1992)	"Living Doll" (THE TWILIGHT ZONE, s05e06, CBS 1963) [credited to Charles Beaumont, written by his ghostwriter Jerry Sohl]
"Terror at 5 ½ Feet" (TREEHOUSE OF HORROR IV, s05e05, Fox 1993)	"Nightmare at 20.000 Feet" (THE TWILIGHT ZONE, s05e03, CBS 1963) [based on the 1961 short story "Alone by Night" by American writer Richard Matheson]
"Homer³" (TREEHOUSE OF HORROR VI, s07e06, Fox 1995)	"Little Girl Lost" (THE TWILIGHT ZONE, s03e26, CBS 1962) [based on the short story "The Shores of Space" by American writer Richard Matheson]
"The Genesis Tub" (TREEHOUSE OF HORROR VII, s15e01, Fox 1998)	"The Little People" (THE TWILIGHT ZONE, s03e28, CBS 1962) [based on the teleplay by Rod Serling]
"Stop the World, I Want to Goof Off" (TREEHOUSE OF HORROR XIV, s08e01, Fox 2003)	"A Kind of A Stopwatch" (THE TWILIGHT ZONE, s05e04, CBS 1963) [based on an unpublished story of the same name by the American writer Michael D. Rosenthal]

series which was cancelled again after only one season. Since 2018, THE TWILIGHT ZONE has been made into a web anthology series on the American over-the-top (OTT) streaming media service CBS All Access, developed by executive writer producers Simon Kinberg (DEADPOOL, THE MARTIAN) and Jordan Peele (GET OUT, US, BLACKKKLANSMAN) among others.

137 For reasons of space, I decided to leave out a close-reading of "The Genesis Tub" as it does not offer new insights or give information which cannot already be gathered from the other segments' preceding analyses.

Some Historical Notes on the Formula in THE TWILIGHT ZONE

Rod Serling started to settle in television and to create a genre niche market between science and superstition as a television writer. He entered the business during a time that is widely seen as "the heyday of life TV drama" in 1953 (cf. Hill 111). Originally, the anthology format was particularly popular within the context of stand-alone dramas during the fifties and sixties 'heyday.' During the 1950s, the dramatic anthology series drew the attention of various other screenwriters (e.g. Paddy Chayefsky and Gore Vidal) who profited from the narrative format as it enabled them free expression and put focus on narrative diversity (cf. Hill 113). In his book *Complex TV*, Jason Mittell remembers the shift from 1930s' episodic daily plotting (resembling the serialized sitcom and soap storytelling) during the radio era to the 1950s' tradition of the self-contained plot-based anthology programming (cf. 2015: 235). These formats, except for a shared title and a recurring host, stood in stark contrast to the mode of 'serials' and 'series' because they, in each episode, typically introduced a new set of characters, were set in a variable location, and presented ever changing plot lines (cf. Mittell 2015: 235). But unlike the freedom to include political or controversial content that had still been offered to the radio auteurs of earlier times, as the 1950s wore on, dramatists were facing an increasingly reluctant attitude on the parts of the TV networks (cf. Mittell 2015: 113).

Since America had overcome its need for escapism during the Great Depression by means of Hollywood (see chapter 3.3) and got back on its feet after WWII, Rodney Hill accurately retraces American history by claiming that in the 1960s, Americans were facing new fears as they entered the atomic age, when nuclear weapons threatened the nuclear family (cf. 117). Stephen King argues that the time was ripe for new anxieties, when in 1957 Russia launched Sputnik into the orbit and the Communist menace found a safe haven in the minds of Americans during the McCarthy era (cf. King 186–187). As a consequence, life drama had to make way for an alternative storytelling that examined "the potential of genre TV as an agent of contemporary myth" (Hill 111). In his article "Mapping THE TWILIGHT ZONE's Cultural and Mythological Terrain" (2008), Rodney Hill explains that broadcasters sought to define television genres such as the Western show as one of these myth-producing agents so that the focus for broadcasters lay on the production of television formats that glossed over the rise of the new anxieties (e.g. the Vietnam War). In order to protect audiences from too much reality in the entertainment industry, networks enforced an increasing censorship upon the rather cynical playwrights like Rod Serling, Gore Vidal, Norman Corwin, or Paddy Chayefsky (cf. 111). According to the TWILIGHT ZONE critic Hill, these playwrights ultimately had to work out a new approach (cf. 115). Serling's own scripts gained attention for their "social awareness and critique" (113) – aspects that felt essentially uncomfortable to TV sponsors and network executives.

Rod Serling's urge for relevance and controversy on television made himself known in history as one of television's 'angry young men'.[138] Science-fiction scholar Gordon F. Sanders even sees Serling as "TV's last angry man," who strongly held up to his belief that the "writer's role is to menace the public's conscience," who uses the arts as a "vehicle of social criticism" while always having an eye on the issues of the time (qtd. in Sanders 130, cf. Hill 113). It will be outlined that Treehouse of Horror significantly benefitted from Serling's role to menace the public conscience as an angry innovator of television storytelling. More often than not, The Simpsons' horror show is a daring venture into translating social criticism into animated art. It seemed that horror in animated form was the ideal alternative to the more conventional storytelling within horror's heyday in the early 1990s.

Television researcher Mittell further explains that the anthology format generally forces a series to be simultaneously familiar and original, and in this respect, to be educational (teach audience how to watch) as much as inspirational (convince audience to keep watching). In their book *Critical History of The Twilight Zone*, Don Presnell and Marty McGee point out that "in the Zone, art imitates as well as reflects life, regardless of whether we like the portraits of ourselves" (1998: 7). Keeping this in mind, it seems that The Twilight Zone paved the way for some realism to enter American homes, which the censors obviously did not recognize behind the homely horror stories.

Serling employed his 'monsters' with a feel of reality that was equally educational and inspirational, a reality that stood somewhere between people's attraction to watch fictional evil and their real anxieties. The central argument of American film scholar David Melbye's study *Irony in The Twilight Zone* (2016) is that in The Twilight Zone, even the campiest science-fiction trappings as robots and flying saucers are "encoded or, better yet, *potentiated* with virulent social critique" (xiv; *ital. in orig.*). Simpsons show runner David Silverman said in a 2018 interview, the creative force behind Treehouse "was a real leap of faith that broke all reality of the show" to present audiences with the safely encoded reality of a nuclear family's disturbing nature (qtd. in Horner 2018). Serling followed a similar strategy like Treehouse of Horror, since robots and flying saucers are as suitable as animated monsters (e. g. "Homer The Blob") to serve as containers for social critique.

Although it might be insufficient to subsume the 156 episodes of the original Twilight Zone series under the umbrella category of science fiction, the genre proved being a safe space to cover up Serling's subtext and social commentary. By using science fiction as the new language of seriously critical content, Serling built

---

138 This refers to the title of the Blog-article "The 'angry young man' of Hollywood, Rod Serling became something of a personal hero to us" by Mark Deming and Joel Sanderson on *Cinephilia & Beyond.org* (undated).

a house above standard also with respect to the time. In the opening narration to "The Fugitive" (1962), Serling introduces with the question: "It's been said that science fiction and fantasy are two different things: science fiction, the improbable made possible; fantasy, the impossible made probable. What would you have if you put these two different things together?" For the context of 1960s' network television, Serling answered those question himself by experimenting with genre-mixing. By doing so, he further paved the way for the horror genre and made the impossible more possible for later decades in television history.

Following Hill, science fiction, on the one hand, drew on the flexibility and dramatic quality that was known from the anthology tradition. On the other hand, the seemingly out-of-timeness of science-fiction content allowed challenging subject matters to be showcased without censorship (cf. Hill 114). In a famous quotation, Rod Serling allegedly said that "a Martian can say things that a Republican or Democrat can't" (quoted in Hill 114). Hill points out that Serling's comment speaks to the new form of THE TWILIGHT ZONE's "keen awareness of carefully working with a formula and format – how it might work best, how far one might go" (114). This insight opened Serling the path to a completely new form of self-conscious television narrative, that of THE TWILIGHT ZONE, a path which the core creators of the TREEHOUSE have explored, too, but did so by means of animation.

Serling's self-consciousness Hill sees surfacing throughout the series (cf. 114) had a positive influence on THE TWILIGHT ZONE to expand science fiction across a variety of genres, preferably to that of horror, the supernatural, and fantasy. With the advantages of the portmanteau structure, the narrator introduces and comments on the ever changing plots with characters that could be killed without consequences, since the new episode will host a new cast in a new studio setup. Serling's 'opening' and 'closing narrations,' which can be defined as narrative brackets at the episode's beginning and end, were used to set the mood of audiences that were about to enter "a fifth dimension beyond that which is unknown to man." Rod Serling used these words, for the first time, when the series premiered on CBS in 1959. Serling's innovative TWILIGHT ZONE show created a fifth dimension which the science-fiction TV scholars J. P. Telotte and M. Keith Booker consider to have "marked the maturation of science-fiction television as a genre" (cf. Telotte 12; Booker 6). I see an equal maturation process in TREEHOUSE OF HORROR which helped to define the phenomenon of cult television with a highly dedicated core audience (cf. Booker 1). THE TWILIGHT ZONE is an early predecessor to TREEHOUSE OF HORROR that set the aesthetic standards and narrative patterns to establish TV's animated horror and significantly contributed to the visibility of the genre on television (e. g. when thinking of popular science-fiction animations such as Adult Swim's RICK AND MORTY or Cartoon Network's ADVENTURE TIME).

As pointed out in the previous paragraphs, one essential ingredient of Serling's formula is THE TWILIGHT ZONE's unique understanding of genre as a TV format.

Media studies scholar David Melbye writes in 2016 that, as one of the first television programs, THE TWILIGHT ZONE has been, as I have already remarked, "somewhat erroneously, categorized within the science fiction genre" (xi). Similar to the difficulty of simplifying TREEHOUSE OF HORROR as simply belonging to the horror genre, the umbrella term of science fiction equally does not suffice to grasp the great generic as well as thematic ambitions of and in THE TWILIGHT ZONE. What distinguishes Serling's show from other popular programs of the time such as ABC's THE OUTER LIMITS (ABC 1963–1964) and the mystery show ALFRED HITCHCOCK PRESENTS[139] is, according to David Melbye, its "vast eclectic range of narrative contexts" (2016: xi); contexts which will be examined in the following paragraphs.

Already a look at the examples at hand shows a thematic trajectory ranging from family drama with supernatural horror elements in "Living Doll" and "It's A Good Life," to classical science-fiction themes like the alien menace in "To Serve Man" and time travel in "A Kind Of A Stopwatch," to the surreal horror scenarios in "The Masks" and "Nightmare At 20,000 Feet." The predecessor of the television show runner, Rod Serling, did what Stephen King considers as defying a clear-cut categorization since THE ZONE simply "was its own thing" (145). Similar to Matt Groening's approach to both subvert and entertain American culture, Serling saw THE TWILIGHT ZONE "as a way of going underground and keeping his ideals alive in television" (King 145). During the 'golden age' of 1960s television, CBS offered Serling the alternative to deal with questions of fascism and Cold War issues, dysfunctional parents and their nasty children, or of American society between political hubris and social hypocrisy "under the comforting guise of 'it's only a make-believe'" (*ibid*.:146). Because of CBS's 'déclassé' denigration of much of the show's subject matter, Serling almost stubbornly made deliberate use of serious content, but kept it strategically under the radar of network executives, sponsors, and partly critics to address various cultural problems more easily (cf. Hill 115). Although the creators of THE SIMPSONS have always had full creative control over the subject matter and production processes, the show's "comforting guise" may derive from audiences' basic misconception of rating animation as a supposedly harmless children's medium which is often used to insert the reflexive turn of a twist. The strategy of the reflexive turn and how it addresses issues surrounding the nuclear family's fragility will be scrutinized in my first example of "The Bart Zone" from ToH II (1991).

---

139 The show was produced by film director Alfred Hitchcock and originally aired as a weekly serial on CBS between 1955 and 1965. In 1962, the title was changed to THE ALFRED HITCHCOCK HOUR including serialized stories each of which required three 30-minute episodes to complete. For more information, see Martin Grams and Patrik Wikstrom's *The ALFRED HITCHCOCK PRESENTS Companion* from 2001 or Thomas Leitch and Leland Poague's *A Companion to Alfred Hitchcock* from 2011.

Disintegrating American Ideology with TREEHOUSE OF HORROR's "The Bart Zone" (Fox 1991)

In addition to the generic flexibility that also mixed horror and fantasy into its science fiction-inspired narration, Serling's recurring themes and motifs guideline audiences along what film scholar Robin Wood has defined as the "disintegration of American ideology" (1979, 23; qtd. in Waller 1987: 150). A substantial part in Serling's attempt to challenge stiff ideologies becomes visible in TREEHOUSE's "The Bart Zone." The segment features the kind of 'existential weirdness' Serling commonly employed and which Bart captures in the riff of "It's A Good Life." The gist of the episode is that a whole town does not dare to even think about whether the world exists beyond their own narrow borders. As will be shown in the following close reading, TREEHOUSE's "The Bart Zone" makes things appear even more non-mainstream. This is because in the particular segment, the show draws Serling's often rather implied ironic twists to an explicit conclusion (cf. Rabin 2011).

In "The Bart Zone," the narrating voice of Harry Shearer sets up the mood for THE ZONE as he informs that the "average little American town" is ruled by a "not so average monster" and its juvenile whims of having psychic powers and the ability to read minds. "If displeased," says the voice, the demonic 10-year-old boy "turns people into grotesque walking terrors."

The almighty Bart almost acts as a visual metaphor of himself because, as Nathan Rabin remembers, at the time of the episode's airing, "in 1991, Bart Simpson towered over the sum of pop culture like a colossus. He came; he saw; he conquered. During the period of 'Bartmania,' it seemed as if the very world bowed at his feet" (2011). The great popularity and public attention which Bart received in the real world becomes the theme of "The Bart Zone." This is why Springfield's psychiatrist Dr. Marvin Monroe asks Bart the question "You like attention, don't you Bart?" Bart self-consciously answers with the words "Do I ever" which attests to how Bart defined himself as a pop-cultural phenomenon the character had become in the real-world practically overnight. This fact might have inspired the segment's writers to think Bart as animated reincarnation of Anthony Fremont, with whom he shares the ability to control the thoughts of the people of his hometown, in this case not Peaksville but Springfield. His mind-controlling skills, of course, also affect his family. They are even more distressed because Bart puts great emphasis on them to think happy thoughts and say happy things.

Springfield's adults are exhausted and humiliated by debasing themselves for the grotesquerie of Bart's amusement. For example, Bart forces his TV hero Krusty the Clown to be on air with "The Krusty the Clown Show" past the point of exhaustion for his private entertainment. Such behavior can be seen as mirroring the exhausted parents of America who helplessly observed how their children identified with Bart as their new '90s' anti-role model. Only Homer tries to dispel Bart but is consequently turned into a Jack-in-the-Box by him. Since the audience is familiar with the problematic relationship between father and son, TREEHOUSE allows Bart to fight his 'oedipal Cold War' (here without weapons but telekinetic powers) against Homer even more efficiently than in the regular SIMPSONS reality. Psychiatrist Dr. Marvin Monroe consequently recommends "more positive attention" for Bart and tells Homer to spend some quality time with his son to get to know him better. Homer consequently tries to undo his bad thoughts by suddenly being a real and caring father who goes fishing with his first-born and takes Bart to a baseball match, following the patterns of what is widely considered a picture-perfect U.S.-American father figure.

Nathan Rabin from *The A. V. Club* considers the segment as "almost too dark to be funny" as it "somewhat subversively suggests that the fundamental nature of childhood is cruel and bored, not innocent and sweet" (2011). Jerome Bixby, author of the original short story, contributed to Serling's cynical vision on rural American family life. The Fremont family lives in a claustrophobic village of Peaksville, Ohio which does not give any hint to whether there is life beyond the borders of the family's property. Because of the fact that the special effects are quite limited, the episode delivers its uncanny atmosphere through extreme close-ups and shadows on the wall that show the transformed neighbor Dan, and sets on viewers' ability to anticipate, for example, when Anthony causes snowfall in the summer. The viewer is invited to anticipate that the snow will have a disastrous effect on the crops and that the cut-off of Peaksville from the rest of the world will experience starvation.

Serling's claustrophobic interpretation of "It's a Good Life" dared to scratch on the façade of a family's supposed immunity towards its destruction from within. At the end, the Fremonts and their friends resign and keep up their worried smiles to avoid that Anthony transforms them into similar "grotesque walking terrors" as he did with Dan (who now can neither walk nor think 'outside the box' anymore). "The Bart Zone" attempts to disintegrate American ideology by creating a nightmarish oedipal dystopia; a no-place of Springfield that is built on the omnipotence of a child to cause adult America's "mortal fears of suffering a worse fate" and enslave them to "painfully strained fake happiness" (Rabin 2011).

On a metalevel, Bart's omnipotence in pop culture thereby reaches beyond the limits of the series. It is a well-known fact that, in the 1990s, America's concerned parents saw a threat in their children's new hero Bart Simpson. That is why one of both series' thematic anchors is the portrayal of how moral decay in a suburbanite society triggers certain fears. My next close-reading will further investigate on the issue of existential weirdness and identity slippage that envisions what happens if the common American angst of non-conformity becomes a person's bitter fate.

Do 'Gen Xers' Dream of the Future? — TREEHOUSE OF HORROR's "Stop the World, I Want to Goof Off"

The segment "Stop the World, I Want to Goof Off," an homage to THE TWILIGHT ZONE's "A Kind of a Stopwatch," shows Bart Simpson and his friend Milhouse van Houten in another context of TREEHOUSE's subversive method to translate the pop-culture phenomenon of Bartmania into public terror. While killing time in front of the TV, Marge suggests the children to read, offering them a box full of old comics from the 1970s. Flipping through a comic edition of "Batman and Rhoda," Bart sees an advert that offers a magic stopwatch. Four weeks later, Bart and Milhouse finally receive the watch and quickly realize its power when used as a device of ultimate pranking. They stop time mainly to compromise authorities and make fun of Principal Skinner, Homer, or Mayor Quimby when they are caught in the public with their pants down, naked or in awkward costumes, hence undermining their respective authority.

Of course, the Springfieldians catch Bart and Milhouse red-handed. The angry mob decides to kill Bart and Milhouse, but is stopped by the stopwatch which suddenly falls down and breaks into pieces. Bart and Milhouse need 15 years to learn how to fix the watch. When they finally manage to continue the course of time, Bart looks like the typical '90s' 'slacker'[140] and Milhouse looks like his own father, since the years have left their marks on them, regarding Bart's mullet and Milhouse's circular hair loss. The watch is fixed and when the two young men press the button, the angry mob continues unhindered. Unaware about whom the mob is actually chasing, they pounce on a placeholder which Bart and Milhouse had positioned earlier. Since no one remembers what happened 15 years ago, the mob's unfiltered aggression now hits Bart and Milhouse's overachieving classmate Martin Prince, Jr..

What Bart and Milhouse originally planned as a childish prank can be read as the call of Gen Xers' deep desire to stop time moving forward, preserving their ontological innocence as careless slackers who will never have to think about tomorrow or the future in general. After 'goofing off' the world for too long, Bart quickly realizes, "I miss being a regular kid in a real world" and Milhouse admits, "I work better in a structured environment." The cartoon stopwatch in this case becomes the agent of ironic justice in Bart and Milhouse's reality. Because as soon as their

---

140 The image of the 'slacker,' that stands synonymous for someone who refers to him-/herself as 'coole loser' (as American singer Beck phrased it in his world hit "Loser:" "I'm a loser baby, so why don't you kill me?!"), was sort of a charming political statement during the 1990s, referring to someone who provokes by showing off his/her ignorant, anti-neoliberal attitude toward success; someone who can be defined as the postmodern version of Bartleby the Scrivener. For more discussion, see Juliane Reil's article "Der 'Slacker' ist nur noch eine leere Pose," published on *Deutschlandfunk Kultur.de* on 07 Aug. 2020 under URL: https://bit.ly/3cfQANo.

wish has come true it is only their surrounding that stops evolving, while their own time moves on. Bart and Milhouse have aged, while being stuck in the 1990s.

At the end of the original "A Kind Of A Stopwatch"[141] episode, the main character Patrick McNulty, a generally disliked, self-righteous bigmouth, breaks the watch and is doomed to a life entirely cut-off from moving forward. McNulty is isolated within a frozen world that will never again have the chance to pay him the respect he desired so deeply. Unlike Bart and Milhouse, all of McNulty's attempts to reactivate the world around him show no avail. But even if McNulty had shared the same fate as Bart and Milhouse, who eventually managed to fix the pocketwatch, the segment subversively suggests that even moving on with time doesn't change anything. Also fifteen years later, "Stop the World, I Want to Goof Off" seems to criticize that people continue as before, remain the 'mob' as they hardly learn from situations, are ignorant, and simply don't care about guilt and innocence as long as they can take revenge and the law into their own hands.

The two Bart-centered segments of "The Bart Zone" and "Stop the World, I Want to Goof Off" make subversive suggestions about the horror of growing up as a child in the 1990s. Bart and Milhouse gained the power to stop time, but are stuck in the 1990s, halting between Gen Xers desire to make up for their attention deficit symptoms and drop out of the system on the one side, and the baby boomers' enthusiasm to raise their children in a structured environment on the other. On the one side, this subversion is translated into Bart's power of imposing supernatural terror onto his social environment, and, on the other side, into a science-fiction inspired parable. This parable centers on a straightforward melancholic dimension of being a part of the no-future generation and a child such as Bart Simpson in 1990s America who just misses being "a regular kid in a real world," as Bart regretfully says.

It is worth noting that the motif of freezing time is a special effect which was meant as a technique of visual terror for the owner of the stopwatch, Patrick McNulty. Although the motif appears rather conventional to us nowadays, it was something of a genre novelty in 1960s' television. In an *A. V. Club* review of "Kind

---

141 In the original "A Kind of a Stopwatch," the protagonist Patrick McNulty is a self-righteous, know-it-all nag, who generally annoys people at work, his boss, and the bar folk and forces them to flee before he can open his mouth. In the local bar, the strange patron Potts gives him a magic stopwatch which can literally stop time itself. Soon, McNulty realizes that "with great power comes a lot off hassles" (Murray 2013). He robs a bank to have all the money in the world to buy him the respect of his boss and others which however only he thinks he deserves. While pushing an overflowing cart of cash, the stopwatch falls out of his pocket and breaks into pieces. The people at his work place, in the bar, and on the street remain frozen. McNulty now has money which is of course not what he really wanted. All the money in the world has no value without anyone recognizing it. IMDB critic Dane Youssef suggests that his doomed fate presents itself as divine karmatic justice because he always felt cut off from the world, but now he really is (cf. *IMDB.com*, undated).

Of A Stopwatch," editor Emily Todd VanDerWerff explains: "We're so used to the idea of people who can stop time being able to mess with other people without those other people knowing that this can drag a bit when you're just waiting for McNulty to come to the same conclusion." (*The A. V. Club.com*, 2014) Although the motif suffers from the logic error that seemingly only animate and just some inanimate objects can be frozen (e.g. McNulty steels the money from the bank and is able to move a cart, but a helicopter is shown being frozen in the air), Todd VanDerWerff assumes that Serling invented the TV trope of freezing time which "has trickled into our pop cultural collective unconscious" (2014).[142] Hence, TREEHOUSE OF HORROR not only ties in with the tradition of adaptation by selling the audience older stories through the appeal of an animated horror show. "Stop the World, I Want to Goof Off" is further an example that pays tribute to Rod Serling's visual realization of a motif which was popularized within a variety of television productions from I DREAM OF JEANNIE (Jeannie could stop people's motion, NBC 1965–1970) to STAR TREK's "Wink Of An Eye" (NBC 1968), but was also used in different TWILIGHT ZONE episodes such as "Time Enough At Last" (CBS 1959) and "A Little Peace of Quiet" (CBS 1985).

Thwarting Audience Expectation with Open Closure in TREEHOUSE OF HORROR's "Terror at 5 1/2 Feet"

From a contemporary perspective, the freezing of time can be classified as an established television-specific special effect. In case of THE TWILIGHT ZONE, Serling implemented the device to visually translate the horror-genre lineages into proper TV-tailored formulae. Another important formulaic device is Serling's opening narration. In the premiering episode, for example, Rod Serling provided the basic definition of THE TWILIGHT ZONE by saying that it is a dimension "between science and superstition" (1959). This liminal space indicates that THE TWILIGHT ZONE fell into a generic niche category between science fiction and fantasy. Such a genre niche would set new standards to the growing demands of its television audience and to the increasingly more eclectic genre hybridity in American TV.

In the non-fiction essay simply titled "Serling," novelist Jonathan Lethem writes that Serling was "a paradigmatic figure of that monstrous new medium's

---

142 A quick internet research reveals that one of the earliest visual examples to use the image freeze technique was René Clair's 1925 silent film PARIS QUI DORT. In literary fiction, however, the motif was applied by H. G. Wells in his short story "The New Accelerator" from 1901. But aside from cinema and fiction writing, the technique of stopping the movement in the background while the movement in the foreground continues was new to the medium of television in the 1960s. VanDerWerff points out that the way McNulty has to learn how his power works in the episode essentially resembles what was required from the larger genre audience to learn how this basic idea would play out for TV generations to come (cf. 2014).

potential and decline; an assimilated Jew whose vision of grey-flannel alienation helped to define postwar American discontent" (1999). Since American audiences of the postwar era were first and foremost trained by the classic Hollywood formula to expect narrative closure, Serling translated the nation's growing discontent into surprise twist endings he himself referred to as "snappers" (Melbye 2016: xii). Those 'snappers' were part of the "atypically formulaic show" (*ibid.*: xii) that favored reflexive turnarounds instead of narrative closure as we have already seen in "It's A Good Life" and "A Kind Of A Stopwatch." Melbye writes about THE TWILIGHT ZONE: "[W]hichever period – past, present, or future – and in whatever context between probable technologies and metaphysical whimsies, the weekly episodes sought to thwart audience expectations by overturning their logical finales" (*ibid.*: xii). Serling's "atypically formulaic" strategy thereby violated the common dramatic practice as much as the audience's viewing habits.

The overturning of audience expectations is another essential element of the anti-climactic endings which TREEHOUSE OF HORROR adapted from THE TWILIGHT ZONE. In "Nightmare at 20,000 Feet," for example, when the mentally distressed Bob Wilson (William Shatner) is finally wheeled away, only the audience knows that the former psychiatry patient was actually right: there really was a sabotaging gremlin tampering outside on the plane's wing.

Other TWILIGHT ZONE examples of anti-climactic twists are the already examined "A Kind of a Stopwatch" which also leaves the audience with the bitter irony-of-fate taste about Patrick McNulty's self-inflicted perdition; or the rope-a-dope strategy in "To Serve Man" in which is only finally revealed that the intergalactic Kanamits from outer space just came to entice, force-feed, and eat the Earthlings (see my analysis of ToH's "Hungry Are The Damned"). During the 1960s, these were all science-fiction future scenarios that stirred up anxious visions of what Lethem called "grey flannel alienation" surrounding the Cold War and the space race, creating a lasting imagery of America's common fears.

TREEHOUSE's homage "Terror At 5 ½ Feet" puts Bart into a comparable situation as Bob Wilson in "Nightmare At 20,000 Feet." The only change is that the plane that is flying 20,000 feet above the ground was replaced by the school bus which has a height of approximately 5 ½ feet. One thing that both locations share is the claustrophobic quality of the spatial limitation of plane and bus. Whereas the plane's constricted mise-en-scène shows Bob Wilson in a trapped situation, tied up to his window seat, TREEHOUSE reimagines the story in the school bus that takes a restless Bart on a terrifying journey. The TREEHOUSE segment reimagines the 1960s' climate of fear close to the original teleplay by Richard Matheson. In the TREEHOUSE version, Bart resembles Bob as he is the only passenger who sees a creepy gremlin dismantling the bus from the outside too. Whenever the increasingly panicking Bart tries to expose the threat to his school mates, they burst into laughter and the gremlin disappears.

The question the segment's narrative course poses is whether the madness and horror lie in the gremlin outside the bus or in the infantile paranoia and delirium inside Bart's mind, writes Nathan Rabin from *The A. V. Club* in his review of the TREEHOUSE segment (cf. 2012). Bart eventually rescues the bus passengers by breaking a window and throwing an emergency flare at the gremlin that sends it into the path of Ned Flander's car right behind the bus. Viewers finally get to know that the Simpson neighbor Ned experiences an even worse fate by being decapitated by the gremlin. When after their arrival bus driver Otto and Principal Skinner watch from the outside how the bus finally completely falls apart, Bart, due to his "disruptive behavior," is tied to a strait jacket and wheeled away to the "New Bedlam Rest Home for the Emotionally Interesting." Although everyone eventually has to acknowledge that Bart was right, in a society in which children do not have much to say, Principal Skinner suggests that a lifelong stay in the madhouse will teach Bart "some manners."

Similar to Matheson's anticlimactic resolution, the viewer is the only one who can decide whether Bart is or is not a paranoid monster in disguise because no one (except dead Ned Flanders) has actually seen the 'hideous monster' on the bus. Much like the pitiful Bob Wilson, Bart is rather believed to have risked the life of all other passengers. But as it might have been the case with Bob Wilson, we almost feel a similar pity for poor Bart, whom no one believes because, in contrast to the really mentally stroke Bob, he is Springfield's well-known deceptive prankster and usually in full control of his actions.

In a genre-specific context, Serling's concept of 'snapper' endings, as exemplified in Matheson's "Nightmare At 20,000 Feet," follows a clear purpose which has been fully ingrained into TREEHOUSE's idea of an open closure too. In *Film Genre* (2006), film scholar Barry Keith Grant explains that, in a genre-specific context, the extent to which a movie achieves narrative closure is an important factor when reading its political implications (cf. 2006: 16). Closure is mostly achieved in form of a conventional, artificial, and constructed upbeat- or happy ending which is aimed to create a constructed sense of security in the viewer. But as Grant concludes, life, unlike such artificial stories, continues (*ibid.*: 16). He argues that a lack of closure is suggestive of a higher realism because the lives of the characters continue after the ending.

When Bart is shown in the ambulance, believing that he can get some rest after the terrors on the bus, the gremlin jumps on the car, premonitorily holding up Ned's head to the window. As the ending of "Terror At 5 ½ Feet" suggests, Bart's life will continue (he is animated), but it will probably be haunted by persistent hallucinations. The implied critical reading of "Terror At 5 ½ Feet" is a statement about, or even an obvious mockery at the authorities (here: Principal Skinner) who ignore Bart's concerns and instead prefer to punish the ten-year-old for his antisocial, maladjusted behavior as well as his character's general refusal to assimilate to the expected social norms. So instead of drawing the social debates and tensions to the same formulaic closure as in the dramatic conflict-condensing of Hollywood films, THE TWILIGHT ZONE squelched audience's expectations to leave the individual viewer ultimately alone with the unsolved tension in the twilight between right or wrong.

Rope-a-Dope with American Angst in TREEHOUSE OF HORROR's "Hungry are the Damned"

The segment "To Serve Man" features Damon Knight's TWILIGHT ZONE eponymous short story which, as already the title suggests, is a play on words.[143] In the English language, 'to serve' has two different meanings. Firstly, 'to serve man' can refer to the servile notion of putting oneself in the service of, in this context, mankind. When the extraterrestrial Kanamits arrive, they only seemingly put their galactic intelligence (their hydrocephalic heads forebode a superior intelligence) into the service of the UN. The highly advanced aliens, represented by their Kanamit delegate, offer safe solutions in terms of natural resources such as oil and water that are almost too good to be true. A second meaning of 'to serve man' is to have him for dinner, which is the actual 'rope-a-dope'[144] of the final twist in Damon Knight's script.

The rope-a-dope tactic means that a joke suggests one thought just to set up a twist. One striking example is provided by the episode's final revelation, when the governmental translator Patty 'decodes' the actual intention of the Kanamits: "Mr. Chambers! Don't get on that ship! The rest of the book 'To Serve Man,' it's … it's a cookbook!" Patty desperately tries to prevent his colleague Michael Chambers from his worse fate, as she was the first to realize that the Kanamits have not come to rescue, but to force-feed and eat mankind after taking them to their unknown planet.

---

143 Only a quick look into the episode's title list of TREEHOUSE OF HORROR reveals that here the device of the play on words becomes especially visible, e.g. when titles of famous films are parodied as "Citizen Kang" (Orson Welles' CITIZEN KANE) or "King Homer" (Ernest Schoedsack's KING KONG), when Darwin's evolution theory 'survival of the fittest' serves as the segment's title for "Survival of the Fattest," and STARSHIP TROOPERS (Paul Verhoeven) is changed to "Starship Poopers," etc.

144 The phrase "rope-a-dope" is actually a boxing technique which is credited to Muhammad Ali's famous fight from 1974, 'Rumble in the Jungle,' against George Foreman. Ali let himself fall back into the ropes to fake a defensive moment that allowed Foreman to punch until getting tired to then be attacked by massive offensive maneuvers. For more information, see the entry on *Wikipedia.org*. (URL: https://en.wikipedia.org/wiki/Rope-a-dope, undated). In the first entry on *Urban Dictionary.com* 'rope-a-dope' is not only associated with a general strategy "to appear weak to convince an opponent to attack and fall into a trap". As a joke, 'rope-a-dope' is also suggested to mean "a joke that suggests one thought just to set up a twist" (cf. MichealJonSnow, URL: https://bit.ly/304n7z5, 22. Mar. 2010).

In the TREEHOUSE episode "Hungry Are The Damned" the rope-a-dope tactic plays with the shocking climactic course of Serling's "To Serve Man." In this regard, the aliens use many double entendres. Kang, for example, slobbers over Marge's attractivity as "a dish" and Kodos announces that the Simpsons will be the "guest of honor" – both comments leave open whether their motives are honestly charming or rather alarmingly smarming. Kang and Kodos abducted the Simpson family to take them to their paradisiacal planet Rigel IV, which they announce being "a world of infinite delights." This promise appears to me like an ironic reference to the Hieronymus Bosch triptych painting that depicts Bosch's medieval vision on the Garden Eden, titled "The Garden of Earthly Delights" (1503–1515). En route, the Rigelians serve the Simpsons a considerable amount of food until Lisa discovers their cookbook in the kitchen.

By deliberately misdirecting the viewer's expectations to see an equal climax of entrapment as in "To Serve Man," the segment does something else. Whereas the first book that Lisa discovers reads *"How to Cook Humans,"* a slight veil of dust obscured that it actually reads *"How To Cook For Humans."* Lisa however remains skeptical and blows more dust off the book that now reads *"How To Cook Forty Humans,"* but the aliens once more blow at the book that finally reveals *"How to Cook For Forty Humans."* The segment's play on words ultimately leaves the viewer uncertain about the alien's secret and sinister agenda and upsets the aliens due to Lisa's mistrust so that they promptly return the Simpsons to their home. Baffled by the benevolent aliens' dramatized rejection, Lisa suddenly changes her doubtful mind and wearily concludes the segment with the precocious words: "Truly there were monsters on that ship, and truly we were them."

As startling as Patty's final outcry "It's a cookbook!" may have been for protagonist Michael Chambers and audiences in the 1960s, episode and line have become an iconic and much referenced joke in popular-culture productions. Beyond all the wisecracking use of the "It's a cookbook" revelation, however, in "To Serve Man" Serling portrayed an American culture that was completely caught up in the sum of Cold War problems of the 1960s; problems which caused a ubiquitous paranoia, the feeling of being supposedly guilty, based on an omnipresent anti-intellectualism, political naivety, and an inflated political overestimation (cf. Hill 124).

Similar to Matt Groening's agenda to always have an eye on the concerns of the time, novelist Jonathan Lethem writes about Serling that his "realist writing was grimly topical," rendered in THE TWILIGHT ZONE's metaphorical vocabulary and wrapped in the medium of fantasy, allegory, and parable. All of these aspects fuel the TREEHOUSE segment with a backstabbing humor when Lisa and her know-it-all attitude takes over the role of Patty and disrupts her family's unsuspicious naivety as the only 'intellectual' whom her mother Marge disappointedly labels being "too smart for her own good." "Hungry Are The Damned" can be seen as an echo of Serling's timeless voice to engage with the great American subjects of alienation, identity, conformity, censorship, and racism on American network television in the 1960s.

As the example illustrates, one striking feature of most TWILIGHT ZONE stories is that Serling translated the "homegrown vernacular of alienation, identity slippage, and paranoia" into an elaborate and sometimes even sarcastic vocabulary that expresses his general skepticism towards the current state of political and social affairs. In TREEHOUSE OF HORROR this vocabulary is further complemented with the candy-colored familiarity of the Simpsons that hold up the mirror and reveal that even thirty years later not much seems to have changed in American culture. Despite Serling's cynical portrayal of the, by nature, distrustful but pretentious politicians at the UN in "To Serve Man," specifically the American politicians become the target of the episode's inherent comedy because they think they are smarter than the Kanamits with their elaborate rhetoric, their convincing promises, and futuristic technology.

In an act of almost reactionary sarcasm, Serling's closing narration of "To Serve Man" wraps up his darkly comic view on current affairs. Chain-smoking Chambers is shown grudgingly accepting his damnation in his new home, a small cell on the spaceship, while Serling's off-voice sardonically ponders about "the evolution of man," "the cycle of going from dust to dessert," and "the metamorphosis from being the ruler of a planet to an ingredient in someone's soup." Both episodes resonate with Western culture's relatively lasting insecurity and angst about whether extraterrestrial existence is a threat or aid for mankind, or at least might cater to the Simpson family's individual salvation in "Hungry Are The Damned."

In THE TWILIGHT ZONE, Serling has a point that the threat on the often archetypal American characters doesn't necessarily have to derive from the outside menace of scheming alien invaders. As my next example will demonstrate, the pressure, for example, on the American family can also emerge from the inside, when the stability of the family eventually reveals its fragility due to mothers, fathers, and children who don't behave in accordance with their expected social role.

Revenge on the Baby Boomers:
Dysfunctional Masculinity in TREEHOUSE OF HORROR's "Clown Without Pity"

Blogger Arlen Schumer associates Rod Serling's recurring theme of "the obsolete man" with the idea of dysfunctional masculinity which I will investigate in the following close-reading of the TWILIGHT ZONE episode "Living Doll." Within the American collective mindset it seems that distinct concepts of masculinity are thoroughly implanted. These masculinity concepts derive from 19th-century texts by political writers such as John O'Sullivan (*The Great Nation of Futurity*, 1839) or Frederick Jackson Turner (*The Significance of the Frontier in American History*,

1893). O'Sullivan and Turner for example define the character of the new American man as being shaped along the myth-making narratives that persisted over time since the American settlement and the frontier.

With respect to these landmark texts from 19th century, a specific type of masculinity exists in American culture which is associated with (mainly WASP's) invulnerability, whiteness, power, or leadership qualities. Within postwar America, these notions of how a man was expected to behave in the 1950s were portrayed in Sloan Wilson's novel *The Man in the Gray Flannel Suit* (1955). In the widely acclaimed novel, the protagonist Tom experiences a crisis of his own masculinity while being torn between his traumatic war experiences during WWII and the societal pressure to find agency in postwar suburbia and corporate America.

This is also how Rod Serling frequently envisioned his male protagonists as those American men who are unable to overcome their crucial self-doubts and toxic self-indulgence. Serling's male protagonists such as Patrick McNulty in "Kind Of A Stopwatch," Dan Hollis in "It's A Good Life," or Erich Streator in my following example, "Living Doll," strive to achieve positive recognition, but are metaphorically castrated by a stopwatch, by a six-years-old boy, or, as in the next example, by a talking doll, any of which acts as a moral agent of ironic justice. So the reason that renders these male protagonists as obsolete is in the fact that they are awkward social bodies, bad fathers, or simply infertile husbands.

"Clown Without Pity" from the third Treehouse Special features the Twilight Zone episode "Living Doll." In the adaptation of Charles Beaumont's teleplay, Telly Savalas plays the frustrated father Erich Streator, whom we immediately see projecting his rage over his literal impotence (he is unable to have children of his own) onto Christie, the daughter of his new wife Annabelle. Christie suffers from her stepfather's ill-tempered hostility and intolerance (e.g. he shouts at little Christie: "I'm not your father!") so that her mother comforts her with Talky Tina, a wind-up doll which Streator instantly dislikes.

Every time he is alone with Talky Tina, the doll raises her syrupy voice and starts an almost elaborate conversation with the wary stepfather. Tina says things like "I don't like you," "I think, I could even hate you" or "I'm gonna kill you" so that Streator misses no chance to dump, burn, or saw the doll. But Talky Tina always returns. His wife Annabelle doesn't believe her husband and his growing paranoia, and instead advises him to see a psychiatrist. Annabelle even reproaches him because she is annoyed about his obvious reluctance towards her daughter Christie. One night, Streator is confused whether he is just hallucinating about the strange noises outside. But when he goes downstairs, Tina magically has already positioned herself on one of the treads. Erich stumbles over the doll and falls down headways, succumbing to his deadly injuries.

Although the audience doesn't learn what had caused the patriarch's infertility, reactions to this subtle anomaly of maleness were certainly ambivalent because,

I suggest that male infertility still belongs to one of the few cultural taboo topics.[145] Television networks rather glossed over the fact that there was a downside of the 1950s' idealized nuclear TV families of the Cleavers of Leave It To Beaver (CBS 1957–1963), the Nelsons of Ozzie and Harriet (ABC 1952–1966), and the Andersons of Father Knows Best (CBS 1954–1960). The new family arrangement in "Living Doll," however, presents its audience a single mother, who is obviously troubled to reconstruct the nuclear family ideal, because she gets married to an infertile man, whose predisposition disables him to protect his new wife and daughter. This domestic scenario was quite unconventional on television of the 1960s because the Streators deconstruct the idea of an ideal(ized) nuclear family.

During the 1960s' heyday of the baby-boomer generation the poor parental custody of Eric Streator must still have felt terrifying to TV audiences of that time. Erich Streator's infertility and lack of parental influence, a disposition which the doll in return immediately claims, somewhat mirrors American anxieties of being a man in the 1960s who is incapable of catching up to the ideological demands of founding and protecting a family. While Christie has probably lost her real father in a war, her stepfather supposedly lost his manliness there as well. In the episode "Living Doll," the supposed domestic safety of the family is defenselessly threatened by a female doll which asserts power over the dysfunctional breadwinner.

At the same time, "Talky Tina" presents us with a motif which is rather known from the horror-film genre but which Beaumont and Serling have translated into a child-focused nightmare made-for-television.[146] Concerning Serling's closing narration, the audience couldn't even be sure whether or not Christie herself has committed the murder on the stepfather, since the doll couldn't have gone to the stairs by itself unless it is equipped with supernatural powers:

> Of course, we all know dolls can't really talk, and they certainly can't commit murder. But to a child caught in the middle of turmoil and conflict, a doll can become many things: friend, defender, guardian. Especially a doll like Talky

---

145 In a related analysis of "Living Doll," David Melbye suggests a comparable reading since the episode exemplarily focuses on children's experience within a destabilized nuclear family, in which a child's toy becomes an "agent of justice and a nightmarish deterrent to any further parental transgressions" (*Irony in* The Twilight Zone, 2016: 182).

146 Killer toy dolls are a staple of horror film plots led by iconic talking puppets like Chucky (Child's Play, 1988), Joey (Joey, 1985), or Annabelle (Annabelle, 2014). On television, however, the motif has only found entrance into selected episodes of popular-horror anthology series such as The Twilight Zone (which was the first show that showcased a cursed doll in the 1962 episode "The Dummy"). Doctor Who aired "The Celestial Toymaker" (1966), Night Gallery had "The Doll" (1971), and even The X-Files' episode "Chinga" (1998) had a doll at its center. As the *Wikipedia* list of killer toy appearances on TV proves, the motif seems to enjoy great popularity in children's-horror fictions by R. L Stine and his related TV anthologies Goosebumps and R.L. Stine's Haunting Hour: The Series as well.

Tina, who did talk and did commit murder – in the misty region of the Twilight Zone. *(Opening narration of "Living Doll." THE TWILIGHT ZONE, CBS 1963)*

Child-focused nightmares slowly spilled over from the silver screen to the intimate space of the home, making evil dolls become stock icons for domestic terror in television since the 1960s. In THE TWILIGHT ZONE, a huge part of the show's terror was based on its most terrifying characters, the 'enchanted objects,' in the forms of dolls, mannequins, domestic devices as well as other items of everyday life (cf. Stanyard 2007: 53). Since Tommy Lee Wallace's two-piece TV horror adaptation of Stephen King's IT (ABC 1990), Tim Curry's performance as the wicked clown Pennywise populated people's worst nightmares and almost outperformed the role of talking dolls. Maybe this insight has been reason enough for the writers of "Clown Without Pity" to install Bart's greatest hero Krusty the Clown not as himself, but infuse his horrific appeal into a cursed and talking doll; a combination which has probably been used to amplify the horror.

The segment from ToH III (1992) introduces us to Homer who forgot to get Bart a birthday present. Homer immediately leaves the party in a rush to go gift-shopping in the House of Evil that bills itself being "your one stop evil shop," selling forbidden objects and frozen yogurt. The shop's interior as well as its owner Mr. Wing are obviously designed after Spielberg's Chinatown shop in GREMLINS (1984).

At the beginning of Spielberg's movie, the father Billy Peltzer is shown in a clichéd studio version of Chinatown, where he buys the wolf in a sheep's clothing, i. e. the cuddly creature Gizmo for his son. The strange location is yet another fact that forestalls what sort of evil will probably happen in the TREEHOUSE segment. Homer leaves the place with what the shopkeeper announced as a "cursed doll" which makes Bart have the best birthday ever, turning Homer into the last-minute father of the year. The volatile quality a toy has for a ten-year-old is similarly reflected in the father-son relationship between Homer and Bart, since both are more often shown fighting than hugging each other.

Later, we see Homer sitting alone next to the Krusty doll which, after being wind up, says similar things as Talky Tina: "I don't like you!" and "I'm going to kill you!" Since Homer still laughs at the doll's high-pitched menace, Krusty gets livelier and attacks Homer with a butcher's knife, attempts to drown him in the dog's water bowl, and to tear out his tongue. The doll turns out to be a pure threat to Homer's life and safety up to the point when Marge calls the service hotline she finds on the doll's box. A technician arrives and solves the problem, revealing that the doll was set to "EVIL." But as soon as it is switched to "GOOD," doll Krusty utters his deep love for Homer. In return, Homer starts to exploit and domesticate Krusty as his personal house slave who is eventually forced to live in Lisa's Malibu Stacy dollhouse. By forcing Bart's single hero Krusty to live in the doll house, which is rather connoted with being a domain for girls' play, Homer symbolically castrates Krusty, indicating that Homer is ironically the man who rules over the house and its inhabitants.

In the audio commentary to the ToH segment,[147] Matt Groening explains the team of writers have had long discussed how to end the doll's murder attempts and did the twist "in a loved American style" (cf. 2004). In the moment when Krusty is switched to "GOOD," Homer's idle lethargy of sitting on the couch and drinking beer is just confirmed by the enslaved Krusty. In other words, Homer settles the score in reversal of Bart's oedipal Cold War which the almighty ten-year-old boy fought with his father in "The Bart Zone." Finding a stressed-out Homer, Bart sarcastically comments: "I'd say the pressure's finally gotten to dad, but what pressure?" In the end, Homer symbolically exploits Bart's ultimate hero, hence he corrupts Krusty's role as Bart's fatherly role model. Metaphorically speaking, Homer hijacks Krusty's service as he takes the clown as his personal hostage.

Different to Erich Streator's high social pressures as an infertile member of the baby-boomer generation, Homer's dysfunctionality merely consists of his hedonistic self-indulgence and lethargic indifference because, as this segment makes clear, most of the time Homer doesn't care if he is a good father, husband, or social being as long as he can watch TV or go to Moe's Tavern. Even if doll Krusty had killed Homer, the segment suggests that Homer's death would not be a big loss for the family under the rules of TREEHOUSE OF HORROR. During the time of ToH III's original airing in 1992, such dysfunctional fathers already existed on TV in form of the hapless male anti-hero of MARRIED... WITH CHILDREN, Al Bundy. Yet, Al Bundy was never threatened by killer toys. The working-class vendor rather suffered from his wife's unquenchable thirst for intercourse and his children's insatiable hunger for cash.

In terms of riffing from other filmic sources, the TREEHOUSE segment is a cross-generational, "macabre riot of smart cinephile homages," as online journalist Al Horner called it (2018). "Clown Without Pity" does not only appeal to the media literacy of TWILIGHT ZONE fans familiar with the 1963 "Living Doll," but also to those viewers who remember the voodoo-fetish doll in the made-for-TV anthology horror film TRILOGY OF TERROR from 1975, and the more contemporary audience that had grown up on the Chucky franchise CHILD'S PLAY, beginning its hype in 1988.

TREEHOUSE's insightful layering of references from different kind of media resources demonstrates how older and newer motifs and themes from television and cinema also express different forms of media convergence. TREEHOUSE OF HORROR's repurposing of 1950s' nuclear family concerns translated into scenarios of

---

147 Cf. Matt Groening, THE SIMPSONS Season 4 DVD commentary for the episode "Treehouse of Horror III" (DVD), 20th Century Fox, 2004.

the 1990s' American family life and stories of uncanny terror were examined in terms of concepts of ideal masculinity on public network television. In the next paragraph, I will investigate how these narrative time shifts have become used in TREEHOUSE OF HORROR in order to create the triangular connection between THE TWILIGHT ZONE as a format from the pre-digital age of television, THE SIMPSONS as a 2-D animated television cartoon, and the age of 3-D digital animation. The form of cross-generational 'riffing,' which will be explored in my final close-reading, shows how TREEHOUSE OF HORROR's archive operates with forms of media convergence across different periods of television and film production.

Science Fiction Becomes Real: 3-D Animation and TREEHOUSE OF HORROR's "Homer3"

My final close reading presents the last element of Serling's legacy to TREEHOUSE OF HORROR. His bequest consists of his pioneer spirit by which he significantly influenced not only 1960s' television; the former playwright also encouraged members of future generations like Matt Groening and his team to advance into regions of animation which were entirely new and unaffordable for most animated TV shows on the networks in the mid-1990s. Whereas the decade of the '60s saw a real transformation in science-fiction-/horror television in terms of genre-specific special effects such as the frozen image technique in "Stopwatch," TREEHOUSE's 1995 "Homer^3" (often pronounced "Homer Cubed") offers another innovation. "Homer^3" is an homage to Richard Matheson's teleplay "Little Girl Lost" – a ToH segment which marks another milestone in the technological development from two-dimensional cel animation to CGI (i. e. computer generated image) 3-D animation.

In the original TWILIGHT ZONE episode, six-year-old Tina Miller mysteriously vanishes in something like an invisible wormhole inside her bedroom so that only her voice can be heard by her parents. After the alarmed Millers call their friend Bill, luckily a physicist, he is able to demarcate the entrance to the fourth ("or fifth," Serling is himself not entirely sure in the opening narration) dimension which Tina is assumed to have entered in her bed room. In the TREEHOUSE adaptation, Homer finds a similar portal, a "mystery wall" in the living room which instantly appears to him like "something out of that twilight show about that zone." Owed to the new 3-D technology of CGI animation, the fantastic ride beyond THE SIMPSONS' unknown 2-D boundaries of cartoon production takes viewers even further, beyond the blurred, crystalline, upside-down landscape which THE TWILIGHT ZONE imagined being the fourth (or fifth) dimension.

What audiences of "Homer^3" get to see instead is Homer ostensibly falling off the 2-D cartoon dimension into a parallel universe of an imagery of the third dimension and our reality "between science-fiction and fantasy" (Serling 1959). *A. V. Club* TV editor Les Chappell explains that Homer digresses "through an interdimensional rift and drool in state-of-the-art-for-1995 computer animation" (*The A. V. Club.com* 2014). The editor suggests that the segment forces Homer and Bart to see their world from a different perspective (2014). But more importantly, Treehouse's pushing forward into 3-D computer animation also enables the audience to see the ordinary Homer and Bart in an extraordinary situation.

"Homer^3" ends with Homer being sucked into a wormhole which rapidly absorbs everything in its close vicinity, so that Homer falls from our real-world sky into a backyard trash container of some Los Angeles supermarket. *A. V. Club*'s Simpsons expert Erik Adams concludes that the segment's twist generally proves the show's horror at a basic, fundamental level, when everything you know gets suddenly disproven. Or, more clearly, when everything we thought familiar turns suddenly into something entirely unfamiliar, for example, when Homer feels "bulgy" for the first time and walks along a shopping street under the heavily irritated looks of real-life pedestrians.

Erik Adams says that the show's "aesthetic boldness" does not only consist of an exploration of new animated horizons. The segment was state-of-the-art in order to show off because "Homer^3" was a million-dollar investment (as was Disney's Tron when it experimented with the CGI aesthetics already in the 1980s). The segment does not only convince due to its intelligent background items, raising an awareness for several mathematical problems of the real-world. "Homer^3" is also an early example that could afford to create a surface of 3-D simulated water in which Homer's face is mirrored. Homer comments The Simpsons' walk on new grounds of animation of Treehouse's cartoon storytelling with the words: "Man, this place looks expensive. I feel I'm wasting a fortune just standing here!"[148] In comparison to the other Twilight Zone adaptations, "Homer^3" is not only the most expensive, but also the most expressive example of how Treehouse's aesthetic boldness extended its scope also in terms of aesthetic layering and converging media across different periods of television history, from black-and-white television to innovations in the animation medium in the digital age.

The Treehouse segment utilizes the narrative twist, which I have talked about in the example of "The Bart Zone," as an off-putting technique to amplify the horror, and, by way of this, evolve a form of maturation in the context of horror slash cartoon television. Speaking in the context of 1990s' science-fiction and horror tv, Treehouse of Horror proved more than once that the Halloween installment is a driving force for animated horror innovations. Inspired by Rod Serling's bold-

---

148 The segment focusing on Lisa, "The Genesis Tub," from 1998, featuring Serling and Matheson's episode "The Little People," proved that at this point the show was accustomed to the use of computer animation. In the DVD audio commentary to ToH VII, the segment's executive producer, Mike B. Anderson, explains that the tiny spaceships which attack Bart were later added to the animation. See Mike B. Anderson, *The Simpsons* Season 8 DVD commentary for the episode "Treehouse of Horror VII" (DVD), 20th Century Fox, 2006.

ness in the 1960s' TWILIGHT ZONE, "Homer[3]" is a milestone reflecting the show's commitment to move forward while looking what popular horror culture has left for the generation of auteurs working on TREEHOUSE OF HORROR.

Conclusion: The Treehouse That Matt Built on Rod's Property

Throughout my readings of THE TWILIGHT ZONE, I intended to dispel any doubt that TREEHOUSE's adaptations of some of THE ZONE's most memorable episodes are perhaps based on a pure nostalgia for a time in which television was still an upscaling medium, a time when it was easy to be controversial or to struck a wrong chord with censors, sponsors, and insecure audiences. I even preferred to read the inspired TWILIGHT ZONE segments not as parodies, but as skillfully animated homages to a landmark show in early broadcast television without which also TREEHOUSE OF HORROR would probably not exist. TREEHOUSE's TWILIGHT ZONE archive helps us to remember where some important aesthetic formulae and narrative techniques have their onset. TREEHOUSE OF HORROR appreciates the comprehensive legacy of Serling's science-fiction, horror, and fantasy parables that were concerned with American discontent after WWII.

My analyses above exemplified how TREEHOUSE OF HORROR rides on the coattails of Rod Serling's formula of telling "imaginative tales" as he himself defined them (cf. Presnell/McGee 1998: 15). As one of the first iconic faces of TV horror, Serling not only blurred the genre lines between science fiction, horror, and fantasy; his tales were further largely unseen on TV of the '60s. In addition, he foregrounded the role of the horror host as the speculative fiction auteur, a group of genre writers to which Serling also belonged himself as he is credited to over ninety teleplays of the overall 156 episodes of the original TWILIGHT ZONE series. The series' themes and motifs were preoccupied with the liminal space between the familiar and the strange, the known and the unknown, focusing on the everyday terror of middle-class America; a formula which TREEHOUSE OF HORROR's original creators Matt Groening, Mike Reiss, Sam Simon, David Silverman, and James L. Brooks infused into their own fascination with the domestic terrors of the Simpson family; a fascination which is sometimes more beastly than whatever is meant to be terrorizing the Simpson family (cf. Horner 2018).

So if anything has inspired the idea factory of TREEHOUSE OF HORROR, it is probably Serling's plan to seriously question the immunity and stability of the American nuclear family by looking for their phobic pressure points. I have discussed "Hungry are the Damned" in which not the aliens but the Simpsons are the monsters on board of the spaceship; "Stop the World" presented viewers with Bart's omnipotence expressed by his ability to control time itself, which in "The Bart Zone" becomes even more pinching because Bart owns another god-like skill to control people's thoughts. The 'obsolete man' tale "Clown without Pity" further confirmed what has come off the image of American masculinity. This is because in this adapted tale, Homer gives up on an idealized image of Western masculinity while terrorizing his family with his carelessness. He even takes revenge on his own son by forcing Bart's role model hero, or better, Krusty's stand-in, the Krusty doll, to find domestic bliss in Lisa's dollhouse. According to Treehouse critic Erik Adams, the unifying element across these segments "is the way they each end on a moment of darkness" (2015). In my close-readings I have outlined the specific aspects which Treehouse inherited from The Twilight Zone. The anthology format of self-contained stories and the anti-climactic twist endings were adapted as a means to amplify dysfunction to unknown extremes, since the Simpsons' have honestly threatened the American television-family ideal as the flawed and dysfunctional underside of '90s' horror TV.

Rod Serling's Twilight Zone helped a new generation of TV viewers to take up a new perspective on things, cutting the cord to the preceding popular medium of the radio and visually confronting American people with their own fears of middle-class terrors amidst their own living rooms. Treehouse of Horror caught up on the formulaic essentials from Serling only to twirl ever harder towards the freedom of bringing the domestic terrors of dysfunctional fathers, killer clowns, and infantile mind-controllers to primetime TV.

Treehouse's direct homages to The Twilight Zone don't play for the mere ironic twists and the often corny humor of the original episodes (remember Patty's "It's a cookbook!" exaggerated reaction in "To Serve Man"). Treehouse of Horror's animated versions of The Twilight Zone in fact mirrors in what the show actually was successful. In my opinion, The Twilight Zone has been a great inspiration to Treehouse of Horror because Serling created his house on solid concepts. He formed a vital link between EC Comics and the old pulp fictions of the '50s and the 'what-if' radio-play trends that came to set the standards for new horror, fantasy, and science-fiction storytelling. The close alliance between The Twilight Zone and Treehouse of Horror expressed each show's understanding that, as I have repeatedly pointed out, "it doesn't take much for the normal to shift just a bit and become abnormal," as Noel Murray suggested (*The A. V. Club.com*, 2013). Whereas The Simpsons regular series keeps an eye on the issues of its time by employing a lot of realism and topical issues (e.g. presidential election, climate debate, etc.), Treehouse inspired a new generation of TV viewers to explore their own culture by watching the show's "barrage of riffs on horror from across media genre history" (cf. Horner 2018).

In conclusion, Dana Gould's suggestion that The Simpsons moved simply in the house that Rod had built twenty years earlier must be corrected. Treehouse of Horror claims its own property with an independent treehouse full of twilight zones; an open archive from which audiences can get an instructive view on the outer- and inner sites that Rod Serling has left for us.

4 Conclusion | A Popular-Culture History of the Digital Age

In the 21ˢᵗ century, complex storytelling has become an essential characteristic of television and a well-established subject in the academy. ACA fans crowd today's universities, trying to raise cultural capital by way of popular TV texts. But what have THE SIMPSONS contributed to TV as we know it in the 2020s? Fans assume that the yellow creatures from Springfield began to change popular culture and its study in 1989. This book explored both popular-culture criticism and one of the most popular TV series ever, THE SIMPSONS. I began by studying THE SIMPSONS, but then became more and more interested in the series' anthology cycle, TREEHOUSE OF HORROR, which until now hasn't been scrutinized by cultural-studies research. So it became my quest to find out how pop-culture criticism and THE SIMPSONS meet in the famous series' rather underestimated Halloween Special. In order to study TREEHOUSE, I had to take my position as an ACA fan seriously. Only as a fan and academic I could approach the overarching questions: What is TREEHOUSE OF HORROR's prime concern? And what is its overall function?

In order to bring this project to a final conclusion, I will first wrap up my most general findings by recapitulating the results of each chapter. Throughout my project, I was led by what TREEHOUSE OF HORROR has taught me: To approach television attentively, to study what it has to offer, to learn from it, and become part of a 'TV intelligentsia' who is able to activate pop-cultural capital they have gained from TREEHOUSE's large archive of pop-culture knowledge. Finally, I will provide an outlook on potential future research in the field of television seriality conducted by ACA fans about the poetics, concerns, and functions of the art of contemporary television narration.

4 Conclusion | A Popular-Culture History of the Digital Age

In their book *The Simpsons in the Classroom* (2010), Carma Waltonen and Denise Du Vernay confront their readers with the question: "Why THE SIMPSONS?" They don't find a conclusive answer to this question until eight years later, in the introduction to their next coedited volume *THE SIMPSONS' Beloved Springfield: Essays on the TV Series and Town That Are Part of Us All* (2019). There they give several reasons why it has become increasingly important to focus on THE SIMPSONS not merely in education, but also in popular-culture studies. As their later title suggests, the authors' central claim is that THE SIMPSONS is a part "of us all," indicating that the series not only changed the standards for reading popular art. Rather, Waltonen and Du Vernay go one step further and declare that THE SIMPSONS changed the world of television by bringing to the small screen a cartoon for adults, a sitcom without a laugh track, an imperfect lower-upper-middle-class family,[1] a mixture of high and low comedy, and satire for the masses (cf. Waltonen / Du Vernay 2019: 3).

Waltonen and Du Vernay are right with respect to THE SIMPSONS, but overlook the many changes TREEHOUSE OF HORROR has not only brought *to* TV, but also to the reception of popular culture *through* TV. On my way to developing my own aesthetic category for TREEHOUSE OF HORROR, I shifted the focus from THE SIMPSONS towards TREEHOUSE OF HORROR. TREEHOUSE is not only a series which is part of us all, but which creates an intimate connection to its audience by re-presenting their pop-culture heritage. I began to suspect that the Halloween special continues a practice initiated by the regular SIMPSONS series which librarian Moritz Fink describes in the conclusion to *THE SIMPSONS: A Cultural History*: "THE SIMPSONS has provided a rich image bank through which popular culture generates its own mutations, mythologies, and memes." (2019: 176) I hypothesized that TREEHOUSE OF HORROR has complemented this image bank with its own look at the past which itself is becoming part of America's cultural history, has influenced people's reading of this history and their ways of re-membering it.

By staging encounters with classic American literature, Hollywood films, and broadcasting traditions of the radio play or the television-anthology series, many stories told in TREEHOUSE OF HORROR reveal that the series looks for more universal cultural patterns behind popular myths than THE SIMPSONS. Thus, the Hal-

---

1   Although the family is set in an American upper-middle class suburb (a neighborhood in which also ex-president George Bush, Sr., once lived), Homer can be described as a member of the blue-collar working class who happens to work in a white-collar job, as underqualified and often clueless safety inspector in Springfield's nuclear power plant while Marge is the classical housewife who takes care of their three children. Throughout the series, however, the Simpsons oscillate between alternating class registers, e.g. when viewers get to know that Marge has studied art history or when Lisa is send to an elite school, etc. As the Simpsons are shown in different class concepts, I refer to the family by means of the category "lower-upper-middle class" which fiction writer George Orwell used to define himself in his essayistic documentary *The Road to Wigan Pier* from 1937.

loween Special tells stories about the past that even hardcore fans of the show don't necessarily remember or know. The horror series thus has been establishing a collection of texts which, put together, present American popular-culture history from today's standpoint. Based on this thought, I decided to provide a comprehensive introduction to THE SIMPSONS' critical history of American everyday life. After all, THE SIMPSONS set out by criticizing classical TV sitcoms' hegemonic tendencies and their re-affirmative conservatisms, TREEHOUSE OF HORROR by inspiring the dialogue between practices of the digital age and U. S.-America's pop-cultural past. THE SIMPSONS can be understood as an animated parody of the television sitcom. But the Halloween Special has always led viewers beyond the aesthetic traditions and generic conventions THE SIMPSONS offered its fans. How, then, was I to classify TREEHOUSE OF HORROR?

I explore this question in the two main chapters of this book. Firstly, I looked at THE SIMPSONS and TREEHOUSE OF HORROR through postmodernist theories from the second half of the 20th- as well as from the 21st century and read these theories through the two series. Secondly, I pointed to differences between the main series and TREEHOUSE by analyzing their respective aesthetic and distinct medial practices in parts and episodes from both series. Each chapter looked at THE SIMPSONS' regular series alongside TREEHOUSE OF HORROR in order to show how their respective formats work differently.

THE SIMPSONS' TREEHOUSE OF HORROR under the Microscope of Postmodern Pop-Culture Theory

In retrospect, much of the research related to THE SIMPSONS basically follows the cultural-studies approach of closely reading an example from the animated archive and put it under the microscope of different postmodern popular-culture theories. This is what I did in my theoretical chapter. The study of popular-culture products not only took me on travels in time and sent me through America's pop-culture- and media *history*, but also into popular-culture *theory*.

Whereas I largely analyzed THE SIMPSONS in the light of classical postmodern theory, I soon realized that the theories don't go far enough to get to the bottom of TREEHOUSE OF HORROR's narrative driving forces that set the series apart from the regular continuity of THE SIMPSONS. I followed the advice of Mark Dery and Kalle Lasn and started some "culture jamming," meddling with these popular-culture theories, for example, in 2.1 when I reconsidered Eco's semiological guerrilla tactics between originality and plagiarism in the arts and discussed them with the SIMPSONS / FAMILY GUY crossover episode "The Simpsons Guy." In subchapter 2.2, I took up Angela McRobbie's investigating practices of contemporary American culture by means of what the *L. A. Times* termed "a SIMPSONS worldview"

(Baker 2003). I applied traditional postmodern theories and their notions of representation to the culture-wars debate of 1990s America to explore how the 'surfaces' of Lisa, Bart, and Homer Simpson developed a cultural life of their own by entering into processes of continuous becoming. For my next subchapter 2.3 I used a comparative approach to the different animation styles and traditions of Walt Disney and Matt Groening to see where these might shed new light on the cultural life and historical function of parody as a myth-revealing instrument of the digital age. At the intersection of the two artists, who both played a pioneering role in the field of animation, I came to the insight that THE SIMPSONS' concept of parody has in fact bettered our understanding of the show and its cultural life. Linda Hutcheon's findings concerning the field of postmodern parody helped me to realize that parody follows a different purpose in THE SIMPSONS than in TREEHOUSE OF HORROR. THE SIMPSONS makes use of parody in order to satirize and subvert U.S.-American culture along its ideological fault lines. TREEHOUSE OF HORROR instead uses parody as an archival tool that enables the show not only to expose or ridicule traditions, but rather to re-member and re-view popular texts from the past. In order to explore how TREEHOUSE OF HORROR reaches out to its fans in different ways than THE SIMPSONS, I applied Foucault's concept of the archive to the popular-culture context in my subchapter 2.4. The French philosopher was among the first to liberate the archive from its ties to the written word in libraries organized by librarians and archivists only. Foucault read the archive "as a site from which to clarify what is at stake in the claims of cultural studies to be an interdisciplinary project" (Robertson 2004: 450). Foucault turned the archive into what German media theorist Oliver Fahle calls a "wandelbare Kontaktzone" (2010: 3), a 'convertible contact zone.' In my analyses of episodes from the TREEHOUSE series, I found that the traditional archival 'site' can be turned into an alternative 'space' of disorder and non-conformity in which knowledge of the past can be re-membered and its fractal pieces can be re-constructed *in* and *in the interest of* the present. Step by step, my analytical interest shifted towards the TREEHOUSE OF HORROR because the more closely I looked at this show, the better I understood its prime concern: It offers itself to its viewers as a 'convertible contact zone,' a re-animated archival space inviting a reconsideration of (popular) culture practices of the past.

It became obvious to me that TREEHOUSE OF HORROR functions as a space in which rediscovered texts newly resonate with ever new generations of fans and their situational knowledge. TREEHOUSE demonstrates how the archive's function has changed in its relation to 21st-century popular culture. Supported by Henry Jenkins' insights into convergence culture, I concluded that archival work has turned into a collective process and an alternate source of democratic power of the digital age. As such, TREEHOUSE OF HORROR's archive is an example for the re-membering, re-writing, and re-purposing of America's popular-culture history tying together past, present, and future according to the needs of today's audiences.

As an ACA fan, a fan who uses a popular text to produce academic content, I continued by making use of popular-culture theories to shed light on my pop material. TREEHOUSE OF HORROR offers a new understanding of cultural practices. My various readings of examples from the TREEHOUSE OF HORROR cycle evidenced that the show does archeological work on media that helps us "understand new and emerging media cultures through the past" (Parikka 2011). The dialectics of parody and the popular-culture implications of the archive have enabled TREEHOUSE OF HORROR to "speak *to* a discourse from *within* it" (Hutcheon, *Poetics* 35) and created a dialogue between the visual culture of the past and ways to read them through digital-age cultural practices. In this regard, parody refers to continuity (of the past) and change (in the present) that inspires new forms and functions of seriality and open continuity.

TREEHOUSE OF HORROR: Lessons to re-member

I finished this project in July 2020. At this time I keep wondering why nothing has been published yet on THE SIMPSONS' seasonal special TREEHOUSE OF HORROR besides committed fan contributions which can be found all over the internet. There exists no academic analysis, no research paper, and no book that is dedicated in its entirety to bettering the academic understanding of TREEHOUSE OF HORROR, or rather, to bettering the academic understanding of popular-culture- and media studies through TREEHOUSE OF HORROR. However, after thirty years of THE SIMPSONS' seasonal special, the Halloween show has proved its commitment to the American horror genre which has been manifesting itself in literature, film, and television texts for over 200 years.

Based on the results I had gathered in the previous chapters, I finally engaged in the close reading of the series' 'history lessons,' arranged as didactic historical units which I see realized in each of TREEHOUSE's four broader narrative sections. Firstly, In 3.1, I investigated the origins of TREEHOUSE OF HORROR's aesthetics and discussed in how far it can be seen as a simulation of digital age media practices by looking at the show's narrative structure and exemplify TREEHOUSE's references to EC Comics as well as Rod Serling's anthology pattern. My findings strengthened the assumption that TREEHOUSE OF HORROR can legitimately be read as a history text that teaches viewers lessons to remember. Those thoughts paved the way for the subsequent four close readings, in which I read the Halloween show as a collection of lessons for viewers to re-member about their medial past.

The opening sequence, better known as the 'couch gag,' was described in 3.2 as a collaborative site for the animation auteur and his (traditionally masculine) auteur animation practices, inviting cultural jammers to experiment with different guerrilla tactics through animation. My look at diverse couch-gag practices helped me understand what this specific TREEHOUSE OF HORROR section can tell us about the developments of the consumption, production, and reception of television content. As examples I analyzed couch gags made by three artists coming from different medial domains: street artist Banksy, independent claymation video artist Lee Hardcastle, and fantasy-film auteur Guillermo del Toro were chosen to examine what kinds of subversive acts of resistance are possible within the commercially successful cartoon enterprise of TREEHOUSE OF HORROR. The resulting couch gags were useful to exemplify how my idea of the 'fan auteur' successfully opened up a new dimension of participatory culture as well as new directions for contemporary television production. The Halloween Special offers a space for individual practices of culture jamming by cartoon auteurs.

Chapter 3.3 deals with TREEHOUSE OF HORROR's third history lesson concerning the Halloween show's literary legacy. I focused on TREEHOUSE's adaptations from its 19th-century Gothic-fiction archive: How does this postmodern animated cartoon for a mainstream TV audience negotiate 19th-century writing? Following Jason Mittell's poetics of contemporary complex serial TV, I came to the conclusion that TREEHOUSE's serial format is important firstly to keep up the dialogue between past texts and present medial practices and secondly to strengthen the connection between the series and its audience. The cycle's ongoing confrontations with different hegemonic tendencies in pop-culture media help create a form of seriality that returns to the past in order to keep it fluid, to return it to its constant state of becoming. My close readings of some of the most memorable "cultural echo chambers" – the TREEHOUSE segments "The Raven," the FRANKENSTEIN adaptation "If I Only Had A Brain", and the H. G. Wells' parody "The Island of Dr. Hibbert" – illustrate to what extent Groening's literary archive opens new ways of looking at U. S.-American culture and developing new ways of understanding the complexity of seriality in the digital age.

The fourth part of chapter three (3.4) is committed to shedding light onto the role of the American horror film in contemporary television. By looking at exotic islands, haunted houses, and home invasions, I was interested in the question how TREEHOUSE OF HORROR makes use of America's horror-cinema archive to renegotiate the objects, motifs, and themes of horror filmmaking in and through a domestic television context. According to my findings, the modern horror film has served throughout cinema history as a sensitive instrument to display the nation's common fears and critically investigate their ideological framing. The interlinkage between the different incarnations of the nation's wider anxieties throughout diverse examples from TREEHOUSE's horror-film archive has supported my claim that all American horror begins at home which turns television and especially the sitcom into an ideal site to spread fear and terror.

The final history lesson is discussed in chapter 3.5: "A Treehouse Full of Twilight Zones" re-members an era of television broadcasting in which the images were still black and white. Even prior to my detailed analysis, it was a widely known fact that THE SIMPSONS' creators drew much inspiration for TREEHOUSE OF HORROR from the radio- and television playwright Rod Serling, or more precisely, from Serling's most notable creation, the landmark TV-anthology series THE TWILIGHT ZONE. My comparative reading oscillates between Serling's portrayal of moral extremes negotiated in his "fifth dimension" stories on the one hand and TREEHOUSE's two-dimensional take on these dystopian tales on the other. Both series turn conventional TV storytelling on its head by working with techniques like ironic twists, archetypal characters, open ends, rope-a-dope tactics leading the audience astray, and innovative special effects to challenge and even irritate the viewer's capacity to see behind the surface and uncover the messages behind the shows' social parables. How, then, did Serling rewire the American psyche to terrors close to home? And what could the re-animation of THE TWILIGHT ZONE tell me about TREEHOUSE OF HORROR and its view on U.S.-American culture and its ideological fault lines in its respective network-TV format? My close readings of seven animated TWILIGHT ZONE adaptations showed that both series strike a balance between intelligent storytelling and staying commercially attractive for sponsors and audience alike. Thus, TREEHOUSE OF HORROR's re-membering of Rod Serling's landmark TV series shows many interconnections between both shows' historically specific medial practices; the respective framing of their narrations as well as their tv formats connect the past of television art to the present of the animated show in the direction of the future of television storytelling.

Finally: What Comes After THE SIMPSONS?

With TREEHOUSE OF HORROR, SIMPSONS' inventor Matt Groening created not only a special cycle that revolves around past popular productions and coincides with Halloween television programming. Groening created a series about pastness and about how U.S.-American history influences our imagination of the past in the present. THE SIMPSONS' horror show makes visible that America's cultural past primarily exists in the medial images popular culture has created, be it in films or television, on photographs, paintings or the radio. Sometimes these images may be too painful, too traumatic to be addressed directly in live-action film. But translated into an animated cartoon, Groening's team manages to draw attention to the pains and pleasures of the past by provoking viewers' capacity to re-member what they cannot recall themselves or never knew. This is what Groening means by reiterating, time and again, that the point of his work is to entertain and subvert (qtd. in Turner 2012).

It turned out that TREEHOUSE OF HORROR works best in those moments when there are challenges to overcome; challenges which can be confronted more effectively in an animated horror show than in a live-action program. One of these challenges became especially evident in the series of online shorts which I have come to label "White House of Horror" stories. Posted on YouTube between 2015 and 2019, the eight "Donald Trump Shorts,"[2] as they are called on *Wikisimpsons*, are speculative cartoon satires presenting what possibly could have been going on behind the walls of the White House since Donald Trump had moved there in 2017. The first "Trumptastic Voyage," posted on July 7, 2015, went viral once some attentive fans had revealed that the clip included a déjà-vu scene which shows Trump riding down a Trump Tower escalator and waving to his fans after his candidacy was announced in June 2015. And SIMPSONS fans had already encountered this scene fifteen years earlier in the episode "Bart To The Future" from 2000! In a 2016 interview with *The Guardian* that preceded Trump's actual election, Groening says about Trump:

> If by chance he gets elected, […] I think we'll suddenly be very inspired. Mr. Trump's election, as horrible as it would be, would be great for comedy. […] If Trump wins there will be an exodus of people. I won't leave the U.S. because I actually think it will be amazing in all its horror.
> *(Groening qtd. in First Dog on the Moon [Andrew Marlton] 2016)*

To a larger degree than THE SIMPSONS, TREEHOUSE OF HORROR has not only taught us how inspiring horror can be for comedy, but also how amazingly complex the re-membering of past pop material can become when it reveals its formerly hidden horror. Watching a TREEHOUSE episode can become a highly complex undertaking, inviting not only academic, but non-academic hardcore fans of the series to take the cultural-studies practice of close reading seriously. With respect to the

---

2   Wikisimpsons lists all eight "Donald Trump shorts" posted on *YouTube* between July 7, 2015, and August 20, 2019. Beginning with "Trumptastic Voyage" in which Homer goes on a surrealist, Meliès-inspired trip into Trump's hair and continuing with "The Debateful Eight" (2016) which is related to the 2016 presidential election; "3 a.m." (2016) which shows that the election causes Homer and Marge sleepless nights; "Donald Trump's First 100 Days In Office" in which Trump twitters about the accomplishments of his first days in the White House; "125 Days: Donald Trump Makes One Last Try To Patch Things Up With Comey" shows Trump as not only being haunted by accusations of fraud during the election campaign, but also by former president Richard Nixon; "Mueller Meets Trump" which shows how Trump tries to bribe former FBI director and special counsel for the Department of Justice Robert Mueller; "A Tale Of Two Trumps" about the question whether Trump has a bad conscience after having fired so many people or whether his actions can be explained by his little ego; and finally "West Wing Story" in which Democratic Congress member Alexandria Ocasio-Cortez and the politicians Ilhan Omar, Ayanna Presley, and Rashida Tlaib start chasing Trump around the White House. For more information, see URL: https://simpsonswiki.com/wiki/Donald_Trump_shorts.

multi-layered complexity of TREEHOUSE OF HORROR, Jenkins, MacPherson, and Shattuc's remark about pop culture that "sticks to our skin" is only too true: Indeed it is impossible to examine this Halloween show from a distance (cf. 2002: 3). Even the "Donald Trump Shorts" take us inside the White House where Trump's character is haunted by the ghosts of American leadership. My detailed analyses aimed to show that TREEHOUSE OF HORROR has answered to the challenges of culture jamming long before television critics and media scholars began calling them cultural practices of the digital age.

The show's poetic travels into the past and present of U.S.-American popular culture will continue. On the news platform *Digital Spy.com*, journalist Rianne Houghton quotes the president of Fox Entertainment, Michael Thorn, who said that "there is no immediate plan" for ending the show, albeit "preparations for a post-SIMPSONS world" are said to exist, preparations that would put a full stop behind Fox's flagship (2020). But not yet.

Since Disney's major takeover of large market shares from 20th Century Fox in 2017, however, it has been uncertain what will happen to THE SIMPSONS in the future. At the moment of writing, the series is between season 31, concluding its batch of episodes in May 2020, and season 32, confirmed to debut in September 2020, which is predicted to contain the show's 700th overall episode. On the occasion of the Corona-pandemic inspired "Comic-Con@Home" event, a group of SIMPSONS producers, writers, animation directors, and voice actors met with committed fans in "THE SIMPSONS Panel," where a fifty-minute video recording on the future episode of TREEHOUSE OF HORROR XXXI was shown (cf. Squires 2020).

"The Simpsons Panel" was a teaser for "Into The Homerverse,"[3] which portrays Homer encountering himself as "Homer Barbera," i.e. a blending of Yogi Bear and Homer who claims that he is "smarter than the average Homer." In the blink of an eye, a pumpkin-shaped carriage falls from the ceiling and the stage is opened for "Disney Princess Homer" who looks like Homer dressed as Cinderella and immediately starts to sing like a heroine in a Disney feature film. This cross-dressing moment shows Homer bereft of his original identity and under the influence of other major American animation traditions, namely Hanna Barbera Productions and the Disney Corporation. The small preview somehow speculates about the spectre of THE SIMPSONS' artists' loss of creative control when Disney will expand its command over the show. But not yet.

Rumors on the Internet are getting louder and louder proclaiming the end of THE SIMPSONS under the supervision of Disney executives on the new streaming

---

3 The segment is actually a SPIDERMAN: INTO THE SPIDER-VERSE (2018) parody and part of TREEHOUSE's thirty-first installment (S32E04) surrounded by the "2020 Election" intro couch gag, the TOY STORY parody "Toy Gory," and "Be Nine, Rewind," a spoof of Michael Gondry's mind-bending comedy BE KIND, REWIND (2008). The thirty-first Halloween and 688th episode overall was aired on All Hallows Day 2020 on Fox Network television.

269

service Disney+, at least after Disney announced in April 2019 that it will become the exclusive streaming home of THE SIMPSONS (cf. *Vulture.com* 2019). Online journalists Stefan Sirucek and Ramsey Ess complain on Vulture: "Yes, Disney+ has provided an online hub for the entire SIMPSONS catalogue, furnishing every season of the iconic series to diehard fans and streaming-era newcomers alike, but it's initially done so with an aesthetic bastardization that would make Santa Claus himself vomit with rage" (2019). Sirucek and Ess's outcry was motivated by Disney's cutting the show's original 4:3 aspect ratio to a 16:9 standard, resulting in amputations of several visual gags which are now missing. Disney further took season three's Michael Jackson episode "Stark Raving Dad" (1991) from broadcast circulation after HBO had commissioned the controversial LEAVING NEVERLAND documentary about the pedophilic history of the deceased King of Pop in 2019. Fans the world over consider this act of curtailing an affront. According to major online-news feeds such as BBC,[4] *The New York Times* (Itzkoff 2020), or *Entertainment Weekly* (Aquilina 2020), the third and most recent change concerns the lasting criticism of THE SIMPSONS for using white actors to voice characters portraying other ethnicities. Hank Azaria, for example, has come under pressure for racial stereotyping primarily due to his voicing of the Indian convenience-store owner Apu Nahasapeemapetilon, a character Azaria has been voice-acting since Apu was created in 1990.[5] The producers consequently decided to provide more opportunities for non-white performers.

All three examples from the recent history of THE SIMPSONS since Disney's ownership that culminated in Disney+, the show's aspect-ratio formatting and corpus curtailing, as well as the matters of political correctness in the wake of Black Lives Matter protests will open new directions for future research on THE SIMPSONS as long as the series keeps moving with its fans. This book provides fertile ground for research on the future dialogue between new generations of audiences in the digital age and the popular culture of the past. U.S.-American traditions of discrimination on the basis of gender, sexuality, race, class, age, or 'deficiencies' of any sort will become more pressing.

Trick, Treat, Transgress has found many answers to questions which remained untouched in the field of SIMPSONS research for a long time. TREEHOUSE OF HORROR provided me with a vast amount of Easter Eggs, hidden cues, and background histories that stimulated this study. I would like to complement Waltonen and Du Vernay's list of how THE SIMPSONS changed the world of television with TREE-

---

4   See, for example, the article on *BBC.com*: "Simpsons actor Hank Azaria says he will no longer voice Apu" posted on 18 Jan. 2020 or Dave Itzkoff's *New York Times* interview with Hank Azaria "Why Hank Azaria Won't Play Apu on 'The Simpsons' Anymore" published on 25 Feb. 2020.

5   Hank Azaria is a white actor who further provides the voice of other ethnic characters, including black police officer Lou and the Mexican-American Bumblebee Man.

House of Horror. According to my findings, the show brought to screen a proof for the necessity of participatory culture in an age of media convergence; it further evidences that cartoons can extend the concept of complex-TV storytelling and sustain the relevance of the television medium. In short, Treehouse of Horror has changed the way we look at the past of popular culture. By means of the horror genre, the cycle helps people re-member the significance of past media as it provides old and new generations of viewers with a popular-culture history of the digital age.

I hope this study will serve future cultural- and media-studies scholars as a starting point to spawn new thinking about the confrontation of viewers with different political positions through popular-culture texts. By continuing the dialogue between audience and series, The Simpsons will probably come to an end one day. But not yet. Not as long as both The Simpsons and Treehouse of Horror stick to the skin of their fans. As continuity narratives both formats are archives of broad cultural knowledge; archives which remain in a constant state of becoming. They will move on to entertain and subvert as complex works in progress which may control their own input, but not our intake of their pop-culture archive.

In the future, it will be necessary to widen our gaze to receptions of iconic (and not so obviously iconic) 18th- or 19th-century texts across media throughout the past until today. This is already being done in contemporary Seriality- and Fan Studies. At the same time, this kind of research has emerged with Martina Pfeiler's habilitation thesis "Ahab in Love: The Creative Reception of Moby-Dick in Popular Culture" at my home university on Herman Melville's *Moby-Dick*, but was also done for other widely remediated texts such as Harriet Beecher Stowe's *Uncle Tom's Cabin*, for Mary Shelley's *Frankenstein* as well as for African American slave narratives whose heritage has been repurposed across the range of yesterday's as well as today's media. The extensive research on the world-wide influence of Walt Whitman's poems is another example for a field that has to offer results feeding into a more extensive understanding of archival practices across U.S.-American and eventually global cultures. I hope that this study may challenge other researchers to investigate how recent and possibly older texts and media have cultivated an archival practice in ways comparable to The Simpsons' Treehouse of Horror.

5 References

Aarseth, Espen. "Computer Game Studies, Year One." *The International Journal of Computer Game Research. Games Studies.org*, Vol 1, No. 1 (July 2001). 20 Feb. 2020. URL: http://gamestudies.org/0101/editorial.html.

——. "Playing Research: Methodological approaches to game analysis." *Games Approaches*. Conference Paper from Aug. 2003. 26 May 2020. PDF-Download from URL: https://bit.ly/306KF6p.

Abelman, Robert / David J. Atkin. *The Televiewing Audience: The Art and Science of Watching TV*, 2nd ed. New York [et al.]: Peter Lang, 2011.

Abramson, Seth. "Ten Basic Principles of Metamodernism." *Huffpost.com*, 27 Apr. 2017. at 20 Aug. 2019. URL: https://bit.ly/3sMQNwN

——. "Five More Basic Principles of Metamodernism. (VIDEOS)" *Huffpost.com*, Updated 12 May 2016. at 20 Aug.2019. URL: https://bit.ly/3uOBPbr.

——. "Metamodernism: The Basics II." *Huffpost.com*, Updated 14 Dec. 2014. 20 Aug. 2019. URL: https://bit.ly/387sgdS.

——. "Metamodernism: The Basics." *Huffpost.com*, Updated 12 Dec. 2014. 20 Aug. 2019. URL: https://bit.ly/307UVem.

Adams, Erik. "The Simpsons (Classic): 'Treehouse of Horror VIII.'" *The A. V. Club.com*, 19 Jul. 2015. URL: https://bit.ly/30bDQ3f.

Alberti, John. Ed. *Leaving Springfield. The Simpsons and the Possibility of Oppositional Culture*. 2nd Ed. Detroit: Wayne State UP, 2005.

Archer, Neil. *Beyond a Joke: Parody in English Film and Television Comedy*. London / New York.: I. B. Tauris, 2017.

Ashley, Leonard R. N. *Halloween: Everything Important About the Most Popular Secular Holiday*. Bloomington: Xlibris, 2012.

Ashlin, Scott. "Island of Lost Souls (1933)." *Movie Review* / Blog. *1000 Misspent Hours*, undated. 20 Dec. 2019. URL: https://bit.ly/2NP0lIZ.

Aylesworth, Gary. "Postmodernism." *Stanford Encyclopedia of Philosophy*, subst. revision 5 Feb. 2015. 9 May 2019. URL: https://stanford.io/3bcTIcn.

Baker, Bob. "The Real First Family." *The L. A. Times.com*, 16 Feb. 2003. 09 Jan. 2020. URL: https://lat.ms/3sN65Sk.

Baldick, Chris. Ed. "Introduction." *The Oxford Book of Gothic Tales*. Oxford / New York: Oxford UP, 1993. xi-xxiii.

Barker, Chris. *Cultural Studies: Theories and Practice*, 3rd edition. London [et al.]: SAGE Publications, 2008.

Barney, Brooks. "Disney Moves From Behemoth to Colossus With Closing of Fox Deal." *The New York Times.com*, 20 Mar. 2019. 24 Sept. 2019. URL: https://nyti.ms/3bcL6SK.

Barnouw, Erik. *Tube of Plenty: The Evolution of American Television*, 2nd Rev. Ed. New York / Oxford: Oxford UP, 1990.

Barry, Peter. *Beginning Theory: An Introduction to Literary and Cultural Theory*, 2nd ed. Manchester UP, 2002 [1995].

Barth, John. "Lost in the Funhouse." *Idem. Lost in the Funhouse*: Fiction for Print, Tape, Live Voice. New York: Bantam Books, 1980. 69–94.

Baudrillard, Jean. *Simulacra and Simulations*. Trans. Sheila Faria Glaser. Ann Arbor: The U of Michigan P, 1994 [1983].

— . "The Precession of Simulacra." Storey, John. Ed. *Cultural Theory and Popular Culture: A Reader*, 4th ed. Harlow: Pearson, 2009. 409–415.

Bell, Amanda. "Here are all the Halloween Marathons hitting TV this year." *TV Guide.com*, 23 Oct. 2018. 23 Jan. 2019. URL: https://bit.ly/3bfcQXb.

Bergetz, Carl. "It's Not Funny 'Cause It's True: The Mainstream Media's Response to Media Satire in the Bush Years." Timothy M. Dale. Ed. *Homer Simpson Marches on Washington. Dissent Through American Popular Culture*. Lexington: University Press of Kentucky, 2010. 257–76.

Berman, Pat. "H.G. Wells' Influence Still Ripping Through Popular Culture." *Local Journalism.com*, 29 Jun. 2006. 20 Aug. 2018. URL: https://bit.ly/3rdzK6B.

Bernard, Mark. Halloween: *Youth Cinema and the Horrors of Growing Up*. London / New York: Routledge, 2020.

Bhattacharya, Sanjiv. "Homer's odyssey." *The Guardian.com*, 06 Aug. 2000. 12 Jan. 2020. URL: https://bit.ly/309d7EB.

Binoche, Bertrand. "Perfectibility." Barbara Cassin. Ed. *Dictionary of Untranslatables: A Philosophical Lexicon*, Transl. ed. by Emily Apter, Jacques Lezra, and Michael Wood. Princeton/Oxford: Princeton UP, 2014. 796–771.

Blau, Sheridan. "Performative Literacy: The Habits of Mind of Highly Literate Readers." *Voices from the Middle*, Vol. 10, 3 (2003): 18–22.

Bloom, Harold. Ed. *Bloom's Modern Critical Views: Stephen King*. Infobase Publishing, 2006.

Bolter, Jay David / Richard Grusin. *Remediation. Understanding New Media*. MIT Press, 2000.

Botting, Fred. *Gothic*. London / New York: Routledge, 1996.

Booker, M. Keith. *Science Fiction Television*. Westport [*et al.*]: Praeger, 2004.

— . *Drawn to Television. Prime-Time Animation from* THE FLINTSTONES *to* FAMILY GUY. Westport [*et al.*]: Praeger, 2006.

Bouchard, Norma. "Eco and Popular Culture." Peter Bondanella. Ed. *New Essays on Umberto Eco*. Cambridge: Cambridge UP, 2009. 1–16.

Bosky, Terry. "The Simpsons at 30." [Book Reviews]. *Library Journal.com*, 12 Jun. 2019. 23 Feb. 2020. URL: https://bit.ly/3883RF1.

Bould, Mark. *Film Noir: From Berlin to Sin City*. London / New York: Wallflower Press, 2005.

Bowman, Jessica. "The Controversial Halloween Scene That Was Cut From 'THE OFFICE'." *Floor 8.com*, 28 Oct. 2019. 04 May 2020. URL: https://bit.ly/389oTTX.

Bradbury, Ray. *A Sound of Thunder*, [PDF-Download], 1952, 1–11. 20 Nov 2018. URL: https://bit.ly/2Pnz6W8.

Brunsdon, Charlotte / Lynn Spigel. Eds. *Feminist Television Criticism. A Reader*, 2nd. Ed. Berkshire: McGraw Hill Open UP, 2008.

Burgin, Victor. *Fiction Film*. (A Portfolio of 9 Screenprints), 1991. *Paragonpress.co.uk*, 26 Jan. 2020. URL: http://paragonpress.co.uk/works/fiction-film.

Burton, Graeme. *Talking Television. An Introduction to the Study of Television*. New York: Oxford UP, 2000.

Burwick, Frederick L. "Edgar Allan Poe: The Sublime, the Picturesque, the Grotesque, and the Arabesque." *Amerikastudien / American Studies, JSTOR.com*, Vol. 43,

No. 3, (1998): 423–436. URL: www.jstor.org/stable/41157397.

Cambridge English Dictionary. "Palimpsest." *Cambridge Dictionary.org*, undated. 20 Apr. 2020. URL: https://dictionary.cambridge.org/dictionary/english/palimpsest.

Cantor, Paul A. "THE SIMPSONS: Atomistic Politics and the Nuclear Family." *Political Theory*, Vol. 27, No. 6, (Dec. 1999): 734–49.

Caughie, John. Ed. "Andrew Sarris." *Theories of Authorship*, 10th ed. *A Reader*. London / New York: Routledge, 2001. 61–67.

Chappell, Les. "THE SIMPSONS (Classic): 'TREEHOUSE OF HORROR VII.'" *AV Club.com*, 05 Oct. 2014. 15 Nov. 2019. URL: https://bit.ly/3sLHQE6.

Chilton, Martin. "The War of the World panic was a myth." *The Telegraph.co.uk*, 6 May 2016. 20 Nov. 2019. URL: https://bit.ly/2OflZpw.

Chow, Valerie Weilunn. "Homer Erectus: Homer Simpson As Everyman... and Every Woman." Alberti, John. Ed. *Leaving Springfield. THE SIMPSONS and the Possibility of Oppositional Culture*, 2nd Ed. Detroit: Wayne State UP, 2005. 107–126.

Chun Kyong, Wendy Hui. "Introduction: Did Somebody Say New Media?" Chun Kyong, Wendy Hui and Thomas Keenan. Eds. *New Media, Old Media*: A History and Theory Reader. London / New York: Routledge, 2006.

Cohen, Jeffrey Jerome. Ed. "Monster Culture (Seven Theses)." *Monster Theory: Reading Culture*. London/Minneapolis: The U of Minnesota P, 1996. 3–25.

Cohen, Paula Marantz. "Conceptual Suspense in Hitchcock's Films." Thomas Leitch and Leland Pague. *A Companion to Alfred Hitchcock*. Wiley-Blackwell, 2011. 126–136.

Collins, Jim. "Postmodernism and Television." Robert C. Allen. Ed. *Channels of Discourse, Reassembled: Television and Contemporary Criticism*, 2nd ed. U of North Carolina P, 1992. 327–353.

Conard, Mark T. "Thus Spake Bart: On Nietzsche and the Virtues of Being Bad." William Irwin, Mark T. Conard, and Aeon J. Skoble. Eds. *THE SIMPSONS and Philosophy: The D'OH! Of Homer*, 2001. 86–118.

Coulthart, John. "Uncharted Islands and Lost Souls." *John Coulthart.com* ['Feuilleton' Blog], 23 Dec. 2013. 11 Oct. 2019. URL: https://bit.ly/30bGJkA.

Creeber, Glen. Ed. *The Television Genre Book*. London: BFI, 2001.

Critical Commons Manager. "THE SIMPSONS opening by Banksy." *Criticalcommons.org*, undated. 20 Jan. 2019. URL: https://bit.ly/30idPiJ.

Cronin, Brian. "TV Legends Revealed: How Congress Inspired an Extra-Violent 'TREEHOUSE OF HORROR.'" *Comic Book Review.com*, 28 Oct. 2015. 20 Jul. 2017. URL: https://bit.ly/3sMSQ3P.

Croxton, Katie. "Snow White, the Grimm Brothers and the Studio the Dwarfs Built." Mark I. West. Ed. *Walt Disney, from Reader to Storyteller: Essays on the Literary Inspirations*. Jefferson: McFarland, 2015. 21–30.

Currie, Mark. Ed. "Introduction." Ibid. *Metafiction*, 2nd Ed. London / New York: Routledge, 2013.

Dalton, Mary M./ Linder, Laura R. eds. *The Sitcom Reader: America Viewed and Skewed*. State U of New York P, 2005.

Dannenberg, Nadine. "Queering the Archive – The Lesbian Archives of Cheryl Dunye's *The Watermelon Woman* and *The Owls*." Conference Talk at the Michel Foucault Symposium at the Georg-August-University Göttingen. 12 Jul. 2016. 12 Jan. 2020. URL: https://foucaultsymp.wordpress.com/.

Darke, Stephanie. "John Barth – 'Lost in the Funhouse' (1968): Writing about Writing about Writing." *Postmodernstudies.weebly.com*, 2014. 26 Jan. 2020. URL: https://bit.ly/30bIRZH.

Davenport-Hines, Richard. *Gothic: 400 Years of Excess, Horror, Evil and Ruin*. London: Fourth Estate, 1998.

5 References

Day, Patrick Kevin. "'The Simpsons' at 500: Show runner talks angry Homer, Julian Assange." *L. A. Times.com*, 18 Feb. 2012. 20 Dec. 2018. URL: https://lat.ms/3qbBufj.

Dean, Rob. "The Simpsons meets You're Next in this Claymation couch gag." *The AV Club.com*, 18 Dec. 2015. 19 Jan. 2019. URL: https://bit.ly/389kuQU.

Delaney, Tim. "The Simpsons as an Idealized Traditional Family." *Connecting Sociology to our Lives: An Introduction to Sociology*. London / New York: Routledge, 2016. 343.

DeLaure, Marylin, Moritz Fink & Mark Dery. Eds. *Culture Jamming: Activism and the Art of Cultural Resistance*. N. Y.: New York UP, 2017

Densham, Pen. "Reopening the Door of Imagination." Stewart T. Stanyard. Ed. *Dimensions Behind the Twilight Zone: A Backstage Tribute to Television's Groundbreaking Series*. Toronto: ECW Press, 2007. 271–273.

Dery, Mark. "Culture Jamming: Hacking, Slashing, and Sniping in the Empire of Signs." *Open Magazine Pamphlet Series*, No. 25 (1993). Reprinted in Marilyn DeLaure / Moritz Fink. Eds. *Culture Jamming: Activism and the Art of Cultural Resistance*. New York: New York UP, 2017. 39–61.

Diederichsen, Diedrich. "Die Simpsons der Gesellschaft." Michael Gruteser, Thomas Klein und Andreas Rauscher. Hgg. *Subversion zur Prime-Time. Die Simpsons und die Mythen der Gesellschaft*. 2. überarb./erw. Aufl.. Marburg: Schüren Verlag, 2002. 1–18.

Doherty, Thomas. "Nightmare Pictures: The Quality of Gruesomeness." *Pre-Code Hollywood: Sex, Immortality, and Insurrection in American Cinema, 1930–1934*. New York [et al.]: Columbia UP, 1999. 295–318.

Dunleavy, Trisha. *Complex Serial Drama and Multiplatform Television*. London / New York: Routledge, 2018.

Dunning, John. *On The Air: The Encyclopedia of Old-Time Radio*, rev. ed. New York: Oxford UP, 1998.

Ebert, Roger. "The Day of the Dolphin [Review]." *Roger Ebert.Com*, 21 Dec. 1973. Retrieved 20 Oct. 2019. URL: https://www.rogerebert.com/reviews/the-day-of-the-dolphin-1973.

Eco, Umberto. "The Ugliness of Others, Kitsch and Camp." *On Ugliness*. Trans. Alastair McEwen. London: Harvill Secker, 2007. 391–420.

— . "Towards a Semiological Guerrilla Warfare." *Travels in Hyperreality*. Trans. William Weaver. New York: Picador, 1997. 135–144.

— . "Apocalyptic and Integrated Intellectuals: Mass Communication and Theories of Mass Culture." Robert Lumley. Ed. *Umberto Eco: Apocalypse Postponed*. Bloomington & Indianapolis: Indiana UP; BFI Publishing, 1994. 17–35.

— . "Reading Things." *Travels in Hyperreality: Essays*. Trans. William Weaver. San Diego [et al.]: Harvest, 1986. 181–219.

— . *Faith in Fakes: Travels in Hyperreality*. Trans. William Weaver. London: Vintage, 1986.

— . *Semiotics and the Philosophy of Language*. Bloomington/Indianapolis: Indiana UP, 1984.

Edmundson, Mark. "American Gothic". *Nightmare on Main Street: Angels, Sadomasochism, and the Culture of Gothic*. Cambridge [et al.]: Harvard UP, 1999[2]. 1–69.

Ernst, Wolfgang and Jussi Parikka. *Digital Memory and the Archive*. Minnesota: U of Minnesota Press, 2013.

Evans, Noëll / K. Wolfgram. "Matt Groening: The Populist Hippie." *Animators of Film and Television: Nineteen Artists, Writers, Producers, and Others*. Jefferson: McFarland, 2011. 76–85.

Fahle, Oliver. "Die Simpsons und der Fernseher." Arno Meteling, Isabell Otto & Gabriele Schabacher. Hrsg. *Previously on … Zur Ästhetik der Zeitlichkeit neuerer*

TV-Serien. München: Fink, 2010. 231–242.

Falero, Sandra M. "'Sorkin Situations:' The Television Auteur Meets the Digital Age." *Digital Participatory Culture and the TV Audience: Everyone's a Critic.* Palgrave Macmillan, 2016. 77–100.

Felluga, Dino. "Modules on Hutcheon: On Parody." *Introductory Guide to Critical Theory.* Purdue U, 17 July 2002. 29 Jan 2019. URL: https://bit.ly/3bhbsTC.

Fiedler, Leslie. *Love and Death in the American Novel.* 2nd Ed. Dalkey Archive Press, [1997] 2003.

Fink, Moritz. *The Simpsons: A Cultural History.* Lanham [et al.]: Rowman & Littlefield, 2019.

First Dog on the Moon, Andrew Marlton. "The Simpsons' Matt Groening: 'President Trump? It's beyond satire.'" *The Guardian.com*, 13 Oct. 2016. 20 Oct. 2018. URL: https://bit.ly/2Onhf1e.

Fiske, John / John Hartley. *Reading Television.* 2nd Ed. London / New York: Routledge, 2001.

Fiske, John. *Television Culture.* London [et al.]: Methuen, 1987.

Folsom, Ed. "Archive." Sascha Bru, Ben de Bruyn & Michel Delville. Eds. *Literature Now. Key Terms and Methods for Literary History.* Edinburgh: Edinburgh UP, 2016. 23–35.

Foster, Hal. Ed. "Postmodernism: A Preface." *Anti-Aesthetic: Essays on Postmodern Culture.* Bay Press, 1983. ix-xvi.

Foucault, Michel. "The Historical *a priori* and the Archive." Transl. from the French by A. M. Sheridan Smith. Charles Merewether. Ed. *The Archive.* Cambridge: MIT Press, 2006.

— . *The Archaeology of Knowledge.* Transl. from the French *L'Archéologie du Savoir.* New York: Pantheon Books, 1972 [1969].

— . "Of Other Spaces (1967)." Transl. by De Cauter & Dehaene. Michiel Dehaene & Lieven De Cauter. Eds. *Heterotopia and the City: Public space in a postcivil society.* London / New York: Routledge, 2008. 13–29.

Fowler, Alastair. *Kinds of Literature: An Introduction to the Theory of Genres and Modes.* Oxford: Oxford UP, 1982.

Freud, Sigmund. "The Uncanny." First published in *Imago*, bd. V., 1919; repr. in *Sammlung*, Fünfte Folge. Transl. By Alex Strachey. URL: https://web.mit.edu/allanmc/www/freud1.pdf.

Friedman, Sam and Giselinde Kuipers. "The Divisive Power of Humour: Comedy, Taste and Symbolic Boundaries." *Cultural Sociology* 7 (2013): 179–195.

Funk, Wolfgang. *The Literature of Reconstruction: Authentic in the New Millennium.* London / New York: Bloomsbury Academic, 2015.

Gabler, Neal. *Walt Disney: The Triumph of the American Imagination* [Biography]. New York: Alfred A Knopf, 2006.

Geerhart, Bill. "Mutated Television." *Cornelrad.com*, 2006. 23 May 2020. URL: https://bit.ly/2PpWT7S.

Gilbride, Paige. "The Movement: The Banksy Effect." *Medium.com*, 13 May 2018. 20 Jan. 2019. URL: https://bit.ly/3bZQzvp.

Glenn, Cerise L. "White Masculinities and the TV Sitcom: Tracing the 'Progression' of Portrayals of Fatherhood." Ronald L. Jackson II & Jamie E Moshin. Eds. *Communicating Marginalized Masculinities: Identity Politics in TV, Film, and New Media.* New York / London: Routledge, 2013. 174–188.

Goertz, Allie / Julia Prescott. 100 Things Simpsons Fans Should Know & Do Before They Die. Triumph Books, 2018.

Gould, Dana. "The House that Rod Built." Stewart T. Stanyard. Ed. *Dimensions Behind the Twilight Zone: A Backstage Tribute to Television's Groundbreaking Series.* Toronto: ECW Press, 2007. 257–259.

Grant, Barry Keith. *Film Genre – From Iconography to Ideology.* [Short Cuts Series.] London / New York: Wallflower Press, 2007.

Gray, Jonathan. *Watching With The Simpsons. Television, Parody, and Intertextuality.* London / New York: Routledge, 2006.

—. "Television Teaching: Parody THE SIMPSONS, and Media Literacy Education." *Critical Studies in Media Communication*, 22, No. 3 (2005): 223–238. URL: https://bit.ly/2NSdK31.

—. "The State of Satire, The Satire of State." Jonathan Gray, Jeffrey P. Jones, and Ethan Thompson. Eds. *Satire TV: Politics and Comedy in the Post-Network Era*. London / New York: New York UP, 2009. 3–36.

Grixti, Joseph. *Terrors of Uncertainty: The Cultural Contexts of Horror Fiction*. London / New York: Routledge Revivals, 1989.

Grote, David. *The End of Comedy. The Sit-Com and the Comedic Tradition*. Hamden: Archon Books, 1983.

Grossberg, Lawrence, Ellen Wartella, D. Charles Whitney, and J. McGregor Wise. *MediaMaking: Mass Media in a Popular Culture*. Thousand Oaks [et al.]: SAGE Publications, 2006.

Gruteser, Michael, Thomas Klein und Andreas Rauscher. Hgg. *Subversion zur Prime-Time. DIE SIMPSONS und die Mythen der Gesellschaft*. 3. überarb. Aufl.. Marburg: Schüren: 2014.

Gunzenhäuser, Randi. "'All plots lead toward death': Memory, History, and the Assassination of John F. Kennedy." *Amerikastudien / American Studies*, Universitätsverlag Winter GmbH, Vol. 43, No. 1; "Media and Cultural Memory" (1998): 75–91.

Hall, Dennis. "Couch." Dennis R. Hall & Susan Grove Hall. Eds. *American Icons: An Encyclopedia of the People, Places, and Things that Have Shaped Our Culture*, Vol 1. Westport / London: Greenwood Press, 2006. 156–165.

Hall, Stuart. *The Hard Road to Renewal: Thatcherism and the Crisis of the Left*. London: Verso, 1988.

Hamamoto, Darrell Y.. *Nervous Laughter. Television Situation Comedy and Liberal Democratic Ideology*. 2nd Ed. New York [et al.]: Praeger, 1991.

Harrington, Claudia. "10 Incredible SIMPSONS Couch Gags Created by Guest Animators." *Idearocketanimation.com*, 23 May 2016. 20 January 2018. URL: https://bit.ly/3c3cVvZ.

Harris, Dan. *Film Parody*. London, 2000.

Hartley, John. "Situation Comedy, Part 1." Glen Creeber. Ed. *The Television Genre Book*. London: BFI, 2001. 96–98.

Hawkes, Terence. *Structuralism and Semiotics (New Accents)*. U of California Press, 1977.

—. "Preface." *The Empire Writes Back: Theory and Practice in Post-Colonial Literatures*. 2nd Ed. Bill Ashcroft, Gareth Griffiths, and Helen Tiffin. London / New York: Routledge, 2002 [1989], ix-x.

Heidelberg, Jermain. "Excavating Media." Conference Talk at the Michel Foucault Symposium at the Georg-August-University Göttingen. 12 Jul. 2016. 12 Jan. 2020. URL: https://foucaultsymp.wordpress.com/

Henry, Matthew A. Ed. "Introduction: THE SIMPSONS, Satire, and American Culture." *THE SIMPSONS, Satire, and American Culture*. New York: Palgrave Macmillan, 2012. 4–18.

—. "The Triumph of Popular Culture: Situation Comedy, Postmodernism and THE SIMPSONS." *Studies in Popular Culture* 17, No. 1 (1994): 85–100. Repr. in Joanne Morreale. Ed. *Critiquing the Sitcom: A Reader*. New York: Syracuse UP, 2003. 262–273.

Hildreth, Richard. "SILLY SYMPHONIES, 1929–1935." Presented at the *San Francisco Silent Film Festival* 2006. Silentfilm.com, 2006. 10 Dec. 2019. URL: http://www.silentfilm.org/archive/silly-symphonies-19291935.

Hill, Rodney. "Mapping THE TWILIGHT ZONE's Cultural and Mythological Terrain." J. P. Telotte. Ed. *The Essential Science Fiction Reader*. Lexington: The UP of Kentucky, 2008. 111–126.

Hills, Matt. "TV Horror". *The Pleasures of Horror*. London / New York: Continuum, 2015. 111–128.

Hogan, Michael. "21 things you never knew about THE SIMPSONS." *Sydney Morning*

Herald.com, 28. Dec. 2014. 10 Dec. 2019. URL: https://bit.ly/3cg8vlV.

Holtzen, Curtis Wm. "'So, you're calling God a liar?': An Unbiased Comparison of Science and Religion." Karma Waltonen & Denise Du Vernay. Eds. THE SIMPSONS *Beloved Springfield. Essays on the TV Series and Town that are Part of Us All*. Jefferson: McFarland, 2019. 130–142.

Honeyman, Susan. *Consuming Agency in Fairy Tales, Childlore, and Folkliterature*. London / New York: Routledge, 2010.

Hooton, Christopher. "Coen brothers confirm FARGO is a true story after all, or at least based on some." *The Independent.co.uk*, 09 Mar. 2016. 15 Oct. 2019. URL: https://bit.ly/2Qi5UAu.

Horner, Al. "The terrifying tale of TREEHOUSE OF HORROR." *Little White Lies.com*, 26. Oct. 2018. 15 Nov. 2019. URL: https://lwlies.com/articles/the-simpsons-treehouse-of-horror-halloween-specials/.

Horner, Avril and Sue Zlosnik. "Comic Gothic." Punter, David. Ed. *A New Companion to the Gothic*. Chichester: Wiley, 2012. 321–334.

Houghton, Rianne. "THE SIMPSONS boss is preparing for when the show ends." *Digital Spy.com*, 09 Jan. 2020. 24 Jul. 2020. URL: https://bit.ly/38aqtVw.

Hughes, William, David Punter, and Andrew Smith. Eds. *The Encyclopedia of the Gothic*. Wiley Blackwell, 2016.

Huhtamo, Erkki / Jussi Parikka. *Media Archaeology: Approaches, Applications, and Implications*. Berkeley/L. A.: U of California P, 2011.

Hunter, James D. *Culture Wars: The Struggle to Define America*. New York: Basic Books, 1991.

Hutcheon, Linda. *A Theory of Adaptation*, 2nd Ed., with Siobhan O'Flynn. London / New York: Routledge, 2013 [2006].

— . *The Politics of Postmodernism,* 2nd Ed.. London / New York: Routledge, 2002 [1989].

— . *A Theory of Parody. The Teachings of Twentieth-century Art Forms*, 2nd Ed.. Urbana/Chicago: Illinois UP, 2000 [1985].

— . "Historiographic Metafiction. Parody and the Intertextuality of History." *A Poetics of Postmodernism*. London / New York: Routledge, 1988. 3–33.

Hutchings, Peter. *The Horror Film*. Edinburgh: Pearson Education Limited, 2004.

Huyssen, Andreas. "Modernism after Postmodernity." *New German Critique 99*. Duke UP: Vol. 33, No. 3 (Fall 2006): 1–5.

— . *Present Pasts: Urban Palimpsests and the Politics of Memory*. Stanford: Stanford UP, 2003.

— . *Twilight Memories: Marking Time in a Culture Of Amnesia*. London / New York: Routledge, 1995.

Irwin, William, Mark T. Conrad, and Aeon J. Skoble. Eds. THE SIMPSONS *and Philosophy: The D'oh! Of Homer*. Illinois: Open Court Carus Publ. Comp., 2001.

Itzkoff, Dave. "Why Hank Azaria Won't Play Apu on 'THE SIMPSONS' Anymore." *The New York Times.com*, 25 Feb. 2020. 27 Jul. 2020. URL: https://nyti.ms/3uSRmXE.

— . "'THE SIMPSONS' Explains Its Button-Pushing Banksy Opening." *New York Times Arts Beat.Blog*, 11 Oct. 2010. 10 Jan. 2019. URL: https://nyti.ms/2O2iZNl.

Jansen, Ele. "Performance – Performatism – Postmodernism." *Ele Jansen.com*, May 2013. 12 Feb. 2020. URL: https://bit.ly/3kNPTxd.

Jasper, Gavin. "FAMILY GUY: 'The Simpsons Guy' Review." *Den of Geek.com*, 29 Sept. 2014. 22 Aug. 2019. URL: https://bit.ly/3kJuhSI.

Jameson, Fredric. *The Cultural Turn. Selected Writings on the Postmodern, 1983–1998*. London / New York: Verso, 1998.

— . "Postmodernism, or The Cultural Logic of Late Capitalism." [PDF-Download], *New Left Review*, 146 (July-August 1984): 53–92. URL: https://bit.ly/3rbolUZ.

Jeffords, Susan. *Hard Bodies: Hollywood Masculinity in the Reagan Era*. New Brunswick / New Jersey: Rutgers UP, 1994.

Jenkins, Henry, Tara McPherson, and Jane Shattuc. *Hop on Pop: the Politics and*

Pleasures of Popular Culture. Durham/London: Duke UP, 2002.

Jenkins, Henry. *Convergence Culture. Where Old and New Media Collide*. New York / London: New York UP, 2006a.

—. *Fans, Bloggers, and Gamers. Exploring Convergence Culture*. New York / London: New York UP, 2006b.

—. *Confronting the Challenges of Participatory Culture. Media Education for the 21st Century*. Cambridge: MIT Press, 2009.

—. *Textual Poachers: Television Fans and Participatory Culture*, 2nd ed. London / New York: Routledge, 2013 [1992].

Jones, Kent. "Hail the Conquering Hero." *Film Comment.com*, Film Society of Lincoln Center. May/June 2005 Issue. 20 Jan 2019. URL: https://bit.ly/3bfh7Kf.

Jowett, Lorna / Stacey Abbott. *TV Horror: Investigating the Dark Side of the Small Screen*. London / New York: I. B. Tauris, 2013.

Kelleter, Frank & Andreas Jahn-Sudmann. "Die Dynamik serieller Überbietung. Amerikanische Fernsehserien und das Konzept des Quality-TV." Frank Kelleter. Hg. *Populäre Serialität: Narration – Evolution – Distinktion. Zum seriellen Erzählen seit dem 19. Jahrhundert*. Bielefeld: transcript, 2012. 205–224.

Kellner, Douglas & Steven Best. *The Postmodern Turn*. New York: The Guilford Press, 1997.

Kelly, Adam. *American Fiction in Transition: Observer-Hero Narrative, the 1990s, and Postmodernism*. New York, [et al.]: Bloomsbury, 2013.

Kern, Kathleen. "Heterotopia of the theme park street." Michiel Dehaene & Lieven De Cauter. Eds. *Heterotopia and the City: Public Space in a Post-Civil Society*. London / New York: Routledge, 2008. 105–116.

King, Stephen. *Danse Macabre – Die Welt des Horrors*. Heyne, 2011.

—. *Danse Macabre*, 2nd Ed.. New York: Gallery Books, 2010 [1981].

Klatt, Jöran. "Die Schildbürger von Springfield: DIE SIMPSONS, eine amerikanische Politikserie." *INDES. Zeitschrift für Politik und Gesellschaft*, 4 (2014): 110–120.

Kurp, Joshua. "Ranking Every SIMPSONS TREEHOUSE OF HORROR Segment, From Worst to First" *Vulture.com*, 25 Oct. 2018. 22 Aug. 2019. URL: https://bit.ly/2Pnpivh.

Laemmerhirt, Iris-Aya and Randi Gunzenhäuser. "Romance and Gothic." Christine Gerhardt. Ed. *Handbook of the American Novel of the Nineteenth Century*. Berlin: Walter de Gruyter, 2018. 34–57.

Laham, Nicholas. *Currents of Comedy on the American Screen. How Film and Television Deliver Different Laughs for Changing Times*. North Carolina: McFarland, 2009.

Landay, Lori. *I Love Lucy*. [TV Milestones Series]. Detroit: Wayne State UP, 2010.

Lethem, Jonathan. "Serling." *Jonathan Lethem.com*, 1999. 22 Nov. 2019. URL: http://jonathanlethem.com/serling/.

Luebering, J. E. "Portmanteau word." *Encyclopedia Britannica.com*, undated. 04 Aug. 2020. URL: https://www.britannica.com/topic/portmanteau-word.

McClellan, Jim. "Who the Hell is Bart Simpson?" *The Face.com*, No. 30 (1991): 66–67. 17 Apr. 2019. 9 May 2019. URL: https://theface.com/archive/who-the-hell-is-bart-simpson.

Manoff, Marlene. "Theories of the Archive from Across the Disciplines." *Libraries and the Academy*. Baltimore: The Johns Hopkins UP, Vol. 4, No. 1 (2004): 9–25.

Marc, David. *Demographic Vistas. Television in American Culture*. Rev. ed. Philadelphia: U of Pennsylvania P, 1996.

—. *Comic Visions: Television Comedy and American Culture*, 2nd ed. Massachusetts: Blackwell, 1998.

—. "Television Comedy." Nancy A. Walker. Ed. *What's So Funny? Humor in American Culture*. Wilmington: American Visions, 1998. 249–70.

Marcuse, Herbert. *Art and Liberation: Collected Papers, Vol. 4. London / New York: Routledge, 2007.

Marlton, Andrew / First Dog on The Moon. "THE SIMPSONS' Matt Groening: 'President Trump? It's beyond satire.'" The Guardian.com, 13 Oct. 2016. 20 June 2018. URL: https://bit.ly/2OkgSEH.

Martens, Lisa. "Bart is Nww Homer: Reflections on THE SIMPSONS Binge." Medium.com, 11 Dec. 2016. 12 Jan. 2020. URL: https://bit.ly/30eTTgV.

McCabe, Janet / Kim Akass. Eds. Quality TV: Contemporary American Television and Beyond. London / New York: I. B. Tauris, 2007.

McLevy, Alex. "Filmmaker Don Hertzfeldt on his SIMPSONS couch gag and the pains of animation. [Interview]" The AV Club.com, 14 Apr. 2015. 20 June 2018. URL: https://bit.ly/3e7IOpU.

McLuhan, Marshal. Understanding Media: The Understandings of Man. Cambridge Massachusetts: MIT Press, 1994.

McRobbie, Angela. Postmodernism and Popular Culture. London / New York: Routledge, 1994.

Melbye, David. Irony in THE TWILIGHT ZONE: How the Series Critiqued Postwar American Culture. Lanham/London: Rowman & Littlefield, 2016.

Meteling, Arno. Monster: Zu Körperlichkeit und Medialität im modernen Horrorfilm. Bielefeld: transcript, 2006.

Milburn, Colin Nazhone. "Monster in Eden: Darwin and Derrida." MLN 118 (2003): 603–621. Baltimore: The Johns Hopkins UP, 2003. 26 Jan. 2020. URL: https://bit.ly/2OkgZQD.

Mills, Brett. The Sitcom. Edinburgh UP, 2009.

— . Television Sitcom, 2nd Ed.. London: BFI, 2008.

Mittell, Jason. Complex TV: The Poetics of Contemporary Television Storytelling. New York / London: New York UP, 2015.

— . "Narrative Komplexität im amerikanischen Gegenwartsfernsehen." Frank Kelleter. Hrsg. Populäre Serialität. Narration – Evolution – Distinktion. Zum seriellen Erzählen seit dem 19. Jahrhundert. Bielefeld: transcript, 2012. 97–122.

— . Television and American Culture. New York [et al.]: Oxford UP, 2010. Print.

— . "Narrative Complexity in Contemporary American Television." The Velvet Light Trap / The U of Texas P, 58 (2006): 29–40.

— . "Making Fun of Genres – The Politics of Parody and Genre Mixing in SOAP and THE SIMPSONS." Genre and Television. From Cop Shows to Cartoons in American Culture. London / New York: Routledge, 2004. 147–95.

— . "Cartoon Realism: Genre Mixing and the Cultural Life of THE SIMPSONS." The Velvet Light Trap, The U of Texas P, 47 (2001): 15–28.

Morreale, Joanne. Ed. Critiquing the Sitcom: A Reader. Syracuse / New York: Syracuse UP, 2002.

Mufson, Beckett/ Zach Sokol. "The 8 Best SIMPSONS Couch Gag Artist Collaborations." VICE.com, 25 Apr. 2014. 12 July 2018. URL: https://bit.ly/386UN3u.

Murphy, Bernice M. "'It's Not the House That's Haunted!': Demons, Debt, and the Family in Peril Formula in Recent Horror Cinema." Murray Leeder. Ed. Cinematic Ghosts: Haunting the Spectrality From Silent Cinema to the Digital Era. New York [et al.]: Bloomsbury Academic, 2015. 235–252.

Murray, Noel. "10 episodes that take viewers into the depths of THE TWILIGHT ZONE." The AV Club.com, 13 Feb. 2013. 5 Nov. 2019. URL: https://bit.ly/3sLKMAw.

— . "It's a cookbook, or something: 14 types of TWILIGHT ZONE endings." AV Club.com, 26 Oct. 2009. 5 Nov. 2019. URL: https://bit.ly/3sNEYX5.

N. N. "Word created by THE SIMPSONS added to U. S. dictionary." BBC.com, 6 Mar. 2018. 12 Nov. 2018. URL: https://www.bbc.com/news/newsbeat-43298229.

N. N. "Words We're Watching: 'Cromulent.'" Merriam Webster.com, undated. 12 Nov. 2018. URL: https://bit.ly/389QZ1g.

N. N. "The Serious History of Silly Symphonies." Oh My Disney.com, 19 May 2016. 10 Dec. 2019. URL: https://bit.ly/3rcuDUi.

Neale, Steve / Frank Krutnik. 1990. *Popular Film and Television Comedy*. London / New York: Routledge, 1990.

Nelmes, Jill. Ed. *Introduction to Film Studies*, 5th Ed. London / New York: Routledge, 2012.

Nelson, Voctoria. "Gothicka." Siegbert S. Prawer. *Caligari's Children: The Film as Tale of Terror*. Oxford: Oxford UP, 1980.

Neu, Robert. "Banksy: The 'Biography' of a Graffiti Street Art Legend." *Stencilrevolution.com*, 10 Nov. 2017. 20 Jan. 2019. URL: https://www.stencilrevolution.com/blogs/profiles/banksy.

Newcomb, Horace. M. *Television: The Critical View*. 6th Ed. New York: Oxford UP, 2000 [1976].

—. "American Television Criticism, 1970–1985." *Critical Studies in Mass Communication* 3, No. 2 (1986): 217–228.

—. *TV: The Most Popular Art*. Garden City: Anchor Press / Doubleday, 1974.

Newcomb, Horace and Robert S. Alley. *The Producer's Medium: Conversations with Creators of American TV*. New York: Oxford UP, 1983.

Newman, Michael Z. / Elana Levine. *Legitimating Television: Media Convergence and Cultural Status*. London / New York: Routledge, 2012.

Newman, Michael Z. *Video Revolutions: On the History of a Medium*. New York: Columbia UP, 2014.

Newsweek Special Editions. "The 1980s: The Best (and Worst) of the Decade that Defined Pop Culture." *Newsweek;* Single Issue Magazine. Publisher: Newsweek, 2018.

Olsen, Mark. "TV horror vs. movie horror: Guillermo del Toro an telling scary stories across different mediums." *L. A. Times.com*, 12 Oct. 2017. 01 Feb. 2018. URL: https://lat.ms/3sLN6Yc.

Olsson, Jan / Lynn Spigel. Eds. *Television after TV. Essays on a Medium in Transition*. Durham/London: Duke UP, 2004.

Ortved, John. *Simpsons Confidential: The uncensored, totally unauthorized history of the worlds' greatest TV show by the people that made it*. London: Ebury Press, 2009.

Page, Susan. "Most Influential People." *USA Today*, 03 Sept. 2007. 09 Jan. 2020. URL: https://bit.ly/3kHf1Wy.

Palmer, Daniel. "Explainer: What is Postmodernism?" *The Conversation.com*, 2 Jan. 2014. 02 Jan.2020. URL: http://theconversation.com/explainer-what-is-postmodernism-20791.

Parikka, Jussi. "'With each project I find myself reimagining what cinema might be:' An interview with Zoe Beloff." *Electronic Book Review.com*, 24 Oct. 2011. Accessed 07 Mar. 2020. URL: https://bit.ly/3rlsPII.

Perkins, Dennis. "THE SIMPSONS: 'TREEHOUSE OF HORROR XXIV.'" *The A. V. Club.com*, 10 Jun. 2013. 22 Jul. 2019. URL: https://bit.ly/2PaAeNl.

Phillips, Kendall R. *A Place of Darkness: The Rhetoric of Horror in Early American Cinema*. Austin: U of Texas P, 2018.

Pinsky, Mark I. *The Gospel According to Disney. Faith, Trust, and Pixie Dust*. Louisville: Westminster John Knox Press, 2004.

Plante, Chris. "How an episode of 'THE SIMPSONS' is made." *The Verge.com*, 25 Oct. 2015. 8 Apr. 2018. URL: https://bit.ly/308Auhw.

Platthaus, Andreas. "Der Anti-Paranoiker." *FAZ.com*, rev. 08 May 2017. 02 Jan. 2020. URL: https://bit.ly/3c4CSve.

Poe, Edgar Allen. *The Philosophy of Composition*. [PDF-Download], 1999. 24 July 2019. URL: http://faculty.wiu.edu/M-Cole/PhilComp.pdf.

Polson, Laura. "Aussie duo's pixel art SIMPSONS tribute to become the show's next opening." *The Sydney Morning Herald.com*, 12 Feb. 2015. 20 Aug. 2019. URL: https://bit.ly/3sOSfPj.

Presnell, Don & Marty McGee. *A Critical History of Television's THE TWILIGHT ZONE, 1959–1964*. Jefferson: McFarland, 1998.

Rabin, Nathan. "THE SIMPSONS (Classic): 'TREEHOUSE OF HORRORS III.'" *The AV Club*, 29

Apr. 2012. 20 Sept. 2019. URL: https://bit.ly/3sNH4pZ.

—. "The Simpsons (Classic): 'Treehouse of Horrors II'." *The AV Club*, 03 Apr. 2011. 20 Sept. 2019. URL: https://bit.ly/3e9E6rG.

—. "The Simpsons (Classic): 'Treehouse of Horrors'." *The AV Club*, 26 Sept. 2010. 27 July 2017. URL: https://bit.ly/3qhjgJA.

Rabotnikof, Nora. "Huyssen, A.; Modernismo después de la posmodernidad (Modernism After Modernism)," [Review]. *Metropolis Barcelona: City Information and Thoughts*, Autumn 2010. 03 Feb. 2020. URL: https://bit.ly/3kRBtwg.

Ritzer, Ivo. "Charisma und Ideologie: Zur Rückkehr des Autors im Quality-TV". Jonas Nesselhauf & Markus Schleich, Hg. *Quality-Television: Die narrative Spielwiese des 21. Jahrhunderts?!* Berlin: LIT, 2014.

Robertson, Craig. "The Archive, Disciplinarity, and Governing: Cultural Studies and the Writing of History." *Cultural Studies / Critical Methodologies*, [Sage Publications] Vol 4, No. 4 (2004): 450–472. URL: https://bit.ly/385OdKf.

Rosenberg, Howard. "TV REVIEWS: 'The Simpsons' Get a Show of Their Own for Christmas." *Los Angeles Time.com*, 16 Dec. 1989. 27 July 2017. URL: https://lat.ms/3sOSji1.

Roy, Elodie A. "For a radical media archaeology: A conversation with Wolfgang Ernst." *NECSUS.org*, 28 May 2017. Accessed 07 Mar. 2020. URL: https://bit.ly/3e9a4ED.

Salam, Maya. "'The Simpsons' Has Predicted a Lot. Most of It Can Be Explained." *The New York Times.com*, 2 Feb. 2018. 20 Aug. 2019. URL: https://nyti.ms/3bdbJqH.

Salmela, Markku. "Beyond the Couch Gag: Reading the Suburb and Its Consumerist Discontents." Maarit Piipponen and Markku Salmela. Eds. *Topographies of Popular Culture*. Newcastle Upon Tyne: Cambridge Scholars Publishing, 2016. 59–76.

Sammond, Nicholas. *Babes in Tomorrowland: Walt Disney and the Making of the American Child, 1930–1960*. Durham & London: Duke UP, 2005.

Sander, Gordon F.. *Serling: The Rise and Fall of TV's Last Angry Man*. Cornell UP, 2011.

Savage, Emily. "There's a Lisa Simpson Reaction for Every Stage of Going Vegan." *PETA.org*, 29 Sept. 2017. 09. Jan. 2020. URL: https://bit.ly/388EiUt.

Savorelli, Antonio. *Beyond Sitcom: New Directions in American Television Comedy*. Jefferson: McFarland, 2010.

Sawyer, Diane. "Person of the Week: Matt Groening." *ABC World News with Diane Sawyer*. 27 Ju. 2007. 09 Jan. 2020. URL: https://bit.ly/3bTmWMc.

Schedeen, Jesse. "The Simpsons: Treehouse of Horror XXX Spoofs The Omen & Stranger Things – Comic-Con 2019." *IGN.com*, 20 Jul. 2019. 18 Sept. 2019. URL: https://bit.ly/2MLQq6p.

Schlegel, Johannes. *Michel Foucault: Discourse Theory and the Archive*. [Symposium at the Georg-August-University Göttingen], 08 Jul. 2016. 12 Jun. 2018. URL: https://bit.ly/3bdZdHr.

Schmidt, Siegfried J. "Gedächtnis – Erzählen – Identität." *Mnemosyne: Formen und Funktionen der kulturellen Erinnerung*. Aleida Assmann and Dietrich Harth. Eds. Frankfurt am Main: Fischer, 1993. 378–97; 384.

Schumer, Arlen. "The Five Themes of The Twilight Zone." *Arlenschumer.com*, undated. 10 Sept. 2017. URL: https://bit.ly/3bbBlEt.

Sconce, Jeffrey. "What if?: Charting Television's New Textual Boundaries". Lynn Spigel and Jan Olsson. Eds. *Television After TV. Essays on a Medium in Transition*. Durham/London: Duke University Press, 2004. 93–112.

Screen Rant. "15 Dark Facts About The Simpsons' Treehouse Of Horror." *YouTube.com*, undated. 18 Sept. 2019. URL: https://www.youtube.com/watch?v=ULt7BJPL7pw.

Sepinwall, Alan / The Star-Ledger. "'The Simpsons' hits 450 episodes – Sepinwall on TV." *NJ.com*, 8 Jan. 2010. 20 June 2018. URL: https://bit.ly/3e7Wod9.

Sharlet, Jeff. "The Blob." *The Family. The Secret Fundamentalism at the Heart of American Power*. New York. HarperCollins Publishers, 2008. 181–204.

Shattuc, Jane M. "Television Production: Who Makes American TV?" Janet Wasko. *A Companion to Television*. Chichester [*et al.*]: Wiley-Blackwell Publications. 142–154.

Shelton, Joseph. "Lee Hardcastle mixes 'You're Next' with 'The Simpsons.'" *1428Elm.com* [by FanSidedNetwork], 20 Dec. 2015. 20 Jan. 2019. URL: https://bit.ly/3bcGNXN.

Sims, David. "Treehouse of Horror: An Appreciation." *The Atlantic.com*, 28 Oct. 2015. 22 Aug. 2019. URL: https://bit.ly/38r7lTx.

—. "The Simpsons (Classic): 'Treehouse of Horror V' [Review]." *AV Club.com*, 14 Jul. 2013. 27 Oct. 2019. URL: https://bit.ly/3rltUQM.

Sirucek, Stefan / Ramsey Ess. "16 Cropped Simpsons Jokes You Can't See on Disney+." *Vulture.com*, 20 Nov. 2019. 05 Jul. 2020. URL: https://bit.ly/30d9wFu.

Slethaug, Gordon E. *Adaptation Theory and Criticism: Postmodern Literature and Cinema in the USA*. New York [*et al.*]: Bloomsbury, 2014.

Sloane, Robert. "Who Wants Candy? Disenchantment in The Simpsons." John Alberti. Ed. *Leaving Springfield: The Simpsons and the Possibility of Popular Culture*. Detroit: Wayne State UP, 2004. 137–171.

Smith, Allan Lloyd. "19th Century American Gothic." David Punter. Ed. *A New Companion to the Gothic*. Chichester: Wiley, 2012. 163–175.

Snierson, Dan. "'The Simpsons:' Guillermo del Toro on 'Treehouse of Horror XXIV' opening." *Entertainment Weekly.com*, 03 Oct. 2013. 11 Jan. 2019. URL: https://bit.ly/389RPLs,

—. "Simpsons Treehouse of Horror: Ren & Stimpy creator's couch gag, Sideshow Bob killing Bart." *Entertainment Weekly.com*, 08 Oct. 2015. 12 Nov. 2018. URL: https://bit.ly/3uTtJOR,

—. "Simpsons 600th episode couch gag can be seen in virtual reality." *Entertainment Weekly.com*, 06 Oct 2016. 12 Nov. 2018. URL: https://bit.ly/3rgbGQP,

—. "Simpsons producer explains Homer's disturbing self-cannibalism in 'Treehouse of Horror.'" *Entertainment Weekly.com*, 22 Oct. 2017. 16 Oct. 2019. URL: https://bit.ly/3ea4PEG,

—. "The Simpsons: A somewhat complete history of 'Homer[3]' from 'Treehouse of Horror VI'." *Entertainment Weekly.com*, 19 Oct. 2018. 24 Sept. 2019. URL: https://bit.ly/3bZB2Mn.

Snow, Jennifer. "Analysis of the Seven Dwarfs." *Disnability; Tumblr.com*, undated. 12 Jan. 2020. URL: https://bit.ly/2Om5qbs.

Spangler, Todd. "Netflix Plans to Release 80 Original Films in 2018." *Variety.com*, 16 Oct. 2017. 01 Feb. 2018.

Spooner, Catherine. *Contemporary Gothic*. London: Reaction Books, 2006.

Squires, John. "'The Simpsons:' Preview This Halloween Season's 'Treehouse of Horror XXXI' With Two Clips." *Bloody Disgustig.com*, 25 Jul. 2020. 27 Jul. 2020. URL: https://bit.ly/3rg2nQR.

Stabile, Carole A. / Mark Harrison. *Prime Time Animation: Television Animation and American Culture*. London / New York: Routledge, 2003.

Stamper, Kory. "The Simpsons is right: 'Embiggen' is perfectly cromulent word | Pop Lexicon." *YouTube.com / The AV Club Channel*, 26 Oct. 2017. 22 Aug. 2019. URL: https://www.youtube.com/watch?v=WTzGnRQ9cfA

Stanhope, Kate. "Exclusive Sneak Peek at The Simpsons Season Finale: Couch Gag Contest Winner Revealed!" *TV Guide.com*, 17 May 2013. 20 Aug. 2019. URL: https://bit.ly/3kWo46d.

Stephens, Emily L. "'They're here': Television invades the home." *The AV Club.com*, 29 Oct. 2014. 24 March 2019. URL: https://bit.ly/2NZHvPj.

Stewart, Jamie. "Bibbity Bobbity Bigot: Addressing the Rumors of Walt Disney's Anti-Semitism." *Jamstew and the Popular Culture* [Blog]. 17 May 2015. 7 Mar. 2020. URL: https://bit.ly/30bBxgJ.

Stice, Joel. "A Brief History of 'THE SIMPSONS' Love Affair with Alfred Hitchcock." *Uproxx.com*, 15 August 2016. 20 January 2018. URL: https://bit.ly/2MK81vl.

Storey, John. "What is Popular Culture?" *Cultural Theory and Popular Culture*, 5th Ed. Harlow: Pearson, 2009. 1–15.

Surman, David. *CGI Animation: Pseudorealism, Perception and Possible Worlds*, [PDF Download]. *Academica.edu*, 2003. URL: https://bit.ly/2O0czyo.

Sullivan, Robert David. "THE SIMPSONS: 'TREEHOUSE OF HORROR XXIII [Review]." *AV Club.com*, 07 Oct. 2012. 27 Oct. 2019. URL: https://bit.ly/3qgYhX2.

Thompson, Ian. "Umberto Eco Obituary." *The Guardian.co.uk*, 20 Feb. 2016. 04 Jan. 2020. URL: https://bit.ly/30bMf6R.

Thompson, Robert J. *Television's Second Golden Age: From "HILL STREET BLUES" to "ER"*. New York: Syracuse UP, 1996.

Tibbetts, John C. "Summit Meetings: Mickey Mouse's Culture Wars." Mark I. West. Ed. *Walt Disney, from Reader to Storyteller: Essays on the Literary Inspirations*. Jefferson: McFarland, 2015. 195–212.

Turner, Chris. *Planet Simpson. How A Cartoon Masterpiece Documented an Era and Defined a Generation*. Random House, 2004.

VanDerWerff, Emily Todd. "THE TWILIGHT ZONE: 'Nightmare at 20,000 Feet' / 'A Kind of a Stopwatch." *The A. V. Club*.com, 14 Jun. 2014. 27 Dec. 2019. URL: https://bit.ly/3bfjMDJ.

Vary, Adam B. "The 100 Greatest Characters of the Last 20 Years." *Entertainment Weekly.com*, 01 Jun. 2010. 09 Jan. 2020. URL: https://bit.ly/388aOWT.

Venable, Nick. "Why We Can Thank Congress For THE SIMPSONS' Most Violent Episode." *Cinemablend.com*, 15 Nov. 2015. 20 Jul. 2017. URL: https://bit.ly/3sN0paT.

Wallace, David Foster. "E Unibus Pluram: Television and U.S. Fiction." *Review of Contemporary Fiction*, 13:2 (Summer 1993): 151–195.

Waller, Gregory A. "Made-for-Television Horror Films." Gregory A. Waller. Ed. *American Horrors: Essays on the Modern American Horror Film*. Urbana/Chicago: U of Illinois P, 1987. 145–161.

Waltonen, Karma / Denise Du Vernay. Eds. *The Simpsons Beloved Springfield. Essays on the TV Series and Town that are Part of Us All*. Jefferson: McFarland, 2019.

—. *THE SIMPSONS in the Classroom: Embiggening the Learning Experience with the Wisdom of Springfield*. Jefferson: McFarland, 2010.

Writing Across Media. "Remediation." *WAM.Fandom.com*, undated. 20 Aug. 2019. URL: https://bit.ly/3kKAXQH.

Ward, Glenn. "'There Is No Such Thing:' Del Toro's Metafictional Monster Rally." A. Davies, D. Shaw & D. Tierney. Eds. *The Transnational Fantasies of Guillermo del Toro*. New York: Palgrave Macmillan, 2014. 11–28.

Watson, Paul. "Critical Approaches to Hollywood Cinema: Authorship, Genre and Stars." Nelmes, Jill. Ed. *An Introduction to Film Studies*, 3rd Ed. London / New York: Routledge, 2003. 129–184.

Wells, Paul. *Animation and America*. 2nd Ed. Edinburgh: Edinburgh UP, 2008.

—. *Animation: Prinzipien, Praxis, Perspektiven*. München: Stiebner, 2007.

—. *Animation. Genre and Authorship*. London / New York: Wallflower Press, 2002.

West, Mark I.. Ed. *Walt Disney, from Reader to Storyteller: Essays on the Literary Inspirations*. Jefferson: McFarland, 2015.

Westfahl, Gary. Ed. "Dimensions." *Science Fiction Quotations: From the Inner Mind to the Outer Limits*. New Haven / London: Yale UP, 2005. 91–94.

Wheatley, Helen. *Gothic Television*. Manchester: Manchester UP, 2006.

Wise, Macgregor J.. *Surveillance and Film*. London / New York: Bloomsbury Academic, 2016.

5 References

Wolfe, Jennifer. "VR Couch Gag Set for Landmark 600th Episode of 'THE SIMPSONS.'" *Animation World Network.com*, 6 Oct. 2016. 27 Dec. 2019. URL: https://bit.ly/3uWu82T.

Wollen, Peter. *Signs and Meaning in the Cinema*, 2nd Ed. Bloomington: Indiana UP, 1972.

Wood Krutch, Joseph. *Edgar Allan Poe: A Study in Genius*. New York: Alfred A. Knopf, 1926.

Wood, Robin. *American Nightmare: On the Horror Film. Collected Essays and Reviews*. Detroit: Wayne State UP, 2018 [1979].

Wulff, Hans Jürgen. "Heterotopie." *Lexikon der Filmbegriffe.org*, 30 Jul. 2011. 07 Mar. 2020. URL: https://bit.ly/3uW7J63.

6 Appendix

TREEHOUSE OF HORROR Episode Guide

ToH	Segment/Title	Scary Names / Selected Credits	Season/Episode	
I	S01 "Bad Dream House" S02 "Hungry are the Damned" S03 "The Raven"	Written by Jay Kogen, Wallace Wolodarsky & John Swartzfelder, Edgar Allen Poe & Sam Simon	S02E16 [7F04]	25 Oct.1990
II	S01 "Lisa's Nightmare" ("The Monkey's Paw") S02 "Bart's Nightmare" ("The Bart Zone") S03 "Homer's Nightmare" ("If I Only Had a Brain")	Written by Atrocious Al Jean and Morbid Mike Reiss, Jittery Jeff Martin, Gasping George Meyer, Slithering Sam Simon and Spooky John Swartzwelder	S03E07 [8F02]	31. Oct. 1991
III	S01 "Clown Without Pity" S02 "King Homer" S03 "Dial 'Z' For Zombies"	Written by Atrocious Al Jean, Morbid Mike Reiss, Warped Wally Wolodarsky, Johnny Katastrophe Koen, Sacrifying Sam Simon, Vicious Jack Vitti	S04E05 [9F04]	29 Oct. 1992
IV	S01 "The Devil and Homer Simpson" S02 "Terror At 5 ½ Feet" S03 "Bart Simpson's Dracula"	Written by Watch Conan O'Brien, The Late Bill Oakley, The Estate of Josh Weinstein, Disfigured Dan McGrath, Greg "It's Alive!" Daniels, Bilious Bill Canterbury	S05E05 [1F04]	28 Oct. 1993
V	S01 "The Shinning" S02 "Time and Punishment" S03 "Nightmare Cafeteria"	Written by Count Greg Danula, Dearly Departed Dan McGrath, David S. Cohen's Severed Hand, Blob Kushell	S06E06 [2F03]	30 Oct. 1994
VI	S01 "Attack of the 50 Foot Eyesores" S02 "Nightmare on Evergreen Terrace" S03 "Homer[3]"	Written by Scary John Swartzfelder, Steve Tombkins, David[2]+S.[2]+Cohen[2]	S07E06 [3F04]	29 Oct. 1995

6 Appendix

ToH	Segment/Title	Scary Names / Selected Credits	Season/Episode
VII	S01 "The Thing and I" S02 "The Genesis Tub" S03 "Citizen Kang"	Written by The Incredibly Strange Creatures Who Stopped Living and Became... Ken Keeler, Dan Greaney, David S. Cohen	S08E01 [4F02] 27 Oct. 1996
VIII	S01 "The Homega Man" S02 "Fly vs. Fly" S03 "Easy-Bake Oven"	Ghostwritten by Mike Scully, David S. Cohen, Ned Goldreyer	S09E04 [5F02] 26 Oct. 1997
IX	S01 "Hell Toupé" S02 "The Terror of Tiny Toon" S03 "Starship Poopers"	Written by Donick "I Still Know What You Did Last Summer" Cary, The Bride of Lichtenstein, David S. Coffin	S10E04 [AABF01] 25 Oct. 1998
X	S01 "I Know What You Diddily-Iddily-Did" S02 "Desperately Xeeking Xena" S03 "Life's a Glitch, Then You Die"	Written by Donick Cary, Tim Long, Ron Hauge	S11E04 [BABF01] 31 Oct. 1999
XI	S01 "G-G-Ghost D-D-Dad" S02 "Scary Tales Can Come True" S03 "Night of the Dolphin"	Developed by Maims Hell Brooks, Bat Groin Injury, Sam "Sayonara" Simon / Written by Rob LaZebnik, John Drink & Don Payne, Carolyn Omine	S12E01 [BABF21] 01 Nov. 2000
XII	S01 "Hex and the City" S02 "House of Whacks" S03 "Wiz Kids"	Written by Joel H. Cohen, John Frink & Don Payne, Carolyn Omine	S13E01 [CABF19] 06 Nov. 2001
XIII	S01 "Send in the Clones" S02 "The Fright to Creep and Scare Harms" S03 "The Island of Dr. Hibbert"	Written by Marc Wilmore, Brian Kelley, Kevin Curran	S14E01 [DABF19] 03 Nov. 2002
XIV	S01 "Reaper Madness" S02 "Frinkenstein" S03 "Stop The World, I Want to Goof Off"	Developed by James "Just One Hug" Brooks, Bat Groening, Sam "Sayonara" Simon / Written by Triple Admiral John Swartzfelder	S15E01 [EABF21] 02 Nov. 2003
XV	S01 "The Ned Zone" S02 "Four Beheadings and a Funeral" S03 "In The Belly of the Boss"	Written by Bill Odenkirk	S16E01 [FABF23] 07 Nov. 2004

TREEHOUSE OF HORROR Episode Guide

ToH	Segment/Title	Scary Names / Selected Credits	Season/Episode	
XVI	S01 "B.I. Bartificial Intelligence" S02 "Survival of the Fattest" S03 "I've Grown A Costume On Your Face"	Show Runner Al Jean / Written by Marc Wilmore	S17E04 [GABF17]	06 Nov. 2005
XVII	S01 "Married to the Blob" S02 "You Gotta Know When to Golem" S03 "The Day the Earth Looked Stupid"	Show Runner Al Jean / Written by Peter Gaffney	S18E04 [HABF17]	05 Nov. 2006
XVIII	S01 "E.T., Go Home" S02 "Mr. and Mrs. Simpson" S03 "Heck House"	Show Runner Al Jean / Written by Marc Wilmore	S19E05 [JABF16]	04 Nov. 2007
XIX	S01 "Untitled Robot Parody" S02 "How to Get Ahead in Dead-Vertising" S03 "It's the Grand Pumpkin, Milhouse"	Show Runner Al Jean / Written by Matt Warburton	S20E04 [KABF16]	02 Nov. 2008
XX	S01 "Dial 'M' for Murder or Press '#' to Return to Main Menu" S02 "Don't Have a Cow, Man" S03 "There is No Business Like Moe Business"	Show Runner Al "20 re Years" Jean / Written by Edward Danielchunhands	S21E04 [LABF14]	18 Oct. 2009
XXI	S01 "War and Pieces" S02 "Master and Cadaver" S03 "Tweenlight"	Show Runner Al Jazeena / Written by As Predicted, Joel Cohen Just Died	S22E04 [MABF16]	07 Nov. 2010
XXII	S01 "The Diving Bell and The Butterball" S02 "Dial D for Diddily" S03 "In the Na'vi"	Directed by Merciless Matthew Faughnan / Written by Carolyon? Oh. Mean, Eh?	S23E03 [NABF19]	30 Oct. 2011
XXIII	S01 "The Greatest Story Ever Holed" S02 "Un-Normal Activity" S03 "Bart And Homer's Excellent Adventure"	Directed by Steven "Freaking" Moore / Written by David Boogie Man-del & Brian Death Knelley	S24E02 [PABF17]	07 Oct. 2012
XXIV	S01 "Oh, the Places You'll D'oh!" S02 "Dead and Shoulders" S03 "Freaks, No Geeks"	Show Runner Al "Lucky 13" Jean / Directed by The Thing that Ate Rob Oliver / Written by Curse of Werebrook	S25E02 [RABF16]	06 Oct. 2013

289

6 Appendix

ToH	Segment/Title	Scary Names / Selected Credits	Season/Episode	
XXV	S01 "School is Hell" S02 "A Clockwork Yellow" S03 "The Others"	Directed by The Infernal Matthew Faughan / Written by Stephanie "Got Moloko?" Gillis	S26E04 [SABF21]	19 Oct. 2014
XXVI	S01 "Wanted: Dead, Then Alive" S02 "Homerzilla" S03 "Telepaths of Glory"	Show Runner Emojean / Directed by Uneven Steven Moore / Written by Joel Cohen's Credit 2: The Squeakquel	S27E05 [TABF18]	25 Oct. 2015
XXVII	S01 "Dry Hard" S02 "BfF R.I.P." S03 "Moefinger"	Show Runner Al "You're Next, Gunsmoke" Jean / Directed by Steven Mean Mooredor / Written by Jowl H. Corpulent	S28E04 [VABF16]	16 Oct. 2016
XXVIII	S01 "The Exor-Sis" S02 "Coralisa" S03 "Mmm.... Homer"	Show Runner Al "Don't Find Me On Facebook" Jean / Directed by Bubble Headed Bailey / Written by Fhrek	S29E04 [WABF18]	22 Oct. 2017
XXIX	S01 "Intrusion of the Pod-Y" S02 "Multiplisa-Ty" S03 "Geriatric Park"	Show Runner Electoral College Jean / Directed by The Ancient Unnameable Matthew Faughnan / Written by Jor-El H. Krypton	S30E04 [XABF16]	21 Oct. 2018
XXX	S01 "Danger Things" S02 "Heaven Swipes Right" S03 "When Hairy Met Slimy"	Show Runner Constitutional Crisis Jean / Directed by Grimothy Bailey / Written by J. Stewart's Urn	S31E04 [YABF18]	20 Oct. 2019
XXXI	S01 "Into The Homerverse" S02 "Be Kind, Rewind S03 "What Happened to the Halloween Candy?"	Show Runner Antiviral Jean / Directed by Egregious Steven Dean Moore / Written by Julia "Ghoulia" Prescott	S32E04 [ZABF17]	01 Nov. 2020

Treehouse of Horror Reference Guide

ToH	Segment/Title	Genre	Theme/Motif	Parody References
I	S01 "Bad Dream House"	Film / Horror	U.S. Mortgage Crisis / Haunted House	AMITYVILLE HORROR (Dir. Stuart Rosenberg, USA 1979; Remake by Andrew Douglas, USA 2005)
	S02 "Hungry are the Damned"	TV / SF Anthology	THE TWILIGHT ZONE / Alien Invasion	"To Serve Man" (CBS 1962; short story adaptation O. S. N. from Damon Knight, USA 1950)
	S03 "The Raven"	Lit / 19th-Century Gothic	Narrative Poem	"The Raven" (written by E. A. Poe, 1845)
II	S01 «Lisa's Nightmare» («The Monkey's Paw»)	Short Story / European Gothic	Supernatural Horror	"The Monkey's Paw" (W. W. Jacobs; published in the collection *The Lady of the Barge* from 1902)
	S02 «Bart's Nightmare» («The Bart Zone»)	TV Anthology / Supernatural	THE TWILIGHT ZONE / Isolationism	"It's a Good Life" (CBS 1961; short story adaptation O. S. N. from Jerome Bixby, 1953)
	S03 «Homer's Nightmare» («If I Only Had a Brain»)	Lit / Film Gothic Horror	Pre-Code Monster / Blaxploitation	FRANKENSTEIN (James Whale, USA 1931) / THE THING WITH TWO HEADS (Lee Frost,USA 1972) (both based on the Novel *Frankenstein, Or The Modern Prometheus* by Mary Shelley, 1818)
III	S01 "Clown Without Pity"	TV Anthology / Horror	THE TWILIGHT ZONE / Jealousy, Impaired Masculinity	"Living Doll" (CBS 1963; screenplay by Jerry Sohl Credited to Charles Beaumont)
	S02 "King Homer"	Film Horror	Pre-Code Monster Horror	KING KONG (Merian C. Cooper & E. B. Schoedsack, USA 1933)
	S03 "Dial 'Z' for Zombies"	Film Horror	Monster / Zombie	THE RETURN OF THE LIVING DEAD (Dan O'Bannon, USA 1985; Comedy Zombie-Horror Spin-Off from Romero's NIGHT OF THE LIVING DEAD, USA 1968)

6 Appendix

ToH	Segment/Title	Genre	Theme/Motif	Parody References
IV	S01 "The Devil and Homer Simpson"	Short Story / 20th-Century American Gothic	Soul-Selling Faustian Fantasy Tale	"The Devil and Daniel Webster" (written by Stephen Vincent Benét 1936; inspired by W. Irving's "The Devil And Tom Walker", in the collection *Tales of a Traveller* from 1824; adaptation from ALL THAT MONEY CAN'T BUY (Dir. William Dieterle, USA 1941)
	S02 "Terror at 5 ½ Feet"	TV Anthology / Horror	THE TWILIGHT ZONE / Paranoia	"Nightmare at 20.000 Feet" (Dir. Rod Serling, CBS 1963; short story adaptation O.S.N. from Richard Matheson, USA 1961)
	S03 "Bart Simpson's Dracula"	Film / Gothic Romance	Monster / Vampire Melodrama	BRAM STOKER'S DRACULA (Dir. Francis Ford Coppola, USA 1992; based on Bram Stoker's 1897 Novel *Dracula*)
V	S01 "The Shinning"	Film / Psychological Horror	Auteur: Stephen King / Stanley Kubrick	THE SHINING (Dir. Stanley Kubrick, UK / USA 1980; based on the novel O.S.N. by Stephen King, USA1977)
	S02 "Time and Punishment"	Short Story / Speculative Fiction	Dystopian Science Fiction / Butterfly Effect	"A Sound of Thunder" (written by Ray Bradbury, USA 1952)
	S03 "Nightmare Cafeteria"	TV Anthology / Horror	Telefantastic Cannibalism	"Nightmare Café" / SOYLENT GREEN (Dir. Wes Craven, NBC 1992 / Dir. Richard Fleischer, Usa 1973)
VI	S01 "Attack of the 50 Foot Eyesores"	Film / SF	Cold-War Indie Fantasy	ATTACK OF THE 50 FT. WOMAN (Dir. Nathan H. Juran, USA 1958; independent B/W SF 1950S B-Movie takeoff from THE AMAZING COLOSSAL MAN, Usa 1957, THE INCREDIBLE SHRINKING MAN, USA 1957 & WAR OF THE COLOSSAL BEAST, USA 1958)]
	S02 "Nightmare on Evergreen Terrace"	Film Horror	Slasher Horror Franchise	NIGHTMARE ON ELM STREET (Wes Craven, USA 1984);
	S03 "Homer³"	TV / SF Anthology	THE TWILIGHT ZONE / National Security / Fantasy Action	"LITTLE GIRL LOST" / TRON (Dir. Rod Serling, CBS 1962; shortstory adaptation O.S.N. from Richard Matheson, USA 1953 / Dir. Stephen Lisberger, USA 1982)

Treehouse of Horror Reference Guide

ToH	Segment/Title	Genre	Theme/Motif	Parody References
VII	S01 "The Thing And I"	TV Movie	80s Home-Video Family Horror	Basket Case (Dir. Frank Henenlotter, USA 1982)
	S02 "The Genesis Tub"	TV / SF Anthology	The Twilight Zone / Imperialism	"The Little People" (Dir. Rod Serling, S03E28, CBS 1962)
	S03 "Citizen Kang"	Film / Political Mystery Drama	American Dream / Political Satire	Citizen Kane (Dir. Orson Welles, USA 1941)
VIII	S01 "The Homega Man"	Novel / Film SF Horror	Post-Apocalypse / Dystopia	The Omega Man (Dir. Boris Segal, USA 1971; Novel adaptation from Richard Matheson's *I Am Legend*, 1954)
	S02 "Fly vs. Fly"	Film / SF Horror	Monster	The Fly (Dir. Curt Neumann, USA 1958; Remake by David Cronenberg, USA 1986; based on the short story O. S. N. by George Langelaan, 1957)
	S03 "Easy-Bake Oven"	Stage Drama / Gothic Romance	Salem Witch Trials / Puritan Mock History of Halloween	The Crucible (Arthur Miller, USA 1953)
IX	S01 "Hell Toupée"	TV Anthology / Fantasy Horror	Telekinetic Monster	Amazing Stories: "Hell Toupee" (Steven Spielberg, S01E21, NBC 1986)
	S02 "The Terror of Tiny Toon"	Telefantasy / Action Adventure	Telekinetic Fantasy	Stay Tuned (Peter Hyams, USA 1992)
	S03 "Starship Poopers"	Novel / Film / SF Action	Dystopian Satire	Starship Troopers (Paul Verhoeven, USA 1997; loosely based on Robert A. Heinlein's novel O. S. N. from 1959)
X	S01 "I Know What You Diddily-Iddily-Did"	Film / Horror	Serial Killer / Teenage Slasher	I Know What You Did Last Summer (Dir. Jim Gillespie, USA 1997; loosely based on the novel by Lois Duncan O. S. N. from 1973)

293

6 Appendix

ToH	Segment/Title	Genre	Theme/Motif	Parody References
	S02 "Desperately Xeeking Xena"	TV-Fantasy Action	Female Superhero	XENA – WARRIOR PRINCESS (Created by Robert G. Tapert, John Schulian, Sam Raimi, USA/NZ 1995-2001)
	S03 "Life's A Glitch, Then You Die"	Film / SF Action	Dystopia / Y2K Anxiety	WHEN WORLDS COLLIDE (Dir. Rudolph Maté, USA 1951; adaptation from novel of O.S.N. by Phillip Wylie & E. Balmer, 1933)
XI	S01 "G-G-Ghost D-D-Dad"	Telefantasy	African-American Family Ghost Haunting	GHOST DAD (Dir. Sidney Poitier, USA 1990)
	S02 "Scary Tales Can Come True"	Lit / Fantasy	Fairy-Tales	Mashup Of Fairy-Tales by Brothers' Grimm, e. g. *Rapunzel* (KHM 12, 1857), *Hansel & Gretel* (KHM 15, 1857), *Goldilocks* (KHM 21, 1857)
	S03 "Night of the Dolphin"	Film / Novel / SF Drama	Animal Dystopia	THE DAY OF THE DOLPHIN / THE BIRDS (Dir. Mike Nichols, USA 1973; loosely based on the Robert Merle's novel *Un Animal Doué De Raison* from 1967 / Dir. Alfred Hitchcock, USA 1963)
XII	S01 "Hex and the City"	Film / Novel / Horror	Auteur: Stephen King	THINNER (Dir. Tom Holland, USA 1996; based on the novel O.S.N. by Stephen King from 1984)
	S02 "House of Whacks"	Film / SF Teenage Horror	Home Invasion	DEMON SEED / A SPACE ODYSSEY (Dir. Donald Cammell, USA 1977; based on the novel O.S.N. by David Koontz from 1977 / Dir. Stanley Kubrick, USA 1968)
	S03 "Wiz Kids"	Film / Novel / Fantasy Multiverse	Fantasy Adventure	HARRY POTTER AND THE PHILOSOPHER'S STONE (Dir. Chris Columbus, UK/USA 2001; based on the youth novel series by J.K. Rowling, 1997)
XIII	S01 "Send in the Clones"	Film / SF Comedy	Human Hubris / Mad Scientist	MULTIPLICITY (Dir. Harold Remis, USA 1996; based on the short story O.S.N. by Chris Miller, 1993)
	S02 "The Fright to Creep and Scare Harms"	Film / SF Action	Gun Control / Time Travel	THE TERMINATOR (Dir. James Cameron, USA 1984)

Treehouse of Horror Reference Guide

ToH	Segment/Title	Genre	Theme/Motif	Parody References
S03 "The Island of Dr. Hibbert"		Film / Horror	Pre-Code / Human Hubris / Mad Scientist	THE ISLAND OF LOST SOULS (Dir. Earl C. Kenton, USA 1932); based on the novel *The Island of Dr. Moreau* by H. G. Wells from 1896
XIV	S01 "Reaper Madness"	TV / Cartoon	FAMILY GUY Parody	"Death is a Bitch" (FAMILY GUY, Writ. by Ricky Blitt, S02E06, Fox 2000)
	S02 "Frinkenstein"	Film / Horror	Pre-Code Monster	FRANKENSTEIN (Dir. James Whale 1931)
	S03 "Stop the World, I Want to Goof Off"	TV / SF Anthology	THE TWILIGHT ZONE / Isolationism	"A Kind of a Stopwatch" (Dir. John Rich, CBS 1963)
XV	S01 "The Ned Zone"	Film / Telekinetic Horror	Auteur: Stephen King	THE DEAD ZONE (Dir. David Cronenberg, USA 1983; based on the novel O. S. N. by Stephen King from 1979)
	S02 "Four Beheadings and a Funeral"	Film / Graphic Novel / Horror	Gothic Mystery	FROM HELL (Dir. Albert & Allen Hughes, USA 2001; based on the graphic novel O. S. N. by Alan Moore & Eddie Campbell from 1999)
	S03 "In The Belly of the Boss"	Film / SF Adventure	Body Venture	FANTASTIC VOYAGE (Dir. Richard Fleischer, USA 1966; based on the screenplay by Otto Klement & Jerome Bixby)
XVI	S01 "B.I. Bartificial Intelligence"	Film / SF Drama	Utopia / Humanoid Robots	A. I. ARTIFICIAL INTELLIGENCE (Dir. Stephen Spielberg, USA 2001)
	S02 "Survival of the Fattest"	Film / Horror Adventure	Pre-Code / Manhunt	THE-MOST DANGEROUS GAME (Dir. Irving Pichel / Ernest B. Schoedsack, USA 1932; based on the short story O. S. N. by Richard Connell from 1924)
	S03 "I've Grown a Costume on Your Face"	TV Anthology / Fantasy	THE TWILIGHT ZONE / Greed	"The Masks" (based on the script by Rod Serling, Dir. Ida Lupino, CBS 1964)

6 Appendix

ToH	Segment/Title	Genre	Theme/Motif	Parody References
XVII	S01 "Married to the Blob"	Film / Sf Monster Horror	Cold War Propaganda	THE BLOB (Dir. Irvin Yeaworth, USA 1958)
	S02 "You Gotta Know When to Golem"	Film / German Expressionism	Silent Monster Horror	DER GOLEM (U.S. Title: THE MONSTER OF FATE, Dir. Paul Wegener / Henrik Galeen, USA 1915)
	S03 "The Day the Earth Looked Stupid"	Sf Radio Play	Alien Invasion	THE WAR OF THE WORLDS (Orson Welles, CBS Radio, 1932; based on the novel O.S.N. by H.G. Wells,1898)
XVIII	S01 "E.T., Go Home"	Film / Sf	Action-Adventure	E.T. THE EXTRATERRESTRIAL (Dir. Stephen Spielberg, USA 1982)
	S02 "Mr. and Mrs. Simpson"	Film / Crime Thriller	Spy Action Comedy	MR. AND MRS. SMITH (Dir. Doug Liman, USA 2005)
	S03 "Heck House"	–	Morality Tale	No Reference / inspired by religious fundamentalist hell houses in american evangelical churches to teach sinners in morals of good behavior
XIX	S01 "Untitled Robot Parody"	Film / Sf Monster Action	Robot Adventure	TRANSFORMERS (Franchise) (e.g. Dir. Michael Bay, USA 2007)
	S02 "How to Get Ahead in Dead-Vertising"	Tv Drama	Serial Killer	MAD MEN (created by Matthew Weiner, AMC 2007-2015)
	S03 "It's the Grand Pumpkin, Milhouse"	Tv / Halloween Special	Revenge	IT'S THE GREAT PUMPKIN, CHARLIE BROWN (Charles M. Schulz, CBS 1966)
XX	S01 "Dial "M" for Murder or Press # to Return to Main Menu"	Film / Suspense Thriller	Auteur: Alfred Hitchcock / Revenge	STRANGERS ON A TRAIN (Dir. A. Hitchcock, USA 1951; based on the novel O.S.N. by Patricia Highsmith from 1950)
	S02 "Don't Have a Cow, Man"	Film / Horror	Social Zombie Drama	28 DAYS LATER (Dir. Danny Boyle, UK 2002)
	S03 "There is No Business Like Moe Business" (Musical Section)	Film / Gothic Musical	Mystery Musical	SWEENEY TODD: THE DEMON BARBER OF FLEET STREET (Dir. Tim Burton, UK/USA 2007; based on the Broadway Musical O.S.N. by Stephen Sondheim)

TREEHOUSE OF HORROR Reference Guide

ToH	Segment/Title	Genre	Theme/Motif	Parody References
XXI	S01 "War and Pieces"	Film / Fantasy	Action Adventure	JUMANJI (Dir. Joe Johnston, USA 1995)
	S02 "Master and Cadaver"	Film / Thriller Drama	Irony of Fate	DEAD CALM (Dir. Phillip Noyce, AUS/USA 1989; based on 1963 novel O.S.N. by Charles Williams)
	S03 "Tweenlight"	Film / Gothic Fantasy Romance	Vampire Teenage Drama	TWILIGHT (Dir. Catherine Hardwick, USA 2008); based on Stephenie Meyer's 2005 fan-fiction novel O.S.N.)
XXII	S01 "The Diving Bell and the Butterball"	Film / Marvel Superhero	Comic Action	SPIDERMAN (FRANCHISE) (Dir. Sam Raimi, Marvel Films 2002)
	S02 "Dial D for Diddily"	Tv Drama	Serial Killer	DEXTER (Dir. James Manos, Jr., Showtime 2006–2013)
	S03 "In The Na'vi"	Film / Sf Action Adventure	Fantasy	AVATAR (Dir. James Cameron, USA 2009)
XXIII	S01 "The Greatest Story Ever Holed"	–	–	No reference / Nuclear Supercollider Creates Miniature Black Hole
	S02 "Un-Normal Activity"	Film / Horror	Supernatural Movie Franchise	PARANORMAL ACTIVITIES (Franchise) (orig. credited to Oren Peli, 2009–2015)
	S03 "Bart and Homer's Excellent Adventure"	Film / Comedy	Action Adventure	BACK TO THE FUTURE (FILM SERIES) / BILL AND TED'S EXCELLENT ADVENTURE (Dir. Robert Zemeckis USA 1985–1990)/ (Dir. Stephen Herek, USA 1989)
XXIV	S01 "Oh, The Places You'll D'oh!"	Children & Youth Literature	Coming-of-Age Morale	THE CAT IN THE HAT (1957) & OH, THE PLACES YOU'LL GO (1990) (written by Dr. Seuss)
	S02 "Dead and Shoulders"	Film / Blaxploitation	Frankenstein complex	THE THING WITH TWO HEADS (Dir. Lee Frost, USA 1972)
	S03 "Freaks, No Geeks"	Film / Horror	Pre-Code Monster	FREAKS (Dir. Tod Browning, USA 1932)
XXV	S01 "School is Hell"	–	–	No reference / Bart & Lisa discover the entrance to a school in Hell where Bart gets A-Grades throughout

6 Appendix

ToH	Segment/Title	Genre	Theme/Motif	Parody References
XXVI	S02 "A Clockwork Yellow"	Film / Dystopian Crime Drama	Auteur: Stanley Kubrick	A Clockwork Orange / Eyes Wide Shut (u.a.) (both Dir. Stanley Kubrick, UK 1971; UK/USA 1999)
	S03 "The Others"	Film / Gothic Mystery	Haunted House / Home Invasion	The Others (Dir. Alejandro Amenábar, E/F/I USA 2001)
	S01 "Wanted: Dead, Then Alive"	Film / Horror	Frankenstein Complex	Re-Animator (Dir. Stuart Gordon, USA 1985); [loosely based on H. P. Lovecraft's episodic novella *Herbert West – Reanimator* (1922)]
	S02 "Homerzilla"	Film / Horror	Monster / Japan	Godzilla (Franchise) (Dir. Ishiro Honda, JAP 1954)
	S03 "Telepaths of Glory"	Film / Thriller	Found Footage	Chronicle (Dir. Josh Trank, USA 2012)
XXVII	S01 "Dry Hard"	Film / Book Dystopian Thriller	Speculative Fiction	Mad Max: Fury Road / Hunger Games, Part I (Dir. George Miller, USA 2015) / (Dir. Gary Ross, USA 2012)
	S02 "Bff R.I.P."	Film / Supernatural Horror	Coming-of-Age Drama	Lights Out (Dir. David F. Sandberg, USA 2016)
	S03 "Moefinger"	Film / Thriller	Spy Action	James Bond: Goldfinger (Dir. Guy Hamilton, UK 1964)
XXVIII	S01 "The Exor-Sis"	Film / Supernatural Horror	Demonic Possession	The Exorcist (Dir. William Friedkin, USA 1972)
	S02 "Coralisa"	Film / Book Stop-Motion Horror	Animated Dark Fantasy Family Tale	Coraline Dir. (Henry Selick, USA 2009)
	S03 "Mmm Homer"	Short Story / Horror	Self-Cannibalism	Survivor Type (based on the short story by Stephen King, USA 1985)
XXIX	S01 "Intrusion of the Pod-Y Switchers"	Novel & Film / Sf Horror	Home Invasion	Invasion of the Body Snatchers (Dir. Don Siegel, USA 1956)
	S02 "Multiplisat-Ty"	Film / Psychological Horror Thriller	Dissociated Personality Disorder	Split (Dir. M. Night Shyamalan, USA 2016)

Treehouse of Horror Reference Guide

ToH	Segment/Title	Genre	Theme/Motif	Parody References
	S03 "Geriatric Park"	Film / Action Adventure	Human Dinosaurs	Jurassic World (Dir. Colin Trevorrow, USA 2015)
XXX	S01 "Danger Things"	Tv / Science-Fiction Fantasy Horror	80s Retro	Stranger Things – Season I (Dir. The Duffer Brothers USA 2016)
	S02 "Heaven Swipes Right"	Film / Fantasy Comedy	Screwball	Heaven Can Wait (Dir. Warren Beatty / Buck Henry, USA1978)
	S03 "When Hairy Met Slimy"	Film / Fantasy Horror	Romantic Gothic Drama	The Shape Of Water (Dir. Guillermo del Toro, USA 2017)
XXXI	S01 "Toy Gory"	Film / Cgi-Animation Adventure	Toys' Revenge	Toy Story (Dir. John Lasseter, USA 1995)
	S02 Into the Homerverse	Film / Marvel Cgi-Animation Adventure	SF Nuclear Transformation	Spider-Man: Into the Spider-Verse (Dir. Bob Persichetti / Peter Ramsey / Rodney Rothman, USA 2018)
	S03 "Be Nine, Rewind"	Tv / Comedy Drama Series	Time Lapse 'Groundhog Night'	Russian Doll (Dir. Leslie Headland / Jamie Babbit / Natasha Lyonne, USA 2019)

Guest-Animated Couch-Gag Guide:
THE SIMPSONS & TREEHOUSE OF HORROR

Banksy. (Untitled). In: "MoneyBART"
(THE SIMPSONS, s22e03, Fox 2010)

Kricfalusi, John. (Untitled). In: "Bart Stops to Smell the Roosevelts."
(THE SIMPSONS, s23e02, Fox 2011)

Plympton, Bill. (Untitled). In: "Beware my Cheating Bart."
(THE SIMPSONSs, s23e18, Fox 2012)

del Toro, Guillermo. (Untitled). In: "TREEHOUSE OF HORROR XXIV."
(THE SIMPSONS' TREEHOUSE OF HORROR, s25e02, Fox 2013)

Plympton, Bill. (Untitled). In: "Black Eyed, Please."
(THE SIMPSONS, s24e15, Fox 2013)

Stoopid Buddy Stoodios. "Robot Chicken Couch Gag." In: "The Fabulous Faker Boy."
(THE SIMPSONS, s24e20, Fox 2013)

Plympton, Bill. (Untitled). In: "Married to the Blob."
(THE SIMPSONS, s25e10, Fox 2014)

Chomet, Sylvain. (Untitled). In: "Diggs."
(THE SIMPSONSs, s25e12, Fox 2014)

Plympton, Bill. "Inside Homer's Brain." In: "What to Expect When Bart's Expecting."
(THE SIMPSONS, s25e19, Fox 2014)

Hertzfeldt, Don. "The Sampsans Epasode Numbar 164.775.7." In: "Clown in the Dumps."
(THE SIMPSONS, s26e01, Fox 2015)

Robertson, Paul, Ivan Dixon, and Jeremy Dower. "Simpsons Pixels" In: "My Fare Lady."
(THE SIMPSONS, s26e15, Fox 2015)

Harmon, Dan & Justin Roiland. "Rick and Morty." In: "Mathlete's Feat."
(THE SIMPSONS, s26e22, Fox 2015)

Kricfalusi, John. "Treehouse of Horror XXVI."
(THE SIMPSONS' TREEHOUSE OF HORROR, s27e05, Fox 2015)

Cutts, Steve. "LA-Z Rider." In: "Teenage Mutant Milk-Caused Hurdles."
(THE SIMPSONS, s27e11, Fox 2016)

Plympton, Bill. "Roomance." In: "Lisa the Veterinarian."
(THE SIMPSONS, s27e15, Fox 2016)

Goldberg, Eric. "The Disneys." In: "Fland Canyon."
(THE SIMPSONS, s27e19, Fox 2016)

Socha, Micha. "IKEA Coüch Gag." In: "Orange is the New Yellow."
(THE SIMPSONS, s27e22, Fox 2016)

Ward, Pendleton. "Simpsons Time." In: "Monty Burns' Fleeing Circus."
(THE SIMPSONS, s28e01, Fox 2016)

Plympton, Bill. (Untitled). In: "22 For 30."
(THE SIMPSONS, s28e17, Fox 2017)

— . "Homer's Face." In: "3 Scenes Plus a Tag from a Marriage."
(THE SIMPSONS, s29e13, Fox 2018)

List of Figures

Fig. 1: Screenshot from THE SIMPSONS' opening sequence since the episode "Take My Life, Please" from 2009.

Fig. 2: The Griffins meet the Simpsons: Screenshot from FAMILY GUY's crossover episode "The Simpsons Guy" (Fox 2014).

Fig. 3: Nelson Muntz ball-gagged in a torture-porn scenario: Screenshot from FAMILY GUY's crossover episode "The Simpsons Guy" (Fox 2014).

Fig. 4: Screenshot from Disney's THE SKELETON DANCE (USA 1929), included in the SILLY SYMPHONIES series.

Fig. 5: The Big Bad Wolf as the Jewish Peddler: Screenshot from Disney's THREE LITTLE PIGS (USA 1933)

Fig. 6: The Big Bad Wolf and the Three Little Pigs meet Animatronics: Screenshot from THE SIMPSONS' "Lisa the Vegetarian" (Fox 1995).

Fig. 7: 'She whistles when she works:' Screenshot from Disney's SNOW WHITE AND THE SEVEN DWARFS (USA 1937) compared with Lisa's Snow White in THE SIMPSONS' "Four Great Women and a Manicure" (Fox 2009).

Fig. 8: Theater promotion for the release of James Whale's FRANKENSTEIN (Universal 1931).

Fig. 9: Orson Welles' performs his radio play WAR OF THE WORLDS: Screenshot from TREEHOUSE OF HORROR's "The Day the Earth Looked Stupid" (ToH XVII, Fox 2007).

Fig. 10: Bloody lettering as usual: Screenshot from TREEHOUSE OF HORROR XVII's title card (Fox 2006).

Fig. 11: "A Clockwork Yellow:" Title card from ToH XXV (Fox 2014)

Fig. 12: Screenshot from the "Hung couch gag" of ToH VI (Fox 1996)

Fig. 13: "Scary Names:" Screenshot from TREEHOUSE OF HORROR's credit sequence.

Fig. 14: Still from an EC Comics' *Tales From the Crypt* issue No. 41 (1950): cover design inspired Bongo Comics "Bart Simpson's Treehouse of Horror" issue no. 11 (2005)

Fig. 15: The couch gag's 'all in the family:' Screenshot from the empty brown couch in the Simpsons' living room.

Fig. 16: Marge kills the pop-up ads: Screenshots from ToH XVII (Fox 2007).

Fig. 17: THE SIMPSONS feat. John Kricfalusi: Screenshots from THE SIMPSONS' couch gags in "Bart Stops to Smell the Roosevelts" (Fox 2010) and to ToH XXVI (Fox 2015)

Fig. 18: Screenshot from Bill Plympton's YOUR FACE (USA 1987) compared to his Simpsonized opening "Homer's Face" (Fox 2018).

List of Figures

Fig. 19: Screenshot from Cartoon Network's ADVENTURE TIME opening sequence compared to "Simpson Time" opening couch gag (Fox 2015).

Fig. 20: THE SIMPSONS, a 20th-Century Sweat Shop: Screenshots from Banksy's couch gag opening in "MoneyBart" (Fox 2010).

Fig. 21: A claymated massacre: Screenshots from Lee Hardcastle's "100 % Unofficial" Play-Doh couch gag.

Fig. 22: "Simpsons Pixels:" Screenshot from the fan-art couch gag opening of "My Fare Lady" (Fox 2015).

Fig. 23: Springfield under popular-culture ruins: Guillermo del Toro's opening couch gag to ToH XXIV (Fox 2013).

Fig. 24: Screenshot from the first Halloween episode, "The Raven" (ToH I, Fox 1990).

Fig. 25: The Bust of Pallas: Still from Gustave Doré's steel-plate engraving compared to ToH I depiction in "The Raven" (Fox 1990).

Fig. 26: "Asseroles" and "Pastra-Me:" Screenshot from "Mmm… Homer" (ToH XXVIII, Fox 2017).

Fig. 27: Screenshots from "Unnormal Activity" (ToH XXIII, Fox 2012)

Fig. 28: Screenshot from "Freaks, No Geeks" (ToH XXIV, Fox 2013)

Index

#

"60 Seconds With Clay" (stop motion, USA 2010-present) 157
$64,000 Question, The (TV, CBS 1955–1958) 236
7th Voyage of Sindbad, The (film, USA 1958) 162

A

Aarseth, Espen J. 16-17, 105
Abbott and Castello Meet Frankenstein (film, USA 1948) 213
Abbott, Stacey 199, 212, 214, 217 f., 201 f., 205–07
ACA fan 16 f., 19, 27, 40, 73, 98, 261, 265
Adams, Erik 205, 257, 259
'adaptation traffic' 214
Addams Family, The (sitcom, ABC 1964–1966) 181, 199, 259
adult animation 21 f., 47 f., 135, 145, 150
Adventure Time (TV, Cartoon Network 2010–2018) 150, 240, 302
Adventures of Tom Sawyer, The (novel, 1876) 46f.
Akass, Kim 142
Aladdin (film, USA 1992) 69, 185
Alberti, John 19–21, 31, 89
Alcott, John 229
Alexander, Julia 230
ALF (TV, NBC 1986–1990) 36
Alfred Hitchcock Presents (TV, CBS 1969–1975) 119, 127, 140, 235, 241

Alias (TV, ABC 2001–2006) 22
Alley, Robert 141
Althusser, Louis 37
American Dream 37 f., 63, 293
American family, the 10, 77, 182, 202 f., 224–26, 234, 243, 251, 256, 294
American Gothic 5, 26, 90, 111, 114, 129, 165, 170, 173–75, 178, 191, 224 f., 292
American Horror Story (TV, FX, since 2011) 125 f., 216
American Idol (TV, Fox, since 2002) 144
Amityville Horror (film, USA 1979) 25, 84 f., 202, 222, 224 f., 312
Animal Doué de Raison, Un (novel, 1967) 220, 294
animation auteur 5, 86, 118, 137 f., 142, 146–49, 155, 161, 165 f., 168 f., 265
Anson, Jay 225
anthology 6, 22 f., 26, 32, 84 f., 109, 112, 114, 116, 121 f., 224–27, 131, 133 f., 140, 142 f., 157, 172, 180, 184, 196, 201, 202, 216, 231 f., 235–40, 253, 255, 259, 262 f., 267, 291–93, 295
Appadurai, Arjun 17
archive, the 5, 13 f., 26, 33, 40, 70, 74, 86–92, 95–97, 99, 101–103, 123, 127, 132, 134, 146, 162, 168, 170, 173, 175, 178, 197, 201 f., 218, 227, 230 f., 236, 256, 258 f., 261, 263–66, 271
Argento, Dario 133 f., 224, 226
Arrested Development (TV, Fox 2003–2006) 173

303

Index

'art horror' 218, 226 f., 229 f.
Astruc, Alexandre 139 f., 168
At the Mountains of Madness (novella, 1931) 163
auteur 5, 86, 138–40, 142–46, 148–50, 152 f., 155–57, 160–62, 166–69, 180, 186, 202 f., 225–27, 229 f., 258, 292, 294–96, 298
auteur animation 145 f., 150, 162, 169, 266
'Auteur-Dieu' 148, 168
auteur television 5, 137 f., 144, 168
Avventure di Pinocchio, Le (novel, 1883) 72 f.
Azaria, Hank 270
baby-boomer generation 59, 253, 255

B

Back To The Future (film, USA 1985) 37, 297
'bad place' 228–31
Banksy 145, 150–54, 168 f., 266, 300, 302
Barker, Chris 38
Barnouw, Erik 126
Barth, John 103
Barthes, Roland 81, 148
Bartmania 46, 58, 242, 244
Batali, Mario 197 f.
Baudrillard, Jean 17, 42, 52, 58, 105
Bava, Mario 133 f.
Bazin, André 139 f.
Beaumont, Charles 124, 126, 235, 237, 252 f., 291
Beavis and Butt-head (TV, MTV 1993–1997, 2011) 205
Beecher Stowe, Harriet 271
Beetlejuice (film, USA 1988) 223
Bennett, Arnold 89
Behind the Music (TV, VH1 1997–2014) 100
Benét, Steven Vincent 174 f., 178, 292
Berkowitz, Joe 158, 160
Berman, Pat 176
Betty Boop (TV, CBS 1930–1939) 76
Bhattacharya, Sanjiv 11, 21, 25
Big Three 10
'Billboard gag' 118
Birds, The (film, USA 1963) 162, 165, 221 f., 294
Birmingham School 14, 52
Bixby, Jerome 127, 236 f., 243, 291, 295
Black Lives Matter 270

Blade I (film, USA 1998) 162
Blade II (film, USA/D 2002) 162, 180
Blau, Sheridan 43
Blaxploitation 186 f., 291, 297
Blob, The (film, USA 1958) 24, 95, 182, 239, 287, 289, 296
Bloch, Robert 165
'board gag' 118, 137, 153, 160
Bob's Burgers (TV, Fox, since 2011) 204
body horror 197 f., 201 f., 205, 215, 217 f., 226
Bolter, Jay David 17, 98–100, 105 f.
Bongo Comics 4, 116, 123, 301
Booker, M. Keith 240
Bosch, Hieronymus 250
Botting, Fred 97, 189
Bouchard, Norma 42 f., 49, 51
Bould, Mark 99
Bourdieu, Pierre 12
Bradbury, Ray 116, 124, 163, 165 f., 212, 292
Brady Bunch, The (TV, ABC 1969–1974) 137
Breaking Bad (TV, AMC 2008–2013) 140
Brecht, Bertolt 38
Bride of Frankenstein, The (film, USA 1935) 164, 190, 213, 288
Brooks, James L. 10, 121, 124, 141, 234, 258, 297
Brothers' Grimm, The 78, 294
Brown, Charlie 42, 60, 112, 296
Browning, Tod 164, 166, 201, 215–18, 233, 297
Brunsdon, Charlotte 12
Buffy the Vampire Slayer (TV, The WB 1997–2003) 13, 227
Buggles, The 39
Burgin, Victor 80 f.
Burke, Edmund 93, 176
Burton, Tim 114, 175, 296
Bush, Sr., George 32, 47, 55, 59, 70, 204, 262

C

"Call of Cthulhu" (short story, 1928) 176
'caméra stylo' 168
'camp' 42, 54, 192, 196, 239
Cannibal Capers (film, USA 1930) 66 f.
canon 16, 23 f., 32, 34, 65, 67, 79, 81, 83 f., 92, 100, 109, 115, 139, 193,
Cantor, Paul A.

cartoon auteur 26, 115, 118, 203, 266
cartoon realism 9, 13, 21, 31, 70, 72, 78, 85, 100, 132, 148, 209, 234
CASABLANCA (film, 1942) 42 f.
CAT PEOPLE, THE (film, USA 1942) 212
Catch-22 (novel, 1961) 43
cautionary tale 189, 233
CCTV 209 f., 231
cel animation 151, 159, 256
Century, Sara 124 f., 133 f.
CGI animation 77, 256, 299
Chabrol, Claude 139
Chappell, Les 256
Chase, David 142
Chayefsky, Paddy 238
CHEERS (TV, NBC 1982–1993) 36
chiaroscuro effect 181
CHILD'S PLAY (film, USA 1988) 253, 255
CHILLING ADVENTURES OF SABRINA (TV, Netflix, since 2018) 108
Chomet, Sylvain 145, 147–49, 300
CHORUS LINE, A (musical, USA 1985) 97
Chow, Valerie 43, 62
CITIZEN KANE (film, USA 1941) 117, 249, 293
claymation 99, 146, 149, 157–59, 161, 168 f., 266
'cliché' 43 f., 45, 47, 51, 57, 82, 99, 102, 148, 179, 184 f., 206, 214, 254
Clinton, Bill 117
CLOCKWORK ORANGE, A (UK/USA 1971) 113, 290, 298
close reading 25 f., 55, 86, 120, 146, 154, 168, 184, 191 f., 202, 225, 231, 235, 237, 242 f., 251, 256, 259, 265–68
Coen Brothers, The 126, 144
Cohen, David X. 30, 69, 117, 287
Cohen, Jeffrey Jerome 213 f., 220, 222
Colbert, Stephen 21
Cold War 83, 85, 95, 107, 125, 221 f., 241, 243, 247, 250, 255, 292, 296
Collins, Jim 32, 50
Collodi, Carlo 72 f.
complex TV 13, 22, 140 f., 146, 170, 172 f., 178, 183 f., 195 f., 238, 271
Conard, Mark T. 19, 61
convergence culture 14, 97 f., 107, 137, 264
coolness 37
CORALINE (film, USA 2009) 197, 298

Corliss, Roger 125
Corman, Roger 224
Corwin, Norman 238
Cosby, Bill 11
COSBY SHOW, THE (TV, NBC 1984–1992) 10 f., 14, 137
'couch gag' 5 f., 24, 26, 99, 118–20, 137 f., 145–63, 166–69, 181, 203, 265 f., 269, 300–02
Craven, Wes 193, 292
'creature feature' 163–65, 232
CREATURE FROM THE BLACK LAGOON, THE (film, USA 1954) 164
credit sequence 117
Creeber, Glen 227
Cronenberg, David 109, 113, 207, 293, 295
CRONOS (film, MEX/USA 1993) 164
Croxton, Katie 74
Crucible, The (novel, 1953) 175, 293
Cthulhu mythology 165
'cultural echo chamber' 176, 184, 196, 212 f., 266
'culture jamming' 16 f., 146, 152, 168, 263, 266, 269
'culture wars' 55 f., 63, 67, 264
'cumulus clouds' 118
Curry, Tim 254
Curtiz, Michael 42
Cushing, Peter 133 f., 205
cyberpunk 35

D

de Certeau, Michel 12
DAILY SHOW, THE (TV, Comedy Central, since 1996) 21
DALLAS (TV, CBS 1978–1991) 36
Dannenberg, Nadine 88
Darwin, Charles 113, 249
DAY OF THE DOLPHIN, THE (film, USA 1973) 97, 220 f., 294
Day, Patrick 152, 155
DAY THE EARTH STOOD STILL, THE (film, USA 1951) 164, 199
DEAD ZONE, THE (film, USA 1983) 109, 113, 295
del Toro, Guillermo 107, 114, 119, 146, 161–69, 175, 180, 186, 266, 299, 300, 302
'dénouement' 193 f.
Densham, Pen 234

Department of Standards and Practices 204 f., 225
Derleth, August 165
Derrida, Jacques 91 f., 97, 183
Dery, Mark 17, 263
Dettmar, Kevin 89
"Devil and Daniel Webster, The" (short story, 1936) 174 f., 178, 292
DEVILS BACKBONE, THE (film, E/Mex/USA 2001) 164, 166
DIAL 'M' FOR MURDER (film, USA 1954) 113
Diederichsen, Diedrich 31, 40, 102
'discursive heterogeneity' 167
Disney 34, 55, 64–83, 85, 168, 185, 193, 223, 257, 269 f., 301
Disneyland 43, 71, 87
Disney, Walt 64 f., 66–69, 72, 74, 77, 79–82, 102, 168, 264
Dixon, Ivan 146, 155, 159–61, 300
Doctor Sleep (novel, 2019) 108
Dole, Bob 117
domestic sitcom 99, 131
Doré, Gustave 4, 23, 194 f., 302
'doxa' 81
DR. JEKYLL AND MR. HYDE (film, USA 1931) 188
Dracula (novel, 1897) 174 f., 182, 216, 292
DRACULA (film, USA 1931) 94, 129, 201, 216, 232 f.
Du Vernay, Denise 18, 20, 30, 107, 262, 270
Duffer Brothers, the 108, 207, 299
DUMBO (film, USA 1941) 69
Dunning, John 111, 199

E

Easter Eggs 195, 270
EASY RIDER (film, USA 1969) 168
Ebert, Roger 220, 228 f.
EC Comics 4, 116, 120–25, 133–35, 259, 265, 301
Eco, Umberto 5, 25, 41–43, 102
ED SULLIVAN SHOW, THE (TV, CBS 1948–1971) 236
'edutainment' 170
Elsaesser, Thomas 87
'enchanted objects' 254
Ernst, Wolfgang 87 f.
Ess, Ramsey 270

E. T. THE EXTRATERRESTRIAL (film, USA 1982) 36
Evans, Noëll 64 f., 68
EXORCIST, THE (film, USA 1973) 109, 180, 197, 202, 222, 224, 298

F

Fahle, Oliver 95, 98
'fake' 43 f., 47–49, 51, 62 f., 72, 95, 102, 117, 243, 249
Falcone, Alex 141
Falero, Sandra 141, 143, 146
family sitcom 10, 31, 115
FAMILY TIES (TV, NBC 1982–1989) 10 f., 14
FAMILY GUY (TV, Fox, since 1999) 23, 44-46, 48-51, 263, 295, 301
fan culture 14, 107
fan auteur 155, 161, 168 f., 266
fandom 19 f., 45, 101, 155, 191, 195, 209
FARGO (TV, Netflix 2014–2017) 22, 126, 142, 144
FATHER KNOWS BEST (TV, CBS 1954–1960) 253
Federal Communications Commission (FCC) 202
Fiction Film (photography, 1991) 80
Fincher, David 142, 144
Fink, Moritz 16, 18, 122, 138, 262
Finn, Huckleberry 46 f., 58
Fischinger, Oscar 67
Fiske, John 12
Fleischer, Richard 116, 292
FLINTSTONES, THE (TV, ABC 1960–1966) 59, 131, 138
Fluck, Winfried 106
FLY, THE (film, USA 1958) 164, 293
FOG, THE (film, USA 1980) 111
Folsom, Ed 90, 92, 103
'forensic fandom' 191
Foster, Hal 33
Foucault, Michel 5, 26, 41, 86 ff., 91, 97, 102, 264
'found-footage style' 209 f., 298
Fox Broadcasting Company (FBC) 10
Fox, Michael J. 11, 37
Fox Network 10, 16, 40, 141, 160 f., 269
Francis, Freddie 125
FRANKENSTEIN (film, USA 1931) 94, 129, 164, 186–88, 201, 212, 215 f., 266, 291, 295

FRANKENSTEIN MEETS THE WOLF MAN (film, USA 1943) 212
Frankenstein, Or the Modern Prometheus (novel, 1818) 174 f., 182, 184–87, 271, 291
Frankfurt School 12, 34
FREAKS (film, USA 1932) 164, 166, 201, 215–18, 232, 297
Freud, Sigmund 200
Friedkin, William 197, 224, 298
Friedman, Sam 146
Friend, Tad 20
Frost, Lee 186, 291, 297
'funny tombstones' 77, 115, 119

G

Gabler, Neal 69
GAME OF THRONES (TV, HBO 2011–2019) 7, 197
Game Studies 16, 105
"Garden Eden of Earthly Delight, The" (triptych, 1503–1515) 250
Gen Xers 59, 61, 64, 244 f.
Generation X 59, 61, 63
'generic clustering' 121
'generic mixology' 132
Genette, Gérard 191
genre mixing 9, 21 f., 100, 121, 127 f., 131, 134, 136, 172 f., 175, 192, 206
GHOST OF FRANKENSTEIN, THE (film, USA 1942) 213
Giallo film 133 f.
Gilbride, Paige 153
Gilligan, Vince 140
Glenn, Cerise L. 63
Godard, Jean-Luc 139
GODZILLA (film, *GOJIRA*, JAP 1954) 95, 298
Goertz, Allie 18, 115, 125, 127, 137 f., 141, 169
Gothic cartoon 178, 191, 195 f.
Gothic fiction 5, 26, 101, 114, 170 ff., 174 f., 184, 191, 212, 216, 218, 235, 266
Gothic horror 184, 195, 199, 201, 204, 217, 225, 291
'Gothicization' 180
Gothic poem 23, 25, 195
Gothic poetry 170, 173, 192 f.
Gothic sitcom 181 f., 199, 213, 226
Gould, Dana 232, 259
Gracie Films 10

Gramsci, Antonio 38
Grant, Barry Keith 248
Grant, Elizabeth 190
Gray, Jonathan 19, 92, 154
Great Depression 109, 188, 231, 238
Great Nation of Futurity, The (essay, 1839) 251
Greco, John 188
GREMLINS (film, USA 1984) 36, 254
Groening, Matt 10 f., 15, 17 f., 21, 30, 39 f., 44, 53 f., 61, 64 f., 67 f., 82, 102, 116, 121, 134, 141, 188, 196, 234, 241, 250, 255 f., 258, 264, 267
Grusin, Richard 17, 98 f., 105
Gruteser, Michael 27, 40, 59 f., 88
guerrilla tactics 17, 263, 266
GUNSMOKE (TV, CBS 1955–1975) 236, 290
Gunzenhäuser, Randi 7, 33 f., 102, 178, 180

H

Hall, Dennis 137
Hall, Stuart 38, 52
HAMMER HOUSE OF HORROR (TV, ITV 1980) 224
Hamner, Jr., Earl 236
Hanna-Barbera cartoon 114
Hardcastle, Lee 146, 155–58, 160, 168, 266
Harris, Dan 81
Hartley, John 12, 182
haunted house 5, 85, 94, 96, 197 ff., 202, 223–25, 229 f., 266, 291, 298
Hawkes, Terence 34
Hawks, Howard 139, 142
Hays' Code 188
HE-MAN AND THE MASTERS OF THE UNIVERSE (TV, Cartoon Network 1983–1985) 36
Hebdige, Dick 52, 58
hegemony 38 f.
HELLBOY (film, USA 2004) 114
Heller, Joseph 43
Henry, Matthew A. 19 ff., 55, 89
HEREDITARY (film, USA 2018) 85
heterotopia 87–89, 191
high-concept Hollywood 36
Hildreth, Richard 67 f.
Hill, Rodney 238
HILL STREET BLUES (TV, NBC 1981–1987) 15
Hills, Matt 205, 225 f.

'historiographic metafiction' 82 ff.
Hißnauer, Christian 170–73
Hitchcock, Alfred 113, 119, 127, 139 f., 142, 162, 224, 241, 294, 296
Hoffmann, E. T. A. 200
Hogan, Michael 64
Holtzen, Wm. Curtis 103
HOME IMPROVEMENT (TV, ABC 1991–1999) 23–25
home invasion 5, 146, 156, 197 ff., 200, 207, 266, 294, 298
'Homeric profundity' 43 f., 102
Hooper, Tobe 224
Horner, Al 132, 234, 255
HOSTEL (film, USA/CZE 2005) 48, 159
Houghton, Rianne 269
HOUSE OF CARDS (TV, Netflix 2013–2018) 142, 144
HOUSE OF FRANKENSTEIN (film, USA 1944) 213
HOUSE OF USHER (film, USA 1960) 174, 224
"House That Bled To Death, The" (TV, ITV 1980) 134, 224
HOUSE THAT DRIPPED BLOOD, THE (film anthology, UK 1971) 125, 133 f.
HOW I MET YOUR MOTHER (TV, CBS 2005–2014) 217
Howard, Robert E. 165
Hughes, John 36
Hunter, James D. 55
Hutcheon, Linda 5, 26, 41, 64 ff., 80–83, 85, 102, 128, 195, 264
Hutchings, Peter 108, 129, 218, 224
Huyssen, Andreas 55
hyperconscious intertextuality 31 f.
hypermediacy 99–101
hypermediality 17

I
I Am Legend (novel, 1954) 164, 166, 293
I DREAM OF JEANNIE (TV, NBC 1965–1970) 246
I LOVE LUCY (TV, CBS 1951–1957) 111, 236
ideology 37 f., 40, 59 f., 62, 182, 242 f.
Illustrated Man, The (novel, 1951) 163, 166
independent claymation 169, 266
Indian burial ground 85, 223–25, 227
INSIDIOUS (film, USA 2011) 223
intertextual parody 19

INVISIBLE MAN, THE (film, USA 1933) 164
Irving, Washington 114, 174
Island of Dr. Moreau, The (novel, 1896) 174–76, 184, 295
ISLAND OF LOST SOULS (film, USA 1932) 174, 178, 187–88, 190, 201, 218 f., 295
IT (TV, ABC 1990) 254
IT – CHAPTER 1 (USA 2017) 108
Iwerks, Ub 65

J
Jackson, Michael 34, 270
Jacobs, W. W. 175, 236, 291
Jahn-Sudmann, Andreas 127
Jameson, Fredric. 52, 54
Jasper, Gavin 44
Jaws (film, USA 1975) 71
Jean, Al 107, 109, 112, 117, 120 f., 152 f., 155, 197 f., 287, 289
Jeffords, Susan 59
Jenkins, Henry 14, 16 f., 97 f., 107, 145 f., 152, 264
JETSONS, THE (TV, ABC 1962–1963; 1985–1987) 59
Jones, James Earl 23, 191, 193
Jowett, Lorna 199, 235
Joyce, James 36
JU-ON: ORIGINS (TV, Netflix 2020) 108
JU-ON: THE GRUDGE (film, JAP 2002) 108
JURASSIC PARK (film, USA 1993) 71

K
Karloff, Boris 129, 164, 185, 201, 205, 213, 235
Kellner, Douglas 34 f., 41, 61, 171
Kenton, Erle C. 174, 187, 201
Kinder- und Hausmärchen der Gebrüder Grimm (folktales, 1812) 78
KING KONG (film, USA 1931) 178, 190, 200 f., 218 ff., 249, 291
KING OF THE HILL (TV, Fox 1997–2010) 205
King, Stephen 84, 93, 96, 108 f., 113, 124, 128, 162, 165, 174, 176, 184, 186, 196, 204, 213, 216 f., 220–22, 226–28, 233, 236, 238, 241, 254, 292, 294 f., 298
Kitsch 42 f., 51, 82, 102
Kittler, Friedrich 88
Klein, Thomas 40, 170, 172
Knight, Damon 237, 249, 291

Index

Koenigsberger, Kurt M. 89
Kondabolu, Ari 190
Kricfalusi, John 114, 145, 147 ff., 149, 300
Kubrick, Stanley 113, 128 f., 131, 203, 212, 225, 227–30, 292, 294, 298
Kuipers, Giselinde 146
Kurp, Joshua 108, 181
Kurtzman, Harvey 122

L

Laemmerhirt, Iris-Aya 178, 180
Lambert, Mary 224
Lang, Fritz 139, 142
Lasn, Kalle 263
LATE NIGHT ACTION W/ ALEX FALCONE (TV, undated) 141
Laughton, Charles 190
LEAVE IT TO BEAVER (TV, CBS 1957–1963) 253
LEAVING NEVERLAND (documentary, HBO 2019) 270
Lee, Christopher 133 f., 201
"Legend of Sleepy Hollow, The" (novella, 1809) 114
Life in Hell (cartoon, since 1977) 10
LIGHTS OUT (radio series, NBC Radio, 1935–1947) 111, 298
LOONEY TUNES (cartoon series, Warner Bros. 1930–1969) 114, 132
L-O-Ps ('Least Objectionable Programs') 205 f., 221, 225
LOST (TV, ABC 2004–2010) 22
"Lost in the Funhouse" (short story, 1968) 103
Lovecraft, H. P. 163, 165 f., 174 f., 298
Lugosi, Bela 164, 201
Lynch, David 52, 140–42, 226

M

MAD (magazine, 1952–2018) 122
MAD MEN (TV, AMC 2007–2015) 140, 296
mad scientist 187 f., 190, 201, 204, 213, 294 f.
made-for-TV horror 202
Mamoulian, Rouben 188
Manoff, Marlene 91
Manson, Charles 48
Marcuse, Herbert 171, 173
MARRIED … WITH CHILDREN (TV, Fox 1987–1997) 137, 211 f., 255

Marxism 38, 52
MARY TYLER MOORE SHOW, THE (TV, CBS 1970–1977) 10
mass media 15–17, 35, 42, 80
mass society 12
'material practice' 37
Matheson, Richard 124, 126, 163, 165 f., 175, 236 f., 247 f., 256 f., 292 f.
MATRIX, THE (USA 1999) 105
McCabe, Janet 142 f., 156
McCarthy era 238
McEvoy, Emma 180 f.
McFarlane, Seth 44, 51
McGee, Marty 234, 239, 258
McLuhan, Marshall 42, 106, 205
McPherson, Tara 16
McRobbie, Angela 5, 26, 35, 40 f., 51, 52 ff., 60, 63 f., 82, 102, 263
media convergence 12, 14, 17, 26, 39, 97, 120, 212, 255 f., 271
media literacy 19, 26, 44, 131, 203, 255
mediascapes 17 f.
MEDIC (TV, NBC 1954–1956) 236
Melbye, David 239, 241, 247, 253
Melville, Herman 271
Mercer, Rick 21
Merle, Robert 220, 222, 294
Meslow, Scott 176
'meta-pop text' 50
meta-textual narration 192
Meteling, Arno 204, 208, 211
metteur en scène 141
Metz, Christian 128, 131
Miller, Arthur 175, 293
Miller, Frank 99
MIMIC (film, USA 1997) 164, 166
MINECRAFT (video game, Mojang Studios, since 2017) 150
"Minion Ways To Die" (stop motion, USA 2015) 157
Mirkin, David 115, 128, 227
Mittell, Jason 9, 13, 20–22, 31, 92, 100, 131, 133–35, 143, 170–72, 177, 184, 192, 238, 266
Moby-Dick (novel, 1851) 271
"Monkey's Paw, The" (short story, 1902) 175, 184 f., 198, 236, 287, 291
monster, the 129, 180, 182, 187, 201, 213–15, 217, 220, 222, 232, 258

'monster boom, the' 232
Motion Picture Association of America (MPAA) 202
MTV 35, 38 f., 46, 61, 205
Mummy, The (film, USA 1932) 164
Munsters, The (TV, CBS 1964–1966) 114, 132, 181, 199
Murdoch, Rupert 10, 16, 34, 64
Murnau, F. W. 201
Murray, Noel 233, 245, 259
Muschietti, Andrès 108

N
'narrative Spezialeffekte' 172
Neat Job, The (film, UK 1973) 133
Nelmes, Jill 139 f., 167
Nelson, Robin 142
Neu, Robert 152
Neumann, Kurt 164
'New Trend, the' 120 ff., 124, 135
Newcomb, Horace M. 11, 14
Newman, Michael Z. 39
Nietzsche, Friedrich 61
Nichols, Mike 220–22, 294
Night Gallery (TV, NBC 1969–1973) 109, 114, 120, 127, 235, 253
Nightmare On Elm Street (film, USA 1984) 120, 193, 207, 292
Nightmare On Elm Street III: Dream Warrior (film, USA 1987) 206 f.
non-canon 24, 32
Nosferatu – Eine Symphonie des Grauens (film, D 1922) 164, 201
nostalgia 107, 116, 160, 258
Nouvelle Vague 139 f.
Nyby, Christian 164

O
O'Sullivan, John 251
Oakley, Bill 141, 287
Oboler, Arch 111
'obsolete man, the' 251, 258
Omega Man, The (film, USA 1971) 164, 293
Omen, The (film, USA 1976) 222
'operational aesthetics' 173, 184, 195
Ortved, John 18, 234
Outer Limits, The (TV, ABC 1963–1964) 127, 235, 241

Ozzie and Harriet (TV, ABC 1952–1966) 253

P
Palimpsest 80 f., 83, 130, 132
Palmer, Daniel 31
Pan's Labyrinth (film, E/MEX 2006) 161, 163 f.
Paranormal Activity (film, USA 2007) 209 f.
Parikka, Jussi 87 f., 98, 265
parody 5, 19, 22, 26, 33, 64 ff., 68 f., 73 f., 76 ff., 79, 81–86, 92, 95, 98, 102, 109, 113, 122, 124, 127–36, 170, 172 f., 184 f., 188, 192, 195, 199, 212, 214 f., 229, 263–66, 269, 291 ff.
participatory culture 5, 14 ff., 17, 26, 115, 137 ff., 145 f., 152 f., 155, 161, 167–69, 266, 271
pastiche 128, 165
Peanuts (cartoon strip, 1950) 43, 46
Peirce, Jack P. 129
Penny Dreadful (TV, Showtime/Netflix 2014–2016) 183
'performative literacy' 43, 49, 170
Perkins, Dennis 215
Pet Sematary (novel, 1983) 108
Pet Sematary (film, USA 1989/2019) 108, 224
Peter Pan (film, USA 1953) 69
Pfeiler, Martina 271
PG-13 36, 48
Phillips, Kendall R. 93 f.
"Philosophy of Composition, The" (essay, 1846) 193
'phobic pressure points' 222, 258
Picket Fences (TV, CBS 1992–1996) 12
Pinocchio (film, USA 1940) 72–74, 76, 81
Pinsky, Mark I. 65–67, 73–76
Planet of the Apes (film, USA 1968) 120
Plympton, Bill 4, 145, 147 ff., 300
Poe, Edgar Allen 23, 84 f., 163, 165, 170, 174, 176, 191, 287
political parody 81
Polson, Laura 155, 159 f.
Poltergeist (film, USA 1982) 85, 202, 206–8, 224
Popeye (TV, USA 1933–1942) 76
'pop irony' 43

portmanteau aesthetic 125
post-Enlightenment anxieties 189
post-Fordist network era 9
postmodernism 9, 18, 20 f., 30–33, 42, 50, 52–55, 81 f., 86 f., 101, 131
postmodern parody 5, 22, 26, 64 ff., 81, 86, 102, 264
'postmodern turn' 34
pre-Code Hollywood 188, 201, 212, 215
pre-Code horror 93, 186, 191, 201, 213, 216
'preachies' 124
Prescott, Julia 18, 115, 137, 169
Presnell, Don 234, 239, 258
Price, Vincent 200
Prince, Stephen 108
Problem with Apu, The (documentary, USA 2017) 190
'pseudorealism' 76 f.
Psycho (film, USA 1960) 223 f.
Puppet Master (film, USA 1989) 108
Pynchon, Thomas 35, 155

Q
'quality TV' 12 f., 22, 171 f.

R
Rabin, Nathan 58, 60, 185, 219, 242 f., 248
radio auteur 111, 238
radio play 26, 84, 109–11, 125, 199, 259, 262, 296, 201
Raiders of the Lost Ark (film, USA 1981) 36, 184 f.
Rauscher, Andreas 32, 40
Reagan-Bush era 55, 59
Reaganomics 63, 204
'reality effects' 106–8, 110
'reflexive cinema' 210
Reiss, Mike 109, 116, 258, 287
remediation 17, 22, 39, 97–99, 101, 106 f., 130, 191, 199
remembering 33, 107, 199
Ren & Stimpy Show, The (TV, Nickelodeon 1991–1996) 114, 147
repurposing 26, 97 f., 101, 135, 148, 169, 255
Rick & Morty (TV, Adult Swim, since 2013) 149, 204
Ring, The (film, USA 2002) 206 f.
Ringu (film, JAP 1998) 206
Ritzer, Ivo 140

Robertson, Paul 146, 155, 159
Robot Chicken (TV, Adult Swim, since 2005) 138, 149, 300
Roman numerals 112 f.
'rope-a-dope' 247, 249 f., 267
Roseanne (TV, ABC 1988–1997, 2018) 23–25
Routt, William D. 139 f.

S
Salem's Lot (novel, 1975) 228
Salmela, Markku 153 f.
"Sandmann, Der" (short story, 1816) 200
Sarris, Andrew 166–8
'satire TV' 21
Saturday-morning cartoons 14, 135
Sausage Party (CGI film, USA 2016) 119
Savalas, Telly 252
Savaya, Ray 156
Sawyer, Tom 46 f., 58
'scary names' 120 f., 287 ff., 301
Scary Stories to Tell in the Dark (1981) 114
Schauerroman 200
Scheib, Richard 187, 189
Schickel, Richard 66, 68
Schlegel, Johannes 87
Schmidt, Siegfried J. 33, 102
Schoedsack, Ernest B. 178, 201, 218, 220, 249, 291, 295
Schultz, Charles M. 43
Schumer, Arlen 251
science-fiction TV 6, 232, 240
'scientific racism' 190
Seinfeld (TV, NBC 1989–1998) 173
Selick, Henry 197, 298
Selman, Matt 105–7, 135, 155
'semiological guerrilla warfare' 42
seriality 2, 22, 127, 170 f., 173, 176, 261, 265 f., 271
Serling, Rod 6, 25 f., 84 f., 109, 114, 121, 124–6, 135, 142, 164, 196, 202, 231–41, 246, 251 f., 257–9, 265, 267, 292 f., 295
Shape of Water, The (film, USA 2017) 106 f., 114, 161, 299
Shattuc, Jane 16, 269
Shearer, Harry 242
Sheldon, Joseph 156
Shelley Mary 94, 129, 175, 182, 184, 216, 271, 291

Shimizu, Takashi 108
SHINING, THE (film, USA 1980) 108, 113, 115, 128, 131, 165, 203, 225, 227–30, 292
Shklovsky, Viktor 171, 173
SHOCKER (film, USA 1989) 206 f.
show runner 21, 24, 112, 121, 124, 127, 135, 141–3, 145 f., 152, 155, 198, 227, 234, 239, 241, 289 f.
Significance of the Frontier in American History, The (essay, 1893) 251
Silverman, David 45, 55, 61, 109, 121, 127, 239, 251, 258
Silverstone, Roger 12
Simon, Sam 121, 124, 141, 258, 287
'Simpsonian natives' 19, 27, 64
Sims, David 115, 227
simulacra 42, 58, 105
Simulacra and Simulation (essays, 1994) 105
simulation 17, 105–7, 117, 131, 135 f., 265
SIN CITY (film, USA 2005) 99
Sinatra, Frank 113
SILLY SYMPHONIES, THE (film series, USA 1929–1939) 65–9, 77
Sirucek, Stefan 270
situation comedy 20, 31
SKELETON DANCE, THE (short film, USA 1929) 65, 67, 301
slacker 244
SLEEPY HOLLOW (film, USA 1999) 114
slow-burn narrative 13
Snead, James A. 190
Snierson, Dan 120, 167, 198 f.
Snow, Jennifer 73
SNOW WHITE AND THE SEVEN DWARFS (film, USA 1937) 72–77, 80 f., 301
Socha, Michal 148
social habitus 12
"Sometimes They Come Back" (short story, 1978) 228
SOMETIMES THEY COME BACK ... AGAIN (film, USA 1996) 228
SON OF FRANKENSTEIN, THE (film, USA 1939) 213
SONG OF THE SOUTH (film, USA 1946) 69
SOPRANOS, THE (TV, HBO 1999–2007) 13, 143, 232
Sontag, Susan 42, 54
SOYLENT GREEN (film, USA 1973) 116, 292
Spigel, Lynn 12

Spooner, Catherine 176, 180, 183
"Sound of Thunder, A" (short story, 1952) 116, 212, 292
SOUTH PARK (TV, Comedy Central, since 1997) 23, 138, 149, 204 f.
Southern California Sorcerers 165
Stafford, Jeff 188
Stanhope, Kate 155
STAR TREK (TV, NBC 1966–1969) 107, 116, 232, 246
STAR WARS (film, USA 1977–1983) 23, 36, 168
STEAMBOAT WILLIE (short film, USA 1928) 65, 68
Steedman, Carolyn 90
Stephens, Emily 207
Stevenson, Robert Louis 174–6, 218
Stewart, Jamie 69
Stoker, Bram 94, 129, 174 f., 182, 216, 292
Storey, John 37 f., 42
Strange Case of Dr. Jekyll and Mr. Hyde (novel, 1886) 174 f.
STRANGER THINGS (TV, Netflix, since 2016) 106, 108, 207, 299
street art 145, 150, 152 f., 158, 169, 266
sublime, the 43, 93, 176
sujet 82, 166
Superman (comic, DC, 1938-present) 42
Surman, David 76 f., 79
SUSPENSE (TV, CBS 1949–1954) 202
SUSPIRIA (film, I 1977) 224, 226
Swartzfelder, John 287 f.
syndication 36, 142, 211 f.

T
"T is for Toilet" (stop motion, USA 2012) 157
TALES FROM THE CRYPT (anthology film, UK 1972) 125, 133
TALES FROM THE CRYPT (TV, HBO 1989–1996) 114, 122
television auteur 142 f., 145, 153
Telotte, J. P. 240
textual poaching 14
'textual syllabus' 43
Thatcher, Margaret 38
THING FROM ANOTHER WORLD, THE (film, USA 1951) 164
THING WITH TWO HEADS, THE (film, USA 1972) 186 f., 291, 297

This Island Earth (film, USA 1955) 164
Thompson, Kristin 13
Thompson, Robert 62
Thompson, Robert J. 12 f.
Thorn, Michael 269
Three Little Pigs, The (short film, USA1933) 66–9, 71 f., 301
Thriller (TV, NBC 1960–1962) 202, 235
Tibbetts, John C. 67 f.
Todd VanDerWerff, Emily 246
Tom & Jerry (cartoon series, Hanna-Barbera 1940–1958) 100, 114, 132
'torture porn' 48, 146, 159, 301
Tourneur, Jacques 212
Tracey Ullman Show, The (TV, Fox 1987–1990) 10, 56
trick'r'treating 37
Trilogy of Terror (anthology film, ABC 1975) 255
Tron (film, USA 1982) 257, 292
Truffaut, François 139, 168
Truman Show, The (film, USA 1998) 105 f.
Trump, Donald 7, 32, 268 f.
Turner, Chris 10, 13, 18, 35, 40, 60, 118
Turner, Frederick Jackson 251
Twain, Mark 46, 48
Twilight Zone, The (TV, CBS 1959–1964) 6, 25 f., 84 f., 90, 114, 124, 126 f., 142, 172, 196, 202, 231–41, 244, 246 f., 249–51, 253–60, 267, 291–93, 295
Twin Peaks (TV, ABC 1990–1991, 2017) 13, 15, 140 f., 226

U
uncanny 165, 176, 178, 181, 200, 211, 220, 222, 224 f., 227, 229, 243, 256
Uncle Tom's Cabin (novel, 1852) 271
'unity of effect' 184, 193
unpleasure 224
Up Series, The (TV, ITV et al. 1964–1972) 100

V
Vault of Horror, The (comics, 1950–1955) 122
Vault of Horror, The (anthology film, UK 1973) 133 f.
VCR 203, 231
Victorian Gothic 175, 184

Vidal, Gore 238
video games 44, 87, 105 f., 160
Videodrome (film, USA 1983) 207
VR experience 120

W
Walden, W. G. 143
Wallace and Gromit (claymation, UK, since 1989) 159
Wallace, Tommy Lee 254
Waltonen, Carma 18, 20, 30, 107, 262
Wan, James 223
'wandelbare Kontaktzone' 95, 98, 264
War of the Worlds (novel, 1898) 199
War of the Worlds (radio play, USA 1938) 109 f., 142, 199, 296, 301
Ward, Glenn 164 f., 167
Wartenberg, Thomas 219
WASP 38, 252
Watts, Steven 67
Weiner, Matthew 140, 296
Weird Fantasy (comics, 1950–1953) 122
Weird Science (comics, 1950–1953) 116, 122
Welles, Orson 109 f., 117, 142, 199, 249, 293, 296, 301
Wells, Herbert George 174 f., 184, 187–9, 199, 246, 266, 295 f.
Wells, Paul 79 f., 129, 148 f.
West Wing, The (TV, NBC 1999–2006) 143
Whale, James 129, 186–8, 201, 213, 215, 291, 295, 301
Whannel, Paddy 38
Wheatley, Helen 176 f., 200, 206, 214
Wheel of Fortune (TV, NBC 1975-present) 36
'white trash' 10, 47, 60
Whitted, Qiana 124
Wiene, Robert 164
Williams, Linda 95
Wilson, Sloan 252
Wingard, Adam 146, 156 f.
Wise, Macgregor 210
Wise, Robert 164, 199
Wolf Man, The (film, USA 1941) 164
Wollen, Peter 141, 160
Wood, Robin 108, 180, 242
'wraparound' 97, 112–15, 120
'writer-producer' 143, 234
Wulff, Hans Jürgen 87

X

X-Files, The (TV, Fox 1994–2002) 172, 227, 253

Y

Young, Elizabeth 190

Young Frankenstein (film, USA 1974) 186

You're Next (film, USA 2013) 146, 156–8, 161

Z

Zielinski, Siegfried 87